THE EU AND NANOTECHNOLOGIES

This book investigates the role of law in confronting major societal transformations embodied by the emergence of nanotechnologies. Taking the case of the European Union, it explores who the key decision-makers in the regulation of nanotechnologies are and how they take decisions. The questions are explored through two distinct case studies: the food and chemicals sectors. The book charts an incremental retreat of the European Union to its executive powers, including 'soft law' measures such as agencies' guidelines or implementing measures. This, the author argues, results in the Union's fundamental democratic control mechanisms, the EU legislature and the Court of Justice of the EU, being circumvented. The book recommends several immediate proposals to reform EU risk regulation, advocating a greater reliance on the European Parliament and outlining measures to increase the transparency of guidance drafting by EU agencies. This important work provides a timely examination of how emerging technologies pose both regulatory and democratic challenges.

Volume 75 in the Series Modern Studies in European Law

Modern Studies in European Law

Recent titles in this series:

The Impact of Union Citizenship on the EU's Market Freedoms
Alina Tryfonidou

Equal Citizenship and Its Limits in EU Law
Päivi Johanna Neuvonen

European Law on Unfair Commercial Practices and Contract Law
Mateja Durovic

The European Union's External Action in Times of Crisis
Edited by Piet Eeckhout and Manual Lopez-Escudero

The Legitimacy of Family Rights in Strasbourg Case Law: Living Instrument or Extinguished Sovereignty?
Carmen Draghici

Strengthening the Rule of Law in Europe: From a Common Concept to Mechanisms of Implementation
Edited by Werner Schroeder

The Pluralist Character of the European Economic Constitution
Clemens Kaupa

Exceptions from EU Free Movement Law
Edited by Panos Koutrakos, Niamh Nic Shuibhne and Phil Syrpis

Reconceptualising European Equality Law: A Comparative Institutional Analysis
Johanna Croon-Gestefeld

Marketing and Advertising Law in a Process of Harmonization
Edited by Ulf Bernitz and Caroline Heide-Jörgensen

The Fundamental Right to Data Protection: Normative Value in the Context of Counter-Terrorism Surveillance
Maria Tzanou

Republican Europe
Anna Kocharov

Family Reunification in the EU
Chiara Berneri

EU Liability and International Economic Law
Armin Steinbach

For the complete list of titles in this series, see 'Modern Studies in European Law' link at
www.bloomsburyprofessional.com/uk/series/modern-studies-in-european-law

The EU and Nanotechnologies

A Critical Analysis

Tanja Ehnert

• HART •
PUBLISHING
OXFORD AND PORTLAND, OREGON
2017

Hart Publishing
An imprint of Bloomsbury Publishing Plc

Hart Publishing Ltd
Kemp House
Chawley Park
Cumnor Hill
Oxford OX2 9PH
UK

Bloomsbury Publishing Plc
50 Bedford Square
London
WC1B 3DP
UK

www.hartpub.co.uk
www.bloomsbury.com

Published in North America (US and Canada) by
Hart Publishing
c/o International Specialized Book Services
920 NE 58th Avenue, Suite 300
Portland, OR 97213-3786
USA

www.isbs.com

First published 2017

British Library Cataloguing-in-Publication Data
A catalogue record for this book is available from the British Library.

ISBN: HB: 978-1-50990-850-9
ePDF: 978-1-50990-851-6
ePub: 978-1-50990-852-3

Library of Congress Cataloging-in-Publication Data

Names: Ehnert, Tanja, author.

Title: The EU and nanotechnologies : a critical analysis / Tanja Ehnert.

Other titles: European Union and nanotechnologies

Description: Oxford [UK] ; Portland, Oregon : Hart Publishing, 2017. | Series: Modern Studies in European Law ; v. 75 | Includes bibliographical references and index. | Description based on print version record and CIP data provided by publisher; resource not viewed.

Identifiers: LCCN 2017012593 (print) | LCCN 2017012722 (ebook) | ISBN 9781509908523 (Epub) | ISBN 9781509908509 (hardback : alk. paper)

Subjects: LCSH: Nanostructured materials industry—Law and legislation—European Union countries. | Nanotechnology—European Union countries. | Technology and law—European Union countries. | Food—Composition—Technological innovations. | Food law and legislation—European Union countries. | Chemicals—Law and legislation—European Union countries.

Classification: LCC KJE6777.N36 (ebook) | LCC KJE6777.N36 E36 2017 (print) | DDC 343.2407/86205—dc23

LC record available at https://lccn.loc.gov/2017012593

Typeset by Compuscript Ltd, Shannon
Printed and bound in Great Britain by TJ International, Padstow, Cornwall

Acknowledgements

This book is based on my PhD thesis written at the Maastricht Centre for European Law, which I defended in March 2015. I would like to thank the members of the assessment committee, Bruno de Witte, Chris Backes, Maria Lee and Elen Stokes, for providing me with valuable feedback and further inspiration for the completion of this book.

Apart from its content, the writing of this book turned out to be a truly European project, as it accompanied me in my journeys through four European countries. Firstly, it was written in Maastricht, where my supervisor Ellen Vos guided me with tremendous support through the thorny process of writing a PhD thesis. In Maastricht, I was extremely lucky to share the office with Kathrin and Sabrina, whom I would like to thank for all their encouragement and highly appreciated distractions during these years. Beyond the office, I greatly benefited from debates of and with colleagues from the Maastricht Centre for European Law. In particular, I would like to thank Mark Dawson, Mariolina Eliantonio, Elise Muir and Maria Weimer.

While working in Maastricht, I lived in Brussels. Without my friends there I would not have had the strength to finish this book. My thanks go to Anna, Milena, Stefanie, Katharina, Sarah Melina, Lilli, Silvia, Mariolina, Lucia and Ermis. Brussels is also the place where the idea for this research was born, during my traineeship in the European Commission and through the inspiration of my colleagues Karola, Pierre, Yannis and Paul, and during my time at the law firm, where I was infected by the passion of my supervisor Anna Gergely for the topic of nanotechnologies.

The third country and place of writing was Italy, especially the library of the European University Institute in Florence. I would like to thank Hans Micklitz for giving me the opportunity to visit the EUI in spring 2012 and to benefit from the atmosphere and intellectual curiosity of this gorgeous place. For discussions on my PhD research in Florence I would particularly like to thank Loic Azoulai and Joanne Scott.

Finally, parts of this book were written in Germany, where I had the unconditional support of my family—of my parents, my brother and my grandmother Else. I would also like to thank my colleagues at the Federal Institute for Risk Assessment, who followed the publication of this book with great support and interest.

The person who accompanied me in all these different countries is Antoine. Only his enthusiasm, love, patience and his time for endless discussions gave me the confidence to arrive at the final manuscript. I am incredibly grateful for our daughter Klara, who came into our life just in the middle of the publication of this book. I thank you for making life in all these countries to feel like home.

Table of Contents

Table of Cases

Judgments of the Court of Justice of the European Union

Opinions of Advocates General

Judgments of the General Court

European Ombudsman

Germany

World Trade Organization (WTO)

Table of Legislation

European Union Legislation

Treaties

Council Regulations—Regulations of the European Parliament and the Council

Council Decisions

Other Council documents

Common position

Working documents

Press releases

Directives

Commission Regulations

Commission Decisions

Commission Recommendations

Commission Communications

Commission Staff Working Papers, Reports, White Papers, Green Papers and other preparatory Commission instruments

Other Commission publications

Resolutions of the European Parliament

Other European Parliament publications

Other acts by the European Union institutions

Other official publications by the European Union institutions and bodies

European Food Safety Authority

Non-European Union Legislation

Belgium

Denmark

France

Germany

Introduction

Regulating the Invisible

IN MARCH 2006, the bathroom cleaner *Magic Nano* went on sale in Germany under the slogan: 'Scrubbing? Never again!' Within hours more than 110 incidents of health disorders related to *Magic Nano* were reported to the German poison control and treatment centres. All of the users suffered from breathlessness, several were hospitalised with water in the lungs. Soon, the 'nano' in *Magic Nano* was declared the culprit.[1] Three days later, the product was taken off the market. The case attracted international attention.[2] For the first time, nanotechnologies were publicly discussed. Questions were posed: What actually is 'nano'? Why would the inhalation of nanoparticles lead to adverse health effects? And how could such a product be marketed in Germany? The fact that it transpired in the end that the product did not even contain nanoparticles faded into the background.

At first glance, nanotechnologies seem not to be a big issue, in the truest sense of the word. One imagines something small, something unfathomable, something invisible that escapes the average person's notice. Nanotechnologies denote the manipulation of matter or the creation of structures at the atomic and molecular level.[3] To give a sense of scale, a human hair is 80,000 times the width of a nanometre.[4] And yet, nanotechnologies have recently become associated with big terms. The idea of 'never scrubbing again' is only the tip of the iceberg. It is claimed that inconceivable economic, environmental and health implications are at stake—in positive and negative terms alike, inseparably linked. Nanotechnologies, it is said, will help overcome the economic crisis by creating jobs and growth, save lives through improvements in cancer treatments and resolve energy problems by generating renewable sources. In the same breath, we are told that the impact and possible harms nanotechnologies might inflict upon the human body and the environment are yet unknown. The rise of nanotechnologies hence embraces the

[1] Bundesinstitut für Risikobewertung, *Vorsicht bei der Anwendung von 'Nano-Versiegelungssprays' mit Treibgas!* (Caution in applying 'nano sealing sprays' with propellant!) (2006) www.bfr.bund.de/de/presseinformation/2006/08/vorsicht_bei_der_anwendung_von__nano_versiegelungssprays__mit_treibgas_-7678.html.

[2] See eg The Economist, 'Has All the Magic Gone?' *The Economist* (London, 12 April 2006) www.economist.com/node/6795430 and Barnaby J Feder, 'Technology's Future: A Look at the Dark Side' *The New York Times* (New York, 17 May 2006).

[3] Q Chaudhry, 'Nanotechnology' (Presentation held at ICoMST, Copenhagen, August 2009).

[4] ibid.

fundamental tension between scientific and technical progress and its unsolicited side effects. The arena of this tension is the interface between science, politics and law. Thus the phenomenon of nanotechnologies may be viewed as a proxy for broader challenges contemporary societies are facing.

This book investigates the role of law in confronting these societal challenges. Where, by whom and how are decisions taken? The aim of this book is to critically analyse the current European Union (EU) regulatory developments in the area of nanotechnologies, thereby putting to the test the EU's institutional set-up and decision-making process in the face of risks. The issue is topical. It is not only the financial crisis that has placed the regulation of risk into the spotlight; more and more regulatory activity is being (re)defined in terms of risk: 'Chemicals, pharmaceuticals, GMOs, transport, stem cell research, nuclear power, even financial engineering, all have prompted the development of risk regulation regimes'.[5] Nanotechnologies have joined this list since the early 2000s.

I. DEFINING THE PROBLEM

A. Regulating in the Shadow of Scientific Uncertainty

The emergence of nanotechnologies is accompanied by severe scientific uncertainties. Although the body of knowledge about nanomaterials is developing, significant gaps persist as to their physicochemical properties.[6] These knowledge gaps render it difficult to evaluate, model and predict nanomaterials' ecological and toxicological behaviour.[7] Research has, however, confirmed that nanomaterials may enter the human body via several channels: through ingestion via the digestive tract, through inhalation via the respiratory tract and potentially through the skin in the case of direct exposure.[8] As soon as the tiny particles have entered the body, they may reach various organs.[9] However, what happens once nanomaterials have entered the different parts of the human body is impossible to determine conclusively at present.

[5] J Black, 'The Role of Risk in Regulatory Processes' in R Baldwin, M Cave and M Lodge (eds), *The Oxford Handbook of Regulation* (Oxford, Oxford University Press, 2010) 304.

[6] Scientific Committee on Emerging and Newly Identified Health Risks (SCENIHR), Opinion on 'Risk Assessment of Products of Nanotechnologies' (19 January 2009), www.ec.europa.eu/health/ph_risk/committees/04_scenihr/docs/scenihr_o_023.pdf, in which SCENIHR advocates a case-by-case approach for risk assessment; European Food Safety Authority, 'The Potential Risks Arising from Nanoscience and Nanotechnologies on Food and Feed Safety' (2009) 7 *EFSA Journal* 1; Observatory-Nano, 'Development in Nanotechnology Regulation and Standards' (FP7 Report, May 2009).

[7] Physical-chemical properties of nanomaterials include size, shape, composition, reactivity, surface area, and/or chemistry. ibid.

[8] European Commission, 'Nanotechnologies: A Preliminary Risk Analysis' (Workshop DG Sanco, Brussels, 1–2 March 2004) 19, www.ec.europa.eu/health/ph_risk/documents/ev_20040301_en.pdf.

[9] J Kreuter, D Shamenkov, V Petrov, P Ramge, K Cychutek, C Koch-Brandt and R Alyautdin, 'Apolipoprotein-mediated Transport of Nanoparticle-bound Drugs Across the Blood–Brain Barrier' (2002) 10 *Journal of Drug Targeting* 317.

B. Who Decides When Nobody Knows?

Intrinsically linked to the existence of scientific uncertainty is the question: who regulates, who decides 'how safe is safe enough'[10] in the face of scientific uncertainty and controversial knowledge claims? To be sure, the determination of the adequate level of protection is likely to significantly affect the everyday life of citizens. If the regulator decided to eliminate all risk by banning the development of nanotechnologies altogether, the impact on the competitiveness of industry could be immediate; a moratorium might deprive society of the opportunities to make important breakthroughs in medical treatment or to develop alternative energy sources. Vice versa, if the regulator decided not to interfere with nanotechnological development, people would be exposed to nanomaterials in their everyday lives—through their food, cosmetics, conditions at their workplace—potentially resulting in irreversible adverse effects to public health and the environment.

Decisions are hence required as to 'where and how one draws the line between still acceptable and no longer acceptable exposures', as Ulrich Beck frames it, and whether 'the possibility of an ecological catastrophe [should] be accepted, for instance, in order to satisfy economic interests. What are necessities, supposed necessities, and necessities that must be changed?'[11] Each affected societal actor, ranging from industry to environmental associations, consumer organisations and ethical groups, has its own reply to these questions. The presence of scientific uncertainty enables the diverse actors to interpret the available knowledge differently, pursuant to their own societal perspective. Industry is grasping nanotechnologies in economic terms, while consumers, trade unions and environmental organisations fear the environmental hazards posed by nanotechnologies and are anxious about consumer safety and the workers' health.

This book argues that continued scientific uncertainty renders the answer to the question at which point the regulation of nanotechnologies achieves its desired result, and hence at which point it becomes 'effective',[12] subjective in nature.[13] This turns the regulation of nanotechnologies into a contentious matter.[14] A rational

[10] S Funtowicz, I Shephard, D Wilkinson and J Ravetz, 'Science and Governance in the European Union: A Contribution to the Debate' (2000) 27 *Science and Public Policy* 327, 330 and S Jasanoff, *The Fifth Branch: Science Advisors as Policy Makers* (Cambridge, Harvard University Press, 2004) 232.

[11] U Beck, *Risk Society: Towards a New Modernity* (M Ritter (tr), London, SAGE Publications, 1992) 29.

[12] See further on the rationale of regulatory intervention in the area of nanotechnologies and the desired result of this intervention, chapter 1, section III.

[13] K Purcell, L Clarke and L Renzulli, 'Menus of Choice: The Social Embeddedness of Decisions' in MJ Cohen (ed), *Risk in the Modern Age: Social Theory, Science and Environmental Decision-Making* (Basingstoke, Palgrave MacMillan, 2000) 68. Or, as Giddens puts it, 'there is no risk that can be described without reference to a value', see A Giddens, 'Risk and Responsibility' (1999) 62 *The Modern Law Review* 1, 5.

[14] See for instance M Lee, 'Risk and Beyond: EU Regulation of Nanotechnology' (2010) 35 *European Law Review* 799; GA Hodge, DM Bowman and AD Maynard (eds), *International Handbook on Regulating Nanotechnologies* (Cheltenham, Edward Elgar Publishing, 2010); G Van Calster, 'Regulating

calculation of the 'optimal' result is precluded.[15] The nature of the potential risks at stake is unknown, so too by implication, when these risks are controlled. Where the definition of effectiveness becomes subjective, value judgements naturally enter the debate. Pursuant to Dahl, 'judgements about trade-offs among different ends are not "scientific"'.[16] They should not be left to technicians, to scientists, to 'the experts'. Or, the other way around, 'there is no expert on risk'.[17] Instead, subjective risk perceptions and controversial knowledge claims should be exposed to debate in the political arena.[18] The common interest of citizens in the area of nanotechnologies is yet to be identified. Questions regarding the democratic legitimacy of the regulation of nanotechnologies arise.

C. The Global Impact of the Nano Size

The regulation of nanotechnologies becomes even more complex by virtue of its transboundary, global implications. The potential risks faced by one individual, company or state depend not only on its own choices but equally on those made by others.[19] There are two sides of the coin. On one side, the interdependency of today's world has transformed issues such as food safety and consumer and environmental protection into global concerns. We are confronted with the globalisation of markets and the implied increasingly global nature of the supply chain.[20] To the contrary, the inherently subjective nature of the concept of risk, and its variation according to histories, local politics and value systems,[21]

Nanotechnology in the European Union' (2006) 15 *European Environmental Law Review* 238; E Stokes, 'Regulating Nanotechnologies: Sizing Up the Options' (2009) 29 *Legal Studies: the Journal of the Society of Public Teachers of Law* 281; O Renn and MC Roco, 'Nanotechnology and the Need for Risk Governance' (2006) 8 *Journal of Nanoparticle Research: An Interdisciplinary Forum for Nanoscale Science and Technology* 1; KH Ladeur, 'Kommunikation über Risiken im Rechtssystem. Das Beispiel Nanotechnologie' in C Büscher and KP Japp (eds), *Ökologische Aufklärung* (Wiesbaden, VS Verlag für Sozialwissenschaften, 2010); T Ehnert, 'The Legitimacy of New Risk Governance: A Critical View in Light of the EU's Approach to Nanotechnologies in Food' (2015) 21 *European Law Journal* 44.

[15] S Funtowicz et al, 'Science and Governance in the European Union' (n 10); S Jasanoff, *The Fifth Branch* (n 10) 232.

[16] RA Dahl, *On Democracy* (New Haven, Yale University Press, 1998) 72. Alvin Weinberg would call them 'trans-scientific', see AM Weinberg 'Science and Trans-Science' (1972) 10 *Minerva* 209.

[17] U Beck, *Risk Society* (n 11).

[18] A Giddens, 'Risk and Responsibility' (n 13) 7; J Habermas and M Rosenfeld, 'Paradigms of Law' (1996) 17 *Cardozo Law Review* 771.

[19] O Renn and MC Roco, 'Nanotechnology and the Need for Risk Governance' (n 14) 8 and 29.

[20] F Cafaggi, 'Private Regulation, Supply Chain and Contractual Networks: The Case of Food Safety' (2010) European University Institute Working Paper, RSCAS 2010/10, 6 www.cadmus.eui.eu/bitstream/handle/1814/13219/RSCAS_2010_10.pdf?sequence=1&isAllowed=y.

[21] E Fisher, 'Risk and Governance' in D Levi-Faur (ed), *The Oxford Handbook of Governance* (Oxford, Oxford University Press, 2012) 423. A Giddens, 'Risk and Responsibility' (n 13).

leads to different regulatory regimes in different countries, sectors or 'contexts'.[22] The international trade in nanoproducts may thus result in the presence of nanoproducts subject to potentially less rigorous and precautionary regulatory requirements on the domestic market of countries implementing either considerably higher or entirely different product standards. On the other side of the coin, the externalities of nanotechnologies, most notably their environmental, health and safety risks, are not confined within domestic borders.[23] The risks inherent in nanotechnologies are of a transnational nature.[24]

II. THIS BOOK

A. An EU Lens

Despite the transnational impact of nanotechnologies, not only beyond the confines of the EU Member States but also beyond the territory of the European Union itself, this book focuses on the European Union's regulatory activity in the area of nanotechnologies. The rationale for this choice is a pragmatic one. First, the fields in which nanotechnologies are or will be applied, such as chemicals, food, cosmetics and medicines, affect shared competences, which have already been harmonised at the EU level.[25] Secondly, appropriate institutional structures have not (yet) been developed at a global level. The international governance of nanotechnologies is currently restricted to scientific and technological standardisation and coordination efforts directed by a few Organization for Economic Cooperation and Development (OECD) countries while 'no deeper structures for global governance of nanotechnology have been created'.[26] Research on the potential of coordination efforts through international organisations, such as the OECD, the International Organization for Standardization (ISO) and within the United Nations (UN) framework, is essential in view of the global impact, not

[22] C Hood, H Rothstein and R Baldwin, *The Government of Risk: Understanding Risk Regulation Regimes* (Oxford, Oxford University Press, 2001) 20.

[23] H Nowotny, P Scott and M Gibbons, *Re-Thinking Science: Knowledge and the Public in an Age of Uncertainty* (Cambridge, Polity Press, 2001) 13.

[24] U Beck, *Risk Society* (n 11) 44.

[25] The legislative frameworks identified by the Commission in its Communication 'Regulatory Aspects of Nanomaterials' are predominantly based on art 114 of the Treaty on the Functioning of the European Union (TFEU) (internal market), art 153 TFEU (worker protection), art 43 TFEU (Common Agricultural Policy), art 168 TFEU (public health) and art 192 TFEU (environmental protection), see European Commission, 'Regulatory Aspects of Nanomaterials' (Communication) COM (2008) 366 final.

[26] R Falkner and N Jaspers, 'Regulating Nanotechnologies: Risk, Uncertainty and the Global Governance Gap' (2012) 12 *Global Environmental Politics* 30, 46.

least because of its implications for international trade,[27] but that discussion falls beyond the scope of this book.[28]

B. Research Question and Relevance

The aim of this book is to provide a critical analysis of the current EU risk regulation in the area of nanotechnologies. Thereby, the analysis will be guided by the overall research question:

How does the EU confront the emergence of nanotechnologies?

The objective of this book is to contrast normative demands or ideas of how the law should respond to the challenges of scientific uncertainty, conflicting knowledge claims and legitimacy concerns, which at European level are commonly captured under the loose notion 'new governance', with the empirical reality of the EU's regulatory approach to nanotechnologies. This book thereby strives to fill two gaps in the existent literature. First, it tackles a topic that has so far been largely neglected, at least from a legal point of view, but that is of great economic, social, political and environmental importance. Much more fundamentally, however, this book asks questions which greatly transcend the area of nanotechnologies. These questions touch upon the pressing issues of knowledge production and the creation of legitimate regulation in modern societies, as well as the capacity of the EU's institutional and constitutional set-up to confront those concerns. These broader questions are explored based on the specific—though exemplary, as it will be argued—case of nanotechnologies, thereby providing current, often abstract, academic debates with a detailed empirical foundation.

C. Method

This book undertakes an analysis of the evolving regulatory framework for nanotechnologies—encompassing the relevant EU legislation, provisions in the

[27] As Van Calster predicts, 'the regulation of nanotechnology announces itself as a future battleground for pitching regulatory ambitions against free trade', see G Van Calster, 'The Role of the World Trade Organisation in Nanotechnology Regulation' in G Hodge, D Bowman and K Ludlow (eds), *New Global Frontiers in Regulation: The Age of Nanotechnology*, Monash Studies in Global Movements (Cheltenham, Edward Elgar Publishing, 2007). See also J Black, 'The Role of Risk in Regulatory Processes' (n 5) 314.

[28] For research on international cooperation in the area of nanotechnologies see for instance R Falkner and N Jaspers, 'Regulating Nanotechnologies' (n 26); GE Marchant, DJ Sylvester and KW Abbott, 'Risk Management Principles of Nanotechnology' (2008) 2 *NanoEthics* 43; L Breggin, R Falkner, N Jaspers, J Pendergrass and R Porter, 'Securing the Promise of Nanotechnologies—Towards Transatlantic Regulatory Co-operation' (Project of the London School of Economics and Political Science, Chatham House, the Environmental Law Institute and the Project on Emerging Nanotechnologies, 2009) www.chathamhouse.org/sites/files/chathamhouse/public/Research/Energy,%20Environment%20and%20Development/r0909_nanotechnologies.pdf.

EU Treaties, case law of the EU courts and the pertinent policy documents—following a classical legal methodology. Yet, this book will do this by embedding these processes in their societal context.[29] It thereby follows Snyder's vision of an 'EU law in context':

> So far, EC law has been conceived mainly as 'black-letter law', based on the exposition of legal doctrine and the analysis of judicial decisions. Now, however, it is time to draw upon perspectives from other social sciences and to move in new directions. We must place EC law in its social, economic and political context. Only in this way can we achieve the deeper and broader understanding—both practical and theoretical—of EC law that is required to meet the exciting challenges of our time.[30]

The merit of Snyder's plea has been demonstrated in the preceding introductory sections. In order to study the regulation of nanotechnologies, it seems crucial to comprehend its societal context. Or rather the other way around, the societal context largely determines whether or not a specific regulatory measure can at all be considered effective or legitimate. As well as the legal literature, therefore, this book also draws on insights from political science, sociology and, particularly, on the valuable contributions from science and technology studies. To gauge the general public opinion, it also looks to newspaper articles, reports or position papers drafted by affected societal actors. Furthermore, a handful of semi-structured qualitative interviews were conducted with representatives from the European Commission, EU agencies and stakeholders. These interviews, however, are not taken as a formal source of information. They are used to test assumptions made in this book and to enrich the theoretical study of legal procedures and mechanisms with a practical dimension of more anecdotal than evidential value.

D. Structure of the Book and Case Studies

Chapter one will set the scene for the ensuing theoretical and empirical chapters. Its first aim is to introduce the topic of nanotechnologies and the controversy surrounding it: what actually are nanotechnologies? The chapter subsequently moves to a further fundamental question: does one need to regulate nanotechnologies? After having established the presence of risk as a rationale for regulatory intervention, the chapter closes with a bird's eye perspective on the current EU regulatory developments in the area of nanotechnologies. This overview will serve as a reference—a point of orientation—for the more detailed analysis that will follow in the empirical part of this book.

In line with the 'EU law in context' approach, chapter two opens by considering three concurrent societal transformations—those of globalisation, functional

[29] R Van Gestel and HW Micklitz, 'Why Methods Matter in European Legal Scholarship' (2013) 20 *European Law Journal* 292, 298.

[30] FG Snyder, *New Directions in European Community Law*, Law in Context (London, Weidenfeld & Nicolson, 1990) 2.

differentiation and the rise of the risk society. These societal transformations, it is argued, are exemplified by the emergence of nanotechnologies. Chapter two then introduces two theoretical approaches, Habermas's discourse theory of law and democracy and Teubner's theory of reflexive law, that offer a normative answer to the research question, how should the EU institutions respond to the rise of nanotechnologies. A synthesis of the two approaches will suggest that, in modern societies, the regulator, on its own, increasingly lacks the capacity to master the diffused knowledge and to ensure the legitimacy of its regulatory activities. Close involvement by affected societal actors in the regulatory process is proposed in order to strengthen regulatory capacity. The theoretical approaches not only help to structure the subsequent empirical part, they also put this book into the context of the ongoing scholarly debate. The last section of this chapter will analyse how these societal transformations and theoretical considerations have influenced the discourse on regulation in the EU context. This will constitute an intermediate step between the normative ideas set out in the theoretical accounts and the empirical analysis of the case studies. It will be shown that a reform process was launched towards the end of the 1990s under the label of 'European governance' or, in EU scholarship, 'new governance' with the aim of increasing the EU's capacity to regulate.

Chapter three, with the theoretical foundations of chapter two at its roots, subsequently defines the scope of the empirical analysis in the case studies. To this end, it first delineates the object of analysis—the *what*—by laying down this book's understanding of 'EU regulation'. Thereafter, the chapter establishes the lenses through which the EU regulation of nanotechnologies will be analysed—the *how*. The analytical lenses will be those of 'regulatory capacity'. Regulatory capacity will comprise the two elements identified in the theoretical sections of chapter two, *viz*. the capacity to master the dispersed knowledge and the capacity to ensure legitimate regulation. Chapter three aims to define these elements. It then identifies the 'tangible impacts' of the governance debate, the legal procedures that the EU institutions have put in place in order to achieve these elements—to pool knowledge and ensure legitimacy, ultimately in order to increase the institutions' capacity to regulate.

It is then left to the empirical part, that is, chapters four and five, to test the applicability and practical operation of these legal procedures in two case studies. Whilst a brief description of the EU's overall approach to nanotechnologies was given in chapter one, due to the cross-sectoral range of potential applications of nanomaterials it is impossible to achieve the necessary analytical depth by continuing with a holistic approach. Instead, the regulatory developments in two sectors affected by nanotechnologies are selected as test cases. The food and chemicals sectors have been considered most suitable for these purposes.

The food sector has been selected mainly due to the particular public sensitivity dominating this area.[31] As the consumption of food plays a fundamental and

[31] Q Chaudhry, L Castle and R Watkins, 'Nanotechnologies in the Food Arena: New Opportunities, New Questions, New Concerns' in Q Chaudhry, L Castle and R Watkins (eds), *Nanotechnologies in Food*, RSC Nanoscience & Nanotechnology no 14 (Cambridge, Royal Society of Chemistry Publishing, 2010) 5.

tangible role in people's lives, new technologies in the food sector often meet with scepticism.[32] Nanotechnological applications in food are no exception.[33] Additionally, the food sector has been burdened by several recent food scares. Regulators, stakeholders and the general public are already on the alert, which puts great pressure on the EU institutions to act. It is therefore hardly surprising that EU food legislation is among the first pieces of legislation to contain nano-specific provisions.

The selection of the chemicals sector as the second case study was almost imperative. The EU's legislative framework for chemicals—the Registration, Evaluation, Authorisation and Restriction of CHemical substances (REACH)—is widely considered to constitute the cornerstone for the regulation of nanomaterials as the 'data generated under REACH will serve as input to other regulation'.[34] This is because the chemical sector's output constitutes the manufacturing basis for many other sectors, including the food industry. Furthermore, the regulation of nanotechnologies in REACH will be an instructive case to compare to the food sector. On the one hand, the two sectors are regulated by a similar institutional set-up. In both cases an independent EU agency was created to provide the process with scientific and technical advice. Both sectors also constitute key industries in the EU economy. On the other hand, the comparison of these two sectors will benefit from a chronological asymmetry. While EU food legislation was among the first EU regulatory frameworks to contain nano-specific provisions, REACH has been under review more recently. It will be telling to see whether differences in approach are visible and, if so, what these differences are.

The final chapter, chapter six, contains concluding remarks. It will be seen that this book walks a tightrope between the well-meaning rhetoric of a more inclusive, transparent and expertise-based regulation, often captured under the term 'new governance' in EU scholarship, and the actual applicability and operation of the legal procedures established for these purposes. Rhetoric and practice, it will be shown, diverge substantially. This book hence separates normative ideas from empirical reality, thereby revealing not only significant shortcomings in the application of the procedures by the EU institutions but also in their design, ultimately questioning their very rationale in the face of this book's theoretical foundations.

[32] Science and Technologies Committee, *Nanotechnologies and Food* (HL 2009–10, 22–I) 5.

[33] International Risk Governance Council, 'Policy Brief—Appropriate Risk Governance Strategies for Nanotechnology Applications in Food and Cosmetics' (2009) 11 www.irgc.org/IMG/pdf/irgc_nanotechnologies_food_and_cosmetics_policy_brief.pdf.

[34] European Commission, 'Regulatory Aspects of Nanomaterials' (n 25). This is also the view of the European Commission in its second regulatory review on nanomaterials, see European Commission, 'Second Regulatory Review on Nanomaterials' (Communication) COM (2012) 572 final, 11.

1

Setting the Scene: Nanotechnologies and their Regulation at the EU Level

FOR THE LAYPERSON, the term 'nanotechnologies' suggests something mysterious. Why are people talking about nanotechnolog*ies* and not nanotechnolog*y*, and what does 'nano' refer to in the first place? The first aim of this chapter is therefore to introduce the topic of nanotechnologies in plain language (section I). Thereafter, the debate evolving around the rise of nanotechnologies is introduced—a debate which is presently torn between the two extremes of nanomania and nanophobia (section II). Against this background, section III approaches a question, which is often overlooked but which is, in fact, fundamental. Is there a need to regulate nanotechnologies? So far, a necessity to regulate has been implicitly assumed. Finally, this chapter sets the scene for the EU's regulatory approach to nanotechnologies. The main pillars of this approach are introduced and the central policy documents are discussed. This bird's eye perspective is essential in order to better comprehend the developments in the food and chemicals sectors and to see how the latter relate to the overall EU regulatory framework for nanotechnologies (section IV).

I. WHAT ARE NANOTECHNOLOGIES?

Dwarfs (*nános* in Greek) are on the rise. One nanometre is not more than one billionth of a metre.[1] The crux of the matter is that at this infinitesimal scale, the physicochemical characteristics of matter may significantly change. First, the material structures of chemical elements may alter their mechanical, optical, magnetic and electronic properties in comparison to those of the bulk matter.[2] For instance, while the melting point of silver in its bulk form is approximately 960°C, silver in its nanoform melts by the application of a hairdryer.[3] Secondly, nanomaterials exhibit a relatively bigger surface area, which renders them more chemically reactive than the conventional form.[4]

[1] Q Chaudhry, 'Nanotechnology' (Presentation held at ICoMST, Copenhagen, August 2009).

[2] O Renn and MC Roco, 'Nanotechnology and the Need for Risk Governance' (2006) 8 *Journal of Nanoparticle Research: An Interdisciplinary Forum for Nanoscale Science and Technology* 1.

[3] Science and Technologies Committee, *Nanotechnologies and Food* (HL 2009–10, 22-I) 11.

[4] ibid.

The origin of nanotechnologies goes back to the lecture *There's Plenty of Room at the Bottom* delivered by the physicist and Nobel prize winner Richard Feynman in 1959: 'What I want to talk about is the problem of manipulating and controlling things on a small scale'.[5] The vision Feynman presented was the idea of nanomachines, meaning tiny robots, which are capable of building by atom-by-atom control.[6] By analogy to biology, living cells may be conceived as consisting of countless nanomachines: 'since cells build more cells, biology shows that nanomachine systems can build more nanomachine systems'.[7] Nanomachines would thus be self-replicable.[8]

The vision not only sparked a fever of excitement but also raised profound fears leading to the development of 'grey goo' scenarios in the scientific community and beyond. The American engineer Eric Drexler[9] wrote in his 1986 book *Engines of Creation*:

> Replicating assemblers and thinking machines pose basic threats to people and to life on Earth. Today's organisms have abilities far from the limits of the possible, and our machines are evolving faster than we are. Within a few decades they seem likely to surpass us. Unless we learn to live with them in safety, our future will likely be both exciting and short. … Entire books will no doubt be written on the coming social upheavals: What will happen to the global order when assemblers and automated engineering eliminate the need for most international trade? How will society change when individuals can live indefinitely? What will we do when replicating assemblers can make almost anything without human labor? What will we do when AI [artificial intelligence] systems can think faster than humans?
>
> Among the cognoscenti of nanotechnology, this threat has become known as the 'gray goo problem'. Though masses of uncontrolled replicators need not be gray or gooey, the term 'gray goo' emphasises that replicators able to obliterate life might be less inspiring than a single species of crabgrass. They might be 'superior' in an evolutionary sense, but this need not make them valuable. We have evolved to love a world rich in living things, ideas, and diversity, so there is no reason to value gray goo merely because it could spread. Indeed, if we prevent it we will thereby prove *our* evolutionary superiority. The gray goo threat makes one thing perfectly clear: we cannot afford certain kinds of accidents with replicating assemblers.[10]

In view of such scenarios, Bill Joy, then chief scientist of Sun Microsystems, was the first to call for a moratorium on nanotechnology research in 2000. Titled 'Why the Future Doesn't Need Us', his article warned against the outlook that 'our most powerful 21st-century technologies—robotics, genetic engineering,

[5] R Feynman, 'There's Plenty of Room at the Bottom' (1960) 23 *Engineering and Science* 22.

[6] KE Drexler, 'Nanotechnology: From Feynman to Funding' in G Hunt and MD Mehta (eds), *Nanotechnology: Risk, Ethics and Law*, Science in Society Series (London, Earthscan, 2006) 26.

[7] ibid 26 and 27.

[8] ibid 27.

[9] Eric Drexler was the first researcher to complete a doctoral thesis on molecular nanotechnology at the Massachusetts Institute of Technology (MIT).

[10] KE Drexler, *Engines of Creation* (New York, Anchor Books/Doubleday, 1986) ch 11.

and nanotech—are threatening to make humans an endangered species'.[11] In fear of public outcries and cuts in funding, the immediate response of the nanoscale research community was to distance itself from the Feynman vision of self-replicating nanorobots.[12] Today, as indicated above, a much wider definition of nanotechnologies is employed, which basically fits any technology at the nanoscale.[13] This is why one often refers to nanotechnolog*ies* in the plural. The original vision of Feynman is included in, yet is not the focus of, such a broad definition. In the last few years, the emphasis has been placed on explaining that nanotechnological development has not yet reached a stage at which 'grey goo' scenarios could come true; the magazine *Wired*, which published Bill Joy's article in 2000, reacted with a follow-up eight years later, 'Why the Future Still Needs Us a While Longer'.[14]

In 1959, Feynman modestly ended his lecture with a high school competition: he offered $1,000 to the first student able to put the information of one page of a book on a surface 1/25,000 smaller in linear scale.[15] It was not until 1985, however, that a Stanford student succeeded in reducing the first paragraph of Charles Dickens' *A Tale of Two Cities* to the requested size. It was only in the late 1980s and 1990s, roughly three decades after Feynman's talk, that research in the area of nanotechnologies seriously commenced with the development of new tools which enable the observation and manipulation of materials at the nanoscale.[16]

II. BETWEEN NANOMANIA AND NANOPHOBIA

Fifty years after Feynman's lecture, we find ourselves somewhere between nanomania and nanophobia. Reviewing the international press headlines over the last years, an ambiguous picture of nanotechnologies emerges.[17] On the one hand,

[11] Bill Joy, 'Why the Future Doesn't Need Us' *Wired Magazine* (San Francisco, 1 April 2000) www.wired.com/2000/04/joy-2/.

[12] KE Drexler, 'Nanotechnology: From Feynman to Funding' (n 6) 29.

[13] ibid 31.

[14] Lucas Grave, '15th Anniversary: Why the Future Still Needs Us a While Longer' *Wired Magazine* (San Francisco, 24 March 2008) www.wired.com/2008/03/st-15joy/.

[15] R Feynman, 'There's Plenty of Room at the Bottom' (n 5).

[16] Royal Society & The Royal Academy of Engineering, *Nanoscience and Nanotechnologies: Opportunities and Uncertainties* (London, The Royal Society, 2004) 6.

[17] See eg Honor Mahony, 'Nanofoods—Coming to a Plate Near You?' *EU Observer* (Brussels, 18 October 2011); Patti Waldmeir, 'Brave New Risks of Nanotechnology' *Financial Times* (London, 18 September 2007); AFP, 'Inquiétudes autour des nanomatériaux dans les aliments' *Le Monde* (Paris, 29 February 2012); Lydia Klöckner, 'Wie umweltschädlich sind Nanoteilchen?' *Die Zeit* (Hamburg, 20 November 2012); Ralf Nestler and Juliane Schäuble, 'Wie gefährlich ist die Nanotechnologie?' *Die Zeit* (Hamburg, 19 November 2009); Jenny Booth, 'Scientists Call for Stricter Safeguards on Nanotechnology' *The Times* (London, 29 July 2004); Richard Waters, 'Why Nanotechnology is Next Big Thing' *Financial Times* (London, 29 March 2005); Svantje Wallbraun, 'Immer kleiner, immer feiner' *Die Zeit* (Hamburg, 12 January 2011); Catherine Belton, 'Nanotechnology: Plans for the Next Stage in Humanity's Development' *Financial Times* (London, 14 April 2009); Natasha Singer, 'New Products Bring Side Effect: Nanophobia' *The New York Times* (New York, 3 December 2008); Kenneth Chang, 'In Study, Researchers Find Nanotubes May Pose Health Risks Similar to Asbestos' *The New York Times*

nanotechnologies are heralded as 'the next stage in humanity's development',[18] with great expectations being placed on their development. They are seen as 'a key economic driver for the twenty-first century', involving considerable social benefits.[19] Nanotechnologies are expected to play a major role in responding to climate change[20] or in securing and managing access to clean water.[21] Accordingly, research in nanotechnological applications has been identified by industry and governments worldwide as a priority area.[22] Whilst the European Commission's Seventh Framework Programme[23] had already allocated nanotechnologies an amount of €3.5 billion between 2007 and 2013, its successor Horizon 2020 identified nanotechnologies as one of the 'key enabling technologies' and allocated it a budget of €13.7 billion until 2020.[24] According to the European Commission, the global market of nanomaterials in 2014 was worth €20 billion, with 300,000 to 400,000 direct employees in the European Union.[25]

On the other hand, fears associated with the Feynman vision continue to exist. Warnings against the 'suspicious dwarfs'[26] are growing. Scientific uncertainty is omnipresent.[27] After the false alarm of *Magic Nano*,[28] a public outcry occurred in 2008 when scientists discovered that certain types of carbon nanotubes show the same toxicological behaviour as asbestos.[29] Environmental non-governmental

(New York, 21 May 2008); Eric Burgraff, 'Les nanotechnologies ont envahi notre vie quotidienne' *Le Soir* (Bruxelles, 27 May 2010); DPA, 'Umweltbundesamt warnt vor Nanotechnik-Produkten' *Die Zeit* (Hamburg, 21 October 2009); Adelheid Müller-Lissner, 'Verdächtige Zwerge' *Die Zeit* (Hamburg, 24 June 2009); Jacy Meyer, 'To Czech Industry, Everything Is Nano' *The New York Times* (New York, 22 May 2012); Michael Bauchmüller and Katrin Blawat, 'Rätsel um das Nano-Risiko' *Süddeutsche Zeitung* (Munich, 1 September 2011).

18 See also in academic literature, eg AD Maynard, 'Nanotechnology: The Next Big Thing, or Much Ado about Nothing?' (2006) 51 *The Annals of Occupational Hygiene* 1; GA Hodge, D Bowman and K Ludlow, 'Introduction: Big Questions for Small Technologies' in GA Hodge, D Bowman and K Ludlow (eds), *New Global Frontiers in Regulation: The Age of Nanotechnology*, Monash Studies in Global Movements Series (Cheltenham, Edward Elgar Publishing, 2007).

19 G Hodge et al, 'Introduction: Big Questions for Small Technologies' (n 18).

20 M Esteban, C Webersik, D Leary and D Thompson-Pomeroy, 'Innovation in Responding to Climate Change: Nanotechnology, Ocean Energy and Forestry' (UNU–IAS Report, United Nations University Institute of Advanced Studies, 2008).

21 OECD, 'Fostering Nanotechnology to Address Global Challenges' (Report, OECD, 2011).

22 Council for Science and Technology, 'Nanosciences and Nanotechnologies: A Review of Governments Progress on its Policy Commitments' (Report, 2007).

23 The Seventh Framework Programme is one of the Union's key funding instruments to support research and innovation activities in nearly all scientific disciplines. Framework Programmes are proposed by the Commission and, eventually, adopted by Council and the European Parliament in the ordinary legislative procedure.

24 European Commission, Horizon 2020, The EU Framework Programme—Key Enabling Technologies www.ec.europa.eu/programmes/horizon2020/en/area/key-enabling-technologies.

25 European Commission, Research & Innovation, 'Nanotechnologies: Policy Issues' (2014) www.ec.europa.eu/research/industrial_technologies/policy_en.html.

26 Adelheid Müller-Lissner, 'Verdächtige Zwerge' *Die Zeit* (Hamburg, 24 June 2009).

27 Above Introduction, section I.A.

28 Above Introduction.

29 CA Poland, R Duffin, I Kinloch, A Maynard, WAH Wallace, A Seaton, V Stone, S Brown, W MacNeel and K Donaldson, 'Carbon Nanotubes Introduced into the Abdominal Cavity of Mice Show Asbestos-like Pathogenicity in a Pilot Study' (2008) 3 *Nature Nanotechnology* 423.

organisations (NGOs) and consumer organisations in particular, represented by the seminal report *The Big Down* of the ETC Group in 2003, have called for the application of the precautionary principle.[30]

III. RISK AS A RATIONALE FOR REGULATORY INTERVENTION

Notwithstanding the ongoing and highly controversial debate on the desirability of nanotechnologies, the reality is that consumer products containing nanomaterials are already available on the EU market. They can be found in various product groups, ranging from foodstuffs, textiles and chemicals to pharmaceuticals, electrical equipment and cosmetics.[31] If the existence of nano-enabled products on the EU market is to be taken for granted, how should one respond to this reality? Should the regulator intervene? To be sure, the justification for regulatory intervention changes depending on the perspective, for instance whether one takes an economic or sociological approach. While an economist would reply that the rationale for regulation is the achievement of market efficiency and equitable distribution, ensuring fairness, access to justice and equality in society would probably be part of the response of a sociologist. Indeed, the safety of products available on the market touches upon fundamental rights, the right to life, the right to safety at work, and the right to a clean environment, as protected by the EU Charter of Fundamental Rights.[32]

The existence of 'risk' is increasingly treated not only as the object of regulatory intervention but also as its self-sufficient justification.[33] Risk thereby functions as an umbrella term, encompassing threats to human health, environment, security, and financial stability.[34] Following this rationale, the regulator's charge is to control the risk and it is justified in intervening to achieve that objective.[35] Often, however, the 'risk' rationale is translated into economic language, which is still widely perceived as a more stable foundation for regulatory intervention.[36] From an

[30] ETC Group, 'The Big Down: From Genomes to Atoms' (Report, 2003) www.etcgroup.org/sites/www.etcgroup.org/files/thebigdown.pdf; see also D Fedrigo and R Senjen, 'Shaping Innovation—Policy Approaches on Innovation Governance: The Case of Nanotechnology' (European Environmental Bureau, Issue 4, 2010) www.eeb.org/?LinkServID=FBEF1E68-F364-600E-D2DD41B9CA0FA4EF; European Consumers' Organisation and European Consumer Voice in Standardisation, 'Nanotechnology: Small is Beautiful But is it Safe?' (Joint ANEC/BEUC Position, 2009) www.anec.org/attachments/ANEC-PT-2009-Nano-002final.pdf.

[31] Milieu Ltd and RPA Ltd, 'Proposal for an EU Reporting System for Nanomaterials' (Study commissioned by the European Commission—DG Environment, 2010).

[32] Charter of Fundamental Rights of the European Union (Consolidated version 2016) [2016] OJ C202/389, arts 2 ('right to life'), 31(1) ('every worker has the right to working conditions which respect his or her health, safety and dignity') and 37 ('environmental protection').

[33] J Black, 'The Role of Risk in Regulatory Processes' in R Baldwin, M Cave and M Lodge (eds), *The Oxford Handbook of Regulation* (Oxford, Oxford University Press, 2010) 306.

[34] ibid 305.

[35] ibid 306.

[36] ibid 307 and 308.

economic perspective, the normative justification for regulation becomes the correction of market failures.[37] The presence of risk could also be an example of negative externalities or the occurrence of information failures.

Negative externalities arise where the actions of one individual force a cost on other individuals without an accordant compensation.[38] In the case of nanotechnologies, the placing on the market of nanoproducts implies environmental, health and safety risks for society as a whole—for the consumer, the worker manufacturing the product, as well as for the environment. This means that the placing on the market of nanoproducts by industry *might* result in externalities, which *might* negatively affect society as a whole. Like the risks inherent in nanotechnologies, the negative externalities of the technologies are therefore also uncertain.[39] A linked market failure results from the existence of information asymmetries,[40] of which two different kinds can be observed with respect to nanotechnologies. First, the majority of European consumers still seem to be unaware of nanotechnologies. According to the Eurobarometer report of October 2010, 54 per cent of Europeans have never heard of nanotechnologies.[41] The second information failure refers to the regulator's knowledge about nanoproducts on the EU market. As a report contracted by the European Commission in 2010 concluded, while there is little doubt that nanomaterials can be found on the EU market, 'there are uncertainties as to the precise form in which such nanomaterials are present … and, indeed, whether there are other significant groups of nanomaterials on (or near to) the EU market which have not been identified in this report (or elsewhere).'[42]

The rationale for and the desired result of a regulatory intervention in the area of nanotechnologies is thus to control the inherent risks. Where the regulation of

[37] G Majone (ed), *Regulating Europe*, European Public Policy (London, Routledge, 1996) 28. The market failure approach is based on the fundamental theorems of welfare economics. The first theorem contends that, under certain conditions, a competitive market leads to an efficient allocation of resources—a pareto-efficient allocation. Pareto-efficiency means that no individual in a society can, via a reallocation of resources, be made better off without someone else being made worse off. The existence of the invisible hand has been questioned, see eg JE Stiglitz, 'The Invisible Hand and Modern Welfare Economics' (1991) NBER Working Paper Series no 3641. Accordingly, market failures arise where the conditions of the fundamental theorem are not fulfilled, ie the competitive market does not lead to a pareto-efficient outcome, see G Majone (ed), *Regulating Europe*, European Public Policy (London, Routledge, 1996) 28.

[38] G Majone, *Regulating Europe* (n 37) 28.

[39] We are thus faced with the existence of potential or uncertain negative externalities. The term 'uncertain negative externalties' has been used at least twice before in academic literature: once in the context of the current consumption of products, which generate uncertain negative externalities towards the future self (such as the consumption of tobacco, cholesterol or fatty food), see I Palacios-Huerta, 'Time-Inconsistent Preferences in Adam Smith and David Hume' (2003) 35 *History of Political Economy* 241, 261; and again in the context of the governmental role in technological innovation, see H Brooks, 'National Science Policy and Technological Innovation' in R Landau and N Rosenberg (eds), *The Positive Sum Strategy: Harnessing Technology for Economic Growth* (Washington D.C., National Academy Press, 1986) 149.

[40] JE Stiglitz, 'The Invisible Hand and Modern Welfare Economics' (n 37).

[41] Eurobarometer, 'Biotechnologie' (Eurobarometer 73.1, 2010) www.ec.europa.eu/public_opinion/archives/ebs/ebs_341_de.pdf.

[42] Milieu Ltd and RPA Ltd, 'Proposal for an EU Reporting System for Nanomaterials' (n 31) 19.

nanotechnologies achieves this 'desired result', it can be regarded as 'effective'.[43] Yet, and recalling the earlier discussion in the Introduction to this book,[44] the determination of the point at which nanotechnologies' risks can be considered controlled depends, due to the perseverance of scientific uncertainties, on the eye of the beholder. By implication, the definition of effectiveness also becomes subjective in nature.

IV. THE EU'S APPROACH TO THE REGULATION OF NANOTECHNOLOGIES: A BIRD'S EYE PERSPECTIVE

Against this background, this section turns to a brief overview of the present EU regulatory developments in the area of nanotechnologies. The aim here is not to go into depth about the individual regulatory frameworks but to view them from a bird's eye perspective. A detailed analysis will follow in the empirical part of the book, which will take a careful look at the subtleties of nanotechnologies' regulation in the food and chemical sectors. This section will serve as a reference point to position the later and more specific discussions in the context of the EU's overall approach to the regulation of nanotechnologies.

A. The EU's Incremental Approach to Nanotechnologies

The question of how to deal with the emergence of nanotechnologies was first discussed at the EU level in a workshop with several invited experts,[45] organised by the European Commission's Directorate General for Health and Food Safety (DG SANTE) in 2004.[46] The task given to the invitees was to 'examine the hazards, exposure and risks to human and environmental health potentially associated with materials derived from nanotechnologies within the next 3–5 years'.[47] Part of the examination was to identify feasible policy options. The experts came up with five alternatives: (i) adopting a 'laissez-faire' approach; (ii) imposing a moratorium on nanotechnologies research and commercialisation; (iii) relying on voluntary measures; (iv) developing a specific legislative framework for nanotechnologies; or (v) launching an incremental process based on the existing legislative frameworks.[48]

[43] According to the Oxford English Dictionary, 'effective' is defined as 'producing a desired or intended result'.

[44] Above Introduction, section I.B.

[45] There were 17 experts in the areas of physics, geography, biology, environmental sciences, toxicology, pathology, genetics, applied epistemology, social sciences and economics. There was no lawyer present at the expert meeting. See European Commission, 'Nanotechnologies: A Preliminary Risk Analysis' (Workshop DG Sanco, Brussels, 1–2 March 2004) 7/8 www.ec.europa.eu/health/ph_risk/documents/ev_20040301_en.pdf.

[46] ibid.

[47] ibid 13.

[48] ibid 22–23.

Four out of the five policy options were instantly rejected as 'unwise', 'feasible only if partial', 'ineffective', 'less efficient' and as 'difficult'. The experts perceived the option of 'doing nothing', meaning the adoption of a laissez-faire approach, as 'unwise' given the insufficient scientific evidence to complete a risk assessment; the uncertain negative externalities inherent in nanotechnologies must be regulated. The second option, the imposition of a moratorium, was mainly found to be unworkable for pragmatic reasons: 'nanotechnologies have already entered the market and their ubiquitous and horizontal nature makes them difficult to control'. 'Little appeal' was also attributed to the sole use of voluntary measures—the experts' third policy option. Finally, the launch of new nano-specific legislation was considered 'difficult' because of the technologies' cross-sectoral impact and, beyond that, regarded as unjustified in view of the existence of legislative frameworks which 'already address a number of issues and can be adapted if the need arises'.[49] For the experts, the 'incremental approach' crystallised as the 'only realistic option'.

The core idea of the incremental approach is simple: existing horizontal and sector-specific legislative structures form the basis of the EU's regulatory approach to nanotechnologies,[50] which may have to be adapted where necessary.[51] In addition, the workshop's report advised that the incremental approach should be complemented by five elements: (i) the issuance of recommendations, meaning voluntary measures, in particular as regards standards, guidelines on risk assessment and occupational health and safety; (ii) the commissioning of studies, for instance, on exposure and (eco)toxicology; (iii) the promotion of a lifecycle approach; and (iv) the setting up of an observatory on the scientific, technological, economic and social development of nanotechnologies.[52] Overall, (v) it was recommended that a public dialogue with European citizens, consumers and industry should accompany the incremental approach.[53]

The 2004 expert meeting thus marks the birth of the EU's regulatory strategy on nanotechnologies. The incremental approach was confirmed in the Commission's subsequent Communication 'Towards a European Strategy for Nanotechnology'[54] and in its first action plan, 'Nanosciences and Nanotechnologies: An Action Plan for Europe 2005–2009'.[55] The feedback from the European legislature was initially

[49] ibid 24.

[50] See, for an analysis of the 'incremental approach', A Franco, SF Hansen, SI Olsen and L Butti, 'Limits and Prospects of the "Incremental Approach" and the European Legislation on the Management of Risks Related to Nanomaterials' (2007) 48 *Regulatory Toxicology and Pharmacology* 171.

[51] Particular attention should be paid to current thresholds employed in risk assessment and in the registration and documentation of products, the adjustment of labelling requirements and the adaptation of (eco)toxicity standards, European Commission, 'Nanotechnologies: A Preliminary Risk Analysis' (n 45) 28.

[52] ibid 23.

[53] ibid 26.

[54] European Commission, 'Towards a European Strategy for Nanotechnology' (Communication) COM (2004) 338 final, 17.

[55] European Commission, 'Nanosciences and Nanotechnologies: An Action Plan for Europe 2005–2009' (Communication) COM (2005) 243 final, 11.

supportive. The Council broadly endorsed the Commission's approach.[56] Likewise, the European Parliament supported the 'objectives and initiatives' set out in the Commission's action plan.[57] It was especially the Parliament which stressed the economic importance of furthering research and development in the area of nanotechnologies, particularly in view of Europe's competitiveness, and requested 'the Commission and the Council to remove any barriers in the form of absent standards or unclear legislation, which unnecessarily hold back the adoption of nanotechnologies and nanosciences in Europe, and to do so without imposing any new bureaucratic hurdles'.[58]

B. The Legislative Review

The core idea of the Commission's incremental approach, namely the review of the existing legislative framework, essentially stagnated after 2005.[59] It was only in June 2008 that the Commission resumed this task. In its Communication on 'Regulatory Aspects of Nanotechnology' the Commission stated:

> [O]verall, it can be concluded that current legislation covers to a large extent risks in relation to nanomaterials and that risks can be dealt with under the current legislative framework. However, current legislation *may* have to be modified in the light of new information becoming available, for example as regards thresholds used in some legislation [emphasis added].[60]

The 2008 Communication identified the legislation on chemicals,[61] worker protection,[62] specific product legislation (covering plant protection products,[63]

[56] Council of the European Union, 'Competitiveness (Internal Market, Industry and Research)' (Press Release, 2605th Council Meeting) 12487/04 (Presse 269) 24 September 2004, 4.

[57] European Parliament, 'Resolution of 28 September 2006 on Nanosciences and Nanotechnologies: An Action Plan for Europe 2005–2009' (P6_TA(2006)0392) para 4.

[58] ibid para 12. It was only towards the end of its resolution that the Parliament mentioned the desirability of integrating social, health and safety aspects into nanotechnological development (para 18).

[59] According to Vogelezang-Stoute, 'the "incremental approach" in the short run does not seem to lead to any regulatory changes at all', see E Vogelezang-Stoute, 'Regulating Uncertain Risks of New Technologies: Nanomaterials as a Challenge for the Regulator' in M Peeters and R Uylenburg (eds), *EU Environmental Legislation: Legal Perspectives on Regulatory Strategies* (Cheltenham, Edward Elgar Publishing, 2014) 218.

[60] European Commission, 'Regulatory Aspects of Nanomaterials' (Communication) COM (2008) 366 final, 3.

[61] Regulation of the European Parliament and of the Council (EC) 1907/2006 of 18 December 2006 concerning the registration, evaluation, authorisation and restriction of chemicals (REACH) [2006] OJ L396/1.

[62] Council Directive 89/391/EEC of 12 June 1989 on the introduction of measures to encourage improvements in the safety and health of workers at work [1989] OJ L183/1.

[63] Council Directive 91/414/EEC of 15 July 1991 concerning the placing of plant protection products on the market [1991] OJ L230/1.

cosmetics,[64] animal feed and food additives,[65] novel foods,[66] etc), the General Product Safety Directive[67] and environmental legislation[68] as the relevant existing legislative frameworks. However, to what extent these existing frameworks should be adjusted to the specific characteristics of nanomaterials remained unclear. The Commission postponed its answer for a further three years, referring to the current lack of 'knowledge on essential questions such as characterisation of nanomaterials, their hazards, exposure, risk assessment and risk management'.[69]

This time, however, the EU legislature disagreed among themselves and vis-a-vis the Commission. Contrary to the Parliament's tone in 2006, which was mostly oriented towards the economic aspects of nanotechnological development, the emphasis now turned sharply to its environmental, health and safety risks.[70] Unambiguously, the Parliament clarified that it

> does not agree, before an appropriate evaluation of current Community legislation, and in the absence of any nano-specific provisions therein, with the Commission's conclusions that a) current legislation covers in principle the relevant risks relating to nanomaterials, and b) that the protection of health, safety and the environment needs mostly be enhanced by improving implementation of current legislation, when due to the lack of appropriate data and methods to assess the risks relating to nanomaterials it is effectively unable to address its risks.[71]

Nonetheless, the Commission confirmed its approach in its 'Second Regulatory Review of Nanomaterials' of 2012.[72] Inter-institutional disagreement crystallised, especially between the Commission and the European Parliament, over the very approach taken to the regulation of nanotechnologies.[73] How the legislative review is progressing in practice will be addressed in the case studies.[74]

[64] Regulation of the European Parliament and of the Council (EC) 1223/2009 of 30 November 2009 on cosmetic products [2009] OJ L342/59.

[65] Regulation of the European Parliament and the Council (EC) 1333/2008 of 16 December 2008 on food additives [2008] OJ L354/16.

[66] Regulation of the European Parliament and of the Council (EC) 258/97 of 27 January 1997 concerning novel foods and novel food ingredients [1997] OJ L43/1.

[67] Directive of the European Parliament and the Council 2001/95/EC of 3 December 2001 on general product safety [2002] OJ L11/4.

[68] Directive of the European Parliament and of the Council 2008/1/EC of 15 January 2008 concerning integrated pollution prevention and control [2008] OJ L24/8; Council Directive 96/82/EC of 9 December 1996 on the control of major-accident hazards involving dangerous substances [1997] OJ L10/13; Directive of the European Parliament and the Council 2000/60/EC of 23 October 2000 establishing a framework for Community action in the field of water policy [2000] OJ L327/1 and Directive of the European Parliament and of the Council 2006/12/EC of 5 April 2006 on waste [2006] OJ L114/9.

[69] 'Regulatory Aspects of Nanomaterials' COM (2008) 366 final (n 60) 11.

[70] The Parliament referred directly, in the resolution's very first point, to profound environmental, health and safety concerns related to nanotechnologies, which it felt needed to be tackled 'within a clear regulatory and policy framework', European Parliament, 'Resolution of 24 April 2009 on Regulatory Aspects of Nanomaterials' (P6_TA(2009)03287) para 1.

[71] ibid para 13.

[72] European Commission, 'Second Regulatory Review on Nanomaterials' (Communication) COM (2012) 572 final.

[73] See also E Vogelezang-Stoute, 'Regulating Uncertain Risks of New Technologies' (n 59) 220.

[74] Below chapters 4 and 5.

C. Complementary Elements

The Commission turned its attention to the 'complementary' elements proposed by the experts in 2004. To this end, it focused first on the adoption of non-binding measures, both of a sector-specific and cross-sectoral nature. The most prominent cross-sectoral example is the 2008 'Code of Conduct for Responsible Nanosciences and Nanotechnologies Research' that the Commission adopted in the form of a recommendation.[75] The Code lays down general principles and guidelines on how researchers should cope with scientific uncertainty.[76] In addition, guidance documents have been (and are currently being) updated in different sectors in order to account for the particular characteristics of nanomaterials, for example, in the performance of risk assessments. These sector-specific guidance documents will be analysed more closely in the case studies in chapters four and five.

Secondly, the feasibility of the creation of a mandatory EU-wide public inventory of products containing nanomaterials has been contemplated for several years, with the aim of gathering essential information relevant for the drafting and implementation of a regulatory framework.[77] With the recent introduction of national mandatory reporting systems in France,[78] Belgium[79] and Denmark,[80] and ongoing discussions in several other Member States, including

[75] Commission Recommendation 2008/345/EC of 7 February 2008 on a code of conduct for responsible nanosciences and nanotechnologies research [2008] OJ L116/46. The Commission's recommendation was supported by the Council in its conclusions of September 2008, in which it 'invite[d] Member States and other stakeholders concerned to take note of the Commission Recommendation', see Council of the European Union, 'Council conclusions on responsible nanosciences and nanotechnologies research' 13672/08, para 8. Bowman and Hodge conducted a study on the existing nanotechnology-specific codes of conduct, see DM Bowman and GA Hodge, 'Counting on Codes: An Examination of Transnational Codes as a Regulatory Governance Mechanism for Nanotechnologies' (2009) 3 *Regulation & Governance* 145.

[76] The Code is based on a set of seven broad principles: meaning (research activities should be comprehensible to the public), sustainability, precaution, inclusiveness, excellence in the form of the best scientific standards, innovation, and accountability.

[77] Milieu Ltd and RPA Ltd, 'Proposal for an EU Reporting System for Nanomaterials' (n 31). The need 'to develop harmonized compulsory databases of nanomaterials and products containing nanomaterials' was reconfirmed in a workshop organised by the Belgian EU Presidency 'Towards a regulatory framework for the traceability of nanomaterials' (Workshop organised by the Belgian EU Presidency, Brussels, 14 September 2010). RIVM, 'Development of an inventory for consumer products containing nanomaterials' (Final report, European Commission—DG Environment, 2011) www.ec.europa.eu/environment/chemicals/nanotech/pdf/study_inventory.pdf.

[78] France adopted a decree for the mandatory reporting of products containing nanomaterials in February 2012, which came into force on 1 January 2013, Décret n° 2012–232 du 17 février 2012 relatif à la déclaration annuelle des substances à l'état nanoparticulaire pris en application de l'article L. 523–4 du code de l'environnement.

[79] The Belgian Council of Ministers validated the national mandatory register on 7 February 2014 and the registration of substances began on 1 January 2016. See www.presscenter.org/fr/pressrelease/20140208/la-belgique-met-en-place-un-registre-des-nanomateriaux.

[80] See Statutory Order no 644 of 13 June 2014 on an inventory of mixtures and products that contain nanomaterials and the duty of manufacturers and importers to report to the inventory www.eng.mst.dk/topics/chemicals/nanomaterials/.

Germany[81] and Sweden,[82] the Commission is under pressure to act in order not to jeopardise the functioning of the internal market.[83] Finally, since the adoption of the Commission's Action Plan in 2005, various official attempts have been launched to engage affected actors in a dialogue on nanotechnological development and regulation at the European level—in the form of citizens' conferences,[84] scientific hearings,[85] public consultations[86] and multi-stakeholder dialogues.[87]

V. CONCLUSION

The current controversy surrounding the emergence of nanotechnologies oscillates between the two extremes of nanomania and nanophobia. In the case of nanotechnologies, the most promising and the most disastrous appear to be inextricably linked, with severe risks accompanying their emergence. The presence of these risks, in turn, was found to constitute a justification for regulatory intervention. Yet, in view of the scientific uncertainty dominating the area, the point at which these risks can actually be considered to be controlled and, hence, at which the regulation of nanotechnologies can be considered 'effective' was found contingent upon how much risk a society is willing to take.

[81] The SPD fraction of the German Bundestag requested in December 2011 'ein öffentliches Produktregister und eine Meldepflicht erforderliche und angemessene Maßnahmen' (a public product register and an obligation to notify necessary and proportionate measures), see Antrag der SPD Fraktion, *Chancen der Nanotechnologien nutzen und Risiken für Verbraucher reduzieren* (Exploiting the opportunities of nanotechnologies and reducing their risks for consumers), Drucksache 17/8158, 14 December 2011.

[82] Swedish Chemicals Agency, 'Förslag om utökad anmälningsplikt för nanomaterial' (Proposal for expanded notification requirements for nanomaterials) (Rapport från ett regeringsuppdrag, 2015).

[83] In 2013, the Commission launched a call for tenders for an impact assessment of a nano register—for a 'study to assess the impact of possible legislation to increase transparency on nanomaterials on the market'—see www.ec.europa.eu/enterprise/newsroom/cf/itemdetail.cfm?item_id=6735&lang=en.

[84] The Commission's DG Sanco organised the 'Nanosafety for Success Dialogue' annually between 2007 and 2011, see for further information on the 'Safety for Success Dialogues' the respective website of the organiser DG Sanco www.ec.europa.eu/health/nanotechnology/events/index_en.htm.

[85] In September 2009, DG Sanco held a scientific hearing on nanotechnologies risk assessment, see www.ec.europa.eu/health/nanohearing_en.htm.

[86] In recent years, the Commission, and also its scientific committees and agencies, have launched dozens of public consultations with respect to nanotechnological policy and development. These will be analysed more closely in the case studies in chapters 4 and 5.

[87] In January 2010, the Commission launched the NanoCode project with the aim of supporting the implementation, adoption and potential revision of its recommendation on a nano code of conduct. NanoCode is financed by the FP7 programme. For more information, see www.nanocode.eu/mos/Frontpage/Itemid,1/. One of its mandates was to develop suggestions for revision within the scope of a 'multi-stakeholder dialogue', taking place at the European and national level. For the final report, including its recommendations, see A Grobe, N Kreinberger and P Funda, 'Synthesis Report—Stakeholder's Attitudes towards the European Code of Conduct for Nanosciences & Nanotechnologies Research' (Report, FP7 NanoCode Project, March 2011).

At the European level, the regulation of nanotechnologies has its origin in an expert workshop organised by the Commission in 2004. In this workshop, an 'incremental approach' to the regulation of nanotechnologies—meaning the adaptation of the existing legislative framework to the intricacies of the nanoform—was proposed. This was to be accompanied by further elements, such as the instigation of voluntary measures and public involvement. Whilst the Commission has pursued this approach in its official policy documents to the present day, the EU legislature, especially the European Parliament, has expressed its strong discontent at such an approach. In the case studies of chapters four and five, the incremental approach will be carefully scrutinised in two sectors. First, however, chapters two and three will establish the theoretical and conceptual foundation necessary to accomplish this task.

2

Regulating in Today's Nano Society

THIS CHAPTER LAYS down the theoretical foundations of this book. To that end, in line with the 'EU law in context' approach, section I strives first to embed the emergence of nanotechnologies in its societal context. The objective is to present this book's guiding image of 'today's nano society'. The overarching argument will be that the rise of nanotechnologies exemplifies fundamental transformations in modern societies, namely those of globalisation, functional differentiation and the rise of the risk society.

Section II will go on to provide normative perspectives on how to regulate given the changing societal context that is embodied by the emergence of nanotechnologies. The foundation for these considerations will be Habermas's discourse theory of law and democracy and Teubner's account of reflexive law. The theoretical considerations will suggest that the regulator, on its own, increasingly lacks the capacity to regulate in today's nano society. Close involvement of affected societal actors in the decision-making process, a proceduralisation of the production of norms, has been advocated by Habermas and Teubner in order to strengthen the capacity to regulate.

Finally, section III will take the discussion to the EU level. The argument will be that the theoretical considerations presented in section II also stimulated the 'governance debate' at the EU level in the late 1990s. The scholarly debate, which evolved around the Commission's White Paper on European Governance, focused on the development and desirability of 'new modes of governance' that are supposedly more inclusive, flexible and transparent than the traditional method of regulation at the EU level, the 'Community method', in order to increase the EU's capacity to regulate. The aim of section III is to deconstruct the debate in order to discern the original ideas and theoretical roots underpinning its concepts and reform proposals.

I. EMBEDDING THE REGULATION OF NANOTECHNOLOGIES IN ITS SOCIETAL CONTEXT

Contemporary societies are witnessing a number of fundamental transformations. Three interrelated transformations, which imply far-reaching social changes and which take place at the European, national and/or global level, are considered: globalisation, functional differentiation and the rise of the risk society. It is argued that the emergence of nanotechnologies exemplifies these developments.

A. Globalisation

Since the 1980s, Europe, like any other part of the world, has been confronted with a new era: the era of globalisation.[1] Globalisation in its widest sense refers to a variety of connected processes of change, leading to a gradual global interdependence of people, economic activity and culture.[2] The boundaries of the concept of globalisation are blurred.[3] It is associated with phenomena of an economic, political, technological, cultural and environmental nature, all but coined by an experience of acceleration.[4] Globalisation has been shaped by developments in means of communication, notably television and the Internet, which render the increasing speed and volume of (economic, social and cultural) exchanges possible.[5] It embraces a revolution in the systems of transportation, which has led to an unprecedented mobility of freight and people. Goods containing nanomaterials can reach destinations thousands of kilometres away from their production site in no time. Indeed, for many commentators the impact of globalisation appears most significant when looking at it as an economic phenomenon: 'global economic transactions, if measured against nationally limited economic activity, are reaching a level achieved in no other previous epoch, and directly affect national economies on a previously unknown scale'.[6] Overall, this complex set of processes comes down to an increasing interdependence among social and political actors, of a public and private nature, beyond the boundaries of the territorial state. The actions of one society impact on the room for manoeuvre left to another society.

[1] Most of the phenomena associated with globalisation, such as the communication revolution, are arguably restricted (or at least to a great extent reserved) to the OECD countries, F Kratochwil, 'Globalization: What It Is and What It Is Not. Some Critical Reflections on the Discursive Formations Dealing with Transformative Change' in D Fuchs and F Kratochwil (eds), *Transformative Change and Global Order: Reflections on Theory and Practice*, Fragen politischer Ordnung in einer globalisierten Welt no 2 (Hamburg, Litt, 2002) 33 and 34.

[2] See eg J Habermas, *The Postnational Constellation: Political Essay*, Studies in Contemporary German Social Thought (M Pensky (tr), Cambridge, Polity, 2001) 65 and F Kratochwil, 'Globalization' (n 1) 26.

[3] As Kratochwil puts it, globalisation does not refer to a 'fixed thing in the outer world' but rather constitutes a 'discursive formation', F Kratochwil, 'Globalization' (n 1) 26.

[4] A Giddens, *Runaway World: How Globalisation is Reshaping Our Lives* (London, Profile Books, 1999) 10; F Kratochwil, 'Globalization' (n 1) 27 and A Dunsire, 'Modes of Governance' in J Kooiman (ed), *Modern Governance: New Government-Society Interactions* (London, SAGE Publications, 1993) 21.

[5] A Giddens, *Runaway World* (n 4) 11; F Kratochwil, 'Globalization' (n 1) 28; A Sens and P Stoett, *Global Politics: Origins, Currents, Directions*, 3rd edn (Scarborough, Nelson Thomson Learning, 2004) ch 1.

[6] J Habermas, *The Postnational Constellation* (n 2) 66.

B. Functional Differentiation

With his appraisal of the 'disenchantment of the world' in the early twentieth century, Max Weber laid the theoretical foundations for the move away from a unifying worldview based on belief and mysticism towards a secular society based on rationality and predictability.[7] Knowledge achieved a fundamentally new status, as it became the precondition for rational action.[8] Scientific and technical input in the decision-making process rose exponentially, marking the beginning of the technocratic movement.[9] Rationalisation encouraged the division of labour into increasingly specialised tasks. Beyond the manufacturing process every area in human life became rationalised or 'functionalised'.[10] Since Weber, the incremental fragmentation of modern societies into different functions has been one of the main themes in modern social theory. Jürgen Habermas, building on Weber and Luhmann, proceeds from the assumption that modern societies are characterised by an ever-increasing pluralisation and differentiation of functional spheres, which are 'defined by specific tasks of social reproduction'.[11] The high level of complexity of modern societies has, according to Luhmann, led to their differentiation into functional systems.[12] Each functional system would fulfil one specific task in society. In his works, Luhmann has referred, among others, to the economy, politics, science, law, religion and education as functional systems.

Because each system monopolises a specific knowledge, it becomes more and more difficult for the individual systems to understand the operation, the rationality, of the other systems.[13] The meta-rationality in the Weberian sense is lost. That way, the systems become increasingly autonomous from their environment, caught in their own restricted perspective of society. They are no longer able to recognise the norms and knowledge produced by other social systems. Yet, even if a system operates according to its own rationality, this does not entail that the systems are isolated from their respective environments.[14]

[7] M Weber, 'Wissenschaft als Beruf' in D Kaesler (ed), *Max Weber Schriften 1894–1922* (Stuttgart, Kröner, 2002) 488 and 510.

[8] SH Kim, 'Max Weber', *The Stanford Encyclopedia of Philosophy* (Fall edn, 2008), www.plato.stanford.edu/archives/fall2008/entries/weber/.

[9] Sheila Jasanoff defined 'technocracy' as 'support for skill-centred forms of policymaking, especially on matters concerning science and technology', see S Jasanoff, *The Fifth Branch: Science Advisors as Policy Makers* (Cambridge, Harvard University Press, 1991) 9.

[10] M Weber, *The Protestant Ethic and the Spirit of Capitalism* (T Parsons (tr), Mineola, Dover Publications, 2003) 26.

[11] J Habermas, *Between Facts and Norms: Contributions to a Discourse Theory of Law and Democracy*, Studies in Contemporary German Social Thought (W Rehg (tr), Cambridge, The MIT Press, 1996) xvii.

[12] N Luhmann, 'Differentiation of Society' (1977) 2 *The Canadian Journal of Sociology/Cahiers canadiens de sociologie* 29.

[13] G Teubner, 'Introduction to Autopoietic Law' in G Teubner (ed), *Autopoietic Law: A New Approach to Law and Society*, European University Institute—Series A Law no 8 (Berlin, De Gruyter, 1987).

[14] N Luhmann, 'Closure and Openness: On Reality in the World of Law' in G Teubner (ed), *Autopoietic Law* (n 13).

The economic system, for example, can process scientific communication, such as a chemical formula, when translating it into its own economic communication, that is, into the monetary profits resulting from the innovation. Thus, there are interdependencies within society at large.[15]

Being fragmented along functional lines, the different systems in society are also no longer confined to national borders but may transcend territorial lines.[16] In these times of increasing interdependence and globalisation, the economic system is the prime example of cross-border functional operations.[17] Beyond the confines of the individual Member States, which have traditionally played an essential role in integrating a differentiated society, European integration has assumed a more functionalist approach, starting off as a project based purely on economic integration.[18] Yet, variations in the degree to which the functional systems differentiate materialise. Whilst the economic and scientific systems in particular appear to be truly globalised, other systems, such as the cultural and health spheres, are much more territorially embedded.[19] The mingling of truly globalised and differentiated rationalities with those that are (still) locally and socially rooted creates an intrinsic friction.

C. The Rise of the Risk Society

Since the end of the nineteenth century, society has been confronted with the negative side effects of modernisation.[20] Depicting this evolution, Ulrich Beck coined the famous term of the 'risk society'—a society which is faced with the uncertain and above all man-made consequences of scientific and technological progress.[21] 'Risk' traditionally referred to the calculation of risk as probability times effect.[22] This equation goes back to Frank Knight, in the 1920s, who distinguished between

[15] G Teubner, 'Introduction to Autopoietic Law' (n 13).

[16] A Fischer-Lescano and G Teubner 'Regime-Collisions: The Vain Search for Legal Unity in the Fragmentation of Global Law' (2004) 25 *Michigan Journal of International Law* 999. See also G Teubner, 'Fragmented Foundations: Societal Constitutionalism Beyond the State' in P Dobner and M Loughlin (eds), *The Twilight of Constitutional Law: Demise or Transmutation?*, Oxford Constitutional Theory (Oxford, Oxford University Press, 2009).

[17] J Black, *Critical Reflections on Regulation* (ESRC Centre for Analysis of Risk and Regulation, London School of Economics and Political Science, 2002) 5.

[18] EB Haas, *The Uniting of Europe: Political, Social and Economic Forces 1950–1957* (Stanford, Stanford University Press, 1958) and see also PF Kjaer, 'Rationality within REACH? On Functional Differentiation as the Structural Foundation of Legitimacy in European Chemicals Regulation' (2007) European University Institute Working Paper, LAW 2007/18, 17 www.cadmus.eui.eu/bitstream/handle/1814/6948/LAW-2007-18.pdf?sequence=1.

[19] I would like to thank Mark Dawson for pointing this out to me.

[20] U Beck, *Weltrisikogesellschaft* (Frankfurt am Main, Suhrkamp, 2008) 24 and 25.

[21] ibid 19 and 45.

[22] See M Van Asselt, E Vos and B Rooijackers, 'Science, Knowledge and Uncertainty in EU Risk Regulation' in M Everson and E Vos (eds), *Uncertain Risks Regulated*, Law, Science and Society (Abingdon, Routledge Cavendish, 2009).

risk, on the one hand, and uncertainty, on the other.[23] According to him, the term risk implies that the probability of an adverse event occurring and the effects this adverse event will bring about are quantifiable. 'Uncertainties', on the contrary, are unquantifiable in nature; they occur in such situations where probability and/or effect are unknown—either because of gaps in scientific knowledge, which make it impossible to determine the hazard, or because the situation is so novel that statistical information on past occurrences is yet to be generated.[24]

With the rise of the risk society, the use of the term risk in public discourse has blurred with uncertainty. New technologies, such as nuclear power, biotechnology and nanotechnologies, are all discussed in terms of risk, even though it is the uncertainties inherent in those technologies that are the focus of concern. More generally, a shift of focus in the traditional basis for risk assessment can be observed; while formerly the analysis of existing statistical data was at the forefront and the main question used to be 'what has happened in the past?', the focal question is now forward-looking: 'what may happen in the future?'.[25] Scientific and technological progress is taking place at such a rapid pace that only in very few circumstances is it possible to rely on existing data; rather, more and more decisions are taken in situations of little information, high uncertainty and low predictability. 'In the risk society', Beck concludes, 'the past loses the power to determine the present'.[26] The search for control, 'man's control over nature and society', which is characteristic of Weber's perception of modernity, is fundamentally shaken.[27] The recognition that every believed certainty bears the aftertaste of an intractable uncertainty questions the foundation of rational decision making.[28] Society is left with an 'uncertain risk',[29] the level of acceptance of which is inherently subjective in nature, varying according to the local, cultural and historical context:[30] who decides 'how safe is safe enough?'[31]

[23] FH Knight, *Risk, Uncertainty and Profit* (Boston, Hart Shaffner and Marx, 1921).

[24] M Van Asselt et al, 'Science, Knowledge and Uncertainty in EU Risk Regulation' (n 22).

[25] ibid.

[26] U Beck, *Risk Society: Towards a New Modernity* (M Ritter (tr), London, SAGE Publications, 1992) 34.

[27] H Nowotny, P Scott and M Gibbons, *Re-Thinking Science: Knowledge and the Public in an Age of Uncertainty* (Cambridge, Polity Press, 2001) 5 and U Beck, *Risk* Society (n 26) 22.

[28] S Jasanoff, *Science and Public Reason*, The Earthscan Science in Society Series (London, Routledge, 2012) 4.

[29] In order to clarify the conceptual distinction between risk and uncertainty, Van Asselt and Vos coined the notion of 'uncertain risks'. According to their definition, an uncertain risk refers to a specific type of situation in which potentially adverse effects are suspected, yet not definitively known as scientific information and/or data on previous events is lacking, see M Van Asselt et al, 'Science, Knowledge and Uncertainty in EU Risk Regulation' (n 22).

[30] E Fisher, *Risk Regulation and Administrative Constitutionalism* (Oxford, Hart Publishing, 2007) 8 and C Hood, H Rothstein and R Baldwin, *The Government of Risk: Understanding Risk Regulation Regimes* (Oxford, Oxford University Press, 2001) 20.

[31] S Funtowicz, I Shephard, D Wilkinson and J Ravetz, 'Science and Governance in the European Union: A Contribution to the Debate' (2000) 27 *Science and Public Policy* 327, 330; S Jasanoff, *The Fifth Branch* (n 9) 232.

According to Alvin Weinberg, the assumption that science and politics are two fundamentally distinct elements, with science providing the means and politics deciding on the ends, does not hold (anymore).[32] The risks created by the modernisation process lay between the different functional spheres, by crossing 'borders of specialities and disciplines', 'values and fact', and 'politics, the public sphere, science and the economy'.[33] At the same time, these risks, while being capable of inducing systematic and often irreversible harm, remain invisible and can thus be 'changed, magnified, dramatized or minimized within knowledge, and to that extent they are particularly open to social definition and construction'.[34] Uncertain risks thereby turn into resources prone to instrumentalisation by different societal actors.[35] At this point, questions regarding the legitimacy of (scientific) expertise arise.

D. Through the Lenses of Nanotechnologies

The main concern associated with the development towards functional differentiation, globalisation and the rise of the risk society is how to regulate, especially in view of democratic aspirations. The area of nanotechnologies exemplifies these concerns. As ever more nanotechnologies-enabled products enter intra-European and international trade, the relevance of individual nation-states in the resolution of nanotechnological challenges decreases. Furthermore, the autonomy, which Luhmann ascribes to the operations of the functional systems, entails the potential for conflicts between the systems' incompatible rationalities.[36] Such conflicts may arise where systems no longer take into account the effects of their operations, that is, their 'externalities', on the operations of other systems.[37] The extent to which and the severity with which the different rationalities clash mostly depends on the area in question, the area's potential for controversy and the number and nature of the conflicting rationalities involved. In the area of nanotechnologies the different rationalities in society become clearly visible when considering the current debate surrounding their emergence. The potential for conflicts is considerable. In chapter one, the state-of-play of the nano debate was described as swaying between nanomania and nanophobia. Inherent conflicts between the different rationalities of the functional systems crystallised. On the one hand, there is the economic rationality grasping the emergence of nanotechnologies in cost-benefit terms. On the other hand, there are rationalities analysing the developments based on

32 AM Weinberg, 'Science and Trans-Science' (1972) 10 *Minerva* 209, 209.
33 U Beck, *Risk Society* (n 26) 70.
34 ibid 23.
35 S Jasanoff, *The Fifth Branch* (n 9) 6 and S Jasanoff, *Science and Public Reason* (n 28) 103 and 106.
36 G Teubner, 'Substantive and Reflexive Elements in Modern Law' (1983) 17 *Law & Society Review* 239, 266 and 267.
37 J Black, 'Constitutionalising Self-Regulation' (1996) 59 *Modern Law Review* 24, 44.

the (adverse) environmental and health effects of nanotechnologies. Finally, the persistence of scientific uncertainty as regards nanotechnologies' human-made environmental, health and safety risks turns their emergence into an incarnation of Beck's 'risk society'.

II. REGULATING IN TODAY'S NANO SOCIETY: TWO THEORETICAL ACCOUNTS

The aim of this section is to introduce two theoretical perspectives on how to regulate in today's nano society: Jürgen Habermas's discourse theory of law and democracy and Gunther Teubner's theory of reflexive law.

It will be noticed in the subsequent discussion that the terms 'regulation' and 'law' are used interchangeably. The situation becomes even more complex when the notion of 'governance' enters the debate in section III. Suffice it to say for the moment, the means or the tool, which is used to alter the behaviour of societal actors, is often generically referred to as 'law', with various understandings as to what 'law' actually denotes. For the purposes of this book, as will be explained further in chapter three, a broadly defined concept of 'regulation' is adopted that is able to capture different understandings of 'law', embracing what are today often labelled as new modes of governance.

A. A Deliberative Account

Jürgen Habermas describes the political system as the 'subsystem specialised for collectively binding decisions', which acts as 'an arena for the perception, identification, and treatment of problems affecting the whole of society'.[38] In Habermas's account, the political system offers a 'safety mechanism' for the solution of problems which threaten social integration, a mechanism which steps in where other mechanisms of social integration have failed.[39]

According to Habermas, the political system operates through the medium of law.[40] He considers the use of legal norms, complementary to moral norms, as a response to the increasing rationalisation and functionalisation of modern society; behavioural expectations can no longer be stabilised merely through common background assumptions: 'the constitution of the legal form became necessary to offset deficits arising with the collapse of traditional ethical life'.[41] According to Habermas, it is the political system of the modern constitutional

[38] J Habermas, *Between Facts and Norms* (n 11) 300 and 301.
[39] ibid 302.
[40] ibid.
[41] ibid 113.

state that decides which norms become 'law'.[42] Furthermore, Habermas understands 'law' as being inevitably coercive in character. Only legal norms, which are enforceable in public courts, can fulfil their function of stabilising behavioural expectations.[43] Yet, Habermas is less concerned with these 'formal characteristics of law', as he calls them, but with how law and thus political power can (and should) be democratically legitimated.[44] This is where he sees law and political power as 'internally connected'.[45] In his discourse theory of democracy, political power is regarded as legitimate only when it is exercised through a law that emanates from formal discursive procedures that enable the public of a highly complex society to voice its opinion: 'the only law that counts as legitimate is one that could be rationally accepted by all citizens in a discursive process of opinion- and will-formation'.[46] Habermas thus introduces the proceduralist paradigm of law.

Proceduralisation has been defined as 'a form of replacing a substantive decision by a legally established process of consultation, participation, or balancing of interests'.[47] The idea of a shift towards a proceduralist paradigm is based on a critique of the two dominant paradigms of law, the bourgeois, formal law of the classical liberal state and the substantive, material law, which is characteristic of the welfare state.[48] This typology goes back to Weber's evolution of law since the industrial revolution. Whilst the bourgeois law reflected the non-interventionist role of the state and provided only a minimalist framework for the protection of individual rights, the shift (or 'social transformation', as Habermas refers to it) towards a substantive orientation of law was a reaction to the increasing recognition of market failures.[49] The shift towards a substantive law aimed at responding to these shortcomings by setting clear policy objectives, the achievement of which was not only commanded but also controlled by the state.

According to Habermas, law is legitimate only if it secures both a citizen's private autonomy and a citizen's public autonomy. The private autonomy of the citizen refers to the protection of his individual freedom of choice (the law's output).[50] Public autonomy, on the other hand, denotes the citizen's rights of political participation, which ensure his 'rational self-legitimation' (the citizen's input).[51] The materialisation of law aimed at securing the citizen's private autonomy, which the bourgeois formal law failed to achieve in an increasingly complex,

[42] ibid 115.
[43] ibid 122 and 125.
[44] ibid 111.
[45] ibid 133.
[46] ibid 135.
[47] KH Ladeur, *Proceduralization and its Use in Post-Modern Legal Theory* (1996) European University Institute Working Paper, LAW 1995/05 www.cadmus.eui.eu//handle/1814/128 3.
[48] J Habermas and M Rosenfeld, 'Paradigms of Law' (1996) 17 *Cardozo Law Review* 771, 772.
[49] ibid 771.
[50] ibid 775.
[51] J Habermas, *Between Facts and Norms* (n 11) xxv.

differentiated society. Yet, Habermas argues that instead of securing the individual's private autonomy, the material law resulted in the opposite: it led to a 'passive followership and conformity' through the welfare state's detailed regulations and prescriptions imposing 'normal patterns' on the citizen, therewith impairing rather than enhancing his or her private autonomy.[52]

The remedy proposed by Habermas is the proceduralist paradigm of law. His idea is that without public autonomy, that is, without the citizen's participation in the law-making process, private autonomy cannot be secured. It is the citizen, him- or herself, who must, through a discursively structured procedure, determine his or her individual choice. Only in this way can the diverging rationalities be accounted for and can the resulting law be accepted by everyone who is asked to abide by it.

To enable such a deliberation to take place, discursively structured procedures should fulfil the conditions of an 'ideal speech situation'.[53] For an ideal speech situation to exist, Habermas identifies four conditions as inevitable: (1) full inclusion of all actors (no actor affected by a decision is excluded); (2) equality (all actors are given the same opportunity to provide input); (3) sincerity of the participants' input; and (4) non-coercion (no sources of coercion are built into the procedures).[54] The conditions of full inclusion, equality, sincerity and non-coercion are to be secured by a system of procedural rights.[55] Referring to the ideal speech situation, Habermas acknowledges that these conditions can rarely be met in practice, in particular not simultaneously; they should be regarded as the standard which participation should strive to approximately satisfy.[56]

Habermas envisions the deliberative ideal to materialise via a 'two track model' of democratic process;[57] via a more 'informal track' of loose, bottom-up communication in the public sphere 'as a necessary condition for joint political will formation'[58] and via a 'formal track' operating through political institutions that respond to the noise made informally by civil society.[59]

Even though Habermas originally developed his theory in the context of the constitutional state, he later formulated analogous normative demands for the European level. In his 'postnational constellation', Habermas finds an increasing permeability of territorial and political boundaries triggered by the pressures of globalisation: 'politics has to catch up with globalised markets, and has to do so in institutional forms that do not regress below the legitimacy conditions

[52] J Habermas, 'Paradigms of Law' (n 48) 775.

[53] J Habermas, *Zwischen Naturalismus und Religion* (Frankfurt, Suhrkamp, 2005) 89.

[54] ibid.

[55] J Black, 'Proceduralising Regulation: Part I' (2000) 20 *Oxford Journal of Legal Studies* 597, 609.

[56] J Habermas, *Between Facts and Norms* (n 11) 316.

[57] See A Verhoeven, *The European Union in Search of a Democratic and Constitutional Theory*, European Monographs no 38 (The Hague, Kluwer Law International, 2002) 45.

[58] J Habermas, 'The Crisis of the European Union in the Light of a Constitutionalisation of International Law' (2012) 23 *The European Journal of International Law* 335, 339.

[59] See A Verhoeven, *The European Union* (n 57).

for democratic self-legitimation'.[60] While so far democratic self-determination has only been realised at the level of the nation-state, Habermas imagines the development of democratic politics beyond the nation-state in an EU context. His normative pretension is the creation of legitimate structures of political deliberation at the European level:[61] 'expanding Europe's political capacity for action has to happen simultaneously with the expansion of the basis of legitimation of European institutions'.[62]

His demands have not passed without criticism. Habermas himself concedes that the conditions for a Europe-wide public sphere are yet to develop, 'jedoch besteht die Erwartung, dass sich aus dem wachsenden gegenseitigen Vertrauen der europäischen Völker zwischen den Unionsbürgern eine transnational ausgedehnte, wenn auch abgeschwächte Form der Bürgersolidarität entwickelt'.[63] This transnational form of civic solidarity would create 'the political-cultural conditions for appropriate communication processes in the political public sphere'.[64] Such a transnational expansion of civic solidarity needs to be stimulated by 'legal-administrative means' and steered by a media that 'help[s] [national populations] to realise how deeply the decisions of the European Union pervade their everyday lives'.[65]

B. A Reflexive Account

Gunther Teubner describes the political system and the legal system as the regulatory systems (*regulierende Systeme*) in society, while the other functional systems are referred to as regulated systems (*regulierte Systeme*).[66] Unlike Habermas, Teubner thus regards the legal system as yet another system in a functionally differentiated society. Like those other systems in society, the legal system also operates according to its own rationality, which is increasingly autonomous from its environment.[67] Teubner's perspective on the potential of the legal system to integrate a society is thus much more negative than that of Habermas. Although Habermas agrees with an increasing functional differentiation of society, he strongly objects to the idea of law as a closed system, 'uncoupled' from all other social systems. Instead, Habermas assumes the possibility of all systems in society

[60] J Habermas, *The Postnational Constellation* (n 2) 61 and 84.

[61] J Habermas, 'Why Europe Needs a Constitution' (2001) 11 *New Left Review* 5, 5.

[62] J Habermas, *The Postnational Constellation* (n 2) 100.

[63] Meaning, 'there is however the reasonable expectation that a transnational although attenuated form of civic solidarity between EU citizens will develop out of a growing mutual trust between the European peoples' (translation by the author), see J Habermas, *Zur Verfassung Europas* (Berlin, Suhrkamp, 2011) 62.

[64] J Habermas, 'The Crisis of the European Union' (n 58) 340.

[65] ibid 347.

[66] G Teubner, 'Das Regulatorische Trilemma: Zur Diskussion um post-instrumentale Rechtsmodelle' (1984) *Quaderni Fiorentini per la Storia del Pensiero Giuridico Moderno* 109, 127.

[67] G Teubner, 'Substantive and Reflexive Elements in Modern Law' (n 36) 249.

communicating with one another in an ordinary language underlying the codes of the different systems, through the medium of law.[68]

More profoundly, Teubner's understanding of 'law' is fundamentally different from that of Habermas. Like Habermas, Teubner's interest is not the question of what 'law' is, that is, what the formal characteristics of law are.[69] Yet, for Teubner, 'law' is the closed discourse of the legal system.[70] Social norms become legal norms as soon as they are communicated according to what Teubner calls the binary code of legal/illegal.[71] He acknowledges that the state used to play a dominant role in determining which social norms are communicated as legal and illegal respectively.[72] However, in a globalising world, diverse legal discourses co-exist, resulting in a legal pluralism.[73] It is 'the—implicit or explicit—invocation of the legal code which constitutes phenomena of legal pluralism, ranging from the official law of the State to the unofficial law of markets and mafia'.[74] Consequently, 'the binary code legal/illegal is not peculiar to the State. … It refutes categorically any hierarchical superior position of the official law of the State, but invokes rather the imagery of a heterarchy of diverse legal discourses'.[75] Accordingly, 'law', based on Teubner's understanding, neither necessarily originates in the political system of the state, nor is it dependent on state-sanctioned coercion—it is not the norms' institutional structure that is relevant but their discourse.

Teubner's theory of reflexive law emerged in the early 1980s. Like Habermas, Teubner builds his theory on a critique of the substantive orientation of the law of the welfare state, which he observes to be increasingly unable to understand and adequately respond, inter alia, to the scientific, economic and cultural complexities and developments of today's society.[76] Yet, instead of striving for more democratic, legitimate and participatory governance, his focus is on capturing the developments and identifying reasons for, what he calls, the 'crisis of the welfare state'.[77]

As the main cause of the crisis, Teubner identifies the inherent conflicts between the different rationalities, and consequently norms, of the functional systems. He holds that the legal system can only effectively regulate by responding to the

[68] Habermas's idea of 'lifeworld', see J Habermas, *Between Facts and* Norms (n 11) 55. See for a critique, J Black, 'Proceduralizing Regulation: Part II' (2001) 21 *Oxford Journal of Legal Studies* 33, 38.

[69] G Teubner, 'The Two Faces of Janus: Rethinking Legal Pluralism' (1992) 13 *Cardozo Law Review* 1443, 1452.

[70] ibid.

[71] ibid.

[72] G Teubner, 'Das Regulatorische Trilemma' (n 66) 120.

[73] G Teubner, 'The Two Faces of Janus' (n 69) 1443.

[74] ibid 1451.

[75] ibid.

[76] G Teubner, 'Substantive and Reflexive Elements in Modern Law' (n 36) 254; G Teubner, 'Regulatory Law: Chronicle of a Death Foretold' (1992) 1 *Social & Legal Studies* 451; see also J Black, 'Constitutionalising Self-Regulation' (n 37) 45 and RA Posner, 'The Decline of Law as an Autonomous Discipline' (1987) 1000 *Harvard Law Review* 761, 769.

[77] G Teubner, 'Substantive and Reflexive Elements in Modern Law' (n 36) 254.

changing reality of a functionally differentiated society. His idea is that the substantive, result-oriented law is no longer able to fulfil this role due to the high internal complexity and ever-increasing autonomy of the systems.[78] More and more, the legal system appears to lack the capacity to understand the structure and ways of operation of the other systems.[79] No single actor, public or private, is then able to produce and master all knowledge and information required to solve problems of a complex, dynamic and diversified nature in an effective way.[80] Teubner hence speaks of the existence of a 'regulatory trilemma' that comprises three different forms of regulatory failure. The first regulatory failure proceeds from the increasing incongruity of law, politics and society.[81] As regulation is no longer compatible with the interactions of the regulated systems, the systems respond with non-reaction; the law becomes irrelevant to the systems' functioning and therewith ineffective.[82] In the second form of regulatory failure, the incompatibility of law, politics and society endangers the internal operation of the regulated systems. Teubner speaks of an 'overlegalisation of society',[83] which comes close to Habermas's critique of the substantive law of the welfare state that intrudes into the private autonomy of the citizen. The third type of regulatory failure refers to the 'oversocialisation of the law'.[84] While the internal organisation of the regulated systems remains intact, it is the organisation of the legal system itself that is jeopardised. The law is 'conquered' and becomes 'politicised', 'economised', 'environmentalised', etc.[85]

To prevent regulatory failure, Teubner's reflexive law strives at 'co-ordinating action within and between the systems' instead of focusing on 'taking over regulatory responsibility for the outcome of social processes', thereby restricting itself to the provision of an institutional and procedural framework for decision making, which stimulates the 'social self-regulation' of the different systems or actors.[86] Reflexive law therefore requires a less comprehensive knowledge about the other systems.[87] In other words, the legal system acknowledges its systemic limits.

[78] ibid 244 and 271.

[79] Others have referred to such observations as the 'disenchantment' of the traditional forms of command and control regulation, see C Scott, 'Reflexive Governance, Regulation and Meta-Regulation: Control or Learning?' in O de Schutter and J Lenoble (eds), *Reflexive Governance: Redefining the Public Interest in a Pluralistic World*, Modern Studies in European Law no 22 (Oxford, Hart Publishing, 2010) 43. Instead of focusing on the hierarchical control of regulation, Scott emphasises the learning element by applying the ideas of reflexive governance to regulation.

[80] J Kooiman, 'Social-Political Governance: Introduction' in J Kooiman (ed), *Modern Governance: New Government-Society Interactions* (London, SAGE Publications, 1993) 4.

[81] G Teubner, 'Das Regulatorische Trilemma' (n 66) 128.

[82] ibid.

[83] ibid 129.

[84] ibid.

[85] ibid.

[86] G Teubner, 'Substantive and Reflexive Elements in Modern Law' (n 36) 239, 242 and 257. See also C Scott, 'Reflexive Governance, Regulation and Meta-Regulation' (n 79) 45, who refers to similar ideas not as 'reflexive law' but as 'meta-regulation', which he defines as 'the self-regulatory capacities of individuals and organisations … subjected to steering'.

[87] J Black, 'Proceduralizing Regulation: Part I' (n 55) 603.

By suggesting how the law's effectiveness is to be enhanced, reflexive law inevitably incorporates a normative element—how law *should* be designed in order to respond to the societal challenges ahead. Although based on a completely different rationale than that of Habermas, Teubner's reflexive law also suggests a shift towards a procedural orientation of law.

C. Grasping the 'Procedural Turn'

For fundamentally different reasons, both theoretical approaches presented above maintain that the societal dynamics of globalisation, functional differentiation and the rise of the risk society have rendered the imposition of a substantive, result-oriented law increasingly inept to respond to the reality of today's nano society. The traditional command-and-control type of regulation displays a deficit in its capacity to regulate in an effective and legitimate way. According to Habermas, who applies the normative standard of democratic self-determination to the discussion, the substantive law of the welfare state, by imposing detailed prescriptions on the citizen, impairs rather than enhances the individual's freedom of choice. Teubner, on the other hand, claims to observe the cognitive failure of substantive law to adequately respond inter alia to constantly changing scientific, economic and cultural conditions. As the main reason therefore, he identifies severe conflicts between the different societal rationalities, which the legal system is no longer able to capture in their entirety.

Although based on fundamentally different approaches, both Habermas and Teubner suggest a shift towards a procedural orientation of law.[88] In simple terms, Habermas advocates such a shift in order to ensure the citizens' self-determination in the decision-making process, while Teubner encourages such a shift in order to enhance the systems' capacity to self-regulate. The idea in both accounts is thereby not to give up law's role in advancing substantive goals, but that these goals are directly articulated by the law's subjects.[89] While for Teubner the question of how a proceduralisation should be designed is not the focus of attention, Habermas maintains that procedural structures should strive to fulfil the conditions of the ideal speech situation in order to produce legitimate law.[90] Taken together, the preceding theoretical debates imply that *the regulator, on its own, increasingly lacks, on the one hand, the capacity to master the specialised knowledge of the various societal actors; on the other hand, the capacity to ensure the regulation's legitimacy.*

[88] I borrow the term 'procedural turn' in the heading of this section from Mark Dawson, see M Dawson, '*New Governance and the Proceduralisation of European Law: The Case of the Open Method of Coordination*' (Law Department PhD, European University Institute, 2009).

[89] ibid 113.

[90] These are (1) full inclusion, (2) equality and (3) non-coercion. His underlying assumption is that, despite the differentiation of society, which Habermas acknowledges, there exists an ordinary language accessible by all the systems' internal discourses, which allows for deliberation to take place.

The various affected societal actors should be involved in a regulatory process through the instigation of adequate procedures.

III. TRANSLATING THE DEBATE TO THE EU LEVEL

How has the evolution towards today's nano society affected the discourse on regulation at the EU level? To answer this question, it will be necessary to go back to the 1990s and early 2000s. At that time, the traditional method of decision making in the Union, the 'Community method', moved into the spotlight of reformist ambitions.[91] There was criticism of both its effectiveness and legitimacy. On the one hand, the discussion was stirred by reflections of a changing societal context resembling those presented above. On the other hand, the ultimate catalyst that led to the debate taking off was a complex interaction of four incidents that coincided in the course of the 1990s. First, the complexity of issues on the EU agenda increased in the wake of the internal market programme, following a significant expansion of the Union's competences, for instance, in the highly technical and scientific areas of environmental and consumer protection.[92] Secondly, public opinion became increasingly sceptical towards the European integration project.[93] Thirdly, the ongoing enlargement of the EU increased its diversity and raised questions as to the continuing appropriateness of its institutions and procedures.[94] These challenges were reinforced by several scandals taking place at the European level, most notably the food crises of the 1990s and the resignation of the Santer Commission in 1999.[95]

The main response of the European Commission was its 2001 White Paper on European Governance.[96] In that White Paper, the Commission attempted to signal to the outside world its willingness to tackle the institution's alleged deficits by proactively reforming European governance. To comprehend the White Paper, it will be necessary to view it in the context of its preparatory phase and the (academic and policy) reactions that followed its adoption. The 'European governance' debate, which reached its peak in the first half of the 2000s, was framed

[91] R Dehousse, 'The Community Method at Sixty' in R Dehousse (ed), *The Community Method: Obstinate or Obsolete?*, Palgrave Studies in European Union Politics (Basingstoke, Palgrave Macmillan, 2011) 4.

[92] R Dehousse, 'Misfits: EU Law and the Transformation of European Governance' in C Joerges and R Dehousse (eds), *Good Governance in Europe's Integrated Market*, Collected Courses of the Academy of European Law XI/2 (Oxford, Oxford University Press, 2002) 207; M Jachtenfuchs, 'The Governance Approach to European Integration' (2001) 39 *Journal of Common Market Studies* 245, 253.

[93] Exemplified by difficulties in the ratification process of the Maastricht Treaty and decreasing levels of turnout for European Parliament elections, see R Dehousse, 'The Community Method at Sixty' (n 91) 9.

[94] ibid 12.

[95] N Lebessis and J Paterson, 'Developing New Modes of Governance' (2000) Forward Studies Unit, European Commission Working Paper, 7 and 13.

[96] European Commission, 'European Governance—A White Paper' COM (2001) 428 final.

in terms of both the necessity and desirability of a development towards 'new modes of governance' (section III.A) and the rise of EU risk regulation (section III.B). This section focuses on the debate and the mute assumptions of Europe's 'governance turn'[97] that coincided with the adoption of the Commission's White Paper in 2001.

A valid question is of course why undertake this effort at all? Why investigate these debates that took place a decade ago? There are two main reasons why travelling back in time to the origins of the European governance debate is indeed necessary. First, it allows for a retracing of the debate's theoretical roots, thereby expounding the original ideas behind the Commission's buzzwords and reform proposals. Secondly, it is precisely now, one decade on, that the tangible impacts of the debate crystallise. What have the EU institutions really done to reform 'European governance'? What legal procedures have been put in place by the EU institutions to increase their capacity to regulate in the aftermath of the White Paper? And it is these tangible impacts, both their formal constitution and their practical operation, that will be scrutinised in the subsequent chapters of this book.

A. The Rise of 'New Modes of Governance'

In 1996, the Forward Studies Unit (FSU)—the European Commission's then internal think tank[98]—launched a project on governance.[99] The 'interpretative framework' of the FSU project was inspired by ideas introduced in the preceding section, particularly by a systems-theoretic approach, but also by elements of a deliberative account.[100] Accordingly, the FSU project identified the

[97] B Kohler-Koch and B Rittberger, 'Review Article: The "Governance Turn" in ES Studies' (2006) 44 *Journal of Common Market Studies* 27.

[98] The Forward Studies Unit (FSU) was established in 1989 by Jacques Delors as a department of the Commission reporting directly to the President, with the 'futurological task' of monitoring and evaluating the European integrations process, see www.ec.europa.eu/archives/cdp/mission/index_en.htm. In 2004, Barroso transformed the FSU into the Bureau of European Policy Advisors (BEPA), with its core task being the 'support and policy advice to the President on specific tasks, outreach to civil society, institutional activities in the field of ethics in science and new technologies, and pursuit of the dialogue with religions, churches and communities of conviction', see www.ec.europa.eu/bepa/about/fresh-start/index_en.htm.

[99] N Lebessis and J Paterson, 'Evolution in Governance: What Lessons for the Commission? A First Assessment' (1997) Forward Studies Unit, European Commission Working Paper; N Lebessis and J Paterson, 'The Future of European Regulation' (1997) Forward Studies Unit, European Commission Working Paper; N Lebessis and J Paterson, 'A Learning Organisation for a Learning Society: Proposals for Designing Tomorrow's Commission' (1998) Forward Studies Unit, European Commission Working Paper; N Lebessis and J Paterson, 'Improving the Effectiveness and Legitimacy of EU Governance: a Possible Reform Agenda for the Commission' (Report CdP(99)750), Forward Studies Unit, European Commission, 1999); N Lebessis and J Paterson, 'Developing New Modes of Governance' (n 95). The main conclusions were published in an edited volume, which appeared in 2001 together with the final version of the White Paper.

[100] The two approaches are explicitly acknowledged in N Lebessis and J Paterson, 'Developing New Modes of Governance' (n 95) 16.

'complexity, diversity and interdependency' of contemporary society as the main societal challenge, which was found to render traditional command-and-control regulation not only ineffective but also illegitimate.[101] Like Teubner and Habermas, the project portrayed the 'crisis of the welfare state', based on an increasing 'segmental differentiation'[102] of society, including a 'fragmentation of knowledge'.[103]

The project inferred that the ongoing societal changes have posed critical challenges for the EU. The normative suggestion was a shift towards 'new forms of governance', which would rest upon a 'proceduralisation of the production and the application of norms'.[104] Five key features were identified to underpin these new forms of governance: participation, transparency and openness of the policy process, a restricted, co-ordinating role for public authorities, collective learning and systemic coherence.[105] A fundamental repositioning of public authorities, including the European Commission, was implied in this shift.[106] The project assumed that government organs could no longer 'themselves adequately define problems, formulate solutions and implement them'.[107] Rather, the Commission's role should be redirected to the procedural establishment and support of participation.[108] 'Participation', according to the FSU project, was to meet four cumulative conditions: all stakeholders must be identified (1) and able to 'participate meaningfully' in the policy process (2), equity in participation (3) and participation must be seen as an ongoing (as opposed to an ad hoc) process (4).[109] Concrete proposals regarding the formalisation of participation rights were put forward through the adoption of a 'European Charter of Political Rights'.[110] Here, analogies to deliberative ideas and Habermas's ideal speech situation are particularly evident.[111]

[101] N Lebessis and J Paterson, 'Evolution in Governance: What Lessons for the Commission? A First Assessment' (n 99) 7.

[102] ibid 8.

[103] N Lebessis and J Paterson, 'Developing New Modes of Governance' (n 95) 22.

[104] N Lebessis and J Paterson, 'Evolution in Governance: What Lessons for the Commission? A First Assessment' (n 99) 14.

[105] N Lebessis and J Paterson, 'Developing New Modes of Governance' (n 95) 27 and 39.

[106] 'The role of the Commission is being transformed. … Greater emphasis comes to be placed on clarifying the issues and enabling the participation of stakeholders; on maintaining a long-term strategic vision and integrating policies while encouraging the collective development of objectives; on seeking to engage broader contextual expertise rather than assuming a monopoly of expertise; on developing mechanisms for achieving the necessary participation; and on developing those mechanisms in such a way that ongoing evaluation and revision is encouraged in the light of new information or emergent problems' and N Lebessis and J Paterson, 'Evolution in Governance: What Lessons for the Commission? A First Assessment' (n 99) 20.

[107] ibid 15.

[108] ibid 19 and 23.

[109] ibid 23 and 24.

[110] A formalisation of participation rights was proposed following the example of the Aarhus Convention on environmental matters, see N Lebessis and J Paterson, 'Developing New Modes of Governance' (n 95) 30 and 32.

[111] Above section II.A.

i. The White Paper on European Governance

Few of the project's reform proposals made it into the White Paper of 2001. Instead of advocating 'new forms of governance', the Commission proposed a return to the traditional mode of regulation, a 'strengthening [of] the Community method'.[112] The Commission clarified that, from its perspective, the traditional way of regulating in the European Union remains the most important tool—and will remain so in the future. Recognising, however, the existence of a crisis in confidence and concerns about the Union's legitimacy and effectiveness,[113] the Commission suggested a reform agenda 'under the treaties as they stand', in order to 'open up policy making to make it more inclusive and accountable', thereby 'connect[ing] the EU more closely to its citizens'.[114] The Commission's stated objective was to achieve 'good governance' in the European Union, following the principles of openness, participation, accountability, effectiveness, and coherence.[115] While the Commission only vaguely defined these principles,[116] they bear a clear resemblance to the FSU's 'features of new forms of governance'. 'Good governance', according to the Commission, however does not condition a shift to the FSU's understanding of 'new governance', viz. to a comprehensive proceduralisation of norms.

Instead, the White Paper envisaged milder reforms, inter alia, those of 'better involvement' and 'better regulation'.[117] With 'better involvement' the Commission understood a greater participation of civil society in the policy process. The Commission, however, was keen to emphasise that consultation was not to replace but only to supplement decision making by the institutions. Also fundamentally different from the FSU project and the underlying deliberative account of participation, the White Paper argued that a 'culture of consultation cannot be achieved by legal rules', as these would 'create excessive rigidity and risk slowing the adoption of particular policies'.[118] The precise role affected actors should take in the policy process remained ambiguous.[119] In its place, a second reform under

112 'European Governance—A White Paper' COM (2001) 428 final (n 96) 8.

113 ibid 11.

114 ibid 8.

115 ibid.

116 JHH Weiler, 'The Commission as Eurosceptic: A Task-Oriented Commission for a Project-Based Union—A Comment on the First Version of the White Paper' in JHH Weiler, C Joerges and Y Meny (eds), *Symposium: Mountain or Molehill? A Critical Appraisal of the Commission White Paper on Governance* (2011) Jean Monnet Working Paper no 6/01, 2 www.jeanmonnetprogram.org/archive/papers/01/010601.html and DM Curtin and I Dekker, 'Good Governance: The Concept and its Application by the European Union' in DM Curtin and RA Wessel (eds), *Good Governance and the European Union: Some Reflections of Concepts, Institutions and Substance*, Ius Commune Europaeum 49 (Antwerpen, Intersentia, 2004) 5.

117 In total, the Commission proposed four reform approaches: those of 'better involvement', 'better policies, regulation and delivery', 'global governance', and 'refocused institutions'.

118 European Governance—A White Paper' COM (2001) 428 final (n 96) 17.

119 *cf* B Kohler-Koch, 'Governing with the European Civil Society' in B Kohler-Koch and C Quittkat (eds), *De-Mystification of Participatory Democracy: EU Governance and Civil Society* (Oxford, Oxford University Press, 2013) 25.

the heading of 'better regulation' was emphasised. To increase the effectiveness of regulation, policy instruments should, among others, be combined in order to be able to react to changing market conditions more rapidly: 'legislation is often only part of a broader solution combining formal rules with other non-binding tools such as recommendations, guidelines, or even self-regulation within a commonly agreed framework'.[120]

Accordingly, the Commission sought to reform 'European governance' by following a dual approach, taking as its point of departure the EU's traditional method of regulation, the Community method.[121] Thus, on the one hand, the Commission proposed to strengthen the Community method by 'following a less top-down approach', for instance through a closer involvement of stakeholders.[122] On the other hand, the Community method should be complemented with 'non-legislative instruments' outside the latter.[123]

ii. The Concept of 'New (Modes of) Governance'

Unsurprisingly, the Commission's shallow reform suggestions triggered more disappointment than excitement. Strong reactions followed in the subsequent public consultation[124] and academic writings.[125] Above all, the Commission was criticised for (mis)using the White Paper to defend its institutional self-interest.[126] Its strong emphasis on a revival of the Community method was widely interpreted as an attempt to secure (and to some extent regain) its influence on policy initiation and implementation.[127] The Commission's approach towards the participation of affected actors was taunted as a 'vulgar version of the Habermasian notion of deliberative discourse'.[128]

Despite the initial disappointment, the White Paper steered discussion on questions regarding the effectiveness and legitimacy of EU governance and instituted debates on the necessity of and a development towards new ways of regulating in Europe. In the years that followed the White Paper, academic literature analysed the 'transformation of European governance',[129] the 'turn' in EU

[120] European Governance—A White Paper' COM (2001) 428 final (n 96) 20.

[121] 'The Union must renew the Community method by following a less top-down approach and complementing its policy tools more effectively with non-legislative instruments', see ibid 4.

[122] ibid.

[123] ibid.

[124] For the results of the public consultation, see European Commission, *Report from the Commission on European Governance* (Luxembourg, Office for Official Publications of the European Communities, 2003).

[125] For a comprehensive review of the White Paper, see JHH Weiler, C Joerges and Y Meny (eds), *Symposium: Mountain or Molehill? A Critical Appraisal of the Commission White Paper on Governance* (2001) Jean Monnet Working Paper no 6/01 www.jeanmonnetprogram.org/archive/papers/01/010601.html.

[126] eg B Kohler-Koch, 'The Commission White Paper and the Improvement of European Governance' in JHH Weiler, C Joerges and Y Meny (eds), *Symposium: Mountain or Molehill?* (n 125).

[127] ibid.

[128] JHH Weiler, 'The Commission as Eurosceptic' (n 116) 7.

[129] R Dehousse, 'Misfits: EU Law and the Transformation of European Governance' (n 92).

governance,[130] the appearance of 'new governance',[131] or 'governance without government'.[132] The amount of literature is immense. Scholars engaged not only in conceptualising new (modes of) governance but also in finding evidence for their existence. Examples range from observations of an increased involvement of civil society in the regulatory process, such as in the area of environmental protection,[133] to findings that private actors themselves have assumed regulatory functions.[134]

In conceptualising 'new modes of governance', scholarship generally proceeded from a shift away from traditional hierarchical regulation associated with 'government'.[135] In their seminal book *Law and New Governance in the EU and the US*, de Búrca and Scott describe as the six 'key characteristics' of new modes of governance the participation of affected actors, the centrality attached to the accommodation of diversity, the emphasis on revisability and flexibility, the attention paid to the objective of policy learning based on ongoing evaluation and review, transparency and the voluntary or non-binding nature of norms.[136]

Often, however, the 'key characteristics' or 'attributes' of new governance have been used, unknowingly or without being admitted as such, in two decisively distinct ways: to describe the emergence of the most varied 'new' regulatory arrangements, such as the Open Method of Coordination, New Approach Directives, the rise of EU agencies and the expansion of comitology structures, but also as normative yardsticks, implying that the possession of the key characteristics is a state to be desired, for example, in order to 'advance

[130] B Kohler-Koch and B Rittberger, 'Review Article: The "Governance Turn" in ES Studies' (n 97).

[131] See J Scott and DM Trubek, 'Mind the Gap: Law and New Approaches to Governance in the European Union' (2002) 8 *European Law Journal* 1 and N Walker and G De Búrca, 'Reconceiving Law and New Governance' (2007) 13 *Columbia Journal of European Law* 519.

[132] See eg M Jachtenfuchs, 'The Governance Approach to European Integration' (n 92) 264.

[133] J Scott and DM Trubek, 'Mind the Gap' (n 131) 3.

[134] F Cafaggi, 'Rethinking Private Regulation in the European Regulatory Space' in F Cafaggi (ed), *Reframing Self-Regulation in European Private Law*, Private Law in European Context Series vol 9 (Alphen aan den Rijn, Kluwer Law International, 2006) 4 and 6 and C Joerges, 'The Law's Problems with the Governance of the European Market' in C Joerges and R Dehousse (eds), *Good Governance in Europe's Integrated Market*, Courses of the Academy of European Law XI/2 (Oxford, Oxford University Press, 2002) 4. Attention hereby focused particularly on the introduction of two specific instruments or processes, the 'New Approach to Harmonisation' of the 1980s and the 'Open Method of Coordination' (OMC) following the adoption of the Lisbon Agenda in 2000. These two examples are also given in P Craig and G De Búrca, *EU Law: Text, Cases, and Materials*, 5th edn (Oxford, Oxford University Press, 2011) 162.

[135] B Kohler-Koch and B Rittberger, 'Review Article: The "Governance Turn" in ES Studies' (n 97) 28 and S Bartolini, 'New Modes of European Governance: An Introduction' in A Héritier and M Rhodes (eds), *New Modes of Governance in Europe: Governing in the Shadow of Hierarchy*, Palgrave Studies in European Union Politics (Basingstoke, Palgrave Macmillan, 2011) 7.

[136] '[N]ew governance forms can be depicted descriptively in terms of some of the key characteristics which they can be said to exhibit', G De Búrca and J Scott, 'Introduction' in G De Búrca and J Scott (eds), *Law and New Governance in the EU and the US*, Essays in European Law no 10 (Oxford, Hart Publishing, 2006) 3.

constitutional and democratic values'.[137] The delineation between descriptive and normative accounts blurs. What exactly 'new modes of governance' in the EU context are (or should be) remains therefore vague. To no surprise, in 2006 Smismans asserted the existence of a 'participatory myth' in new modes of governance. Based on an empirical case study in the field of occupational health and safety, Smismans concluded that: 'more heterarchical, horizontal and flexible modes of governance do not necessarily imply more participation and inclusion in terms of involving all the stakeholders as too quickly taken for granted by some normative claims about the participatory and deliberative democratic character of new governance'.[138]

At a policy level, the Commission's approach stipulated in the White Paper was confirmed and further elaborated on in various documents of the EU institutions after 2001. The approach is thus reflected in the Commission's Better Regulation initiative[139] and was consolidated in the Interinstitutional Agreements on Better Law-Making of 2003 and 2016.[140]

B. The Rise of European Risk Regulation

An integral part of the debate on European governance focused on the integration of technical and scientific expertise in the regulatory process—how should knowledge be collected, imparted and debated? Even though competences in the area of environmental and consumer protection—objects of regulatory activity which are often defined in terms of risk[141]—were not initially envisaged by the drafters of the Treaties of Rome, the completion of the single market entailed the transfer of much more powers to the European level than foreseen.[142] Rapidly, deregulatory pressures were perceived to necessitate the development of positive

[137] See eg K Armstrong and C Kilpatrick, 'Law, Governance and New Governance? The Changing Open Method of Co-ordination' (2007) 13 *Columbia Journal of European Law* 649.

[138] S Smismans, 'New Modes of Governance and the Participatory Myth' (2006) European Governance Paper (EUROGOV) N-06-01, 5.

[139] The origin of the Better Regulation initiative lies in a report of an advisory group of national experts under the chairmanship of the French representative Mandelkern (the 'Mandelkern Report'), see D Mandelkern et al, 'Mandelkern Group on better Regulation Final Report' (European Commission, 2001) www.ec.europa.eu/smart-regulation/better_regulation/documents/mandelkern_report.pdf. Most recently, the Better Regulation was 'revamped' with the adoption of the Commission's 'Better Regulation Package' of 19 May 2015. For a critical discussion of the package, see A Alemanno, 'How Much Better is Better Regulation?' (2015) 3 *European Journal of Risk Regulation* 344 and M Dawson, 'Better Regulation and the Future of EU Regulatory Law and Politics' (2016) 53 *Common Market Law Review* 1209.

[140] Interinstitutional Agreement on better law-making [2003] OJ C321/01 and Interinstitutional Agreement on better law-making [2016] OJ L123/1.

[141] Above chapter 1, section III. See also E Fisher, 'Risk and Governance' in D Levi-Faur (ed), *Oxford Handbook of Governance*, Oxford handbooks in politics & international relations (Oxford, Oxford University Press, 2012) 419.

[142] C Joerges, 'The Law's Problems with the Governance of the European Market' (n 134) 4.

rules at the EU level.[143] Incrementally the EU institutions had to engage in highly technical and scientific issues as functional spillovers from the completion of the internal market.[144] The bovine spongiform encephalopathy (BSE) crisis of the late 1990s shifted attention to precisely these issues and sparked claims for a comprehensive overhaul of the ad hoc science-based decision making in the EU.[145] An Inquiry Report of the European Parliament (the 'Medina Ortega Report') found major shortcomings in the EU's exercise of political power, ranging from a lack of transparency and the blurring of scientific and political decisions to a lack of effectiveness in the implementation of EU policies at the national level.[146]

The FSU project suggested as one essential element of new modes of governance a radical democratisation of scientific expertise in order to enhance the interfaces between policy making, expertise and public debate. In other words, risk regulation should move from a substantive to a procedural rationality. The project maintained that the development of 'pluralistic scientific expertise' is needed for three main reasons. First of all, scientific decision making should become more responsive to societal needs in order to re-establish a connection between science and society. Secondly, the opening up of scientific expertise would contribute to counter the functional differentiation and fragmentation of knowledge by providing a platform for interdisciplinary communication. Finally, trans-scientific issues must be discussed in open political processes in order to expose underlying assumptions and potential uncertainties of various opinions.[147] The overall objective was 'to improve communication between science and society by encouraging the exposure of assumptions … and to make political the choices that have been reserved to experts'.[148]

Although the European Commission, in its White Paper, recognised the significance of taking into account 'a wide range of disciplines and experience beyond the purely scientific',[149] especially moral and ethical issues, it did not support a strict democratisation of scientific expertise as proposed by the FSU. As is clear from the previous section, the Commission rejected a strict shift towards

[143] Especially after the ECJ's *Cassis de Dijon* judgment (Case C-120/78 *Rewe-Zentrale AG v Bundesmonopolverwaltung fur Branntwein* [1979] ECR 649), fears arose that the Court had paved the way for a deregulated free market economy at the expense of consumer protection. See also S Weatherill and P Beaumont, *EU Law*, 3rd edn (London, Penguin, 1999) 600 and R Dehousse, 'Misfits: EU Law and the Transformation of European Governance' (n 92) 227.

[144] For instance, Case C-178/84 *Commission of the European Communities v Federal Republic of Germany* [1987] ECR 1227; S Funtowicz et al, 'Science and Governance in the European Union' (n 31) 328.

[145] M Everson and E Vos, 'European Risk Governance in a Global Context' in E Vos (ed), *European Risk Governance—Its Science, Its Inclusiveness and Its Effectiveness* (Mannheim, CONNEX Report Series, 2008) 7.

[146] European Parliament, 'Report on alleged contraventions or maladministration in the implementation of Community law in relation to BSE, without prejudice to the jurisdiction of the Community and national courts' (A4-0020/97/A, 7 February 1997).

[147] N Lebessis and J Paterson, 'Developing New Modes of Governance' (n 95) 34.

[148] ibid 35.

[149] 'European Governance—A White Paper' COM (2001) 428 final (n 96) 19.

a proceduralisation of norms. Instead, the Commission found European risk regulation to be built on two major principles: the principle of risk analysis and the principle of precaution.[150]

i. Risk Analysis

First, the Commission concentrated its reformist attention on a more 'transparent' decision-making process by disentangling 'the opacity of the Union's system of expert committees' and by institutionally separating the allegedly scientific risk assessment from the political process of risk management.[151] This separation is commonly captured under the principle of 'risk analysis'.[152] The principle denotes a strictly science-based approach to risk regulation consisting of three distinct elements: risk assessment, risk management and risk communication.[153] This separation was first articulated at the European level in the food sector as an immediate response to the BSE crisis.[154] The objective was to counter criticisms voiced in the above-mentioned Medina Ortega Report.[155] Whereas 'risk assessment' is framed in that report as a purely scientific exercise in order to identify and evaluate hazards to health and the environment, the 'risk management' stage would involve the political balancing between the costs and benefits of deciding in different ways. Risk managers are asked to decide, based on the scientific assessment and 'other legitimate factors' such as societal, economic, traditional, ethical, and environmental factors, whether a risk is acceptable to society or not.[156]

[150] ibid.

[151] ibid. Risks and scientific uncertainties identified in the risk assessment should be communicated to citizens and policy makers. To that end, the drafting of guidelines for the selection and use of expertise was proposed, as well as open meetings of scientific committees and the publication of scientific advice. The Commission in December 2002 adopted the principles and guidelines on the 'collection and use of expertise', European Commission, 'Communication from the Commission on the Collection and Use of Expertise by the Commission: Principles and Guidelines' COM (2002) 713 final.

[152] Alemanno refers to the principle of 'risk analysis' as the *Grundnorm* of EU risk regulation, see A Alemanno, 'Regulating the European Risk Society' in A Alemanno, F Den Butter, A Nijsen and J Torriti (eds), *Better Business Regulation in a Risk Society* (New York, Springer, 2013) 41.

[153] O Renn, *Risk Governance: Coping with Uncertainty in a Complex World*, Risk in Society Series (London, Earthscan, 2008) 8. The approach was originally developed by the US National Research Council in 1983; see National Research Council, *Risk Assessment in the Federal Government: Managing the Process* (Washington DC, National Academies Press, 1983).

[154] Accordingly, the Commission's Communication on Consumer Health and Food Safety (1997) first defined the risk regulation process as being split into the aforementioned three stages, see European Commission, 'Communication on Consumer Health and Food Safety' COM (97) 183 final, 7. See also E Vos and F Wendler, 'Food Safety Regulation at EU Level' in E Vos and F Wendler (eds), *Food Safety Regulation in Europe, A Comparative Institutional Analysis*, Ius Commune Europaeum 62 (Antwerp, Intersentia, 2006) 66–71.

[155] A Alemanno, 'EU Risk Regulation and Science: The Role of Experts in Decision-Making and Judicial Review' in E Vos (ed), *European Risk Governance—Its Science, Its Inclusiveness and Its Effectiveness* (n 145) 43.

[156] E Fisher, *Risk Regulation and Administrative Constitutionalism* (n 30) 7. See for the area of food safety, European Commission, 'White Paper on Food Safety' COM (1999) 719 final, 9; A Szajkowska, 'Different Actors, Different Factors—Science and Other Legitimate Factors in the EU and National Food Safety Regulation' (2011) 4 *European Journal of Risk Regulation* 523, 523.

The strict separation between risk assessment and risk management should furthermore be reflected in the EU's institutional structure. The scientific risk assessment should accordingly be left to independent experts sitting either in the Commission's scientific committees or in EU agencies. The political risk management, on the other hand, should be carried out by the Commission and Member State representatives in comitology committees.[157]

Contrary to what this book's guiding image of today's nano society would suggest, the Commission eventually inferred that the scientific rationality could be strictly separated from ethical, moral, economic and social values. This clear distinction between science and politics presupposes the existence of a scientific truth. Rather than 'opening up' scientific expertise, the Commission's rhetoric hence isolates scientific assessment, functionally and institutionally, thereby neglecting questions of a trans-scientific character, such as those marked by uncertainty.

ii. Precaution

Secondly, for situations characterised by scientific uncertainty, the White Paper advocates recourse to the precautionary principle.[158] Although not explicitly defined by the Commission, the principle generally enables the adoption of protective measures even if full scientific certainty as to environmental and health risks is still lacking. In short, it applies to circumstances in which a scientific risk assessment cannot be sufficiently completed.[159] In such situations, regulators are called on to 'err on the side of safety'.[160] Does this mean that the precautionary principle allows for economic, social, moral and ethical values to re-enter scientific assessment? The Commission's official answer to this question is 'no'. A short *excursus* to the historical development of the precautionary principle clarifies the Commission's position.

The principle was formally included in the European legal order with the Treaty of Maastricht in 1992, in Article 130r, now Article 191(2) of the Treaty on the Functioning of the European Union (TFEU) on environmental protection, yet without providing a specific definition.[161] Although the Court of Justice (ECJ) and the Court of First Instance (CFI; now the General Court) were asked to review purportedly precautionary measures adopted by EU institutions and Member States before 1992, the bulk of the case law developed after the entry into force of

[157] E Vos and F Wendler, 'Food Safety Regulation at EU Level' (n 154) 88.

[158] 'European governance—A white paper' COM (2001) 428 final (n 96) 19.

[159] European Commission, 'Communication from the Commission on the precautionary principle' COM (2000) 1 final, 12.

[160] GE Marchant, DJ Sylvester and KW Abbott, 'Risk Management Principles of Nanotechnology' (2008) 2 *NanoEthics* 43, 46.

[161] The roots of the idea of a precautionary approach go back to the German *Vorsorgeprinzip* in the 1970s, see J Zander, *The Application of the Precautionary Principle in Practice, Comparative Dimensions* (Cambridge, Cambridge University Press, 2010) 76.

the Maastricht Treaty.[162] In the years that preceded the BSE crisis, the ECJ and CFI commonly conceded a wide margin of discretion to the EU institutions regarding the application of the precautionary principle when being confronted with Article 263 TFEU challenges to Union acts. First of all, the Courts limited their scope of review to purely procedural issues, to rule whether 'the measure in question is vitiated by a manifest error or misuse of powers, or whether the authority in question has manifestly exceeded the limits of its discretion'.[163] Secondly, the Courts did not require the EU institutions 'to prove the factual basis of their decisions to establish the legal validity of such decisions'.[164] With respect to cases in which Member States took precautionary action in order to derogate from Articles 34 and 35 TFEU on the free movement of goods, in many instances the ECJ found the national derogation to be justified; especially in situations where there was no harmonisation, the Court granted Member States the liberty to autonomously decide on the 'degree of protection of the health and life of humans'.[165]

Following the BSE crisis, the wide discretion granted to EU institutions and Member States in situations of scientific uncertainty was increasingly perceived as compromising the legitimacy and effectiveness of EU policies.[166] Towards the end of the 1990s, clear guidelines on how to act in situations of uncertainty were therefore demanded.[167] The response of the European Commission was its Communication on the Precautionary Principle, which was adopted in 2000, one year before the White Paper on European Governance.[168] In order to counter the perceived arbitrariness denounced in the Medina Ortega Report, the objective of the Communication was to ensure that 'decisions were underpinned by objective and independent science', even under circumstances of scientific uncertainty.[169]

[162] For a detailed analysis, see E Fisher, *Risk Regulation and Administrative Constitutionalism* (n 30) 218ff.

[163] Case C-180/96 *United Kingdom of Great Britain and Northern Ireland v Commission of the European Communities* [1998] ECR I-2265; Case C-331/88 *R v Minister of Agriculture, Fisheries and Food and Secretary of State for Health, ex parte FEDESA* [1990] ECR I-4023, para 8; Case C-284/95 *Safety Hi-Tech Srl v S. & T. Srl* [1998] ECR I-4301, para 37.

[164] E Fisher, *Risk Regulation and Administrative Constitutionalism* (n 30) 218ff; eg Case C-331/88 *R v Minister of Agriculture, Fisheries and Food and Secretary of State for Health, ex parte FEDESA* [1990] ECR I-4023, para 9.

[165] E Fisher, *Risk Regulation and Administrative Constitutionalism* (n 30) 221; Case C-174/82 *Criminal proceedings against Sandoz BV* [1983] ECR 2445, para 11.

[166] Conflicts also arose at the international level in the World Trade Organisation (WTO). eg the US requested consultations in 1996 due to the EU's broad interpretation of the precautionary approach under Art 5.7 of the WTO SPS Agreement, see *European Communities—Measures Concerning Meat and Meat Products (Hormones)*, Mutually acceptable solution on implementation (notified on 25 September 2009) DS26.

[167] In 1999, the Council urged the Commission to 'develop as a priority, clear and effective guidelines for the application of this [the precautionary] principle', Council of the European Union (Press Release, 2171st Council meeting Consumer Affairs) 7212/99 (Presse 98) 13 April 1999, 7.

[168] 'Communication from the Commission on the Precautionary Principle' COM (2000) 1 final (n 159).

[169] E Fisher, *Risk Regulation and Administrative Constitutionalism* (n 30) 225. Some commentators seriously disputed that the Commission's guidelines reduced the EU institutions' and/or Member States' discretion to adopt protective measures, see for instance G Majone, 'What Price Safety? The Precautionary Principle and its Policy Implications' in G Majone (ed), *Risk Regulation in the European*

The rationale was to 'avoid unwarranted recourse to the precautionary principle, as a disguised form of protectionism'.[170]

While the Communication does not provide for a definition of the precautionary principle, it indicates the conditions under which the principle should be used. First, the principle is clearly regarded as part of the management stage of risk analysis.[171] This implies that a scientific risk assessment must already have been conducted.[172] Only if 'the scientific information is insufficient, inconclusive or uncertain and where there are indications that the possible effects on the environment, human, animal and plant health may be potentially dangerous and inconsistent with the chosen level of protection', may the precautionary principle be invoked.[173] Consequently, the precautionary principle does not constitute an opportunity to derogate from the strict science-based approach of EU risk regulation. Hence, it does not allow for economic, social, moral and ethical values to re-enter the scientific assessment.[174] Formally, the principle is thus embedded in the logic of risk analysis, which, as was made clear above, is based on the idea of a scientific truth that can, and must, be separated from social, economic, moral and ethical values.

IV. CONCLUSION AND NEXT STEPS

Today's society is characterised by fundamental societal transformations that have critical implications for the capacity of regulators to alter the behaviour of societal actors. Globalisation, functional differentiation and the omnipresence of uncertain risk in modern societies—developments which were shown to be exemplified by the emergence of nanotechnologies—have challenged not only the regulator's capacity to master the various knowledge(s) of the different affected actors but, linked to this, also to ensure the legitimacy of regulation. To remedy

Union: Between Enlargement and Internationalisation (Florence, European University Institute, 2003) www.cadmus.eui.eu/bitstream/handle/1814/2521/RiskRegulation_Majone.pdf and CR Sunstein, *Laws of Fear: Beyond the Precautionary Principle*, John Robert Seeley lectures no 6 (Cambridge, Cambridge University Press, 2005).

[170] 'Communication from the Commission on the Precautionary Principle' COM (2000) 1 final (n 159) 2.

[171] ibid 12.

[172] ibid.

[173] ibid 7. Furthermore, the Communication requires precautionary measures to comply with the general principles underlying risk management decisions, ie proportionality, non-discrimination, consistency, cost/benefit analysis, and precautionary measures can be of a provisional nature only, ibid 17.

[174] Elizabeth Fisher refers to this understanding of the precautionary principle by the Commission as 'rational-instrumental', in the sense that is constitutes 'a limited exception to action needing to have a firm basis which operates only when certain conditions precedent are met', as opposed to its 'deliberative-constitutional' interpretation 'as an enabling principle which requires deliberation and the flexible exercise of discretion'—an understanding which comes much closer to the idea of 'pluralistic scientific expertise' put forward by the FSU, see E Fisher, *Risk Regulation and Administrative Constitutionalism* (n 30) 209.

this lack in regulatory capacity both theoretical approaches of Habermas and Teubner suggested a closer involvement of affected actors in the (risk) regulatory process. Traditional command-and-control regulation, they infer, must be overcome. These considerations have not spared the EU level. Looking back to the end of the 1990s revealed very similar ideas and concerns to underlie the debate on European governance. This chapter hence retraced the theoretical origins of the debate that culminated in the White Paper on European Governance and that was accompanied by the rise of 'new (modes of) governance' in EU scholarship.

Two sets of questions now arise that will be addressed in the remaining chapters of this book. First, how has the European governance debate affected the 'real world' production of EU (risk) regulation; how have the EU institutions implemented the reforms proposed in the White Paper? In other words, what are the concrete legal procedures that the EU institutions have put in place in the aftermath of the governance debate to increase their capacity to regulate? Secondly, given all this debate, has the (risk) regulatory process at the European level become more effective and legitimate? The first question is addressed in chapter three, in which the legal procedures—or, in other words, the tangible outcomes of the European governance debate—will be identified. Taken together, these procedures will form the framework for the critical analysis of the EU's risk regulation of nanotechnologies in the case studies. The two case studies in chapters four and five will then attend to the second question and analyse, based on this framework, how the identified procedures are applied and how they operate in practice.

3

Analysing EU (Risk) Regulation through the Lenses of Regulatory Capacity

THIS CHAPTER DEVELOPS the analytical frame of this research. It lays down *what* will be analysed in the empirical part ('EU regulation') and *how* this will be done ('through the lenses of regulatory capacity'). Accordingly, section I will first clarify this book's understanding of the concept of 'regulation' in the EU context. Not only will 'regulation' be defined, it will also be embedded in the previous theoretical discussions and related to the (competing) concepts of 'law' and '(modes of) governance'. Subsequently, section II will turn to the *how*. To this end, the section engages with what was referred to as the tangible outcomes of the European governance debate—with the legal procedures that the EU institutions have put in place in order to increase their capacity to regulate: that is, their capacity to master the societally fragmented knowledge and their capacity to ensure legitimate regulation. Together, these procedures will form the framework through which the EU regulation of nanotechnologies is put to the test in the case studies.

I. DEFINING THE OBJECT OF ANALYSIS: 'EU REGULATION'

A. *Excursus*: Law, Regulation and Governance

When asked 'what is law?' Richard Posner once replied that this is 'a question that has little practical significance if, indeed, it is a meaningful question at all'.[1] Without going into the validity of this statement, it is important to clarify how the concept of 'law' is understood within the context of this book, in particular how it is distinguished from the concept of 'regulation'. Posner's statement, however, already indicates the complexity of this endeavour. The fundamental problem is

[1] RA Posner, 'The Decline of Law as an Autonomous Discipline' (1987) 100 *Harvard Law Review* 761, 765.

that both—law and regulation—are heavily contested concepts.[2] Their relationship changes according to the definition adopted of the respective other. As was seen in chapter two, Habermas and Teubner's accounts of 'law' are based on fundamentally different conceptions. While Habermas follows a positivist, state-centred understanding of law, for Teubner 'law' is exclusively determined by the binary code of legal/illegal and therefore independent of any institutional structure.[3] The picture becomes even more complicated when the notion of 'governance' enters the scene.

Whereas the concept of law has been subject to heavy philosophical debates for centuries, ranging from natural law to legal positivism and legal pluralism, the concept of regulation is rather novel and, it could be said, surprisingly underdeveloped. In fact, little is written about its origins and meaning,[4] albeit it is often used in legal scholarship. Where does the concept come from? And why has there been the (perception of a) need to develop such a concept next to the concept of law?

Beyond doubt, the concept of regulation originated in the English-speaking world as—even though the word itself can be found, for instance, in German (*Regulierung*) or French (*régulation*)—an equivalent concept does not exist in most other languages. It was with the Thatcher administration in the UK of the early 1980s that the term regulation became prominent. The slogan was that the extensive regulation of the welfare state interfered with the individuals' freedom of choice.[5] The rhetoric of 'deregulation' dominated the Government's political agenda.[6] Regulation was intrinsically associated with a command-and-control style, synonymous for Weber's substantive orientation of law.[7] A vast amount of literature was written about deregulation and, subsequently, reregulation efforts in the 'regulatory state'.[8]

The regulation rhetoric changed substantially in the UK with the election of Tony Blair and the Labour administration in 1997.[9] Instead of abandoning Thatcher's rhetoric altogether, the new Government kept the term but subjected it to fundamental reform under the motto of 'better regulation'.[10] More

[2] See eg R Baldwin, M Cave and M Lodge, 'Introduction: Regulation—The Field and the Developing Agenda' in R Baldwin, M Cave and M Lodge (eds), *The Oxford Handbook of Regulation* (Oxford, Oxford University Press, 2010) 11; J Black, *Critical Reflections on Regulation* (ESRC Centre for Analysis of Risk and Regulation, London School of Economics and Political Science, 2002) 1 and N Walker and G De Búrca, 'Reconceiving Law and New Governance' (2007) 13 *Columbia Journal of European Law* 519, 519.

[3] Above chapter 2, sections II.A and II.B.

[4] But see J Black, *Critical Reflections on Regulation* (n 2).

[5] S Weatherill, 'The Challenge of Better Regulation' in S Weatherill (ed), *Better Regulation*, Studies of the Oxford Institute of European and Comparative Law no 6 (Oxford, Hart Publishing, 2007) 1, 1.

[6] ibid.

[7] Above chapter 2, section II.A. R Baldwin et al, 'Introduction: Regulation' (n 2) 8 and 9 and J Black, *Critical Reflections on Regulation* (n 2) 2.

[8] See, most prominently, G Majone, 'The Rise of the Regulatory State in Western Europe' in WC Müller and V Wright (eds), *The State in Western Europe: Retreat or Redefinition?*, West European Politics Series vol 17 no 3 (Ilford, Frank Cass, 1994).

[9] S Weatherill, 'The Challenge of Better Regulation' (n 5) 1.

[10] ibid 2.

fundamentally, the concept of regulation itself also altered. The UK Better Regulation Task Force defined regulation as 'any government measure or intervention that seeks to change the behaviour of individuals or groups, so including taxes, subsidies and other financial measures'.[11] Yet, instead of referring exclusively to regulation by the state, the task force also examined alternative options, by questioning the Government's role in regulation generally and by looking into more market-based forms of regulation, involving private actors, such as self- and co-regulation.[12] Furthermore, the examples mentioned in the task force's definition do not exclusively refer to legally binding rules, but include incentive measures more broadly which cannot be enforced by state-sanctioned coercion. Regulation could hence no longer be used interchangeably with 'command-and-control' and, consequently, could no longer be regarded as a synonym for Weber's substantive orientation of law.[13] The concept of regulation as it was used in the UK after 1997 thus broadened significantly, thereby losing its state-centred characteristic.

Also in academic circles, various broad definitions of regulation were subsequently put forward. Probably one of the broadest definitions is proposed by Weatherill, who refers to regulation as 'embrac[ing] practices that serve to constrain or influence the behaviour of individuals or firms. It may accordingly catch not only binding rules, but also measures designed to influence conduct and, more broadly still, any kind of social control or influence, irrespective of its precise legal form or even its intent'.[14] Weatherill's definition of regulation appears to be even broader than Teubner's understanding of law, as it covers 'any kind of social control or influence', thus including purely social norms. Pursuant to Teubner, purely social norms, which are not communicated according to the binary code legal/illegal do not form part of the closed discourse of the legal system, that is, they do not qualify as 'law'. It is precisely this aspect of the legal pluralism debate which has attracted most criticism. One of the main problems that legal pluralists have encountered is that the distinction between law (legal norms) and non-law (social norms) is vague: when do social norms actually become legal in nature?[15] Arguably, this poses a challenge in practice. As Tamanaha puts it, 'nothing prohibits legal pluralists from viewing law in this extraordinarily expansive, idiosyncratic way, although common sense protests against it. When understood in these terms, just about every form of norm governed social interaction is law. Hence, we are swimming, or drowning, in legal pluralism.'[16]

[11] Better Regulation Task Force, *Principles of Better Regulation* (London, Cabinet Office, 1998) 1.

[12] See eg Better Regulation Task Force, *Imaginative Thinking for Better Regulation* (London, Cabinet Office, 2003) ch 8 on self and co-regulation.

[13] R Baldwin et al, 'Introduction: Regulation' (n 2) 5 and 6.

[14] S Weatherill, 'The Challenge of Better Regulation' (n 5) 1.

[15] M Wilkinson, 'Three Concepts of Law: Towards a Jurisprudence of Democratic Experimentalism' (2010) 2 *Wisconsin Law Review* 673, 706.

[16] B Tamanaha, 'Understanding Legal Pluralism: Past to Present, Local to Global' (2008) 30 *Sydney Law Review* 375, 393.

Also broad concepts of regulation, like the one suggested by Weatherill, carry the risk of being unworkable: 'if regulation is everything, then it is nothing'.[17] On the other hand, too narrow definitions, such as those reflecting the command-and-control style, might be unable to accommodate the new social realities and needs brought about by globalisation, functional differentiation and the risk society. A balance between extensively broad and restrictively narrow definitions has therefore been proposed by Julia Black. She understands regulation as 'the sustained and focused attempt to alter the behaviour of others according to defined standards or purposes with the intention of producing a broadly identified outcome or outcomes'.[18] The definition thus captures social control exercised by public and private actors, yet it is restricted to its intentional use.

Thus, depending on whether one employs a narrow or broad understanding of law and, respectively, a narrow or broad understanding of regulation, the relationship between the two concepts changes drastically. In their narrowest understandings, regulation (as 'regulatory law') may simply be considered an orientation of a state-centred law, acting as a steering mechanism of the state's political system; in the broadest interpretation of their meaning, law, from a legal pluralist perspective, and regulation, if understood as 'any kind of control or influence', could also be mere 'redescription[s] of one another'.[19]

How does the term 'governance' now fit into this already complex picture? The unsatisfying answer is that this term's meaning is also rather elusive, as various context-dependent interpretations exist.[20] Many early definitions of 'governance' have been adopted in the context of nation building in developing countries.[21] Accordingly, it was the World Bank in a report on Sub-Saharan Africa in 1989, which first coined the term as 'the exercise of political power to manage a nation's affairs'.[22] In the academic world, as was shown in chapter two, the term has recently been employed in a more normative way, often implying a critique of problems associated with the command-and-control style associated with 'government'.[23]

[17] R Baldwin et al, 'Introduction: Regulation' (n 2) 12.

[18] J Black, *Critical Reflections on Regulation* (n 2) 20.

[19] ibid 23.

[20] *cf* DM Curtin and I Dekker, 'Good Governance: The Concept and its Application by the European Union' in DM Curtin and RA Wessel (eds), *Good Governance and the European Union: Some Reflections of Concepts, Institutions and Substance*, Ius Commune Europaeum 49 (Antwerpen, Intersentia, 2004) 3.

[21] C Möllers, 'European Governance: Meaning and Concept' (2006) 43 *Common Market Law Review* 313, 315.

[22] World Bank, *Sub-Saharan Africa: From Crisis to Sustainable Growth* (Washington, The World Bank, 1989). More recently, the World Bank described governance as 'a process by which authority is conferred on rulers, by which they make the rules, and by which those rules are enforced and modified', World Bank, 'What is Governance?' www.web.worldbank.org/WBSITE/EXTERNAL/COUNTRIES/MENAEXT/EXTMNAREGTOPGOVERNANCE/0,contentMDK:20513159~pagePK:34004173~piPK:34003707~theSitePK:497024,00.html.

[23] J Torfing, BG Peters, J Pierre and E Sørensen, *Interactive Governance: Advancing the Paradigm* (Oxford, Oxford University Press, 2012) 9; B Kohler-Koch and B Rittberger, 'Review Article: The "Governance Turn" in ES Studies' (2006) 44 *Journal of Common Market Studies* 27, 28; S Bartolini, 'New Modes of European Governance: An Introduction' in A Héritier and M Rhodes (eds), *New Modes*

Looking, however, for a more generic definition of governance, the Oxford English Dictionary defines the term as 'the action or manner of governing', 'to govern' meaning 'to conduct the policy and affairs of (a state, organization, or people)'. In the European Union, the Commission in its White Paper on Governance referred to governance as the 'rules, processes and behaviour that affect the way in which powers are exercised at European level'.[24] Similar to the definition put forward by the World Bank and the one found in the Oxford English Dictionary, the European Commission hence also understands governance as *the exercise of political power*.[25] Analogously, a 'mode of governance' would denote *the way political power is exercised*. Political power might then be exercised in various ways—for instance, through law or through regulation. In other words, law and regulation constitute 'modes of governance'. Depending on the respective definition both terms might or might not be able to capture the rise of 'new' as well as the persistence of the 'traditional' mode of governance, the 'Community method', in the European Union.

Keeping all this in mind, this book will be concerned with the 'regulation' of nanotechnologies. There are three main reasons for this. First, employing the term regulation will avoid 'swimming' and potentially 'drowning' in recurring discussions about what law is and the blurred distinction between legal and social norms. Second, the term law appears to be an inappropriate choice to live up to the interdisciplinary approach of this research, thereby neglecting the significant contributions to the debates made not only by lawyers, but also by sociologists and political scientists.[26] Finally, while the term '(modes of) governance' would also allow this interdisciplinarity to be captured,[27] it appears problematic, especially in EU discourse, due to the normative connotations it has carried in recent discussions.

B. Defining 'Regulation'

In order to embrace the diverse tools used to alter the behaviour of affected actors in today's nano society, regulation will be broadly understood as the *intentional attempt to alter the behaviour of others according to defined standards or purposes*, following Julia Black's definition. The definition comprises regulation by public

of Governance in Europe: Governing in the Shadow of Hierarchy, Palgrave Studies in European Union Politics (Basingstoke, Palgrave Macmillan, 2011) 7.

[24] European Commission, 'European Governance—A White Paper' COM (2001) 428 final, 8.

[25] See M De Visser, *Network-Based Governance in EC Law*, Modern Studies in European Law no 19 (Oxford, Hart Publishing, 2009) 4.

[26] R Baldwin et al, 'Introduction: Regulation' (n 2) 4; see also D Levi-Faur, 'Regulation and Regulatory Governance' in D Levi-Faur (ed), *Handbook on the Politics of Regulation* (Cheltenham, Edward Elgar Publishing, 2011) 16.

[27] P Zumbansen, 'Governance: An Interdisciplinary Perspective' in D Levi-Faur (ed), *The Oxford Handbook of Governance* (n 26).

and/or private actors in the form of instruments that may or may not be legally binding.[28] This understanding of regulation not only incorporates different conceptions of law, including Habermas's positivist and Teubner's legal pluralist understanding, it also covers the exercise of political power at the EU level through the Community method, as well as through alternative or 'new' modes of governance.

C. The Regulatory Spectrum at the EU Level

With the adoption of a broad definition of regulation, a spectrum emerges which may be classified according to the public and/or private nature of the regulator and according to the legal effect of a respective regulatory measure.

i. Public–Private

Sketching the regulatory spectrum based on the public/private nature of regulation, one finds on one end a purely private form of regulation. Private regulation is autonomously and independently carried out by private actors.[29] It is the affected actors themselves who regulate. Various different conceptualisations of private or self-regulation have been put forward.[30] In the Interinstitutional Agreement on Better Law-Making (2003) self-regulation was broadly defined 'as the possibility for economic operators, the social partners, non-governmental organisations or associations to adopt amongst themselves and for themselves common guidelines at European level'.[31] Self-regulation, accordingly, does not implement or condition the existence of a legislative act.[32] As this book will be concerned with the *EU* regulatory developments in the area of nanotechnologies, pure self-regulation falls outside its scope of analysis.

Instead, this book will focus on public regulation and, possibly, on co-regulatory arrangements. At the EU level, public regulation refers to rules adopted by the institutions of the EU, its bodies or agencies. It thus includes rule making by the legislature through the Community Method. It also addresses rulemaking by

[28] ie enforceable in public courts.

[29] F Cafaggi, 'Rethinking Private Regulation in the European Regulatory Space' in F Cafaggi (ed), *Reframing Self-Regulation in European Private Law*, Private Law in European Content Series vol 9 (Alphen aan den Rijn, Kluwer Law International, 2006) 18.

[30] See eg J Black, 'Constitutionalising Self-Regulation' (1996) 59 *Modern Law Review* 24; F Cafaggi, 'Rethinking Private Regulation in the European Regulatory Space' (n 29); E Svilpaite, 'Legal Evaluation of the Selected New Modes of Governance: The Conceptualisation of Self- and Co-Regulation in the European Union Legal Framework' (University of Basel, NEWGOV: New Modes of Governance, 2007) 8 www.eu-newgov.org/database/DELIV/D04D41_Self-and_Co-Regulation_in_the_EU_Legal_Framework.pdf.

[31] Interinstitutional Agreement on better law-making [2003] OJ C321/01.

[32] E Svilpaite, 'Legal Evaluation of the Selected New Modes of Governance' (n 30) 9.

the EU executive, by the Commission acting alone or through comitology, and by the EU's 'satellite executive',[33] such as EU agencies or networks.

In between purely public and purely private regulation, the regulatory spectrum provides for different possibilities of regulatory hybrids, meaning that public and private actors collaborate or perform different functions in the drafting or implementation of regulation. Whereas various different terminologies have been suggested to conceptualise such hybrids,[34] they are commonly referred to as 'co-regulation'.[35] Co-regulation, in the EU context, describes a 'mechanism whereby a Community legislative act entrusts the attainment of the objectives defined by the legislative authority to [private] parties'.[36] Contrary to self-regulation, a condition for co-regulatory measures is thus the existence of an EU legislative act. A classic example are the 'New Approach Directives' to harmonisation, which set out the 'essential requirements' necessary to ensure public health and safety, with detailed technical standards being elaborated by private standard setting organisations.[37] These latter co-regulatory arrangements as well as EU executive rulemaking through comitology or EU agencies are commonly referred to as 'new (modes of) governance'—as departures from the classical Community Method.[38]

ii. Legal Effect

On the other hand, the regulatory spectrum can be classified according to the legal effect of a regulatory option. A regulatory measure creates legal effects where it affects the legal position of a person, meaning that it generates legal rights and/or imposes legal obligations.[39] The legal position of a person may be affected by measures that are 'legally binding'. Legally binding measures can be enforced and reviewed by public courts, in the EU context, by the European courts and, as the case may be, by the national courts of the Member States. The legal effect stems from the measure itself.[40] At the EU level, Article 288 of the Treaty on the

[33] D Curtin, *Executive Power of the European Union, Law, Practices, and the Living Constitution*, Collected Courses of the Academy of European Law XII/4 (Oxford, Oxford University Press, 2009) 135.

[34] Cafaggi, for instance, refers to 'co-regulation' (private actors have been called upon to take part in different stages of the regulatory process), 'delegated private regulation' (private authority is empowered by public authority), and 'ex post recognised private regulation' (purely private regulation is subsequently recognised by a public authority), see F Cafaggi, 'Rethinking Private Regulation in the European Regulatory Space' (n 29) 27 and 33. Levi-Faur identifies four hybrid forms of regulation: co-regulation, enforced self-regulation, meta-regulation and multi-level regulation, see D Levi-Faur, 'Regulation and Regulatory Governance' (n 26) 10 and 11.

[35] E Svilpaite, 'Legal Evaluation of the Selected New Modes of Governance' (n 30) 10.

[36] Interinstitutional Agreement on better law-making (n 31).

[37] P Craig and G De Búrca, *EU Law: Texts, Cases and Materials*, 5th edn (Oxford, Oxford University Press, 2011) 162.

[38] Above chapter 2, section III.A.

[39] L Senden, *Soft Law in European Community Law: Its Relationship to Legislation* (Nijmegen, Wolf Legal Publishers, 2003) 264.

[40] ibid 263.

Functioning of the European Union (TFEU) defines regulations, directives and decisions as 'binding', whereas recommendations and opinions have 'no binding force'. Article 288 TFEU, however, conveys a 'misleading simplicity', as a considerably broader array of non-binding measures is used in practice.[41] There are declarations, guidance documents, interpretative notices, White Papers, etc, adopted by the Commission itself, but also by EU agencies and networks. An increasing number of unidentified legal objects (ULOs) are thus flying around the EU's legal space.

Pursuant to Article 263 TFEU, the European courts can review the legality of legislative acts and acts intended to produce legal effects. Measures adopted in the form of a regulation, directive or decision are hence reviewable. But are recommendations and opinions, which are formally barred from having 'binding force', or indeed the array of informal non-binding measures, the ULOs, reviewable? In fact, for all these measures, the EU courts have long insisted that, in determining whether they produce legal effects vis-a-vis third parties, the courts would not look at the form of the measure but at its substance.[42] What is relevant is whether the act was *intended* to have binding force and whether it de facto brings about a change in a third party's legal position.[43] This is largely determined by the actual contents of the act, most notably its wording and terms, but also by the context of the adoption of the act: 'the choice of form cannot alter the nature of a measure'.[44] Even in the case of recommendations and opinions, which are formally considered to be non-binding, the Court in the past looked at the substance of the act before excluding legal effects.[45]

Measures which have no legally binding force per se (and are hence not judicially reviewable) may still entail practical or indirect legal effects, for example when being cited in court in support of a certain interpretation of a legally binding act.[46]

[41] L Senden, 'Soft Post-Legislative Rulemaking: A Time for More Stringent Control' (2013) 19 *European Law Journal* 57, 57.

[42] For instance, Case C-22/70 *Commission of the European Communities v Council of the European Communities (ERTA)* [1971] ECR 263, para 42, in which the Court concludes that 'an action for annulment must therefore be available in the case of all measures adopted by the institutions, whatever their nature or form, which are intended to have legal effects', and Case C-60/81 *International Business Machines Cooperation v Commission of the European Communities* [1981] ECR 2639, para 9. See also Case C-314/11 P *European Commission v Planet AE* [2012] not published. See, for an early analysis, J Klabbers, 'Informal Instruments Before the European Court of Justice' (1994) 31 *Common Market Law Review* 997.

[43] Case C-60/81 *International Business Machines Cooperation v Commission* (n 42) para 9.

[44] Case C-322/88 *Salvatore Grimaldi v Fonds des maladies professionnelles* [1989] ECR 04407, para 14. See also Case C-303/90 *French Republic v Commission of the European Communities* [1991] ECR I-05315, para 10, and a review of the relevant case law by L Senden, *Soft Law in European Community Law* (n 39) 277.

[45] In the landmark *Grimaldi* case, the Court first established whether the recommendation it was confronted with—a Commission recommendation laying down a European schedule for occupational diseases—was a 'true recommendation, that is to say a measure which, even as regards the persons to whom they are addressed, are not intended to produce binding effects', see Case C-322/88 *Salvatore Grimaldi* (n 44) para 16.

[46] FG Snyder, 'Soft Law and Institutional Practice in the European Community' in S Martin (ed), *The Construction of Europe: Essays in Honour of Emile Noël* (Dordrecht, Kluwer Academic Publishers, 1994).

In this way the non-binding measure indirectly affects the legal rights and/or obligations of an individual.[47] The EU courts, for instance, find it increasingly 'useful' for national courts to 'take into account' interpretations of secondary law stipulated in Commission guidance documents,[48] but they also consider such documents themselves when interpreting EU legislation.[49] Further, even if the legal effects of a non-binding measure are restricted, 'there may still be a question of a high degree of de facto persuasiveness and influence of interpretative and decisional acts upon legislative practice in the Member States'.[50]

In academic literature, measures with 'no binding force' are commonly referred to as 'soft law'—as opposed to 'hard law'. Linda Senden developed a definition of soft law in the EU context, which describes such measures as 'rules of conduct that are laid down in instruments which have not been attributed legally binding force as such, but nevertheless may have certain—indirect—legal effects, and that are aimed at and may produce practical effects'.[51] The term 'soft law' is, however, problematic in light of the discussion of law versus regulation as outlined above. Taking, for instance, a broad definition of law such as that put forward in legal pluralism, 'law' must not at all be enforceable in a public court in order to qualify

[47] This became clear in the above-cited *Grimaldi* judgment of 1989. Mr Grimaldi, a migrant worker in Belgium, was suffering from Dudytren's contracture, a disease not recognised by the Belgian Occupational Disease Fund as an occupational disease, see Case C-322/88 *Salvatore Grimaldi* (n 44) para 2. According to a Commission Recommendation of 1962 which established a European schedule of occupational diseases, however, Dudytren's contracture was recommended to be introduced into national law as an occupational disease (para 4). The Court, after clarifying that the measure in question is, as it said, a 'true recommendation' without binding force, concluded that 'it must be stressed that the measures in question cannot therefore be regarded as having no legal effect. The national courts are bound to take recommendations into consideration in order to decide disputes submitted to them, in particular where they cast light on the interpretation of national measures adopted in order to implement them or where they are desired to supplement binding Community provisions' (para 18).

[48] Case C-308/11 *Chemische Fabrik Kreussler & Co. GmbH v Sunstar Deutschland GmbH* [2012] not yet published. In *Chemische Fabrik Kreussler*, the Oberlandesgericht Frankfurt a. M. asked the Court whether, in order to interpret the term 'pharmacological action' laid down in Art 1(2)(b) of Directive 2001/83 on medical devices, a guidance document on medical devices adopted by the Commission's Directorate-General for Enterprise and Industry could be relied upon (para 17). The Court clarified two points before answering the question. First, guidance documents are not part of the Union's legal acts referred to in Art 288 TFEU and, therefore, 'cannot be of a legally binding nature or enforceable against individuals' (para 23). Secondly, only the Court has jurisdiction to give a binding interpretation of EU law (para 24). However, the Court continued by stating that 'the fact remains that, inasmuch as that document was drawn up by a group of experts from the national authorities, the Commission's services and professional associations from industry, it may provide useful information for the interpretation of the relevant provisions of European Union law' (para 25). Consequently, the national court may take account of the definition of 'pharmacological action' as stipulated in the guidance document, as long as 'the interpretation thus derived was derived in a manner consistent with the criteria laid down by the case law' (paras 26 and 27).

[49] See for instance Case C-308/11 *Chemische Fabrik Kreussler* (n 48) para 29.

[50] L Senden, 'Soft Post-Legislative Rulemaking' (n 41) 66. See also M Lee, *EU Environmental Law, Governance and Decision-Making*, Modern Studies in European Law Series vol 43, 2nd edn (Oxford, Hart Publishing, 2014) 45 and 88.

[51] L Senden, *Soft Law in European Community Law* (n 39) 104; see for a similar definition, A Peters and I Pagotto, *Soft Law as a New Mode of Governance: A Legal Perspective* (NEWGOV: New Modes of Governance, 2006) 4 www.ssrn.com/abstract=1668531 or http://dx.doi.org/10.2139/ssrn.1668531.

as 'law'; how it is communicated is decisive.[52] The distinction between 'hard' and 'soft' law would be meaningless in this context. If, however, 'law' was understood to be the exclusive product of the state, and clearly coercive in character, 'soft law' would simply not exist—either it would be law or not. This book's definition of regulation, on the contrary, is able to comprise what Senden (and many other authors) refer to as 'soft law'.

D. The Object of Analysis: 'EU Regulation'

The object of the subsequent analysis will consequently be the *EU regulation* of nanotechnologies. Following the broad understanding of regulation as adopted in this book, EU regulation comprises not only the adoption of measures by the EU legislature. It also includes acts adopted by the EU executive, most notably by the Commission via comitology and by EU agencies. These measures may be of both a binding and non-binding nature.

II. PUTTING ON THE ANALYTICAL LENSES OF REGULATORY CAPACITY

Having defined this book's understanding of EU regulation, that is, the *what*, it is time to move on to the *how* and to put on the analytical lenses of regulatory capacity. Capacity is here functionally understood as constituting 'the ability or power to do or understand something'.[53] Regulatory capacity, accordingly, refers to the ability of an actor to regulate. In the following sections, the two elements of regulatory capacity—those of mastering knowledge and ensuring legitimacy—will first be defined building on the theoretical accounts introduced in chapter two. Thereafter, this section focuses on the question of how the EU institutions have been intending to attain these elements, by identifying the main legal procedures that the EU institutions have set in place in the aftermath of the European governance debate. Their applicability and practical operation will afterwards be put to the test in the analysis of the current EU regulatory developments in the two case studies.

Naturally, the two elements of regulatory capacity are linked. For instance, where societal actors are included in the regulatory process for the instrumental purpose of gathering knowledge, this inclusion affects, positively or negatively, the regulation's legitimacy.[54] Equally, where procedures to pool knowledge structure and

[52] Above chapter 2, section II.B.

[53] Oxford English Dictionary.

[54] D Curtin, H Hofmann and J Mendes, 'Constitutionalising EU Executive-Rulemaking Procedures: A Research Agenda' (2013) 19 *European Law Journal* 1, 11 and J Neyer, *The Justification of Europe: A Political Theory of Supranational Integration* (Oxford, Oxford University Press, 2012) 59.

thereby enhance the transparency of the regulatory process, this also impacts on the ability of affected societal and institutional actors to scrutinise the regulatory output ex post. For the purpose of analytical clarity, however, the two elements will be examined separately.

A. First Element: Pooling Knowledge

Chapter two assumed that in today's nano society the regulator displays a deficit in capacity to master the specialised knowledge of the various affected societal actors.[55] At the same time, knowledge is widely regarded as a crucial regulatory resource. In Dahl's words, 'no government could make satisfactory decisions without the help of highly informed specialists'.[56] Also at the EU level the Commission, in its White Paper on European Governance, stressed that 'scientific and other experts play an increasingly significant role in preparing and monitoring decisions. From human and animal health to social legislation, the Institutions rely on specialist expertise to anticipate and identify the nature of the problems and uncertainties that the Union faces …'.[57] Accordingly, an integral part of the EU governance debate focused on the question of how technical and scientific knowledge should be collected and used in the (risk) regulatory process.[58]

i. Defining 'Knowledge'

In line with the theoretical considerations of chapter two, knowledge is comprehended within the meaning of sociology, as a social attribution or construction.[59] In the place of one rationality, one knowledge and one truth,[60] it is assumed that various rationalities co-exist, and compete, in today's nano society. Each of these rationalities, in turn, produces its own knowledge, its own social reality and

[55] According to Neyer, 'no single governmental or non-governmental body can convincingly claim to have access to all relevant information and to be able to decide autonomously on the proper solutions to the increasingly complex challenges of modern societies', see J Neyer, *The Justification of Europe* (n 54) 59.

[56] RA Dahl, *On Democracy* (New Haven, Yale University Press, 1998) 78.

[57] European Commission, 'European Governance—A White Paper' COM (2001) 428 final, 19.

[58] See chapter 2, section III.B.

[59] U Beck, *Weltrisikogesellschaft* (Frankfurt am Main, Suhrkamp, 2008) 211. Beck clarifies that 'von ‚Wissen' und ‚Nichtwissen' spreche ich nicht im kognitiven Sinne der Philosophie, Wissenschaftstheorie oder der Naturwissenschaft, sondern im Sinne der Soziologie, die ‚Wissen' als Erwartung, als soziale Attribution und Konstruktion begreift' (I am talking about 'knowledge' and 'non-knowledge' not within the cognitive meaning of philosophy, the theory of science or natural sciences, but within the meaning of sociology, which grasps 'knowledge' as an expectation, as a social attribution and construction).

[60] As Renn terms it, 'the [Weberian] meta-rationality of modernity (ie instrumental rationality, efficiency, justice through economic growth, and steady improvement of individual living conditions through scientific and technical progress)', see O Renn, *Risk Governance: Coping with Uncertainty in a Complex World*, Risk in Society Series (London, Earthscan, 2008) 27.

ultimately its own truth.[61] Paradoxically then, while scientific knowledge becomes more and more necessary, at the same time it is 'less and less sufficient for the socially binding definition of truth'.[62] Like society itself, knowledge has become differentiated and fragmented in society, necessarily 'disembedded from the public realm'.[63] To maintain its (legitimate) authority, the regulator 'has to bring together knowledge'; it 'cannot arise at one specific site, or from the views of one specific discipline or group of highly respected researchers, but precisely from bringing together the many different and heterogeneous practice-related knowledge dimensions that are involved'.[64] It is against this background that the theoretical considerations of chapter two inferred the need for procedures that enable the regulator to gather the diverse knowledge(s).

ii. The Impact Assessment as a Procedure to Pool Knowledge

In the aftermath of the European governance debate, the Commission established a set of non-binding procedural rules stipulating how knowledge should be collected and imparted by its services in the preparation of regulation. Of particular interest is the so-called 'impact assessment'—the performance of an ex ante evaluation of the economic, social and environmental effects of major policy proposals before their adoption. The declared aim of this 'information generating procedure'[65] is to contribute to the effectiveness and legitimacy of the regulatory process by rationalising resources and fostering transparency in EU decision making.[66] Since its launch in 2003, commentators have referred to it as 'the most tangible change to the EU law-making procedures that came out of the Governance project'.[67] The procedural rules for the Commission's impact assessment practice were first laid down in the Impact Assessment Guidelines of 2002 and 2009[68] and have been revised most recently within the scope of the Commission's Better Regulation Package in 2015.[69] As the empirical part of this book was carried out in the period before 2015, reference in the following will primarily be made to the 2009 Impact Assessment Guidelines. The Better Regulation Package of 2015 will, however, be commented upon as part of the outlook and reform proposals in the concluding chapter.

[61] See chapter 2, section I.C.

[62] U Beck, *Risk Society: Towards a New Modernity* (M Ritter (tr), London, SAGE Publications, 1992) 156.

[63] H Nowotny, P Scott and M Gibbons, *Re-Thinking Science: Knowledge and the Public in an Age of Uncertainty* (Cambridge, Polity Press, 2001) 229.

[64] ibid 248.

[65] HCH Hofmann, GC Rowe and AH Türk, *EU Administrative Law and Policy* (Oxford, Oxford University Press, 2011) 458.

[66] European Commission, 'Impact Assessment Guidelines' SEC (2009) 92, 4.

[67] A Meuwese, *Impact Assessment in EU Law-Making*, European Monographs no 61 (Alphen aan den Rijn, Kluwer Law International, 2008) 27.

[68] 'Impact Assessment Guidelines' SEC (2009) 92 (n 66).

[69] European Commission, 'Better Regulation Guidelines—An EU Agenda' (Communication) COM (2015) 215 final, Ch III.

According to the Impact Assessment Guidelines, a precondition for the assessment of impacts is the collection of knowledge.[70] To this end, the Commission has committed to undertaking consultations with affected actors, in order to gather knowledge but also in order to 'increase the legitimacy of EU action from the point of view of stakeholders and citizens'.[71] The Commission's minimum standards of consultation are applicable to these consultations and will be introduced in section II.B on legitimacy.[72] As further potential input into the drafting process, the 2009 Impact Assessment Guidelines identified an entire catalogue of 'sources', such as studies carried out by and for the European Commission, knowledge gathered from stakeholders in hearings, conferences, etc, studies and research by the Joint Research Centre, EU agencies, the Commission's expert groups, including its scientific committees, as well as data from Member States, third countries or international organisations.[73]

In pooling knowledge from these sources, the Commission committed to adhere to a further set of self-imposed rules, namely its 2002 guidelines on the collection and use of expertise.[74] The content of these guidelines is confined to the definition of three overarching principles, focusing on the 'quality, openness and effectiveness' of the knowledge gathered. While the quality of the knowledge gathered should be determined by the 'excellence', 'independence' and 'pluralism' of the advice sought, openness is mainly understood in terms of 'transparency', in the way questions are framed, experts are selected and results handled in order to provide for 'more accountability for all involved'.[75] The guidelines thus embody the principle of risk analysis.[76] The incompatibility of the strict separation between science and politics with the theoretical underpinning of this book, especially in view of scientific uncertainties, was discussed in chapter two.[77] Nonetheless, with these guidelines and the principle of risk analysis at its roots, the Commission launched an overhaul of its 'prime sources' of technical and scientific advice by establishing (new) procedural frameworks for the operation of Commission expert groups and EU agencies.[78]

[70] 'Impact Assessment Guidelines' SEC (2009) 92 (n 66) 18; 'Better Regulation Guidelines' COM (2015) 215 final (n 69) 16.

[71] 'Impact Assessment Guidelines' SEC (2009) 92 (n 66) 19. See, similarly, European Commission, 'Better Regulation "Toolbox"' 59 www.ec.europa.eu/smart-regulation/guidelines/docs/br_toolbox_en.pdf.

[72] See European Commission, 'Towards a Reinforced Culture of Consultation and Dialogue—General Principles and Minimum Standards for Consultation of Interested Parties by the Commission' (Communication) COM (2002) 704 final.

[73] 'Impact Assessment Guidelines' SEC (2009) 92 (n 66) 18 and 19.

[74] European Commission, 'Communication from the Commission on the Collection and Use of Expertise by the Commission: Principles and Guidelines' COM (2002) 713 final.

[75] ibid 9.

[76] Above chapter 2, section III.B.i.

[77] ibid.

[78] According to the Impact Assessment Guidelines, '[e]xpert groups and, in particular, scientific committees set up by the Commission and EU Agencies are a prime source of scientific advice', 'Impact Assessment Guidelines' SEC (2009) 92 (n 66) 18.

a. Pooling Knowledge through Commission Expert Groups

In 2005, the Commission designed a new framework of horizontal rules for the creation and operation of its expert groups.[79] Pursuant to this framework, Commission expert groups denote 'consultative entities set up by the Commission or its services, comprising at least six public and/or private sector members, who are foreseen to meet more than once'.[80] Their role is to supply the Commission with specific knowledge in the preparation of legislative and policy initiatives, delegated acts, and the implementation of existing EU legislation, programmes and policies.[81] The groups operate according to a set of horizontal rules, which lay down their establishment, composition and functioning. More detailed rules might be set out in the Commission decisions establishing individual expert groups or in the expert groups' own rules of procedure.[82] The horizontal rules stipulate general provisions on the expert groups' transparency, which have been reinforced with their most recent update in 2016.[83] All expert groups must be included in an online register[84] and the names of their members[85] and information concerning their activities must be published.[86] For expert groups composed of national authorities of the Member States, additional rules apply. First, the Commission commits to sending the same documentation that it forwards to the Member States also to the European Parliament when meetings concern the preparation and implementation of Union legislation.[87] Second, 'upon request of the European Parliament, the Commission services may invite the European Parliament to send experts to attend meetings of [such] expert groups'.[88]

b. Pooling Knowledge through EU Agencies and their Networks

As a second source of technical and scientific knowledge, the Commission announced in its White Paper on European Governance its intention 'to define

[79] The framework is meant to 'supplement the initiatives already undertaken by the Commission on the basis of the White Paper on European Governance', see European Commission, 'Framework for Commission's Expert Groups: Horizontal Rules and Public Register' (Communication) C(2005) 2817. The 2005 procedural rules were revised in November 2010 and May 2016, see European Commission, 'Framework for Commission's Expert Groups: Horizontal Rules and Public Register' (Communication) C(2010) 7649 final, 2 and European Commission, 'Framework for Commission Expert Groups: Horizontal Rules and Public Register' (Communication) C(2016) 3300 final.

[80] 'Framework for Commission's Expert Groups' C(2010) 7649 final (n 79) Annex, rule 2. See, similarly, 'Framework for Commission Expert Groups' C(2016) 3300 final (n 79) 2–3.

[81] 'Framework for Commission's Expert Groups' C(2010) 7649 final (n 79) Annex, rule 3. See, similarly, 'Framework for Commission Expert Groups' C(2016) 3300 final (n 79) 3.

[82] 'Framework for Commission's Expert Groups' C(2010) 7649 final (n 79) Annex, rule 15.

[83] 'Framework for Commission Expert Groups' C(2016) 3300 final (n 79) 4.

[84] 'Framework for Commission's Expert Groups' C(2010) 7649 final (n 79) Annex, rule 17.

[85] ibid Annex, rule 18.

[86] ibid Annex, rule 19.

[87] ibid Annex, rule 12.

[88] ibid Annex, rule 13.

in 2002 the criteria for the creation of new regulatory agencies … and the framework within which they should operate'.[89] The powers and tasks of EU agencies vary greatly.[90] Typically, however, EU agencies provide information and expert advice, are charged with the administration of this information and assist in the implementation of EU policies and the formation of networks.[91] Thereby, agencies occupy a key role in 'supporting the decision-making process by pooling the technical and specialist expertise available at European and national level'.[92] The years that followed the White Paper witnessed a 'mushrooming' of agencies.[93] No less than 20 new agencies were created in the 2000s,[94] among them the European Food Safety Authority (EFSA) in 2002 and the European Chemicals Agency (ECHA) in 2007. EFSA and ECHA are, in line with the principle of risk analysis, formally charged with the provision of independent scientific and technical advice to the Commission,[95] for which they rely on networks with national authorities, in-house (scientific) committees or panels and consultations with affected institutional and societal actors.

Following the commitment in the White Paper, the Commission proposed an operating framework for European regulatory agencies in 2002.[96] In its proposal, the Commission called for a common approach 'in terms of internal structure, their relations with the institutions, responsibilities and powers'.[97] Until then, EU agencies were established on an ad hoc basis.[98] Yet, due to interinstitutional

[89] 'European Governance—A White Paper' COM (2001) 428 final (n 24) 24.

[90] HCH Hofmann et al, *EU Administrative Law and Policy* (n 65) 285.

[91] A Meuwese, Y Schuurmans and W Voermans, 'Towards a European Administrative Procedure Act' (2009) 2 *Review of European Administrative Law* 3, 18 and E Vos, 'Reforming the European Commission: What Role to Play for EU Agencies?' (2000) 37 *Common Market Law Review* 1113, 1120.

[92] European Parliament, Council of the European Union and European Commission, 'Joint Declaration on Decentralised Agencies', 2012, 1 www.europa.eu/european-union/sites/europaeu/files/docs/body/joint_statement_and_common_approach_2012_en.pdf.

[93] D Curtin and R Dehousse, 'European Agencies: Tipping the Balance' in M Busuioc, M Groenleer and J Trondal (eds), *The Agency Phenomenon in the European Union: Emergence, Institutionalisation and Everyday Decision-Making*, European Policy Research Unit Series (Manchester, Manchester University Press, 2012) 193. The emergence of EU agencies has its roots back in 1975 when the first two agencies were established, a trend that continued during the 1990s, see E Vos, 'European Agencies and the Composite EU Executive' in E Everson, C Monda and E Vos (eds), *European Agencies in Between Institutions and Member States*, European Monographs no 85 (Alphen aan den Rijn, Wolters Kluwer Law & Business, 2014) 13 and 14.

[94] E Vos, 'European Agencies and the Composite EU Executive' (n 93) 15.

[95] Art 23 of Regulation of the European Parliament and the Council (EC)178/2002 of 28 January 2002 laying down the general principles and requirements of Food Law [2002] OJ L31/1; Art 77(1) Regulation of the European Parliament and of the Council (EC) 1907/2006 of 18 December 2006 concerning the registration, evaluation, authorisation and restriction of chemicals (REACH) [2006] OJ L396/1. In accordance with the principle of risk analysis and the implied functional separation between risk assessment and risk management, see above chapter 2, section III.B.i.

[96] European Commission, 'Communication from the Commission: The Operating Framework for European Regulatory Agencies' COM (2002) 718 final.

[97] ibid 3.

[98] E Vos, 'European Agencies and the Composite EU Executive' (n 93) 14.

disagreements,[99] a non-binding statement of Commission, Council and Parliament on a common approach to decentralised agencies could only be agreed upon in 2012.[100] In this common approach, the three institutions committed to broad directions as regards the establishment of future EU agencies (hence excluding existing agencies such as EFSA and ECHA), their basic structure,[101] the agencies' work programmes, their funding, budget, reporting requirements, periodic evaluation, and an emphasis on their transparent operation.[102]

How the Commission made use of these sources of knowledge in the development of a regulatory framework for nanotechnologies and how the impact assessment as the Commission's flagship tool to expose the knowledge gathered from these various sources has been applied and has operated in practice will be tested in the case studies.

iii. Extending the Impact Assessment Procedure to Parliament and Council

Although the impact assessment procedure was first and foremost a commitment of the European Commission, it has since expanded further. In 2003, the Parliament, Council and Commission first declared in the Interinstitutional Agreement on Better Law-Making that 'where the codecision procedure applies, the European Parliament and Council *may*, on the basis of jointly defined criteria and procedures, have impact assessments carried out prior to the adoption of any *substantive amendment*, either at first reading or at the conciliation stage …' (emphasis added).[103] Also the new Interinstitutional Agreement of 2016 states that 'the European Parliament and the Council will, when they consider this to be appropriate and necessary for the legislative process, carry out impact assessments in relation to their substantial amendments to the Commission's proposal'.[104] The three institutions furthermore affirmed their intentions in an inter-institutional 'Common Approach to Impact Assessment' of 2005.[105]

[99] Especially as regards the representation of Member States and European Parliament designates on the agencies' Management Boards as well as the very form such a common approach should take (the Commission had proposed an interinstitutional agreement in 2005, see European Commission, 'Draft Interinstitutional Agreement on the Operating Framework for European Regulatory Agencies' COM (2005) 59 final).

[100] 'Joint Declaration on Decentralised Agencies' (n 92).

[101] Most notably the composition of the Management Board and the functioning of scientific committees.

[102] 'Joint Declaration on Decentralised Agencies' (n 92).

[103] Interinstitutional Agreement on Better Law-making [2003] (n 31) para 30.

[104] Interinstitutional Agreement on Better Law-making [2016] OJ L123/4, para 15.

[105] European Commission, European Parliament and Council of Ministers, 'Interinstitutional Common Approach to Impact Assessment' (2005) www.ec.europa.eu/smart-regulation/impact/key_docs/docs/ii_common_approach_to_ia_en.pdf.

a. Parliamentary Impact Assessment

While the Parliament clearly perceives the Commission as the institution in charge of conducting impact assessments of legislative proposals,[106] in 2011 and 2014 it encouraged its committees to rely on this tool more often.[107] In 2008, the Parliament had already adopted its own procedural rules on impact assessments, the 'Impact Assessment Handbook', in which it lays down the procedural steps according to which parliamentary impact assessments on 'substantive amendments' can be requested by individual MEPs or parliamentary committees.[108]

b. Council Impact Assessment

The Council implemented the Inter-Institutional Common Approach to Impact Assessment with a guidance document 'Handling Impact Assessments in Council' in 2006.[109] The guidance document recommends that working party chairs follow three main procedural steps in treating impact assessments. First, it advises the chair to conduct a quality check of the Commission's impact assessment.[110] In case of omissions, the 'presidency may invite the Commission to update and amend its impact assessment'.[111] Secondly, the working party chair should encourage the consideration and discussion of the Commission's impact assessment in the working party meetings.[112] Finally, the working party should contemplate whether a newly introduced Council amendment qualifies as 'substantive' for an additional Council impact assessment to be justified.[113]

[106] European Parliament, 'Resolution of 8 June 2011 on guaranteeing independent impact assessments' (P7_TA- (2011)0259) para 26.

[107] ibid para 24.

[108] 'On a proposal from the rapporteur, the chairman or a member of the committee acting on behalf of his or her political group, the coordinators decide, in consultation with the rapporteur, to request an impact assessment of one or more specific substantive amendments. There must be broad political support for that decision,' see European Parliament Conference of Chairmen, 'Impact Assessment Handbook' (Guidelines) PE380.566 CPG 15.11.2012, para 18. Indeed, the Parliament's General Secretariat disposes of a Directorate G for 'Impact Assessment and European Added Value'. In March 2012, Directorate G also assumed responsibility for the 'Science and Technology Options Assessment' unit (STOA) that had existed since 1992. According to the STOA rules, 'the objectives of STOA are to contribute to the debate and the legislative consideration of scientific and technological issues of particular political relevance'. To that end, STOA shall 'provide Parliament's committees and other parliamentary bodies concerned with independent, high-quality and scientifically impartial studies and information for the assessment of the impact of possibly introducing or promoting new technologies', see STOA Rules (2009) www.europarl.europa.eu/stoa/webdav/site/cms/shared/1_about/rules/200911/rules04may2009_modified_11nov2009_en.pdf.

[109] Council of the European Union, 'Better Regulation—Handling of Impact Assessments in Council' (2006, 9382/06).

[110] ibid para 9.

[111] ibid para 12.

[112] ibid paras 13–15.

[113] ibid para 18.

B. Second Element: Ensuring Legitimate Regulation

i. Defining 'Legitimacy'

Much of contemporary scholarship on legitimacy builds on the descriptive account of Max Weber. Weber's main interest at the beginning of the twentieth century was focused on the question of why people accept and obey the command of a political order even if their personal interest does not correspond to the command's content. Weber's answer was the people's belief in a political order: 'the basis of every system of authority, and correspondingly of every kind of willingness to obey, is a belief, a belief by virtue of which persons exercising authority are lent prestige'.[114] Central to Weber's understanding of legitimacy is thus the notion of *Legitimitätsglaube*.[115] People, he argued, believe in a political regime and accept its authority because they have faith in the sacredness of an enduring order (traditional authority), because they sense an affectionate devotion towards a particular leader (charismatic authority) or because people believe in the legality, the rationality, of an order (legal authority).[116] It is this last type of legitimate authority that is of particular interest in the context of this book. The belief in the legal authority, *die Herrschaft des Gesetzes* or the rule of law, emerged in modern Western civilisation as a result of the advancing rationalisation process.[117] The basic notion is that laws are created and modified through formal procedures on grounds of rationally recognised principles.[118]

Weberian thoughts remain highly influential in current debates. Consciously or unconsciously, scholars have built on Weber's ideas by further developing aspects of his descriptive concept, by either contrasting or complementing it with normative elements. From a normative perspective, legitimacy turns into a reference standard, against which a political regime is evaluated as being justified or unjustified. If an institution is considered unjustified, there is no obligation to obey its commands.[119] Such a normative perspective has been put forward by Habermas,[120] with his reference standard being the democratic self-determination of the citizen: 'citizens should always be able to understand themselves also as authors of the law to which they are subject as addressees'.[121] Habermas thus builds on

[114] M Weber, *The Theory of Social and Economic Organization* (T Parsons and AM Henderson (trs), New York, Free Press 1964) 382.

[115] M Weber, 'Die drei reinen Typen der legitimen Herrschaft' (1922) 187 *Preußische Jahrbücher* 1, 1.

[116] ibid 1, 3 and 6.

[117] J Winckelmann, *Legitimität und Legalität in Max Webers Herrschaftssoziologie* (Tübingen, JCB Mohr, 1952) 34.

[118] M Weber, 'Die drei reinen Typen der legitimen Herrschaft' (n 115) 1.

[119] F Peter, 'Political Legitimacy', *The Stanford Encyclopedia of Philosophy* (Summer edn, 2010) www.plato.stanford.edu/archives/sum2010/entries/legitimacy/.

[120] Above chapter 2, section II.A.

[121] J Habermas, *Between Facts and Norms: Contributions to a Discourse Theory of Law and Democracy*, Studies in Contemporary German Social Thought (W Rehg (tr), Cambridge, The MIT Press, 1996) 449. See above chapter 2, section II.A.

Weber's legal authority. Yet, Habermas regards the formal legality of law as a 'rather hollow value'; it is not the form that is essential but rather the material content of such laws which must correspond to the people's will.[122]

Fritz Scharpf, in turn, operationalised Habermas's reference standard of democratic self-determination to entail the two 'faces' of input and output legitimacy.[123] His distinction offers a well-suited starting point for the development of an analytical tool for this book in order to examine the procedures through which this self-determination is purported to be realised at the EU level. The first face of democratic self-determination is 'input-oriented' in the sense that political choices are legitimate if they reflect the will of the people.[124] Here, Scharpf utilises the notion of 'government *by* the people', which can be achieved by the citizens' participation in the decision-making process.[125] According to Scharpf, input-oriented legitimacy conditions the presence of a collective identity (in historical, linguistic, cultural, ethnic and institutional terms), as it exists in established national democracies.[126] At the European level, however, he contends that such a collective identity, and here Scharpf emphasises the diversity of the EU's Member States, is still absent.[127]

Scharpf concludes that, in the EU, attention should instead be focused on the second face of democratic self-determination, on output legitimacy. In contrast to input legitimacy, output legitimacy is not dependent on the presence of a collective identity but (merely) conditions the existence of a common interest.[128] Where regulation serves this common interest, it can be considered output legitimate ('government *for* the people').[129] Output legitimacy serves two purposes: (1) the prevention of abuse of public power, that is, the holding to account of the regulator for its conduct, and (2) effective problem-solving.[130] According to Scharpf:

> [T]he confusion and frustration of present debates can only be overcome if the distinction between input- and output-oriented democratic legitimacy is accepted, and if it is realised that the European polity is fundamentally different from national democracies since it can, for the time being, only aspire to the latter.[131]

Scharpf's conclusion concerning the absence of input legitimacy and the resulting necessity to decouple input and output legitimacy at the EU level has been

[122] G Poggi, *Weber: A Short Introduction* (Cambridge, Polity Press, 2006) 100. See chapter 2, section II.A.

[123] FW Scharpf, *Governing in Europe: Effective and Democratic?* (Oxford, Oxford University Press, 1999) 6–13. FW Scharpf, *Demokratietheorie zwischen Utopie und Anpassung* (Konstanz, Universitätsverlag, 1970).

[124] FW Scharpf, *Governing in Europe* (n 123) 6.

[125] ibid 7.

[126] Scharpf refers here to Weber's concept of *Gemeinschaftsglaube*, ibid 8.

[127] ibid 9.

[128] ibid 11.

[129] ibid 6.

[130] ibid 13.

[131] ibid 12.

strongly contested, most notably by Habermas.[132] The rationale behind such criticism is that the citizens' input is seen as imperative in order to identify the citizens' interest in the first place, that is, output legitimacy conditions input legitimacy and can only be supplementary.[133] These considerations bear particular weight in the context of this book. Being confronted with the presence of conflicting rationalities in the area of nanotechnologies, Scharpf's 'common interest' cannot be rationally determined. Instead, the 'common interest' or the regulatory intervention's 'desired result' has become subjective.[134] 'Effective problem-solving' hence cannot constitute a stand-alone source of legitimation.[135] Therefore, when discussing 'output legitimacy', the focus of this book will be on the second element of Scharpf's concept, namely on the extent to which abuses of power can be prevented. Indeed, affected actors' participation in the decision-making process would be meaningless if the regulator could afterwards proceed as he or she pleased without the prospect of being held to account for his or her actions.

Taking Scharpf's analytical frame of input and output legitimacy further, the following two sections will define, still with the theoretical reflections of chapter two at their roots, the two components of 'participation' (input, section II.B) and 'accountability' (output, section II.C). Analogous to the preceding section on pooling knowledge, the following two sections will identify the procedures and the tools, set in place at the EU level to foster legitimate regulation in the aftermath of the governance debate.

ii. Participation at the EU Level

Habermas premises the participation of all affected actors in a deliberative decision-making process as the basis for democratic self-determination and, eventually, the production of legitimate regulation.[136] Others have questioned such a generalisation of the desirability to involve affected actors actively in the decision-making process. Such critiques centre around two main arguments. First, it is feared that participation will delay the decision-making process, thereby

[132] *cf* Habermas's claim that the citizen's private autonomy can only be ensured once his public autonomy is given, see above chapter 2, section II.A. See also RA Dahl, *On Democracy* (n 56) 52, who claims that 'you can protect your rights and interests from abuse by government … only if you can participate fully in determining the conduct of government'. See further S Smismans, *Law, Legitimacy, and European Governance: Functional Participation in Social Regulation*, Oxford Studies in European Law (Oxford, Oxford University Press, 2004).

[133] C Harlow, *Accountability in the European Union*, Collected courses of the Academy of European Law Series XI/3 (Oxford, Oxford University Press, 2002) 190; A Follesdal, 'The Legitimacy Challenges for New Modes of Governance: Trustworthy Responsiveness' (2011) 46 *Government and Opposition* 81, 84.

[134] Above Introduction, section I.B and chapter 1, section III.

[135] See contra, G Majone, *Regulating Europe*, European Public Policy (London, Routledge, 1996).

[136] Above chapter 2, section II.A.

interfering with the 'experts' work' and reducing the regulation's effectiveness.[137] Secondly, it is argued that participation should be treated with caution, as it may not adequately reflect the public interest, in particular, where imbalances in power among societal actors prevent equal participation.[138] From a deliberative viewpoint, the response to these concerns is clear. On the one hand, all decisions should be open for deliberation in the political arena. This ties in with the argument made above that the citizens' input is imperative in order to identify the 'common interest' in the first place. On the other hand, imbalances in power are precluded by the requirements of an ideal speech situation, by adhering to the postulates of (1) full inclusion of all affected actors, (2) equality and (3) non-coercion, secured by a system of procedural rights.[139]

The conditions of an ideal speech situation are widely recognised as a normative yardstick for evaluating participation.[140] They have, however, been found to be difficult to apply in practice:[141] Who are the 'affected actors'? How should 'full inclusion' be interpreted? How can it be determined whether the procedures in place indeed provide all actors with an equal opportunity to provide input into the deliberation? Attempts have thus been made to operationalise the standards.[142] First, identifying who qualifies as an 'affected actor' has been acknowledged as one of the most challenging tasks.[143] One is confronted with a potentially huge mass of actors, some of whom it might be impossible to identify. Webler therefore suggests that objective and subjective processes be set in place to identify relevant actors. With objective processes, Webler refers to those that 'reveal the causal links that expose physical, social, economic or value impacts', such as exposure assessments or social impact analyses.[144] Subjective processes, to the contrary, enable actors to identify themselves as affected.[145] It is important that a selection is not made so as to strategically or systematically exclude a certain group of actors.[146] Next to affected actors' access to participation, 'full inclusion' would require participation in agenda setting, including the way potential questions to the participants are

[137] See, most prominently, G Majone, *Regulating Europe* (n 135).

[138] C Scott, 'Reflexive Governance, Regulation and Meta-Regulation: Control or Learning?' in O De Schutter and J Lenoble (eds), *Reflexive Governance: Redefining the Public Interest in a Pluralistic World*, Modern Studies in European Law vol 22 (Oxford, Hart Publishing, 2010) 47.

[139] Above chapter 2, section II.A.

[140] T Webler, '"Right" Discourse in Citizen Participation: An Evaluative Yardstick' in O Renn, T Webler and P Wiedemann (eds), *Fairness and Competence in Citizen Participation*, Technology, Risk, and Society vol 10 (Dordrecht, Kluwer Academic, 1995) 41.

[141] T Dietz, 'Preface: Democracy and Science' in O Renn, T Webler and P Wiedemann (eds), *Fairness and Competence in Citizen Participation* (n 140) xviii.

[142] See most notably T Webler, '"Right" Discourse in Citizen Participation' (n 140) 61–70.

[143] ibid 52.

[144] ibid 53.

[145] ibid.

[146] eg by not distributing information about the participation in a transparent, timely and accessible way or by conducting the participation (in case of a physical meeting) in a location unreachable by certain actors, see ibid 69.

formulated, the ability of affected actors to contribute to the substantive discussion as well as the extent to which they can influence the final decision.[147]

The second postulate requires each actor to participate equally in the discourse. This presupposes, according to Webler, access to information about the substantive contents of the regulatory measure.[148] Otherwise, the societal actor might be 'incompetent' to participate in a meaningful way.[149] Furthermore, affected actors, especially those with comparably fewer resources, should be granted sufficient time in order to participate.[150] The ideal conditions for participation based on these considerations can hence be summarised as follows:

1. 'Full inclusion of all affected actors': Objective and subjective actor identification processes are in place to ensure that 'all affected actors' participate. Furthermore, these affected actors should be involved, first, in agenda setting, second, in the discussion of the regulation's substance and, finally, the actors should be able to influence the final decision.
2. 'Equality': Actors should be given access to information about the regulation, as well as sufficient time to participate.

For analytical purposes, two mechanisms are further distinguished that enable affected societal actors to participate in the decision-making process. First, the will of the affected actors can be determined indirectly via their participation through elected representatives ('political participation'). Secondly, affected actors may directly participate in the decision-making process through administrative procedures ('administrative participation').

a. Political Participation

The participation of affected actors through elected delegates is anchored in the traditional model of representative democracy as it developed in the context of the nation-state. In recent decades, globalisation and the consequent emergence of transnational entities beyond the state have challenged the very functioning of the traditional model, particularly its intrinsic link with the nation-state. The creation of the European Parliament reproduces the model at the European level, as reflected in Article 10 of the Treaty on European Union (TEU). It is well-known that the strength of representative democracy through the European Parliament, and its accordant approximation to the ideal speech situation, has been subject to

[147] ibid 62–65; J Burgess, A Stirling, J Clark, G Davies, M Eames, K Staley and S Williamson, 'Deliberative Mapping: A Novel Analytic-Deliberative Methodology to Support Contested Science-Policy Decisions' (2007) 16 *Public Understanding of Science* 299, 300.

[148] T Webler, '"Right" Discourse in Citizen Participation' (n 140) 65.

[149] Webler refers to this 'metacriterion' as 'competence'; see ibid.

[150] C Quittkat, 'New Instruments Serving Democracy: Do Online Consultations Benefit Civil Society?' in B Kohler-Koch and C Quittkat (eds), *De-Mystification of Participatory Democracy: EU Governance and Civil Society* (Oxford, Oxford University Press, 2013) 101.

substantial criticism.[151] Above all, the low turnout in European elections and the European electorate's continued focus on national politics[152] have led to warnings that a true European *demos*, built on a common identity, or in Scharpf's words a 'collective identity', does not exist at the EU level.[153] The well-known notion, here caricatured by Habermas, is that since 'there is no European people, … a Political Union that deserves the name is built on sand'.[154] Habermas, however, proposes to grasp representative democracy at the EU level as a multi-level construct.[155] In such a multi-level system he argues that sovereignty is 'originally shared' between the EU citizens acting in their roles of citizens of the Union (by electing the European Parliament) and the same EU citizens acting in their roles of citizens of one Member State (by electing their national parliaments).[156]

While the Council of Ministers hence constitutes an important forum in legitimising EU policies through the political systems of the Member States,[157] the European Parliament plays an equally essential role as the only EU institution whose members are directly elected by the totality of EU citizens.[158] Arguably, however, the weight the Parliament takes in this balance is yet underdeveloped. An adjustment would 'require that equal legislative powers be given to the Council and the Parliament in all relevant political fields'[159]—formally but also in practice. More than the Council, it is therefore the role of the European Parliament in the regulatory process at European level that has been the core subject of debates on

[151] See eg the judgment of the German Constitutional Court, BVerfG, Judgment of the Second Senate of 30 June 2009—2 BvE 2/08—paras (1–421) *Gauweiler v Treaty of Lisbon*, para 280; C Harlow, *Accountability in the European Union* (n 133) 180; S Hix and C Lord, 'The Making of a President: The European Parliament and the Confirmation of Jacques Santer as President of the Commission' (1996) 31 *Government and Opposition* 62, 62.

[152] PC Schmitter, *How to Democratise the European Union … And Why Bother?*, Governance in Europe (Lanham, Rowman & Littlefield Publishers, 2000) 65.

[153] Above section II.B. See also A Menon and S Weatherill, 'Democratic Politics in a Globalising World: Supranationalism and Legitimacy in the European Union' (2007) LSE Law, Society and Economy Working Papers 13/2007, 26; B De Witte, 'Executive Accountability under the European Constitution and the Lisbon Treaty' in P Kiiver, S Loeffen and L Verhey (eds), *Political Accountability and European Integration* (Groningen, Europa Law Publishing, 2009) 139; S Smismans, *Law, Legitimacy, and European Governance* (n 132) 12; R Dehousse, 'The Community Method at Sixty' in Dehousse (ed), *The Community Method: Obstinate or Obsolete?*, Palgrave Studies in European Union Politics (Basingstoke, Palgrave Macmillan, 2011) 9; RA Dahl, *On Democracy* (n 56) 117; J Neyer, *The Justification of Europe* (n 54) 61.

[154] J Habermas, 'The Crisis of the European Union in the Light of a Constitutionalisation of International Law' (2012) 23 *The European Journal of International Law* 335, 337.

[155] See for a discussion, A Von Bogdandy, 'The European Lesson for International Democracy: The Significance of Articles 9 to 12 EU Treaty for International Organisations' (2011) Jean Monnet Working Paper no 02/11, 11 www.jeanmonnetprogram.org/wp-content/uploads/2014/12/110201.pdf.

[156] J Habermas, 'Democracy in Europe: Why the Development of the EU into a Transnational Democracy Is Necessary and How It Is Possible' (2015) 21 *European Law Journal* 546, 554; J Habermas, 'The Crisis of the European Union' (n 154) 343.

[157] L Verhey, 'Fostering Executive Accountability in the EU: A Key Issue' in J Wouters, L Verhey and P Kiiver (eds), *European Constitutionalism Beyond Lisbon* (Antwerp, Intersentia, 2009) 243.

[158] ibid 242.

[159] J Habermas, 'The Crisis of the European Union' (n 154) 345.

the European Union's 'democratic deficit'.[160] When analysing political participation in the case studies, the role of the European Parliament, de jure and de facto, will consequently be the focus of attention.

b. Administrative Participation

Administrative participation, as a complement to representative democracy, has been approached cautiously by the EU institutions.[161] Its role seems particularly important where the Parliament's involvement is constrained, for instance due to the delegation of regulatory powers to the EU executive. The Treaty of Lisbon inserted a new Article 11 TEU, which upgrades participation to one of the Union's democratic principles.[162] Yet, unless participation rights are expressly provided for by a relevant Treaty article or secondary legislation, the European courts have in the past consistently denied a general consultation right.[163] Instead, participation in decision-making procedures is dependent upon the willingness of the EU institutions to set self-imposed standards. In chapter two, it became clear that, in its White Paper on Governance, the Commission objected to the adoption of procedural guarantees in a legally binding form, such as those proposed by Habermas.[164] Instead, the Commission adopted non-binding minimum standards for consultation in 2002 in order to 'ensure that all relevant parties are properly consulted'.[165] These standards were confirmed in May 2015 with the Commission's

[160] See JHH Weiler, UR Haltern and F Mayer, 'European Democracy and Its Critique' (1995) 18 *West European Politics* 4. While different descriptions of the 'democratic deficit' exist, the standard version revolves around five interrelated claims about the Union's institutional set-up: First, critics contend that while European integration has resulted in an increase in executive power at Union level, outside the scope of public scrutiny, it has decreased the democratic parliamentary control at the national level. Secondly, the only directly elected institution at the EU level, the European Parliament, is too weak, even after increases in its legislative powers since the Single European Act and up to the Treaty of Lisbon. Thirdly, elections to the European Parliament are still fought over national political issues, as 'second-order national contests', and are not driven by a European agenda. Fourthly, the EU is too distant from its citizens and too complex for them to grasp. Finally, national politicians use the European level to circumvent constraints posed by national parliaments, courts or interest structures; they can thus pursue policy objectives at the European level which do not receive sufficient support at the national level.

[161] See for the historical development, C Quittkat and B Kohler-Koch, 'Involving Civil Society in EU Governance' in B Kohler-Koch and C Quittkat (eds), *De-Mystification of Participatory Democracy: EU Governance and Civil Society* (Oxford, Oxford University Press, 2013) 43–47.

[162] J Mendes, 'Participation and the Role of Law After Lisbon: A Legal View on Article 11 TEU (2011) 48 *Common Market Law Review* 1849.

[163] P Craig, *EU Administrative Law*, Collected Courses of the Academy of European Law vol XVI/1, 2nd edn (Oxford, Oxford University Press, 2012) 292. The leading authority is the *Atlanta* case, Case C-104/97P *Atlanta AG and others v Commission of the European Communities and Council of the European Communities* [1999] ECR I-6983.

[164] Above chapter 2, section II.A.

[165] 'Towards a reinforced culture of consultation and dialogue' COM (2002) 704 final (n 72) 3.

'Better Regulation Package' and the Guidelines on Stakeholder Consultation as laid down in the Better Regulation Guidelines.[166]

According to these minimum consultation standards, the Commission commits itself to safeguarding that all parties affected by the policy, first, have an opportunity to express their opinion and, secondly, are made aware of the consultation through adequate publicity. Furthermore, all communication relating to a particular consultation should be clear and include all necessary information, such as a summary of the context, scope and objectives of the consultation. Moreover, the Commission should grant affected parties sufficient time to reply to a consultation.[167] Finally, the results of the consultation are to be published and 'adequate feedback' provided.[168] These standards could easily be considered to have been inspired by the Habermasian ideal speech situation. The case studies will analyse the extent to which the EU institutions' administrative participation indeed approximates this ideal in practice. It was mentioned above that with the new Article 11 TEU, for the first time participation is explicitly associated with democracy at the EU Treaty level. Whether or not the Commission's self-imposed consultation standards sufficiently meet the demands of participatory democracy has already been questioned.[169] The analysis in the case studies strives to give these current discussions an empirical foundation.

iii. Holding the EU Regulator to Account

Accountability aims at the prevention of abuses of power.[170] Questions of accountability arise from the execution, often following a delegation, of public tasks by a wide spectrum of actors.[171] Such actors may have incentives to use their position

[166] 'Better Regulation for Better Results'—An EU Agenda' COM (2015) 215 final (n 69) 4. See for the minimum consultation standards, European Commission, 'Better Regulation Guidelines' (Staff Working Document) SWD (2015) 111 final, ch VII 'Guidelines on Stakeholder Consultation'.

[167] A period of at least eight weeks. Since 2012, the eight-week requirement has been extended to 12 weeks, see European Commission, 'Smart Regulation in the European Union' (Communication) COM (2010) 543, 10 and 'Better Regulation Guidelines' SWD (2015) 111 final (n 166) 77.

[168] Towards a Reinforced Culture of Consultation and Dialogue' COM (2002) 704 final (n 72) 21–22 and 'Better Regulation Guidelines' SWD (2015) 111 final (n 166) 66.

[169] J Mendes, 'Participation and the Role of Law After Lisbon' (n 162) 1876. Discussions are taking place as to whether legally enforceable participation rights for the EU decision-making process should be adopted as a consequence of its insertion. Conflicting opinions have been expressed as regards the nature of the obligation in Art 11 TEU, whether it is a mere political commitment or whether it may also have legal effects. According to Kohler-Koch, 'the Article may add to the democratic legitimacy of the EU but it may as well just produce a smoke screen of democratic governance and thus contribute to a further disillusionment of the European public' as 'no formal institutions are envisaged, it is a political but no legal obligation', see B Kohler-Koch, 'Colliding Visions of Representation and Participation' (3rd ACELG Annual Conference on 'Postnational Democracy: Beyond Representation in the EU', University of Amsterdam, 22 November 2013). In a similar vein, M Lee, *EU Environmental Law* (n 50) 185.

[170] RO Keohane, 'Accountability in World Politics' in S Gustavsson, C Karlsson and T Persson (eds), *The Illusion of Accountability in the European Union*, Routledge Advances in European Politics (London, Routledge, 2009) 17.

[171] C Scott, 'Accountability in the Regulatory State' (2000) 27 *Journal of Law and Society* 38, 38.

to follow their own self-interest or may be captured by the interests of those being regulated, thereupon compromising their independence.[172] To prevent this, regulators should be held to account for their conduct.[173] In many contexts, accountability functions as an umbrella term, encompassing the virtues of 'good governance' such as transparency, responsibility, openness but also inclusiveness and participation.[174] Following the reconceptualisation of Scharpf's analytical frame of input and output legitimacy, however, a narrower definition of accountability is needed. Accountability is to be clearly distinguished from participation, which provides for input into the regulatory process. Understanding accountability as a mechanism to enhance output legitimacy, it provides an ex post oversight. Actors are held to account for their conduct, which has already taken place. 'Conduct' then comprises, for instance, the way knowledge was collected by the regulator, the way affected societal actors were included in the regulatory process and whether procedures introduced to these ends were (correctly) followed.

An appropriate narrow definition has been provided by Mark Bovens. He defined accountability as 'a relationship between an actor [*who?*] and a forum [*to whom?*], in which the actor has an obligation to explain and to justify his or her conduct [*for what?*], the forum can pose questions and pass judgment, and the actor may face consequences'.[175] Bovens' definition thus consists of three core elements: (1) the account giver, that is, the actor, who needs to inform (explain or justify) her or his conduct to the forum; (2) the forum, which must be allowed to question the actor's conduct; and (3) the taking place of a debate, in which the forum may judge the actor based on her or his conduct and may impose (formal or informal) consequences.[176] Bovens et al identify several kinds of fora to which an actor may render account: (1) the political forum, (2) the legal forum, (3) the administrative forum and (4) the social forum.[177]

[172] M Flinders, 'Distributed Public Governance in the European Union' (2004) 11 *Journal of European Public Policy* 520, 538.

[173] See also RW Grant and RO Keohane, 'Accountability and Abuses of Power in World Politics' (2005) 99 *American Political Science Review* 29.

[174] An example is the Global Accountability Project (GAP), developed by One World Trust, which understands accountability as consisting of four core dimensions: transparency, participation, evaluation and complaint and response mechanisms, see M Blagescu, L De Las Casas and R Lloyd, *Pathways to Accountability: A Short Guide to the GAP Framework* (London, One World Trust, 2005) 2. Another example is the Commission's White Paper on European Governance which describes accountability in the following way: '[r]oles in the legislative and executive processes need to be clearer. Each of the EU Institutions must explain and take responsibility for what it does in Europe. But there is also a need for greater clarity and responsibility from Member States and all those involved in developing and implementing EU policy at whatever level.' The Commission thus understands accountability in a very broad sense, as to embrace a clarification of roles in the policy-making process and responsibility of actors, see 'European Governance—A White Paper' COM (2001) 428 final (n 24) 8 and 10; see also C Harlow, *Accountability in the European Union* (n 133) 185.

[175] M Bovens, 'Analysing and Assessing Accountability: A Conceptual Framework' (2007) 13 *European Law Journal* 447, 450.

[176] M Bovens, D Curtin and P't Hart, *The Real World of EU Accountability: What Deficit?* (Oxford, Oxford University Press, 2010) 36.

[177] ibid 41–44. I left out the 'professional forum'.

a. Political Accountability

Political accountability is the traditional type of accountability of the national constitutional state. In essence, 'the forum' consists of the citizens who hold their politicians to account in elections.[178] In this sense, accountability is intrinsically linked to input legitimacy. Voters in elections not only choose their representatives, but they also hold the incumbent to account for their conduct during the previous legislative period.[179]

Political accountability is referred to as traditional because it operates according to a direct, hierarchical chain of delegation. The delegation of power is often described with the help of the principal–agent framework. According to this framework, the existence of a principal is assumed, who transfers certain powers and tasks to an agent, who, in turn, is expected to act on the principal's behalf.[180] In the national context, a direct chain of delegation between principal and agent emerges (voter–parliament–executive body), through which the agent can be held accountable to the principal.[181] It has proved more complex to apply the framework to the EU's multi-level structure. The multi-level configuration at the EU level has led to the emergence of multiple chains of delegation, implying an analogous proliferation of accountability relations.[182] In view of the broad understanding of regulation adopted in this book, the situation is even more opaque, with tasks potentially being delegated to public and/or private actors in heterarchical, more flexible relationships.[183] The Court of Justice of the EU reacted to these developments as early as 1958. In its *Meroni* judgments,[184] the Court considerably limited the institutions' ability to delegate power. Accordingly, 'only clearly defined executive powers', as opposed to 'discretionary powers', could be delegated to bodies outside the institutions established by the Treaties.[185] The Court justified its decision by reference to the 'balance of powers' that it found to underlie the

[178] D Curtin and L Senden, 'Public Accountability of Transnational Private Regulation: Chimera or Reality?' (2011) 38 *Journal of Law and Society* 163, 175.

[179] FW Scharpf, *Governing in Europe* (n 123) 15.

[180] D Curtin, 'Holding (Quasi-) Autonomous EU Administrative Actors to Public Account' (2007) 13 *European Law Journal* 523, 525.

[181] ibid.

[182] D Curtin, *Executive Power of the European Union* (n 33); PC Schmitter, *How to Democratise the European Union* (n 152). For the concept of multi-level governance, see L Hooghe and G Marks, *Multi-level Governance and European Integration* (Lanham, Rowman and Littlefield, 2001). See also C Harlow and R Rawlings, 'Promoting Accountability in Multi-Level Governance: A Network Approach' (2006) European Governance Papers (EUROGOV) no C-06-02, 6.

[183] C Scott, 'Accountability in the Regulatory State' (n 171) 39; P Lindseth, 'Agents without Principals? Delegation in an Age of Diffuse and Fragmented Governance' in F Cafaggi (ed), *Reframing Self-Regulation in European Private Law*, Private Law in European Content Series vol 9 (Alphen aan den Rijn, Kluwer Law International, 2006) 108; E Fisher, 'The European Union in the Age of Accountability' (2004) 24 *Oxford Journal of Legal Studies* 495, 501.

[184] Case 9/56 *Meroni and Co., Industrie Metallurgiche S.p.A. v Highly Authority of the European Coal and Steel Community* [1957–58] ECR 133 and Case 10/56 *Meroni and Co., Industrie Metallurgiche S.p.A. v Highly Authority of the European Coal and Steel Community* [1957–58] ECR 157.

[185] Case 9/56 *Meroni* (n 184) para 152.

Community's institutional structure.[186] The preservation of this balance would be necessary to ensure the Community's democratic legitimacy, requiring legislation to be made by the politically elected or at least by politically accountable officials.[187]

In spite of these inherent limitations, Verhey et al maintain that national experiences with political accountability form a valuable source of inspiration for the EU level.[188] Taking the European Parliament as the locus of political accountability at the EU level, the regulator should, first, be required to justify his or her conduct to the political forum. Secondly, the Parliament should possess the right to be informed about the regulator's conduct. Thirdly, the European Parliament should be able to make a judgement about the regulator's behaviour and impose sanctions.[189] Political accountability thus refers to the political forum's scrutiny of EU regulatory performance.

The European Commission, as the Union's main executive institution,[190] has been at the centre of debates on accountability.[191] Since the European governance debate, the Parliament has been able to (formally) enhance its capacity to hold the Commission to account. The Parliament approves the President of the Commission and the nominated college of Commissioners.[192] After appointment, the Commission remains answerable to Parliament, which may at any time table a motion of censure upon which the college of Commissioners has to resign.[193] Beyond that, the Commission shall reply to questions posed by the Parliament[194] and submit a general activity report annually.[195] The Parliament furthermore retains the budgetary control.[196] Arguably, these could be labelled the 'grand supervisory powers' that the Parliament possesses over the Commission. Whether, and to what extent, the Parliament is also able to use these powers to scrutinise the EU executive's regulatory output in practice will be analysed in the case studies.

[186] K Lenaerts and A Verhoeven, 'Institutional Balance as a Guarantee for Democracy in EU Governance' in C Joerges and R Dehousse (eds), *Good Governance in Europe's Integrated Market*, Collected Courses of the Academy of European Law XI/2 (Oxford, Oxford University Press, 2002) 37.

[187] D Curtin and R Dehousse, 'European Agencies: Tipping the Balance' in M Busuioc, M Groenleer and J Trondal (eds), *The Agency Phenomenon in the European Union* (n 93) 200.

[188] L Verhey, M Claes and H Broeksteeg, 'Political Accountability in the European Union: Conceptual Analysis and Future Prospects' (2008) in L Verhey, H Broeksteeg and I Van den Driessche (eds), *Political Accountability in Europe: Which Way Forward?* (Groningen, Europa Law Publishing, 2008) 326.

[189] ibid.

[190] See eg HCH Hofmann et al, *EU Administrative Law and Policy* (n 65) 766.

[191] See also A Wille, 'The European Commission's Accountability Paradox' in M Bovens, D Curtin and P't Hart, *The Real World of EU Accountability: What Deficit?* (n 176) 64. See for a more detailed discussion of the Medina Ortega Report above chapter 2, section III.B.

[192] Art 17(7) of the Treaty on European Union 'TEU' (Consolidated version 2016) [2016] OJ C202/13.

[193] Art 17(8) TEU, Art 234 of the Treaty on the Functioning of the European Union 'TFEU' (Consolidated version 2016) [2016] OJ C202/47.

[194] Art 230 TFEU.

[195] Art 233 TFEU.

[196] Art 319 TFEU.

b. Legal Accountability

Legal accountability refers to the review of the regulator's conduct by the judiciary. Regulators are required to justify their decisions before the courts and are faced with the possibility of formal sanctions.[197] At the EU level, the General Court and the Court of Justice act as legal fora which can, pursuant to Article 263 TFEU, review and annul Union acts if they constitute an infringement of the Treaties or an essential procedural requirement, a lack of competence and/or constitute a misuse of power.[198] According to Bovens, 'legal accountability is the most unambiguous type of accountability, as the legal scrutiny will be based on detailed legal standards'.[199] Whether this is indeed the case is questionable in view of this book's broad understanding of regulation, which not only considers new actors in the regulatory process but which may also result in norms of a more flexible, voluntary character with uncertain legal effects.[200] The judicial role in scrutinising the EU institutions' conduct therefore needs to be closely analysed in the empirical part.

c. Administrative Accountability

Administrative accountability refers to supervision exercised by ombudsmen, auditors, controllers and inspectors. At the EU level, three main fora have to be mentioned. First, the Court of Auditors examines the revenues and expenditures of all EU bodies, offices and agencies.[201] In close collaboration with the Court of Auditors, the European Parliament not only approves the Union's annual budget together with the Council,[202] but it also controls the implementation of the budget by the Commission, other institutions and agencies funded by the EU budget according to Article 319 TFEU. Secondly, in case of fraud, corruption and other illegal activities to the detriment of the EU's financial interests, administrative accountability is performed by the European Anti-Fraud Office (OLAF) and its wide investigative powers.[203] Finally, the European Ombudsman, appointed by the European Parliament, has the mandate to investigate complaints concerning cases of maladministration in the EU institutions, bodies, offices or agencies.[204] The Ombudsman may require the institutional actors to explain and justify their

[197] C Harlow and R Rawlings, 'Promoting Accountability in Multi-Level Governance' (n 182) 8 and 15.

[198] D Chalmers, G Davies and G Monti, *European Union Law*, 3rd edn (Cambridge, Cambridge University Press, 2014) 428ff.

[199] M Bovens, 'Analysing and Assessing Accountability' (n 175).

[200] Above section I.C.ii; E Fisher, 'The European Union in the Age of Accountability' (n 183) 505.

[201] Art 287(1) TFEU.

[202] Art 314 TFEU.

[203] OLAF was established by the Commission Decision 1999/352/EC, ECSC, Euratom of 28 April 1999 establishing the European Anti-fraud Office (OLAF) [1999] OJ L136/20.

[204] Art 228(1) TFEU. The European citizens' right to apply to the Ombudsman is laid down in Art 24 TFEU and Art 43 of the Charter of Fundamental Rights of the European Union (Consolidated version 2016) [2016] OJ C202/389.

conduct, question their behaviour and pass judgment.[205] Yet, it cannot impose legal obligations. Instead, it may submit recommendations and, in the final instance, present its findings to the Parliament.[206]

d. Social Accountability

Social accountability refers to the regulator's accountability to affected societal actors.[207] Affected actors may not only play a role in the regulatory process itself, but may also help to hold the regulator to account ex post. One prerequisite for social accountability is a transparent regulatory process. According to Curtin, transparency comprises the accessibility and visibility of information: 'a transparent political system is one where it is possible for people on the outside to acquire the information they need to form opinions about actions on processes within the political and administrative institutions'.[208] Hence, pursuant to Article 11(2) TEU, 'the institutions shall maintain an open, transparent and regular dialogue with representative associations and civil society'. To that effect, Article 15(3) TFEU grants EU citizens the right to access documents of the EU institutions, bodies and agencies. The right of access to documents is also reflected in Article 42 of the Charter of Fundamental Rights and implemented by Regulation 1049/2001 on public access to documents.[209] Next to access to documents, transparent decision making entails a reason-giving dimension.[210] Furthermore, the procedures introduced in section I.A on 'pooling knowledge'—the impact assessment procedure, the horizontal rules on expert groups, the common approach to EU agencies, as well as the guidelines on the collection of expertise—also aim at increasing the transparency of the drafting process by exposing the consulted sources to public scrutiny. Their operation in practice is therefore prone to further increase (or decrease) the transparency of the regulatory process. Finally, the availability of information and documentation on the regulatory process might be difficult

[205] C Harlow and R Rawlings, 'Promoting Accountability in Multi-Level Governance' (n 182) 19.

[206] See further P Magnette, 'Between Parliamentary Control and the Rule of Law: The Political Role of the Ombudsman in the European Union' (2003) 10 *Journal of European Public Policy* 677, 681.

[207] M Bovens et al, *The Real World of EU Accountability: What Deficit?* (n 176) 44.

[208] D Curtin, *Executive Power of the European Union* (n 33) 205.

[209] Regulation of the European Parliament and of the Council (EC) 1049/2001 of 30 May 2001 regarding public access to European Parliament, Council and Commission documents [2001] OJ L145/43. Currently, a Commission proposal to amend the Regulation is at an impasse due to disagreement between Parliament, Commission and Council, see European Commission, 'Proposal for a Regulation Regarding Public Access to European Parliament, Council and Commission documents' COM (2008) 229.

[210] J Scott and S Sturm, 'Courts as Catalysts: Re-Thinking the Judicial Role in New Governance' (2007) 13 *Columbia Journal of European Law* 565, 587.

to access by all affected actors if it is not translated into the official languages of the EU.[211]

Yet, while transparency is a precondition for social accountability, the existence of the former does not guarantee the latter. Transparency does not involve the elements of debate and judgement necessary for accountability. The existence of debate and judgement crucially depends on the organisation and the influence of affected societal actors at the European level. The problem of (the absence of) a European public sphere has already been discussed in section II.B.i. This must be kept in mind when analysing social accountability in the case studies.

III. CONCLUSION

This chapter marked out the scope of the following empirical analysis in two important ways. First, it defined the object of the analysis, the *what*: 'EU regulation'. Accordingly, the case studies will not only address the current legislative developments in the area of nanotechnologies, but, following the broad definition of regulation, they will also explore, beyond legislation, activities in the EU executive sphere of both a binding and non-binding nature. Secondly, this chapter defined the lenses through which the EU regulation of nanotechnologies will be analysed, the *how*: 'regulatory capacity'. Having embedded the elements of regulatory capacity—namely the ability to master knowledge and to ensure legitimate regulation—into the theoretical accounts of chapter two, this chapter identified the legal procedures, the 'tangible impacts' of the European governance debate, that the EU institutions set in place to their attainment. It is the applicability and practical operation of these tools and procedures that will be tested in the analysis of the EU regulatory developments in the food and chemical sectors.

[211] See eg M Lee, *EU Environmental Law* (n 50) 96 and N Vogiatzis, 'The Linguistic Policy of the EU Institutions and Political Participation Post-Lisbon' (2016) 41 *European Law Review* 176.

Table 1: Analysing EU Risk Regulation of Nanotechnologies through the Lenses of Regulatory Capacity

Component of Regulatory Capacity	*Legal Tools and Procedures*
1. Pooling Knowledge	— Impact Assessment Procedure (of Commission, Parliament and Council) — Procedural frameworks for the collection of knowledge from Commission expert groups and EU agencies
2. Ensuring Participation (input legitimacy) a) Political Participation b) Administrative Participation	— Involvement of the European Parliament in the drafting of regulation — Commission's Minimum Standards for Consultations
3. Ensuring Accountability (output legitimacy) a) Political b) Legal c) Administrative d) Social	EU regulator is held to account — by the European Parliament — by the European Courts — by the European Ombudsman, European Anti-Fraud Office, Court of Auditors — by affected societal actors (transparency)

4

Nanotechnologies in Food

AFTER THE THEORETICAL debates of the last two chapters, it is time to plunge into the empirical part of this book. At the heart of this first case study lies the analysis of the current regulatory developments through the lenses of regulatory capacity. Before delving into the analysis, an outline of the present applications of nanotechnologies in the food sector will be given (section I). Subsequently, the relevant EU regulatory framework, and the coverage of nanotechnologies therein, will be identified. The analysis will reveal a preference on the part of the European Commission to address the contentious issue of nanotechnologies in an executive setting—via comitology, Commission recommendations and agency guidance documents (section II). The scene is then set for the chapter's core, that is, the analysis of the applicability and practical operation of the legal procedures—the 'tangible impacts' of the European governance debate—that were identified in chapter three. The chapter will bring to the fore not only severe shortcomings in the applicability of these procedures to executive rule making but also as regards their operation in the drafting of legislation (section III).

I. NANOTECHNOLOGIES IN FOOD

A. Innovating Food Production and Processing

The production and processing of food used to be closely tied to the conditions of the land and the cultural habits of its population. This fundamentally changed in the last two centuries, driven by the increasing pace of scientific and technological innovation, functional differentiation and globalisation.[1] Globalisation turned food—like cars, cosmetics or textiles—into a 'good' or a 'commodity' which is traded around the globe.[2] Food is increasingly detached from its origin. As people are no longer able to determine the quality of their food themselves, novel problems regarding food safety arise.

[1] Above chapter 2, section I. *cf* High-Level Group of the Competitiveness of the Agro-Food Industry, 'Report on the Competitiveness of the Agro-Food Industry' (European Commission, DG Enterprise and Industry, March 2009) 11.

[2] Since 2011, world exports in food have overtaken exports in automotive products, see WTO, 'International Trade Statistics 2012' (2012) 53 www.wto.org/english/res_e/statis_e/its2012_e/its2012_e.pdf.

As well as the loss of individuals' direct control over what they eat, the uncertain and man-made consequences inherent in today's industrialised methods of food production and processing have stirred deep anxieties.[3] Naturally, people are cautious about what they eat. New technologies in the food sector are therefore often regarded with scepticism, distrust and even resistance.[4] Yet, modern food production must also be regarded as another facet of the risk society.[5] A case in point is the outbreak of the cattle disease BSE in the UK in the late 1980s. While cattle are herbivores, the introduction of industrialised animal farming resulted in an expanded use of commercial feeds. Feed processed from animal tissues was commonly used to reduce costs and to increase productivity.[6] Since then, this feed has been identified as the origin of BSE.[7] By artificially changing the feed of the cattle in order to render meat production more profitable, a new, severe danger to human and animal health was unknowingly created.

Regulatory intervention in the food sector is therefore necessary. Food production, processing and consumption belong to the most heavily regulated sectors worldwide.[8] Regulatory frameworks for food exist at the national, supranational (European) and international level, by organisations such as the World Trade Organization (WTO), the United Nations' Food and Agricultural Organisation (FAO), and the World Health Organisation (WHO).[9] It is also the regulatory requirements that have led the food industry to explore new ways to enhance their products, such as reductions in the amount of sugar, salt, fat, artificial colouring and preservatives used.[10]

B. Applications of Nanotechnologies in Food

In its continuous endeavour to innovate, the food industry has discovered the potential of nanotechnologies. The rise of nanotechnologies has steered expectations that these new technologies may tackle many of the current needs of the modern food industry and, even beyond that, address global challenges such as nourishing a growing world population, the need for more sustainable

[3] D Inglis and D Gimlin, 'Food Globalisations: Ironies and Ambivalences of Food, Cuisine and Globality' in D Inglis and D Gimlin (eds), *The Globalisation of Food* (Oxford, Berg Publisher, 2009) 20.

[4] Science and Technologies Committee, *Nanotechnologies and Food* (HL 2009–10, 22-I) 7 www.publications.parliament.uk/pa/ld200910/ldselect/ldsctech/22/22i.pdf.

[5] For an introduction to the 'risk society', see above chapter 2, section I.C. *cf* A Szajkowska, *Regulating Food Law: Risk Analysis and the Precautionary Principle as General Principles of EU Food Law*, European Institute for Food Law series vol 7 (Wageningen, Wageningen Academic Publishers, 2012) 17.

[6] European Food Safety Authority, 'Bovine Spongiform Encephalopathy (BSE)' www.efsa.europa.eu/en/topics/topic/bovinespongiformencephalopathy.htm.

[7] ibid.

[8] D Inglis and D Gimlin, 'Food Globalisations' (n 3) 19.

[9] ibid.

[10] FAO/WHO, *FAO/WHO Expert Meeting on the Application of Nanotechnologies in the Food and Agriculture Sectors: Potential Food Safety Implications* (Rome, FAO/WHO, 2010) 4.

production, food safety, and preventive healthcare.[11] The novel functionalities of nano-sized materials and substances have thus infected the food sector with a wave of nanomania. Yet, it is exactly with these novel functionalities that not only nanomania but also nanophobia begins.[12]

i. Nanomania: Exploiting Nanotechnologies for the Food Sector

Countless potential applications of nanotechnologies in the food sector are imagined. A first core area of application is the development of nanostructured food ingredients.[13] Their main benefit is said to be the availability of comparatively healthier products. For instance, they allow for a smooth dispersal of even water-insoluble ingredients without the use of additional fats or surfactants. This would enable the preparation of products, such as low-fat mayonnaise or ice cream, which promise to be as creamy as the full-fat equivalent.[14] Several consumer products are already available on the global market which incorporate nanostructured food ingredients.[15]

A further area of application is the development of delivery systems based on encapsulation technologies. The idea is that a nano-enabled shell encapsulates additives and supplements to control their release, better preserve them during storage and processing, mask unpleasant tastes,[16] or to ensure an enhanced uptake of the nutrients by the body.[17] Currently and in the foreseeable future the largest share of the market is occupied by nano-enabled food contact materials and packaging.[18] The objective is to generate more lightweight and robust packaging that allows for a prolonged shelf life of the product,[19] thereby reducing the amount of food waste.[20] For example, PET bottles coated with nano-layers minimise the loss of CO_2 and prevent the absorption of O_2 into the packaging.[21] Also,

[11] F Kampers, 'Potential Benefits and Market Drivers for Nanotechnology Applications in the Food Sector' in Q Chaudhry, R Watkins and L Castle (eds), *Nanotechnologies in Food*, RSC Nanoscience & Nanotechnology 14 (Cambridge, Royal Society of Chemistry Publishing, 2010) 103–08.

[12] See, for an introduction to the nano debate, above chapter 1, section II.

[13] Q Chaudhry, M Scotter, J Blackburn, B Toss, A Boxall, L Castle, R Aitken and R Watkins, 'Applications and Implications of Nanotechnologies for the Food Sector' (2008) 25 *Food Additives and Contaminants* 241, 244.

[14] ibid.

[15] FAO/WHO, *FAO/WHO Expert Meeting on the Application of Nanotechnologies in the Food and Agriculture Sectors* (n 10) 10 and 11.

[16] Q Chaudhry et al, 'Applications and Implications of Nanotechnologies for the Food Sector' (n 13) 244.

[17] FAO/WHO, *FAO/WHO Expert Meeting on the Application of Nanotechnologies in the Food and Agriculture Sectors* (n 10) 10 and 11.

[18] ibid 15.

[19] ibid.

[20] M Smolander and Q Chaudhry, 'Nanotechnologies in Food Packaging' in Q Chaudhry, R Watkins and L Castle (eds), *Nanotechnologies in Food* (n 11) 86.

[21] Q Chaudhry et al, 'Applications and Implications of Nanotechnologies for the Food Sector' (n 13) 245.

nanoparticles with antimicrobial activity are used in food contact materials. Nanosilver, for instance, inhibits bacterial growth on refrigerator surfaces, storage bags and kitchenware.[22] Furthermore, nanosensors are integrated into 'intelligent' food packaging to monitor and inform about the quality of the food.[23] Lastly, research has commenced into potential applications of nanotechnologies in the agricultural sector, such as in veterinary medicines, pesticides, and further agrochemicals, such as fertilisers and plant growth regulators.[24]

ii. Nanophobia: Environmental, Health and Safety Risks of Nanofoods

While it is the changing physicochemical properties that enable novel applications, it is the very same properties that have caused great concerns.[25] Several non-governmental organisations (NGOs)[26] have called for a moratorium on the commercialisation of food products and packaging containing nanomaterials 'until nanotechnology-specific safety laws are established and the public is involved in decision-making'.[27] The fear is that the ingestion of nano-sized particles poses hazards to the health of the consumer.[28] The European Food Safety Authority (EFSA) in 2009 identified several uncertainties for the risk assessment of nanotechnologies and their possible applications in the food and animal feed area.[29]

First, EFSA observed difficulties characterising, detecting and measuring engineered nanomaterials in food and feed.[30] Current information on the use of engineered nanomaterials in food can therefore only be provided by the industry itself.[31] Secondly, there is limited information as to the fate and potential adverse effects of engineered nanomaterials in the human body.[32] The smaller the particle, the greater the distribution to organs.[33] Particularly tricky in this regard is the

[22] ibid 246.

[23] FAO/WHO, *FAO/WHO Expert Meeting on the Application of Nanotechnologies in the Food and Agriculture Sectors* (n 10) 9. The application of nanosensors is also expected to contribute significantly to the speed and efficiency of food distribution, as products can be more easily identified and the stock faster controlled, see ObservatoryNano, 'Nanotechnologies for Food Packaging: Reporting the Science and Technology Research Trends' (FP7 Report, August 2010) 3.

[24] FAO/WHO, *FAO/WHO Expert Meeting on the Application of Nanotechnologies in the Food and Agriculture Sectors* (n 10) 18.

[25] European Food Safety Authority, 'The Potential Risks Arising from Nanoscience and Nanotechnologies on Food and Feed Safety' (2009) 7 *EFSA Journal* 1, 1.

[26] eg ETC Group, 'Down on the Farm: The Impact of Nano-Scale Technologies on Food and Agriculture' (Report, November 2004); Friends of the Earth, 'Out of the Laboratory and on to our Plates: Nanotechnology in Food and Agriculture' (Report, March 2008).

[27] Friends of the Earth, 'Out of the Laboratory' (n 26) 3.

[28] Q Chaudhry et al, 'Applications and Implications of Nanotechnologies for the Food Sector' (n 13) 248.

[29] European Food Safety Authority, 'The Potential Risks Arising from Nanoscience' (n 25).

[30] ibid 25.

[31] ibid 13.

[32] ibid 25.

[33] FAO/WHO, *FAO/WHO Expert Meeting on the Application of Nanotechnologies in the Food and Agriculture Sectors* (n 10) 29.

nano-encapsulation technique, which may facilitate the transfer of encapsulated additives into unintended parts of the human body, therewith acting as a 'Trojan horse'.[34] Thirdly, most published studies focus on exposure through the skin or inhalation and not on exposure through the gastrointestinal tract.[35] It is also unclear to what extent nano-components in food contact materials may migrate into the food.[36] While first studies have indicated a low risk of migration,[37] representative testing is lacking.

C. The EU Food Industry and Nanotechnologies

The food industry is torn between nanophobia and nanomania. In recent years, it is notable that major food companies avoided references to 'nano' in their official communications.[38] The fear of a public boycott is omnipresent. At the same time, the largest international food and beverages firms, among them Nestlé, Kraft, Heinz, PepsiCola and Unilever, started research into nanotechnological applications.[39] Already in 2008, it was estimated that more than 400 food companies were active in nanotechnological research and development. This number is expected to increase to more than 1,000 companies in 2018.[40] According to the market research consultancy Cientifica,[41] food applications of nanotechnologies were worth approximately US$ 410 million in 2006. At that time, projections for 2012 had already reached US$ 5.8 billion,[42] so there is no doubt that nanotechnologies in food are rapidly developing into a global, multi-billion Euro industry.[43]

At the EU level, the food sector is one of the key industries in the global market.[44] In order to stay competitive in that market, the European food industry

[34] ibid 12.

[35] European Food Safety Authority, 'The Potential Risks Arising from Nanoscience' (n 25) 18.

[36] ibid 13.

[37] R Franz (Fraunhofer Institute), 'Can nano particles migrate from food contact plastics into foods?' (Lunch Debate European Parliament, 'The function of nanomaterials in food packaging: Safe for the consumer?', Brussels, 26 March 2013) www.publica.fraunhofer.de/documents/N-238837.html.

[38] FAO/WHO, *FAO/WHO Expert Meeting on the Application of Nanotechnologies in the Food and Agriculture Sectors* (n 10) 25; Science and Technologies Committee, *Nanotechnologies and Food* (n 4) 7.

[39] ObservatoryNano, 'Agrifood Sector: Report on Economic Impact of Nanotechnologies' (FP7 Report, April 2010) 9.

[40] ibid.

[41] Several market research consultancies have published estimates on the value of the nano food market. They differ significantly from one another.

[42] Study prepared by consultancy Cientifica, Cientifica, 'Nanotechnologies and Food' (Study, August 2006), quoted in ObservatoryNano, 'Agrifood Sector: Report on Economic Impact of Nanotechnologies' (FP7 Report, April 2010) 8 and 9.

[43] Q Chaudhry et al, 'Applications and Implications of Nanotechnologies for the Food Sector' (n 13) 243.

[44] High-Level Group of the Competitiveness of the Agro-Food Industry (n 1) 4. In 2009, the European agro-food industry represented 2 per cent of the Union's GDP and provided for 13.5 per cent of total employment in the EU's manufacturing sector, see High-Level Group of the Competitiveness of the Agro-Food Industry (n 1) 5.

is under significant pressure to innovate. FoodDrinkEurope, the association representing the food and beverage industry at the EU level, concedes that 'its members are interested in science-based research and development, including the application of nanotechnologies and their potential in food production'.[45] Yet, the association disputes that its members are presently commercialising nanotechnological applications.[46] EFSA, however, suspects that especially nanofood contact materials are already circulating in the EU market.[47] So far, the EU food industry has therefore adopted a cautious approach towards nanotechnologies, at least in its official communications.

II. THE EU REGULATORY FRAMEWORK FOR NANOTECHNOLOGIES IN FOOD

Having introduced the various applications of nanotechnologies in the food sector, the aim of this section is to draw a clear picture of the EU regulatory framework for food, and to discuss the extent to which it has been adapted to the specific characteristics of the nanoform since the Commission's first Communication in 2004, which established the 'incremental approach'.[48] To this end, this section will first analyse the adaptation of the existing EU legislative framework (section A). Thereafter, and in line with this book's broad understanding of regulation,[49] the section will take a careful look at regulatory measures adopted by the EU executive to confront the rise of nanotechnologies outside the legislative review (section B).

A. EU Legislative Framework for Food: Fit for Nano?

The EU legislative framework for food developed as a consequence of the BSE crisis of the late 1990s. Indirectly, the EU had interfered in food safety issues already since the 1960s, mostly due to national food safety provisions that conflicted with EU legislation aimed at the creation of a common market. The EU's approach to food safety regulation bitterly collapsed with the outbreak of BSE, which triggered a comprehensive overhaul of risk regulation in the European Union that reached

[45] FoodDrinkEurope, 'Nanotechnology' www.fooddrinkeurope.eu/our-actions/topic/nanotechnology/.

[46] CIAA (now FoodDrinkEurope) statement in European Food Safety Authority, 'The Potential Risks Arising from Nanoscience' (n 25) 10.

[47] European Food Safety Authority, 'The Potential Risks Arising from Nanoscience' (n 25) 10. See also Science and Technologies Committee, *Nanotechnologies and Food* (n 4) 13. Recently, EFSA reviewed and endorsed three applications for food packaging made with nanotechnologies under Commission Regulation 10/2011. These are silicon dioxide, carbon black and titanium nitride.

[48] For an overview of the EU's regulatory approach to nanotechnologies, see chapter 1, section IV.

[49] See, for the definition of 'regulation' above chapter 3, section I.B.

beyond the food sector.[50] Its regulatory architecture for food safety was newly designed with the Commission's White Paper on Food Safety of 2000.[51]

i. The General Food Law

The blueprint for a new food safety policy was integrated into the EU legislative framework with the adoption of Regulation 178/2002, the 'General Food Law', in 2002.[52] The General Food Law establishes 'common principles and responsibilities, the means to provide a strong science base, efficient organisational arrangements and procedures to underpin decision-making in matters of food and feed safety'.[53] Food, in the General Food Law, is broadly defined as 'any substance or product, whether processed, partially processed or unprocessed, intended to be, or reasonably expected to be ingested by humans'.[54] Its fundamental requirement is that 'food shall not be placed on the market if it is unsafe',[55] a responsibility which rests with the food industry.[56] Failure to comply with this fundamental requirement results in the industry's liability for any damage caused by the unsafe food.[57]

According to the General Food Law, food safety regulation in the EU is based on the principles of risk analysis, precaution and transparency.[58] The division of responsibilities and institutional arrangement for the three stages of risk analysis is clearly laid down. In order to ensure the provision of an 'independent, objective and transparent' risk assessment, the General Food Law set up the European Food Safety Authority, which shall 'provide scientific advice and scientific and technical support for the Community's legislation and policies in all fields which have a direct or indirect impact on food and feed safety'.[59] The political risk management, to the contrary, is conducted by the European Commission together with a comitology committee, the Standing Committee on the Food Chain and Animal Health (SCFCAH).[60]

[50] On the rise of European risk regulation, above chapter 2, section III.B.

[51] European Commission, 'White Paper on Food Safety' COM (1999) 719 final.

[52] Regulation of the European Parliament and of the Council (EC) 178/2002 of 28 January 2002 laying down the general principles and requirements of food law, establishing the European Food Safety Authority and laying down procedures in matters of food safety [2002] OJ L31/1 (hereafter 'General Food Law' or 'GFL').

[53] Arts 1(1) and 5 GFL.

[54] Art 2 GFL.

[55] Art 14(1) GFL.

[56] Art 17(1) GFL.

[57] Art 21 GFL refers to Council Directive 85/374/EEC of 25 July 1985 on the approximation of the laws, regulations and administrative provisions of the Member States concerning liability for defective products [1985] OJ L210/29. See also G Van Calster, D Bowman and J D'Silva, 'Protecting Consumers or Failing Them? The Regulation of Nanotechnologies in the EU' (2011) 1 *European Journal of Consumer Law* 85, 98.

[58] Arts 6, 7, 9 and 10 GFL. For an analysis of the principles of risk analysis and precaution, see above chapter 2, sections III.B.i and III.B.ii.

[59] Art 22(2) GFL.

[60] Art 3(12) GFL; E Vos and F Wendler, 'Food Safety Regulation at EU Level' in E Vos and F Wendler (eds), *Food Safety Regulation in Europe*, Ius Commune Europaeum 62 (Antwerp, Intersentia, 2006) 88.

The General Food Law can thus be understood as the basic structure of EU food law. It applies to all 'food' falling within its broad definition. In principle, this means that the various applications of nanotechnologies in food must also comply with the general safety requirement.[61] Yet, in view of the uncertain risks, several commentators, among them EFSA and the UK House of Lords, have doubted the adequacy of entrusting the responsibility for the safety of nanofoods solely to the food industry: 'the uncertainty that exists with regard to the definition, methodologies, exposure and hazard types is preventing that general safety provision from working properly'.[62] The House of Lords concluded that 'it is essential that any nanomaterial used in a food product should be subject to a formal risk assessment process through the European Food Safety Authority'.[63]

ii. Specific EU Food Law

Specific and more stringent harmonised rules exist at the EU level with respect to particular food, such as food additives, genetically modified foods, novel foods and food packaging, which provide for pre-market approval systems. These foods are considered 'unsafe' a priori; the idea is that only if the contrary is proven can the food be placed on the market.[64] Two specific EU legislative frameworks for food potentially cover the first and second fields of application of nanotechnologies:[65] the legislative regime for novel foods and that for food additives. The coverage of nano-enabled food contact materials needs to be analysed separately, as a specific legislative framework has been in place since the late 1980s.

a. Novel Food Regulation

'Novel foods' were until recently governed by Regulation 258/97, the 'old Novel Food Regulation'.[66] However, in November 2015, the old Novel Food Regulation was repealed by Regulation 2015/2283, the 'new Novel Food Regulation'.[67] As the empirical part of this book was concluded before 2015, reference still needs to be made to both, the provisions of the old and the new Novel Food Regulations.

[61] G Van Calster et al, 'Protecting Consumers or Failing Them?' (n 57) 98.

[62] Science and Technologies Committee, *Nanotechnologies and Food* (n 4) 46; European Food Safety Authority, 'The Potential Risks Arising from Nanoscience' (n 25) 2.

[63] Science and Technologies Committee, *Nanotechnologies and Food* (n 4) 49; European Food Safety Authority, 'The Potential Risks Arising from Nanoscience' (n 25) 2.

[64] A Szajkowska, *Regulating Food Law* (n 5) 62.

[65] ie nano-applications for food ingredients and nano-encapsulation of food additives.

[66] Regulation of the European Parliament and of the Council (EC) 258/97 of 27 January 1997 concerning novel foods and novel food ingredients [1997] OJ L43/1 (hereafter 'old Novel Food Regulation' or 'old NFR').

[67] Regulation (EU) 2015/2283 of the European Parliament and of the Council of 25 November 2015 on novel foods [2015] OJ L327/1 (hereafter 'new Novel Food Regulation' or 'new NFR').

The old Novel Food Regulation established a mandatory pre-market authorisation system. To the present day, novel foods can only be placed on the EU market after a risk assessment has been performed and an accordant authorisation decision been taken, as the case may be, at the national or EU level. As both the old and the new Novel Food Regulations exempt food additives from their scope of application,[68] it is necessary to look separately at the legislative framework for food additives in the next section.

Under both Novel Food Regulations, the first defining criterion of a novel food is that it was not used for human consumption to a significant degree within the Union before 15 May 1997.[69] Since the first nanotechnology laboratory was established by Kraft only in 1999,[70] the first criterion of the definition of novel food is generally fulfilled.[71] Having said that, there remains the possibility that a producer does not consider the food to be novel, for instance, because the same ingredient had already been used in its conventional form before 1997.[72] In this case, a pre-market authorisation would not be undertaken.[73]

If the food or food ingredient is recognised as 'novel', both Novel Food Regulations stipulate a second defining criterion for novel foods that has to be met: The food has to fall within one of several listed exhaustive categories.

The old Novel Food Regulation featured four of these categories. The category which was most likely to cover nanofoods,[74] referred to:

> foods and food ingredients to which has been applied a production process not currently used, where that process gives rise to *significant changes* in the composition or structure of the foods or food ingredients which affect their nutritional value, metabolism or level of undesirable substances [emphasis added].[75]

Obviously, the situation in which the food producer did not recognise the characteristics of the nanofood to be 'significantly changed' was highly problematic[76] and it was not helped by the fact that the concept of 'significant change' was not further

[68] Art 2(1)(a) old NFR; Art 2(2)(b)(ii) new NFR.

[69] Art 1(2) old NFR; Art 3(2)(a) new NFR.

[70] Science and Technologies Committee, *Nanotechnologies and Food* (n 4) 17.

[71] *cf* A Meisterernst, H Daniel and M Thron, 'Nanoparticles in Food and Cosmetics—Scientific and Legal Aspects' (2006) 2 *European Food & Feed Law Review* 69, 74.

[72] Food Standards Agency (UK), 'A Review of Potential Implications of Nanotechnologies for Regulations and Risk Assessment in Relation to Food' (Report, August 2008) 6; A Gergely, D Bowman and Q Chaudhry, 'Small Ingredients in a Big Picture: Regulatory Perspectives on Nanotechnologies in Foods and Food Contact Materials' in Q Chaudhry, R Watkins and L Castle (eds), *Nanotechnologies in Food* (n 11) 155.

[73] The situation is aggravated by the fact that it is currently not possible to detect and measure engineered nanomaterials in food, but that information on the use of engineered nanomaterials in food can only be provided by industry itself, see above section I.B.ii.

[74] A Meisterernst et al, 'Nanoparticles in Food and Cosmetics' (n 71) 75.

[75] Art 1(2)(f) old NFR.

[76] A Gergely et al, 'Small Ingredients in a Big Picture' (n 72).

defined.[77] The uncertainty regarding the applicability of the old Novel Food Regulation to nanofoods was thus mainly related to the absence of a clear definition of nanomaterials in the Regulation.

In 2008, the European Commission adopted a first proposal to revise the Novel Food Regulation[78]—a legislative initiative which eventually failed after three years of negotiation in the ordinary legislative procedure.[79] In December 2013, the Commission reproposed a revision,[80] resurrecting the final draft as negotiated in the conciliation phase of the first legislative proposal. This new Novel Food Regulation was finally adopted in November 2015. As this second attempt at revision builds on the amendments of the legislative procedure of the first attempt, it remains relevant to analyse what nano-specific amendments were proposed and by which institution.

The Commission's original proposal for a revision in 2008 did not contain any nano-specific provisions or requirements. Its Recital 6 merely demanded that nanotechnological applications should be covered by the definition of novel foods. Instead, it was the European Parliament at the first reading stage that claimed substantial changes with respect to the nanoform.[81] Most importantly, the Parliament proposed to rectify the uncertainties surrounding definition by inserting into the definition of 'novel foods' a new, self-contained category which referred to 'food containing or consisting of engineered nanomaterials not used for food production within the Community before 15 May 1997'.[82] In turn, 'engineered nanomaterial' was defined in Article 3(2)(f) of the resolution.[83]

In addition to the definitional clarification, the Parliament suggested a drastic answer to the persisting lack of nano-specific risk assessment methods.

[77] Neither in the Novel Food Regulation nor in its Implementation Guidelines, see Commission Recommendation 97/618/EC of 29 July 1997 concerning the scientific aspects and the presentation of information necessary to support applications for the placing on the market of novel foods and novel food ingredients and the preparation of initial assessment reports under Regulation (EC) 258/97 of the European Parliament and of the Council [1997] OJ L253/1, 5 and 6.

[78] European Commission, 'Proposal for a Regulation of the European Parliament and of the Council on novel foods and amending Regulation (EC) No XXX/XXXX' COM (2007) 872 final.

[79] European Commission, 'Statement by Commissioner Dalli on the lack of agreement in the conciliation procedure on the Novel Food Regulation' MEMO/11/202, 29 March 2011. Interestingly, the revision did not ultimately fail due to questions regarding the regulation of the nanoform but rather because of disagreements between Parliament and Council on animal cloning. See, for a detailed discussion, M Weimer, 'EU Risk Governance of 'Cloned Food'—Regulatory Uncertainty between Trade and Non-Trade' in M Van Asselt, E Versluis and E Vos (eds), *Balancing Between Trade and Risk: Integrating Legal and Social Science Perspectives* (Abingdon, Routledge, 2013).

[80] European Commission, 'Proposal for a Regulation of the European Parliament and of the Council on Novel Foods' COM (2013) 894 final.

[81] European Parliament, 'Legislative resolution of 25 March 2009 on the proposal for a regulation of the European Parliament and of the Council on Novel Foods and amending Regulation (EC) No XXX/XXXX [common procedure] (COM (2007) 0872—C6-0027/2008—2008/0002(COD))' (P6_TA(2009)0171) [2010] OJ C 117E C 236E/95.

[82] ibid Art 3(2)(a)(iv).

[83] ibid Art 3(2)(f).

According to its 2009 report, 'foods to which production processes have been applied that require specific risk assessment methods (eg foods produced using nanotechnologies) may not be included in the Community list until such specific methods have been approved for use'.[84] Further, authorisation of a novel food should be denied in case of scientific uncertainty.[85] The Parliament thus proposed a de facto moratorium on the commercialisation of nanofoods.[86]

Whilst the Council agreed to clarify the definitional question,[87] the Member States did not support the additional parliamentary amendments. This, however, did not prevent the Parliament from reproposing the amendments at the second reading stage.[88] While the Commission also found the inclusion of a regulatory definition of 'engineered nanomaterial' useful 'in order to clarify which products would require a pre-market approval under the Novel Food Regulation',[89] it strongly rejected the further nano-specific requirements demanded by the Parliament.[90] The text that was eventually negotiated in the conciliation phase of the ordinary legislative procedure hence no longer contained the de facto moratorium as requested by the Parliament.[91] In March 2011, the conciliation between the co-legislators failed.[92] The new proposal that the Commission adopted in December 2013 builds on the nano-specific amendments of the failed revision and was finally adopted in November 2015. The new Novel Food Regulation finally includes a definitional category for 'food consisting of engineered nanomaterials',[93] including a definition of 'engineered nanomaterial'.[94]

[84] ibid Art 7(2).

[85] ibid Art 7(4).

[86] Euractiv, 'Parliament calls for EU ban on cloning for food' *Euractiv* (Brussels, 8 July 2010) www.euractiv.com/section/agriculture-food/news/parliament-calls-for-eu-ban-on-cloning-for-food/.

[87] Council of the European Union, 'Proposal for a Regulation of the European Parliament and of the Council on Novel Foods and Amending Regulation (EC) No XXX/XXXX [common procedure] (LA) (First reading)—Political Agreement' (17 June 2009, 10754/09).

[88] European Parliament, 'Legislative resolution of 7 July 2010 on the Council position at First Reading for adopting a regulation of the European Parliament and of the Council on Novel Foods, Amending Regulation (EC) No 1331/2008 and repealing Regulation (EC) No 258/97 and Commission Regulation (EC) No 1852/2001 (11261/3/2009—C7-0078/2010—2008/0002(COD)' (P7_TA(2010)0266) [2011] OJ C351E C298/56.

[89] European Commission, 'Opinion of the Commission pursuant to Article 294, paragraph 7, point (c) of the Treaty on the Functioning of the European Union, on the European Parliament's amendments to the Council's position regarding the proposal for a Regulation of the European Parliament and of the Council on Novel Foods' COM (2010) 570 final, 3.

[90] European Commission, 'Opinion of the Commission pursuant to Article 294, paragraph 7, point (c) of the Treaty on the Functioning of the European Union, on the European Parliament's Amendments to the Council's Position regarding the Proposal for a Regulation of the European Parliament and of the Council on Novel Foods' COM (2010) 570 final, 5.

[91] 'Statement by Commissioner Dalli' (n 79).

[92] ibid.

[93] Art 3(2)(a)(viii) new NFR.

[94] Art 3(2)(f) new NFR.

b. Legislative Framework for Food Additives

Before 2008, EU legislation on food additives consisted of Framework Directive 89/107/EEC, which empowered the Council to issue lists of authorised food additives.[95] Accordingly, the Council adopted three specific Directives on colours, sweeteners and other additives. Only additives which were included in the 'positive list' of one of these Directives could be used in food. A problematic aspect of food additives in nanoform was that a minimum particle size was only specified in the case of two additives on the positive lists.[96] All other listed food additives could therefore be used at nanoscale without a re-evaluation being necessary.

In 2008, the Council and Parliament adopted a new legislative framework for food additives which has been applied in the EU since January 2010.[97] The system works as follows. A common authorisation procedure for food additives, enzymes and flavourings was established by Regulation 1331/2008. Regulation 1333/2008, in turn, lays down the substantive requirements concerning the assessment and authorisation of food additives, by providing for a 'positive list' of approved additives, specifying their conditions of use as well as laying down rules on their labelling.[98]

To what extent does Regulation 1333/2008 address the old legislative framework's shortcomings with respect to food additives in nanoform? According to Article 12 of Regulation 1333/2008, 'when a food additive is already included in a Community list and there is a *significant change* in its production methods or in the starting materials used, or there is a change *in particle size, for example through nanotechnology*, the food additive prepared by those new methods or materials shall be *considered as a different additive and a new entry in the Community lists or a change in the specifications shall be required before it can be placed on the market*' (emphasis added). In other words, a food additive, even though it was already included in the 'positive list' in its conventional size, will still be treated as a 'new' food additive at nanoscale and will therefore require a separate authorisation.

Also in the ordinary legislative procedure that led to the adoption of Regulation 1333/2008, the Parliament emerged as the protagonist in the introduction of nano-specific provisions. The Commission, in its original proposal for the Regulation, referred to the potential necessity of a re-evaluation of already approved food additives if they are 'prepared by production methods or starting materials

[95] Art 3(2)(a), Council Directive 89/107/EEC of 21 December 1988 on the approximation of the laws of the Member States concerning food additives authorised for use in foodstuffs intended for human consumption [1989] OJ L40/27.

[96] Food Standards Agency, 'A Review of Potential Implications of Nanotechnologies for Regulations and Risk Assessment in Relation to Food' (n 72) 6.

[97] Regulation of the European Parliament and of the Council (EC) 1333/2008 of 16 December 2008 on food additives [2008] OJ L354/16; Regulation of the European Parliament and of the Council (EC) 1331/2008 of 16 December 2008 establishing a common authorisation procedure for food additives, food enzymes and food flavourings [2008] OJ L354/1.

[98] Art 1, Regulation (EC) 1333/2008 (n 97).

significantly different from those included in the risk assessment of the Authority' (emphasis added) only in the Recitals. It clarified that 'significantly different production methods or starting materials could mean a change of the production method from extraction from a plant to production by fermentation using a micro-organism or a genetic modification of the original micro-organism'.[99] A change in particle size was not included in the examples. In its Common Position, the Council added 'a change in particle size' to the Recital's examples.[100] At the second reading stage, the Parliament not only approved the Council's amendment but also added 'change in particle size, *including the use of nanotechnology*' (emphasis added).[101] The Parliament, furthermore, inserted the essential Article 12, which triggers the separate authorisation requirement for changes in particle size.[102]

c. Legislative Framework for Food Contact Materials

The third legislative framework, the Food Contact Materials (FCM) Regulation 1935/2004[103] was not revised after 2004. Generally, and in contrast to the legislative frameworks for food additives and novel foods, the FCM Regulation does not per se require a pre-market approval for food contact materials falling within its scope of application. Instead, the Commission has been delegated the task of adopting implementing acts for an exhaustively defined group of articles and materials, such as plastics, ceramics, intelligent materials and articles. In these implementing acts, the Commission may establish authorisation requirements for these particular groups of materials and articles.[104] The main loophole as regards the coverage of nanomaterials in FCM is thus not the fact that they fall outside

[99] European Commission, 'Proposal for a Regulation of the European Parliament and of the Council on Food Additives' COM (2006) 428 final, Recital 13.

[100] Council of the European Union, 'Common Position (EC) No 7/2008 adopted by the Council, acting in accordance with the procedure referred to in Article 251 of the Treaty establishing the European Community, with a view to the adoption of a Regulation of the European Parliament and of the Council on Food Additives' [2008] OJ C111E/10, Recital 13.

[101] European Parliament, 'Position of the European Parliament adopted at Second Reading on 8 July 2008 with a view to the adoption of Regulation (EC) No …/2008 of the European Parliament and of the Council on food additives' 8 July 2008, Recital 13.

[102] A significant factor for the Parliament's sudden focus on the issue of nanotechnologies in the summer of 2008 was surely the Commission's almost simultaneous adoption of its Communication on 'Regulatory Aspects of Nanotechnology', which brought nanotechnologies back onto the regulatory agenda after approximately three years of inaction at the EU level. In comparison, the much more drastic nano-specific amendments of the Parliament in the revision of the Novel Food Regulation were first proposed in March 2009, after the Commission presented its Communication and only one month before the Parliament adopted its own Resolution on Regulatory Aspects of Nanotechnology, in which it strongly rejected the Commission's approach, see further above chapter 1, section IV.

[103] Regulation of the European Parliament and of the Council (EC) 1935/2004 of 27 October 2004 on materials and articles intended to come into contact with food [2004] OJ L338/4.

[104] See ibid Art 5(1) and Annex I.

the scope of Regulation 1935/2004[105] but that the Regulation does not foresee the development of specific implementing acts for a separate category of nano-components.[106] Nano-components are thus only subject to a prior authorisation requirement when they fall within the scope of one of the particular materials listed in Regulation 1935/2004 (see further section II.B.i). The Commission has not yet attempted to address this gap by making use of its right to take the legislative initiative.

iii. State of Play: A Cautious European Commission

The above analysis showed that the Commission has been cautious in introducing nano-specific provisions into the legislative framework for food. It has hardly used its right to take the legislative initiative. The European Parliament and to some extent the Council, however, have opposed the Commission's approach. The analysis revealed an active Parliament, which inserted nano-specific requirements into the legal texts wherever they were under revision in a legislative procedure.[107] By inference, the FCM Regulation, which has not been revised since 2004, does not contain any nano-specific provision. The current state of play of the legislative review thus reflects the interinstitutional disagreement over the Commission's approach to the regulation of nanotechnologies. All in all, the legislative review is advancing at a slow pace. Uncertainties as to the coverage of nanotechnological applications in the legislative framework persist.

As well the slow progress, significant inconsistencies emerged in the treatment of nanotechnological applications across the different legislative frameworks. Most obvious is the definitional issue. The new Novel Food Regulation contains a definition of 'engineered nanomaterial'; the term 'nano' is thus explicitly mentioned, defined and moreover restricted to 'engineered' materials. Food or food ingredients falling within this definition are considered as 'novel' and thus require a separate authorisation. With respect to food additives, however, Regulation 1333/2008 does not explicitly mention 'nano' but instead refers to a 'change in particle size' as triggering the need for a new entry into the positive list. Consequently, a definition of 'nanoscale' is not provided. It is equally not specified whether the

[105] It has been largely acknowledged that Regulation 1935/2004 is drafted in terms broad enough to deal with the migration of nano-components into food from food contact materials, as the Regulation generally requires materials and articles not to transfer any of their constituents to foodstuffs, regardless of the particle size of those constituents, see Food Standards Agency, 'A Review of Potential Implications of Nanotechnologies for Regulations and Risk Assessment in Relation to Food' (n 72) 7. See also, NanoKommission, 'Review of Nanomaterial and Nanoproduct Regulation' (Working Group Report of three of the German Federal Government's NanoKommission, 2010).

[106] Food Standards Agency, 'A Review of Potential Implications of Nanotechnologies for Regulations and Risk Assessment in Relation to Food' (n 72) 9.

[107] On the Parliament as the driver of the legislative review, see E Stokes, 'Nanotechnology and the Products of Inherited Regulation' (2012) 39 *Journal of Law and Society* 93, 98.

authorisation requirement only applies to deliberately engineered particle sizes, or whether it also covers naturally occurring size changes. These inconsistencies are summarised in Table 2.

Table 2: Inconsistencies in the EU Legislative Framework for Food

EU Legislative Framework	Definition		Separate authorisation required	Moratorium until nano-specific risk assessment methods are developed
	'nano' mentioned	'nano' defined		
New Novel Food Regulation (Regulation (EU) 2015/2283)	Yes	Yes (restricted to 'engineered nanomaterials')	Yes	Proposed by European Parliament, rejected by Commission and Council
Legislative Framework for Food Additives (Regulation (EC) No 1333/2008)	No (reference to 'change in particle size')	No	Yes	No
Legislative Framework for Food Contact Materials (Regulation (EC) No 1935/2004)	No	No	No	No

B. Addressing Nanotechnologies via the Executive Route

Instead of using its right of legislative initiative, the Commission has so far focused its regulatory attention on options in the executive sphere. First, the Commission adopted implementing acts under the Food Contact Materials Regulation that attempt to address the loopholes left by the legislative framework with respect to nanomaterials.[108] Secondly, the Commission mandated EFSA

[108] Commission Regulation (EC) 450/2009 of 29 May 2009 on active and intelligent materials and articles intended to come into contact with food [2009] OJ L135/3; Commission Regulation (EU) 10/2011 of 14 January 2011 on plastic materials and articles intended to come into contact with food [2011] OJ L12/1.

to prepare a guidance document for the risk assessment of nanotechnological applications in food and feed.[109] Finally, the Commission issued a recommendation with the aim of eliminating the definitional confusion about what a nanomaterial actually is.

i. Via Comitology: Implementing Acts under the FCM Regulation

Instead of initiating an amendment to the FCM Regulation[110] the Commission decided to address the issue of nanotechnologies by means of implementing acts for certain groups of materials and articles, most notably plastics and intelligent packaging.[111]

Accordingly, in 2009 the Commission adopted an implementing act on intelligent packaging.[112] Commission Regulation 450/2009 establishes harmonised requirements as well as a positive list for the marketing of active and intelligent materials and articles intended to come into contact with food.[113] However, substances used in components of active and intelligent materials which are not in direct contact with food are exempted from the general authorisation requirement, except in two circumstances: first, if the substance is particularly toxic and classified either as 'mutagenic', 'carcinogenic', or 'toxic to reproduction' and, secondly, if substances are 'deliberatively engineered to particle size which exhibit functional physical and chemical properties that significantly differ from those at a larger scale'.[114] While 'particle size' is thus recognised as a factor which might involve risks to health and the environment comparable to those of substances categorised as 'mutagenic', 'carcinogenic', or 'toxic to reproduction',[115] the Commission Regulation does not clarify whether substances in nanoform require a separate entry in the positive list, that is, a separate authorisation.

Two years later, the Commission was more explicit in Commission Regulation 10/2011 on plastics.[116] Like the Regulation on active and intelligent packaging, the new plastics Regulation also excludes 'substances in nanoform' from the scope of exemption of the general authorisation requirement.[117] More importantly, however, Commission Regulation 10/2011 addresses the question which remained unanswered with regard to active and intelligent packaging. It contains an article

[109] European Food Safety Authority, 'Scientific Opinion on Guidance on the Risk Assessment of the Application of Nanoscience and Nanotechnologies in the Food and Feed Chain' (2011) 9 *EFSA Journal* 2140, 2145.

[110] For instance, by introducing a separate 'nano-category' into the exhaustive list of materials and articles subject to a pre-market approval system.

[111] Commission Regulation (EC) 450/2009 (n 108); Commission Regulation (EU) 10/2011 (n 108).

[112] Commission Regulation (EC) 450/2009 (n 108).

[113] ibid Art 1.

[114] ibid Art 5(2)(c).

[115] See ibid Recital 14.

[116] Commission Regulation (EU) 10/2011 of 14 January 2011 (n 108).

[117] See ibid Arts 13(4)(b) and 14(3)(b).

stipulating that 'substances in nanoform shall only be used if explicitly authorised and mentioned in the specifications in Annex I'.[118] Authorisations of a substance in its conventional form hence do not cover nanoparticles. Paradoxically, however, the Regulation does not define 'nanoparticle'.[119] This arguably adversely affects implementation of the nano-specific provisions of the Regulation, especially the separate authorisation requirement.

ii. Via Agency Guidance Documents: EFSA's Guidance on Risk Assessment of Nanotechnologies in Food and Feed

Guidance documents have become familiar occupants of the EU's legal space. They instruct stakeholders on how to interpret and eventually implement the legislative provisions in order to ensure a uniform application. Guidance documents inherently aim to alter and to 'guide' the behaviour of affected actors. Yet, they do not form part of the list of legal acts stipulated in Article 288 of the Treaty on the Functioning of the European Union (TFEU).[120] Guidance documents are hence the prototype of an 'unidentified legal object'.[121] Often, guidance documents fill in the nitty-gritty details that are omitted in the legal text. It is therefore not infrequent that they are put into the drawer of technical specifications.

In July 2009, the Commission mandated EFSA to 'prepare a guidance document for the safety assessment of applications involving the application of nanoscience and nanotechnology to food and feed'.[122] In view of the absence of a specification of nano-specific risk assessment methods in the legislation itself,[123] the guidance document must be considered an attempt to fill this blank in the legislative framework. Are we thus confronted with a technical specification? The form in which the guidance was adopted—a 'scientific opinion'—certainly hints in this direction.

In its guidance document of May 2011, EFSA concludes that, in principle, the current risk assessment paradigm (hazard identification, hazard characterisation, exposure assessment and risk characterisation), as enshrined in the General Food Law,[124] is also appropriate for the assessment of nanotechnological applications.[125] The Agency concedes, however, that there are uncertainties with respect to the appropriate testing methods in each of these four steps.[126] EFSA therefore offers a

[118] ibid Art 9.

[119] See ibid Art 3.

[120] See on 'legal effects' of EU instruments, above chapter 3, section I.C.ii.

[121] See ibid.

[122] European Food Safety Authority, 'Scientific Opinion' (n 109) 2145.

[123] See on the discussion of the necessity of having nano-specific risk assessment methods in the context of the first novel food revision, above section II.A.ii.a.

[124] Art 3(11) GFL.

[125] European Food Safety Authority, 'Scientific Opinion' (n 109) 2142.

[126] ibid 2167–69.

decision tree for industry and regulators that first identifies the parameters to be taken into consideration when determining whether or not one is confronted with an engineered nanomaterial.[127] Secondly, if confronted with an engineered nanomaterial, the Agency indicates how the four steps of risk assessment should be performed.[128] The guidance document thereby evaluates 'at each stage the information and data needed to accomplish the risk assessment'.[129]

A close-up look at the drafting history of the guidance, and more precisely at the comments provided by affected actors on a first draft of the document, attests that EFSA's conclusions in both steps were not uncontroversial. Affected actors not only contested EFSA's definition of nanomaterial and the inherent choice of parameters, they also considered the proposed supplementary testing requirements unfounded in view of the lack of scientific evidence, as too demanding or indeed insufficient, and challenged the Agency's balancing of diverse societal interests, ranging from environmental protection, consumer health to animal welfare and the competitiveness of the EU economy.[130] It is therefore reasonable to assume that the guidance document entails choices that extend beyond a merely technical sphere.

At the same time, the guidance document is of high practical importance. The UK Food Standards Agency stated that 'EFSA's guidance will be used whenever products of nanotechnology are evaluated for food or feed applications in the EU'.[131] In addition, a former EFSA staff member confirmed that industry is following the guidance.[132] Furthermore, as discussed in chapter three, guidance documents are increasingly used before national and EU courts as an aid to interpreting the legal text.[133] EFSA's guidance could thus be relied upon in clarifying a food producer's duties under the above-discussed legislative frameworks for food, thereby also impacting on the legal sphere of the food producer.

iii. Via Commission Recommendations: Defining the Term 'Nanomaterial'

The foregoing sections illustrated the struggle of the legislative review with the absence of definitional agreement.[134] In response, the Commission adopted

[127] ibid 2151–53.

[128] ibid 2156–67.

[129] ibid 2148.

[130] For the various comments by affected actors in the public consultation launched by EFSA, see European Food Safety Authority, Technical Report of EFSA (2011) www.efsa.europa.eu/en/supporting/doc/126e.pdf.

[131] See Food Standards Agency (UK), Nanotechnology, www.food.gov.uk/science/novel/nano/#.U9_3GkKd7ww.

[132] Interview with a former EFSA staff member (Brussels, 28 November 2013), notes on file with the author.

[133] See above chapter 3, section I.C.ii.

[134] *cf* Science and Technologies Committee, *Nanotechnologies and Food* (n 4) 48.

Recommendation 2011/696/EU in October 2011, which lays down a definition of 'nanomaterial'.[135] The recommendation is addressed to Member States, EU agencies and industry, who are invited to use the definition in the adoption and implementation of legislation and policy.[136] According to the Commission, a recommendation was preferable to a legally binding instrument, as it would have the advantage of flexibility, and 'does not contain any direct obligations for Member States and economic operators' but 'implementation will happen through various pieces of specific legislation'.[137]

The recommended definition is, first, not restricted to engineered nanomaterials but also embraces natural and incidental materials; secondly, it is based solely on the size of the material's constituent particles. Two core elements of the recommended definition thereby distinguish nanomaterials from non-nanomaterials: a material is considered a nanomaterial if at least 50 per cent of its constituent particles are in the size range of 1 to 100 nanometres.[138]

Given the scientific uncertainty and the continued debate about, for instance, the appropriate size range, whether size is the only characteristic that needs to be considered, and whether also naturally occurring nanomaterials should be included in the definition's scope,[139] the definition has been contested by various affected actors. As the Dutch National Institute for Public Health and the Environment emphasised, 'at present, the particle size range of 1nm–100nm has no scientific basis'.[140] Also, the chosen particle number threshold of 50 per cent 'has been a political decision because no scientific reasoning can be given for a threshold value'.[141] The European Environmental Bureau (EEB) thus announced in a press release that it 'is deeply disappointed by the European Commission's decision released today to use a narrow definition for the term "nanomaterial", indicating that industry lobbying has won over the Commission's own scientific advisors'.[142] The EEB particularly criticised the chosen threshold of 50 per cent as being too restrictive, stating that it 'had called upon the Commission to stick to a

[135] Commission Recommendation 2011/696/EU of 18 October 2011 on the definition of nanomaterial [2011] OJ L275/38, para 2. The recommendation is based on Art 292 TFEU, the general legal basis for the Commission, Council and European Central Bank (ECB) to adopt recommendations.

[136] Commission Recommendation 2011/696/EU (n 135) paras 1 and 7.

[137] European Commission, 'Questions and answers on the Commission Recommendation on the definition of nanomaterial' MEMO/11/704, 18 October 2011.

[138] Commission Recommendation 2011/696/EU (n 135) para 2.

[139] K Malkiewicz, M, Pettitt, KA Dawson, A Toikka, SO Hansson, J Hukkinen, I Lynch and J Lead, 'Nanomaterials in REACH' (Project Report, SKEP ERA-NET, August 2011) 27. See also RIVM, 'Interpretation and Implications of the European Commission Recommendation on the Definition of Nanomaterial' (RIVM Letter Report 601358001, 2012) 21.

[140] RIVM, 'Interpretation and Implications of the European Commission Recommendation on the Definition of Nanomaterial' (n 139).

[141] ibid.

[142] European Environmental Bureau, 'Nano Definition Too Narrow Says EEB' (Press release, 18 October 2011) www.eeb.org/index.cfm/news-events/news/nano-definition-too-narrow-says-eeb/.

1 per cent threshold of the particle number size distribution as a way to put under scrutiny, certain materials, which may exhibit nano specific hazardous properties in the larger size range'.[143] In a similar vein, the European Consumers' Organisation BEUC considered the Commission's definition to be 'too narrow', which would lead to 'a situation in which products with bigger particles could escape the definition and thereby remain unregulated'.[144] The European Chemical Industry Council, Cefic, to the contrary, criticised the definition as 'too broad in scope', fearing that 'the proposed definition will add unnecessary burden for companies, leading to added costs and less efficient use of resources'.[145]

Despite the resistance, the Commission's definition has found its way into several legislative texts at the EU and national level. It was incorporated almost verbatim into the EU Biocidal Products Regulation.[146] Also, the revision of the Medical Devices Directive that is currently under way in the ordinary legislative procedure contains a definition of nanomaterial, which follows the recommendation.[147] The recommended definition furthermore forms the basis of the first national mandatory reporting scheme for nanomaterials in the EU, set up by France in February 2012.[148] Also in Denmark, the statutory order establishing a comparable register of nanoproducts explicitly states that it follows the Commission's definition of nanomaterial.[149] Belgium is currently developing a similar register, also with the definition at its roots.[150]

However, this automatic 'hardening' process of the recommended definition experienced a setback in February 2014 in the context of EU Regulation 1169/2011 on the provision of food information to consumers. Regulation 1169/2011 was adopted simultaneously with the Commission's recommended definition in October 2011 and originally contained a different definition of nanomaterial.[151]

[143] ibid.

[144] ANEC (European consumer voice in standardisation) and BEUC (European Consumers' Organisation), 'NANO Very Small and Everywhere: A Technological Magic Silver Bullet or a Serious Safety Risk?' (Brochure, 2012) 17.

[145] European Chemical Industry Council (Cefic), *Press Release: Practical nanomaterials definition needed to push forward next great innovation breakthroughs* (18 October 2011).

[146] Art 3(1)(z), Regulation (EU) 528/2012 of the European Parliament and of the Council of 22 May 2012 concerning the making available on the market and use of biocidal products [2012] OJ L167/1.

[147] European Commission, 'Proposal for a Regulation of the European Parliament and of the Council on medical devices' COM (2012) 542 final, Recital 13 and Art 2(1)(15).

[148] Décret n° 2012-232 du 17 février 2012 relatif à la déclaration annuelle des substances à l'état nanoparticulaire pris en application de l'article L. 523-4 du code l'environnement, Art R. 523-12.

[149] Ministry of Environment and Food of Denmark, 'Statutory order on a register of mixtures and articles that contain nanomaterials as well as the requirement for producers and importers to report to the register' no 644 (13 June 2014), para 4 no 1 www.eng.mst.dk/topics/chemicals/nanomaterials/the-danish-nanoproduct-register/.

[150] Belgium notified the Commission in July 2013 of its Draft Decree to create a register of nanomaterials, based on the Commission recommendation for a definition of nanomaterial (COM 2013/368/B).

[151] Art 2(2)(t), Regulation (EU) 1169/2011 of the European Parliament and of the Council of 25 October 2011 on the provision of food information to consumers [2011] OJ L304/18.

After the Regulation's entry into force, the Commission proposed a delegated regulation, which was intended to bring the definition in line with its recommendation. The Parliament, however, for the first time since the introduction of this possibility with the Lisbon Treaty, used its right of objection to a delegated act.[152] The Parliament contested, inter alia, the controversial 50 per cent threshold for 'run[ning] contrary to the basic aim of the directive to pursue a high level of protection of consumers' health and interests'.[153] Instead, the Parliament considered a threshold of 10 per cent 'more appropriate'.[154] Stakeholders also used this opportunity to comment. The European Consumer Organisation BEUC sent an open letter to the Members of European Parliament before the plenary vote, urging them to support the resolution.[155] FoodDrinkEurope, to the contrary, considered the European Parliament's decision 'regrettable'.[156] The Parliament thus exposed the controversy underlying the nano definition.

The Parliament continued its opposition to the Commission's recommended definition in the second attempt to revise the Novel Food Regulation.[157] While the Commission referred in its legislative proposal of 2013 to the definition of nanomaterial as laid down in the Food Information Regulation,[158] the European Parliament inserted a new definition into the Novel Food Regulation, which no longer considers size as the only characterising property of a nanomaterial.[159] The Parliament moreover demanded that this new definition of nanomaterial should replace the current definition in the Food Information Regulation.[160] These amendments were accepted by the Commission and the Council, and are contained in the final text of the new Novel Food Regulation.[161]

At the same time, the Parliament is not always able to scrutinise ex ante this hardening process of the Commission's recommendation, especially where it is not inserted into binding acts via a legislative or non-legislative procedure, but where

[152] European Parliament, 'Motion for a Resolution on the Commission delegated regulation of 12 December 2013 amending Regulation (EU) No 1169/2011 of the European Parliament and of the Council on the provision of food information to consumers as regards the definition of 'engineered nanomaterials' (C(2013)08887—2013/2997(DEA))' (18 February 2014, P7_TA(2014)0218).

[153] ibid para T.

[154] ibid.

[155] European Consumers's Organisation (BEUC), 'Plenary vote on a Resolution opposing the draft European Commission (EC) Delegated Regulation updating the definition of "engineered nanomaterials" in food' (Letter sent to the Members of the European Parliament, 10 March 2014) www.beuc.eu/publications/beuc-x-2014-015_cpe_engineered_nanomaterials_in_food-plenary_vote.pdf.

[156] FoodDrinkEurope, 'MEPs' vote on "engineered nanomaterials" regrettable for Europe's food and drink industry' (Statement, 13 March 2014).

[157] Art 3(2)(f) new NFR.

[158] 'Proposal for a Regulation of the European Parliament and of the Council on novel foods' COM (2013) 894 final (n 81) Art 2(a)(ii).

[159] European Parliament, 'Legislative resolution of 28 October 2015 on the proposal for a regulation of the European Parliament and of the Council on novel foods COM (2013) 0894' (P8_TA-PROV(2015)0380), Art. 3(2)(f).

[160] ibid Art 33(1).

[161] Arts 3(2)(f) and 33(1) new NFR.

it serves to prepare further non-binding measures—such as EU agency guidance documents. Indeed, the definition, as will be seen in chapter five, has served to formulate guidance documents on nanomaterials in EU chemicals legislation.[162] In view of the adoption of the recommended definition from the European to the national context and its development from a non-binding norm to a hard reality for affected actors, it is difficult to overestimate its practical significance.

iv. Synthesis: Towards Executive Rule Making

This section has highlighted a clear preference on the part of the European Commission to address nanotechnologies via the executive route—via comitology, a Commission recommendation and an agency guidance document. Next to the arduous legislative review, the administrative setting emerges as an important stage for settling controversial decisions in the regulation of nanotechnologies. The Commission's implementing acts under the FCM Regulation lack crucial nano-specific provisions, such as a definition of 'nano' or a separate authorisation requirement for the nanoform, which the Parliament and Council were eager to push into the legal texts of the novel food and food additives regulation. Also, the analysis of EFSA's nano guidance and the Commission's definition of nanomaterial revealed that these measures are all but void of political choices. They contain sensitive balancing exercises between the different rationalities at stake, most notably between the economic interest, on the one hand, and environmental, health and safety rationalities, on the other. Topics that were flagged as contentious in the legislative review were taken up: should one wait for nano-specific risk assessment methods before commercialisation? How should the EU define 'nanomaterial' in the absence of scientific certainty? These questions reach beyond a mere technical realm. At the same time, these measures, independent of their formal legal effect, were shown to impact on the rights and interests of affected actors, most notably the food industry and EU consumers, and to inform subsequent (binding) acts adopted by national authorities, the Commission and EFSA.

With respect to EFSA, there is reason to doubt whether the adoption of its guidance is still within the Agency's legislative mandate, which is clearly restricted to the provision of 'scientific and technical advice'. The Agency seems to develop de facto from its formal role as a neutral source of knowledge, which feeds into the regulatory process,[163] into a regulator in its own right. While EFSA is formally denied the power to engage in political choices following the principle of risk analysis[164] and the Court of Justice's *Meroni* doctrine,[165] these limitations appear hollowed

[162] See, for a discussion of ECHA's guidance documents, below chapter 5, section II.C.
[163] On the role of EU agencies as sources of knowledge, see above chapter 3, section II.A.ii.b.
[164] On the principle of risk analysis, see above chapter 2, section III.B.i.
[165] On the *Meroni* doctrine, see above chapter 3, section II.B.iii.a.

out by the practical significance and controversy of the guidance's substance. The fact that contentious decisions are taken at the level of the EU administration, begs vital questions as to the procedures under which these regulatory measures were adopted: how they allowed for the pooling of the fragmented knowledge and how they ensure the legitimacy of the regulatory output, as understood by the theoretical foundations of this book. These questions are examined in the following section.

III. ANALYSING THE EU'S REGULATION OF NANOFOODS THROUGH THE LENSES OF REGULATORY CAPACITY

The above analysis showed that, next to adapting the existing legislation to the intricacies of the nanoform, implementing acts and non-binding regulatory options assume an important role in confronting the challenges posed by nanotechnologies. This raises fundamental questions as to how the EU regulator has addressed the challenges of pooling the socially dispersed knowledge and guaranteeing the legitimacy of the regulatory output. This third section of the chapter therefore turns to the critical analysis of the EU's production of regulation in the area of nanotechnologies through the lenses of regulatory capacity. More precisely, this section will scrutinise the applicability and practical operation of the procedures that the EU regulator installed in the aftermath of the European governance debate with the aim to pool knowledge (section A) and to ensure the input (section B) and output (section C) legitimacy of the identified regulatory measures.

A. Pooling Knowledge

Chapter three identified the impact assessment procedure as the main horizontal tool set in place for the purpose of bringing together societally dispersed knowledge. New procedural frameworks were installed in the wake of the European governance debate for the establishment and operation of Commission expert groups and EU agencies as sources of independent scientific knowledge.[166] This section analyses the applicability of these procedures as well as their operation in practice. It proceeds by asking the following questions:

- Were the identified procedures applicable?
- If they were applicable, were these procedures used in practice to pool knowledge? If yes, did they result in an exposition of the knowledge gathered?

[166] Above chapter 3, section II.A.ii.

— If they were not applicable, were other procedures put in place? If yes, were these other procedures used in practice to gather knowledge? Did these other procedures result in an exposition of the knowledge gathered?

i. The Impact Assessment: A Tool to Pool Knowledge?

The EU institutions' commitment to conducting impact assessments for legislative and policy proposals stems directly from the governance debate of the early 2000s.[167] In the following paragraphs, the merits of this procedure are put to the test in practice. Since the empirical part of this book was concluded before 2015, reference will be made to the 2009 Impact Assessment Guidelines that were applicable at that time. Changes introduced as part of the Better Regulation Package of May 2015 are commented upon in the concluding chapter of this book.

a. The Commission's Impact Assessment Procedure

According to the Commission's 2009 Impact Assessment Guidelines, 'IAs [impact assessments] are necessary for the most important Commission initiatives and those which will have the most far-reaching impacts. This will be the case for all legislative proposals of the Commission's Legislative and Work Programme (CLWP) and for all non-CLWP legislative proposals which have clearly identifiable economic, social and environmental impacts … and for non-legislative initiatives … which define future policies. It will also be the case for certain implementing measures (so called "comitology" items) which are likely to have significant impacts.'[168]

The Guidelines hence applied to all legislative proposals included in the Commission's annual Legislative and Work Programme. The legislative proposals analysed above, that is, the proposals for the Novel Food and Food Additives Regulations, were thus within the scope of their application. Furthermore it is clear that EFSA's guidance document was not subject to the Commission's impact assessment requirement, which is restricted to 'Commission initiatives'.

The answer as regards the two implementing acts of the FCM Regulation is less straightforward. Implementing acts were not per se subject to the Commission's 2009 impact assessment commitment but only where they are likely to have 'significant impacts'.[169] A definition of 'significant impact', however, was not given. The decision of whether or not to conduct an impact assessment, therefore,

[167] ibid.
[168] European Commission, 'Impact Assessment Guidelines' SEC (2009) 92, 6.
[169] ibid.

remained a grey area and to a large extent within the Commission's discretion.[170] And indeed, in the case of the two implementing acts adopted under the FCM Regulation, the Commission used its discretion not to conduct an impact assessment. An open evaluation of the measures' environmental, social and economic effects, inter alia of the inserted nano-specific requirements, did not take place. To say the least, this is surprising given that nanotechnological applications are first and foremost applied in the field of food packaging.[171] For the food industry, and consumer and environmental organisations alike, it therefore seems of great importance whether or not nanocomponents in food packaging require a separate authorisation.

Also, in the drafting of non-binding regulation, such as recommendations, the Commission was bound by its 2009 Impact Assessment Guidelines only if the measure in question 'defines future policies'.[172] Again, what exactly this criterion entailed was not further defined. Does a measure 'define future policies' merely if it contains proposals for legislative or policy action or is the trigger reached where a recommendation defines key concepts that shall be inserted into future legislation or policies, such as the definition of 'nanomaterial'? In its drafting, the Commission considered the impact assessment rules not to be applicable. The Commission nevertheless decided to launch a public consultation outside the impact assessment framework, which will be analysed in section III.B.ii on 'administrative participation'.

Consequently, out of the various regulatory measures identified earlier in this chapter, only the two legislative proposals were subject to the Commission's impact assessment commitment. No impact assessments were performed for the regulatory measures in the executive setting.

Turning to the procedure's operation, a closer look at the contents of the two impact assessments conducted for the first attempt to revise the Novel Food Regulation and the drafting of the Food Additives Regulation[173] reveals that neither of them engaged with the impacts of including (or not) nano-specific provisions in the respective legislative frameworks. Remarkably, in both impact assessments, the matter of nanotechnologies was simply omitted.

[170] The 2011 Guidelines for the Services of the Commission on delegated acts confirm that 'it is the primary responsibility of each service to determine the scale of expertise required to prepare a delegated act. All services should bear in mind the necessity, in certain circumstances, to have recourse to impact assessments', see European Commission, 'Implementation of the Treaty of Lisbon. Delegated Acts. Guidelines for the services of the Commission' (2011) rule 108.

[171] See on the applications of nanotechnologies in food, above section I.B.i.

[172] 'Impact Assessment Guidelines' SEC (2009) 92 (n 168) 6.

[173] European Commission, 'Impact assessment for a regulation replacing Regulation (EC) No 258/97 on novel foods and novel food ingredients' (Staff Working Document) SEC (2008) 12; European Commission, 'Impact assessment—Annex to the proposal for a European Parliament and Council Regulation on food additives' (Staff Working Document) SEC (2006) 1040.

Equally remarkable, for its second proposal to revise the Novel Food Regulation of December 2013, the Commission concluded that a new impact assessment was not necessary since

> the Commission carried out an Impact Assessment in 2007. For each of the measures of the 2008 proposal, several options were examined with regard to their economic, social and environmental impact on the various stakeholders and Member States. … Regarding the current proposal, the 2008 impact assessment is still valid, as the rationale for an in-depth revision of the current legislation … is unchanged.
>
> The main changes compared to the 2008 proposal are primarily those introduced during the Ordinary legislative procedure whose impact is unchanged as they only clarify the purpose of the measures.[174]

The Commission concluded this despite the fact that the impacts of the nano-specific provisions in the second proposal were never subject to an assessment. At the same time, the first impact assessment was conducted in 2007, eight years before the new Novel Food Regulation was finally adopted.

Having said that, a glance at the 2009 Impact Assessment Guidelines could explain these omissions. Pursuant to these Guidelines, the scope and level of knowledge collection, stakeholder consultation, the type of impacts to be examined and their consequent quantification is governed by the overarching principle of a 'proportionate level of analysis'.[175] In order to 'define the right level of analysis of your IA', the Guidelines recommend that the responsible desk officer take into consideration the 'significance of impacts', the proposal's 'political importance', as well as the stage of policy development.[176] Substantial room for variations in length and methodology of impact assessments arises.[177] Strictly speaking, the Commission was thus not required to analyse all aspects and impacts of its legislative proposals, including the (non-)inclusion of nano-specific requirements.

b. The Parliament and Council's Impact Assessment Procedure

Parliament (and Council) nevertheless inserted several nano-specific amendments within the scope of both legislative procedures.[178] Following the interinstitutional 'Common Approach to Impact Assessments', the legislator too is required to 'carry out impact assessments, when they consider this to be appropriate and necessary for the legislative process, prior to the adoption of any *substantive*

[174] Proposal for a Regulation of the European Parliament and of the Council on Novel Foods, COM (2013) 894 final (n 80) 4.

[175] 'Impact Assessment Guidelines' SEC (2009) 92 (n 168) 13.

[176] ibid 14.

[177] A Meuwese, *Impact Assessment in EU Law-Making*, European Monographs no 61 (Alphen aan den Rijn, Kluwer Law International, 2008) 58. The European Parliament in particular has criticised an inconsistency in the quality of impact assessments, see European Parliament, 'Resolution of 8 June 2011 on guaranteeing independent impact assessments' (P7_TA-PROV(2011)0259) para I.

[178] See, for an analysis of these amendments, above sections II.A.ii.a and II.A.ii.b.

amendment' (emphasis added).[179] The definition of what constitutes a 'substantive amendment' is, however, for the respective institution to determine.[180] The Parliament leaves this decision to the relevant parliamentary committee, most notably to the dossier's rapporteur. The Council has also delegated the task to the respective Council working party. In practice, neither of the two legislators conducted an own impact assessment of its—arguably 'substantive'—nano-specific amendments.[181] These amendments found their way into the legal texts without an open assessment of their effects being performed.

c. An Empty Procedure?

The impact assessment procedure was in practice not used to bring together nano-specific knowledge in the drafting of a regulatory framework for nanotechnologies in food. On the one hand, this must be attributed to the ambiguous scope of application of the Commission's 2009 Impact Assessment Guidelines. The same goes for the legislature's elusive impact assessment trigger of 'substantive amendment'. On the other hand, even where the Commission's 2009 Impact Assessment Guidelines were clearly applicable, their operating principle of a 'proportionate level of analysis' left a wide discretion to the Commission in determining the depth of analysis on a case-by-case basis. In practice then, the impact assessment procedure was largely empty.

Table 3: Applicability and Operation of the Commission's 2009 Impact Assessment Guidelines

	Legislative Acts		**Implementing Acts**		**Commission Recommendation on a Definition of 'Nanomaterial'**	**EFSA Guidance on Nanotechnological Risk Assessment**
	Novel Food	**Food Additives**	**FCM Intelligent Packaging**	**FCM Plastics**		
Applicable?	Yes		Grey area ('significant impact')		Grey area ('defines future policies')	No
Applied?	Yes		No		No	No
Operation	Nano not mentioned		—		—	—

[179] European Commission, European Parliament and Council of Ministers, 'Interinstitutional Common Approach to Impact Assessment' (2005) www.ec.europa.eu/smart-regulation/impact/key_docs/docs/ii_common_approach_to_ia_en.pdf.

[180] ibid.

[181] This is in line with a 2010 report of the European Court of Auditors, according to which an IA was carried out for only seven out of 377 acts of secondary legislation adopted by the Parliament and for only one out of 1,946 acts adopted by the Council in relation to the amendments to the initial Commission proposal. The report concludes that 'amendments to the initial Commission proposal are not subject to additional assessments of potential impacts', see European Court of Auditors, 'Impact Assessments of the EU Institutions: Do They Support Decision-Making?' (Special Report no 3, 2010) 24 and 25.

ii. Knowledge Collection through Commission Expert Groups

As one of the sources of knowledge, chapter three identified the consultation of Commission expert groups. The framework for their creation and operation is laid down in the Commission's horizontal rules on expert groups, which were first drafted in the aftermath of the European governance debate.[182] These rules apply to all expert groups falling within their scope of application. The decision to consult, however, is reserved for the Commission in each individual case. The questions arising are therefore, first, whether the Commission made use of expert groups in the drafting of a regulatory framework for nanotechnologies in food and, if so, how their consultation operated in practice.

The Commission referred to an expert group twice—once in the adoption of the implementing act on intelligent packaging under the FCM Regulation and, again, in the drafting of its recommendation for a definition of nanomaterial. First, the Commission decided for the implementing act on intelligent packaging to present a draft to its Advisory Group on the Food Chain.[183] The Advisory Group on the Food Chain was established as an expert group to provide a stakeholder perspective on food and feed safety issues. It consists of 45 stakeholders, comprising representatives from consumer organisations, farms, the food industry and retailers.[184] The register of expert groups explains that its task is to 'provide expertise to the Commission when drafting implementing measures'.[185] The group's own rules of procedure require that minutes of its meetings be drawn up[186] and published on the Commission's website.[187] Accordingly, the minutes of the meeting at which a draft of the measure on intelligent packaging was presented are available online.[188] Yet, although the minutes indicate that questions were raised

[182] See European Commission, 'Framework for Commission's expert groups: horizontal rules and public register' (Communication) C(2005) 2817. The 2005 procedural rules were revised in November 2010 and May 2016, see European Commission, 'Framework for Commission's expert groups: horizontal rules and public register' (Communication) C(2010) 7649 final and European Commission, 'Commission decision of 30.5.2016 establishing horizontal rules on the creation and operation of Commission expert groups' C(2016) 3301 final. See, for a discussion of these rules, above chapter 3, section II.A.ii.a.

[183] The expert group was created by Commission Decision 2004/613/EC of 6 August 2004 concerning the creation of an advisory group on the food chain and animal and plant health [2004] OJ L275/17.

[184] For current membership of the Group, see Commission Decision 2011/242/EU of 14 April 2011 on the members of the advisory group on the food chain and animal and plant health established by Decision 2004/613/EC [2011] OJ L101/126.

[185] See European Commission, Register of Commission expert groups, Advisory Group on the Food Chain and Animal and Plant Health www.ec.europa.eu/transparency/regexpert/index.cfm?do=groupDetail.groupDetail&groupID=860&NewSearch=1&NewSearch=1.

[186] European Commission, Advisory Group on the Food Chain and Plant Health, 'Rules of Procedure' (2005) Art 7 www.ec.europa.eu/dgs/health_food-safety/dgs_consultations/docs/ag/rules_procedure_en.pdf.

[187] ibid Art 10.

[188] European Commission, 'Plenary Meeting of the Advisory Group (AG) on the Food Chain and Animal and Plant Health' (Summary Record, SANCO.03/D(2009), 2008) para 8.

by the group's members, their individual comments are not reported. Further, the topic of nanomaterials is not mentioned in the minutes. It therefore remains unclear whether the Commission gathered nano-specific knowledge via this expert group. It is interesting to note too that the second implementing act, that is, the draft implementing measure on plastics, was not presented at or discussed within this group.

Secondly, in the drafting of its recommendation for a definition of the term nanomaterial, the Commission requested advice from its Scientific Committee on Emerging and Newly Identified Health Risks (SCENIHR).[189] The basic procedural rules and principles of SCENIHR's operation are laid down in its founding decision.[190] Furthermore, DG SANTE's three scientific committees, among them SCENIHR, have adopted common, more detailed rules of procedure.[191] In drafting the requested opinion, SCENIHR made use of the power granted to it in its founding decision to create a working group.[192] As well as members of SCENIHR, a working group may consist of additional experts who can be drawn from the 'Pool of Scientific Advisors' and/or the 'Database of Experts'.[193] SCENIHR then opened a draft of its opinion to public consultation.[194] The rules of procedure specify that the committee may launch a public consultation in order 'to gather specific comments and suggestions on the scientific basis of the opinion, as well as any other relevant scientific information regarding the questions addressed'.[195] A summary report of the contributions, as well as the preliminary and the final SCENIHR opinion are available on DG SANTE's website.[196]

[189] For the request, see Scientific Committee on Emerging and Newly Identified Health Risks (SCENIHR), 'Request for a Scientific Opinion via Accelerated Procedure: Scientific basis for the definition of the term "nanomaterial"' www./ec.europa.eu/health/scientific_committees/emerging/docs/scenihr_q_024.pdf.

[190] Commission Decision 2008/721/EC of 5 August 2008 setting up an advisory structure of Scientific Committees and experts in the field of consumer safety, public health and the environment [2008] OJ L241/21.

[191] DG Sanco Scientific Committees, 'Rules of Procedure of the Scientific Committees on Consumer Safety, Health and Environmental Risks and Emerging and Newly Identified Health Risks' (2009) www.ec.europa.eu/health/scientific_committees/docs/rules_procedure_en.pdf.

[192] Decision 2008/721/EC of 5 August 2008 (n 190) Art 7.

[193] For the Commission's request at issue, SCENIHR established a Working Group consisting of five scientists of SCENIHR, one member of the Scientific Committee on Consumer Safety (SCCS) and five external experts, of which one was selected from the pool of scientific advisors, see the list of experts in SCENIHR, 'Scientific Basis for the Definition of the Term "Nanomaterial"' (Pre-consultation opinion, 6 July 2010) 3; for the pool of scientific advisors, see Commission Decision 2009/146/EC of 19 February 2009 on the appointment of the members and advisors of the Scientific Committees and the Pool set up by Decision 2008/721/EC [2009] OJ HR L49/33, Annex II.

[194] Decision 2008/721/EC (n 190) Art 9(3).

[195] DG Sanco Scientific Committees (n 191) annex IV para 5b.

[196] The committee received 94 contributions from public and private actors: 7 from public authorities, 39 from industry, 7 from trade associations, 4 from academia, 8 from individuals, 14 from NGOs and 15 others, see European Commission, 'Explanatory Note how the Comments received during the Public Consultation were taken into Account for the final SCENIHR Opinion on the Scientific Basis for the Definition of the Term Nanomaterial' (SANCO C7, no date indicated) www.ec.europa.eu/health/scientific_committees/emerging/docs/scenihr_o_032_note.pdf.

Three observations flow from the Commission's use of expert groups. First, the discretion of the Commission to decide whether or not to consult an expert group in each individual case may lead to odd situations, in which, with no reasons given, an expert group is consulted in the adoption of one implementing act but not in the preparation of another. Secondly, expert groups embrace a heterogeneous range of diverse assemblies, ranging from groups composed of stakeholders (comprising social, economic or environmental rationalities) to (allegedly) purely scientific advisors. Finally, the operation of an expert group, especially the way the group generates and communicates its advice, seems to depend to a large degree on its individual founding decision or the respective rules of procedure adopted by each group. This becomes evident by comparing the operation of the Advisory Group on the Food Chain to that of the scientific committee SCENIHR. This is despite the existence of horizontal rules adopted by the Commission. It should be remembered that this must be viewed in the context of the absence of an impact assessment, which, at least in theory, would have summarised the input gathered from these groups.

iii. Knowledge Collection in the Drafting of EFSA's Guidance Document

Chapter three identified EU agencies, next to Commission expert groups, as the second major source of knowledge. Yet, the preceding section showed that EFSA, with the adoption of its nano guidance, de facto developed beyond its formal role. This, in turn, provoked questions as to how the Agency itself, first, gathers knowledge and, secondly, ensures the legitimacy of its regulatory output. The former question is addressed here, whilst the latter question will be addressed below in sections B and C on participation and accountability. As was seen above, EU agencies, including EFSA, are not bound by the impact assessment commitment of the Commission.[197] We will therefore examine whether the Agency set in place its own procedures for the collection of knowledge and, if so, how these procedures operated in practice.

In this context, it must first be noted that EFSA's founding regulation, the General Food Law, does not prescribe any specific procedure for the adoption of scientific opinions, but it has delegated this task to the Agency's Scientific Committee.[198] Accordingly, the Agency published a 'workflow' on its website that it follows in the drafting of scientific opinions.[199] EFSA's Management Board and the Agency's Executive Director have adopted procedures elaborating (most of) the different stages of the workflow (see Figure 1).

[197] See above section III.A.i.a.

[198] According to Art 28(2) GFL, '[t]he Scientific Committee shall be responsible for the general coordination necessary to ensure the consistency of the scientific opinion procedure, in particular with regard to the adoption of working procedures and harmonisation of working methods'.

[199] See European Food Safety Authority, Working Practices www.efsa.europa.eu/en/efsahow/workflow.htm.

According to this workflow, EFSA commences the preparation of a scientific opinion with the creation of a dedicated working group,[200] in case of the nano guidance the Working Group on Nanotechnologies.[201] Scientists from the different EFSA panels are invited to take part in the working group;[202] the involvement of additional actors is at the discretion of the working group's chair. First, 'external experts', who are chosen from the Agency's Database of External Scientific Experts,[203] may be engaged to join the working group.[204] For the preparation of the nano guidance, the Scientific Committee considered the appointment of external experts necessary.[205] Secondly, stakeholders may be involved in the opinion's drafting process via scientific colloquia. There is no record, however, that the Working Group on Nanotechnologies opted to do this. Thirdly, working groups may draw on EFSA's data collection networks or launch an open call for data on its website.[206] While a call for data related to the nano guidance was not launched,[207] the working group presented a draft version thereof to the Agency's 'Scientific Network of Risk Assessment of Nanotechnologies in Food and Feed'.[208] The network was established by EFSA's advisory forum in February 2011[209] and is composed of representatives from national food safety authorities.[210] Finally, after

[200] ibid, for an outline of EFSA's procedure for the adoption of scientific opinions.

[201] Members of the Working Group on Nanotechnologies—Guidance: Mona-Lise Binderup, Qasim Chaudhry, Wim De Jong, Corrado Galli (member until February 2011), David Gott, Rolf Hertel, Akihiko Hirose, Wolfgang Kreyling, Hermann Stamm, Stefan Weigel, and EFSA staff member David Carlander, see European Food Safety Authority, 'Scientific Opinion' (n 109).

[202] Their appointment is conducted in line with a procedure adopted by the Agency's Executive Director, see European Food Safety Authority, 'Decision of the Executive Director Concerning the Selection of Members of the Scientific Committee, Scientific Panels and External Experts to Assist EFSA with Its Scientific Work' (EFSA/SCISTRAT/DEC/01/2014, 14 March 2011) www.efsa.europa.eu/en/keydocs/docs/expertselection.pdf. According to this procedure, scientists are selected based on an open call for applications (Art 2) and scrutinised by an Evaluation Team consisting of EFSA senior staff (Art 3), which in turn is overseen by three independent external evaluators and approved by the Management Board (Arts 6 and 9).

[203] ibid Art 14.

[204] ibid Art 13(2).

[205] European Food Safety Authority, 'Minutes of the 40th Plenary Meeting of the EFSA Scientific Committee Held on 11 December 2009' (2010) 8.

[206] See European Food Safety Authority, 'Workflow Practices' (n 199).

[207] See European Food Safety Authority, 'Call for Data' www.efsa.europa.eu/en/calls/data.htm.

[208] 'David Carlander presented the draft guidance which is out for public consultation until the 25th of February 2011. Member States welcomed the guidance and provided comments and suggestions to clarify various sections. … The comments raised by the Member States will be communicated to EFSA Working Group to be taken into consideration for the finalisation of the guidance document', see European Food Safety Authority, '1st Meeting of EFSA Scientific Network for Risk Assessment of Nanotechnologies in Food and Feed on 22 February 2011' (Minutes Agreed by the Network by written endorsement on 12 May 2011) 3–4.

[209] The overall objective of the Network is to (i) exchange information and data between EFSA and Member States, (ii) facilitate harmonisation of assessment practices and methodologies, and to (iii) achieve synergies in risk assessment activities, European Food Safety Authority, 'Technical Report—EFSA Scientific Network of Risk Assessment of Nanotechnologies in Food and Feed European Food Safety Authority' (Supporting Publications 2012) 246.

[210] For a list of the 2012 membership, see www.efsa.europa.eu/en/scnetworks/docs/scnanotechnologiesnetworklist.pdf.

the adoption of the draft scientific opinion, the working group may launch a public consultation[211] in accordance with 'EFSA's approach on Public Consultation on scientific outputs'[212] (see further section III.B on 'participation'). And, indeed, a draft version of the nano guidance was open to public scrutiny.[213]

To sum up, while EFSA is not bound by the impact assessment procedure, the Agency, in the absence of concrete procedures prescribed in its founding regulation, created for itself a net of procedures for pooling the dispersed knowledge and for exposing the latter to public scrutiny. (Most of) these procedures were also applied in the adoption of EFSA's nano guidance. A summary of the procedure and its operation in practice is given in Figure 1.

iv. Synthesis: Pooling Knowledge in the Drafting of a Regulatory Framework for Nanotechnologies in Food

The impact assessment procedure was identified in chapter three as the main tool introduced by the EU institutions for the purpose of pooling the societally fragmented knowledge. Put to the test in practice, the procedure failed to fulfil its promise. If the Commission (and Parliament and Council) were pooling knowledge, it was not via the impact assessment procedure. First, this is a consequence of the procedure's ambiguous scope of application in the 2009 Impact Assessment Guidelines. The Commission's impact assessment commitment was considered applicable only to the drafting of the two legislative acts. By inference, it was not applied to the regulatory options in the executive sphere. In view of the politically controversial content that these regulatory measures de facto entail in the area of nanotechnologies, it is tempting to argue for a clarification, and possibly an extension, of the impact assessment procedure.

However, a second fundamental problem relates to the practical operation of the procedure. Even though the Commission's 2009 Impact Assessment Guidelines were applicable to the drafting of the Novel Food and Food Additives Regulations, in practice the underlying principle of a 'proportionate level of analysis' allowed them to be neither used to gather nano-specific knowledge nor, by implication, did they result in an exposition of the latter's sources. Whether or not the scope of the procedure should be clarified or potentially extended succeeds or fails with its added value in practice. It goes without saying that it is futile to extend the scope

[211] See European Food Safety Authority, 'Workflow Practices' (n 199).

[212] The website provides a link to the document entitled 'EFSA's approach on public consultation on scientific outputs' www.efsa.europa.eu/en/keydocs/docs/consultationpolicy.pdf.

[213] The working group received comments from 34 interested parties: 9 from national authorities, 1 from an environmental NGO, 1 from a consumer organisation, 3 from animal rights groups, 13 from industry, and 7 from research institutes or universities, see European Food Safety Authority, 'Technical Report of EFSA—Outcome of the Public Consultation on the Draft Scientific Opinion on Guidance on Risk Assessment Concerning Potential Risks Arising from Applications of Nanoscience and Nanotechnologies to Food and Feed' (Supporting Publications 2011) 126.

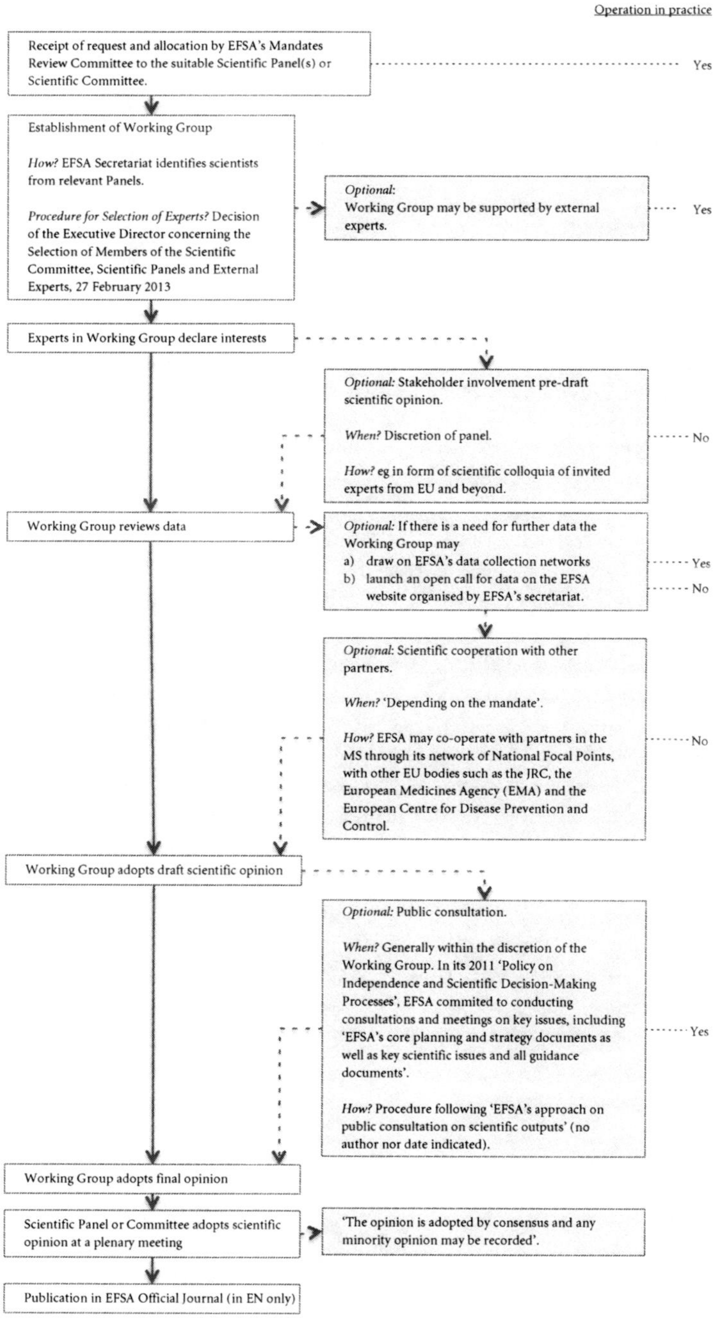

Figure 1: EFSA's Procedure for Adopting Scientific Opinions and its Operation in Practice

of an empty procedure, which would only add a further layer of bureaucracy. Similar conclusions must be drawn with regard to the interinstitutional 'Common Approach to Impact Assessment'. Neither Parliament nor Council conducted an own impact assessment for their nano-specific amendments, even though they could easily have been labelled 'substantive' in nature.

Instead of conducting impact assessments for regulatory measures in the executive sphere, the Commission decided to turn to an expert group on two occasions during the drafting processes of these measures. The documentation about these consultations is mixed. While the consultation of the Advisory Group on the Food Chain did not result in a display of the knowledge gathered,[214] the consultation of SCENIHR led to the adoption of a scientific opinion, which can be accessed online and whose authors are disclosed on the committee's website. Whether an expert group's consultation thus allows for a transparent collection of knowledge seems to depend mainly on the individual procedures applicable to or adopted by the respective group. The Commission's Horizontal Rules on Expert Groups turned out to be too vague in practice in order to result in a more uniform picture.

A special case is the collection of knowledge through the EU agency EFSA. Formally, the agency, like the expert groups, is a source of knowledge that supplies the regulator with scientific advice. Earlier in this chapter, however, it was concluded that EFSA itself has assumed regulatory tasks. This, in turn, raised questions as to how EFSA pools knowledge from affected actors. First, EU agencies, including EFSA, are not bound by the Commission's impact assessment commitment. Secondly, the Agency's founding regulation, the General Food Law, does not prescribe any specific procedure for the adoption of guidance documents. It is the Agency itself that has established a complex net of procedural rules—how to set up working groups, how to select experts and how to consult affected actors. Most of these rules were followed in practice. Yet, EFSA uses the same procedure for the drafting of guidance documents that it has set in place for scientific opinions (which is not surprising in view of the agency's formal mandate). This gives rise to questions about the adequacy of this procedure for the policy choices contained in the nano guidance, which will be considered further in relation to the participation of affected actors (section III.2). Moreover, it will be interesting to compare EFSA's adoption procedure to that of the European Chemicals Agency in chapter five.[215]

[214] This is because the individual comments of the expert group's members are not contained in the meeting's minutes. They can be requested via Regulation 1049/2001 if one applies the Court of First Instance's approach in Case T-121/05 *Borax Europe Ltd v Commission* [2009] ECR II-00027*, in which the Commission refused access to the unabridged minutes of a meeting of one of its expert groups in order to protect the privacy and integrity of the experts. The Court, however, annulled the Commission's decision.

[215] See below chapter 5, section III.A.ii.d.

Overall, the Commission, with its self-imposed procedures introduced in the aftermath of the European governance debate, seems to have created a largely empty procedural net that threatens to collapse once one takes a closer look at its scope of application and practical operation—at least in the case of nanotechnologies in food. This, in turn, has significant consequences for the legitimacy of the employed regulatory options, which will be addressed in the subsequent sections.

B. Participation

This section turns to the inextricably linked discussion on legitimacy. Input legitimacy, meaning affected actors' participation in the decision-making process, is analysed first. For analytical purposes, two types of participation were distinguished in chapter three: political participation through the representation of affected actors in the European Parliament and administrative participation through their direct contribution to the drafting process of individual regulatory measures. Whereas it was assumed that representation through the European Parliament generally approximates the Habermasian ideal speech situation, affected actors' direct participation in the decision-making process requires a closer examination. Following the White Paper on European Governance, the Commission adopted a set of minimum consultation standards.[216] The applicability and practical operation of these standards is analysed, ultimately in order to evaluate their operation based on the criteria derived from the Habermasian ideal speech situation, namely those of (1) 'full inclusion' of 'all affected actors' and (2) 'equality'. The guiding questions of this section are therefore the following:

— Was the European Parliament involved in the adoption of the different regulatory options?
— Did affected actors have the opportunity to directly contribute to the drafting process?
— If so, were the Commission's minimum consultation standards applicable? If they were applicable, were they complied with in (nano) practice?
— If the Commission's minimum consultation standards were not applicable, were other procedures set in place?
— To what extent did administrative participation in the drafting of the regulatory framework for nanotechnologies in food approximate the criteria derived from the ideal speech situation?

[216] European Commission, 'Towards a reinforced culture of consultation and dialogue—General principles and minimum standards for consultation of interested parties by the Commission' (Communication) COM (2002) 704 final and European Commission, 'Better Regulation Guidelines' (Staff Working Document) SWD (2015) 111 final.

i. Political Participation

It is only in the ordinary legislative procedure, which was followed in the revision(s) of the Novel Food Regulation and in the drafting of the Food Additives Regulation, that the European Parliament was involved as co-legislator. In the EU's executive sphere, the influence of the Parliament is, unsurprisingly, constrained. The Parliament hence did not play a role in the adoption of EFSA's guidance document and the Commission's recommended nano definition. The Parliament's involvement in comitology, to the contrary, has long been the stage for an interinstitutional battleground between the Commission, Parliament and Council,[217] which for now has culminated in the Lisbon Treaty's distinction between implementing and delegated acts.[218] To determine the involvement of the Parliament in the adoption of these measures, it is necessary to distinguish between the Commission Regulation on intelligent packaging, on the one hand, and the Commission Regulation on plastics, on the other. This is because the Commission Regulation on intelligent packaging was drafted before the regulatory procedure with scrutiny was introduced for certain implementing acts under the FCM Regulation in June 2009. Accordingly, the regulatory procedure (post-Lisbon examination procedure) was still applicable, meaning that the role of the Parliament was restricted to the right to be informed about the draft measure.[219]

The Commission Regulation on plastics, on the other hand, was drafted after June 2009. Its adoption was therefore subject to the regulatory procedure with scrutiny. Prior to its adoption, the Commission thus had to submit the draft measure to Council and Parliament for scrutiny.[220] However, a closer look at the comitology register reveals that the Parliament did not oppose the draft measure within the set timeframe. What is more, the draft measure does not appear on any agenda or minutes of the meetings of the responsible parliamentary Committee on Environment, Public Health and Food Safety in the relevant three-month period.[221] This is remarkable, since, in the two legislative procedures, it was the Parliament that emerged as the main driver for the inclusion of the essential

[217] HCH Hofmann, GC Rowe and AH Türk, *EU Administrative Law and Policy* (Oxford, Oxford University Press, 2011) 398.

[218] See for a more detailed discussion, eg M Keading and A Hardacre, 'The European Parliament and the Future of Comitology After Lisbon' (2013) 19 *European Law Journal* 382, 382–84.

[219] See Council Decision 1999/468/EC of 28 June 1999 laying down the procedures for the exercise of implementing powers conferred on the Commission [1999] OJ L184/23, art 5.

[220] ibid Art 5a. Following the Parliament's Rules of Procedure, the draft is, once received, forwarded to the responsible parliamentary committee, the ENVI Committee in our case, the chair of which 'set[s] a deadline for Members to propose that the committee object to the draft of measures', see Rule 88(2), European Parliament Rules of Procedure, July 2012. If the committee decides to object to the measure, it needs to table a motion for a resolution. The resolution may eventually be adopted by a majority of MEPs in plenary session, see Rule 88(4b), European Parliament Rules of Procedure, July 2012.

[221] September 2010 to January 2011.

nano-specific requirements.[222] What this implies, however, is that although the Parliament was de jure involved in the drafting of the plastics regulation, even with a veto power, it did not (or could not) make use of its right in practice.[223]

ii. Administrative Participation

Could the weak political participation in executive rule making be compensated for by the involvement of affected societal actors in the drafting process? While it it was clear from the previous sections that affected actors were invited at different stages to participate for the instrumental purpose of pooling knowledge, the endeavour of the following paragraphs is to take a careful look at who these actors were and how they were involved, making it possible also to evaluate their involvement as a source of input legitimacy.

a. Consulting *en vogue*

For nearly all regulatory measures identified in this chapter, affected societal actors were granted the opportunity to contribute their perspectives to the drafting process. Affected actors were hence consulted by the European Commission in the preparation of the first attempt to revise the Novel Food Regulation and in drafting the new Food Additives Regulation. In the drafting process leading to the adoption of the Commission's recommendation for a definition of nanomaterial, affected actors were even given the opportunity to voice their opinion twice: once, on a draft version of SCENIHR's scientific opinion and, again, on the subsequent Commission draft recommendation. Also EFSA, in the process leading to the adoption of the nano guidance, launched a public consultation.[224]

It is these consultations that will form the object of analysis in the following paragraphs. This wave of consultations raises vital questions. Most obvious is whether the Commission as well as EFSA were obliged to conduct these consultations or whether the decision to do so was at their discretion. Moreover, was the regulator bound by the Commission's minimum consultation standards when engaging in these contacts with affected actors? If so, were these standards complied with in practice?

The exceptions to this broad trend towards consultation are the two implementing acts adopted under the FCM Regulation. No public consultations were undertaken in their drafting. This finding has to be seen particularly critical given the de facto absence of the Parliament in their adoption (see section III.B.i).

[222] Most notably definitions of 'nanomaterial' and respective separate authorisation requirements for the nanoform.

[223] The finding that the Parliament seldom exercises its right of scrutiny in the regulatory procedure with scrutiny is supported by more general studies on the Parliament's practical engagement with draft acts adopted under the regulatory procedure with scrutiny, see M Keading and A Hardacre, 'The European Parliament and the Future of Comitology After Lisbon' (n 218) 392.

[224] See above section III.A.iii.

b. Consulting Freestyle? The Erratic Applicability of the Commission's Minimum Consultation Standards

The Commission minimum consultation standards of 2002 are applicable to 'major policy initiatives'.[225] The 'majorness' of a policy initiative, in turn, is indicated by the presence of an impact assessment requirement.[226] While it was seen that the performance of an impact assessment was compulsory for all legislative proposals, comitology items and non-binding acts only fell within its scope when these measures were likely to have 'significant impacts' or, respectively, 'define future policies'.[227] Above, it became clear that the Commission considered that the 2009 Impact Assessment Guidelines were not applicable to the identified regulatory measures in the executive sphere. This means that out of the various public consultations initiated, only two of them, namely those conducted by the Commission for the two legislative acts, were also subject to the minimum consultation standards.

There are thus three categories of consultations that fell outside the scope of the Commission's standards: the consultations launched by EFSA, the consultation conducted by the Commission's scientific committee SCENIHR and the consultation launched by the Commission in the adoption of its recommendation. This last consultation took place without any procedural rules being (considered) applicable. EFSA and SCENIHR, to the contrary, set in place their own standards.

EFSA's website features a document entitled 'EFSA's approach on public consultation on scientific outputs'.[228] Its stated aim is to provide 'for a comprehensive and integrated approach on public consultations to ensure that this process follows common criteria that allow public involvement in a transparent, coherent and timely manner'.[229] It is therefore arguable that EFSA has developed its own consultation standards. But how do these standards compare to those of the Commission? In fact, EFSA's approach reflects two of the Commission's minimum standards—first, the commitment that all communications relating to a consultation should be clear and include all necessary information[230] and, secondly, that the results of a consultation should be available online and 'adequate feedback' should be provided.[231] On the other hand, EFSA's standards remain silent on the inclusiveness of all affected actors. They neither stipulate a minimum consultation period, nor do they contain requirements as to the publicity of the consultation. They are thus considerably less demanding than those of the Commission, which

[225] 'Towards a reinforced culture of consultation and dialogue' COM (2002) 704 final (n 216) 15.
[226] ibid.
[227] See above section III.A.i.a.
[228] The website provides a link to the document entitled 'EFSA's approach to public consultation on scientific outputs' (n 212).
[229] ibid 1.
[230] ibid.
[231] ibid 7.

conflicts with the earlier finding that EFSA itself has—in practice—assumed regulatory functions.

There is no comparable document devoted to the organisation of SCENIHR's public consultations. However, a section in SCENIHR's rules of procedure broadly sketches the general aim of committee public consultations.[232] In comparison to the Commission's consultation standards, there is however no requirement to submit to the public beforehand any background information or to comply with a minimum consultation period. There is also no mention of the consultation's inclusiveness or of its prior publicity. Furthermore, there is no obligation to publish results or to provide feedback to the participants.[233] One might therefore wonder whether the term 'consultation standards' is really adequate for these rules of procedure or whether they rather legitimise the committees' *carte blanche* in involving affected actors.

c. Consulting in Nano Practice: Zooming-in on the Consultations' Operation

The aim of the subsequent paragraphs is to delve into greater detail on the consultations' operation. To this end, we will analyse the extent to which administrative participation approximated in practice the two criteria derived from the ideal speech situation, namely those of 'full inclusion of all affected actors' and 'equality'.

First Criterion: 'Full Inclusion' of 'All Affected Actors'

The first criterion of 'full inclusion' of 'all affected actors' was found to be made up of several components.[234] More precisely, the format and reporting of the diverse consultations will be looked at, including the way affected actors were identified and the consultation publicised, affected actors' representation, as well as the extent to which affected actors disposed of agenda-setting powers and the ability to influence the final decision.

First, the most common format of consultations was an online public consultation open to all affected parties. Four of the consultations listed above formed part of this category.[235] 'Targeted consultations with Member State

[232] 'The objective of public consultations is to gather specific comments and suggestions on the scientific basis of the opinion, as well as any other relevant scientific information regarding the questions addressed, in order to allow the Scientific Committees to focus on issues which need to be further analysed. This consultation process shall not deal with policy or risk management needs and measures', DG Sanco Scientific Committees (n 191) annex IV para 5b.

[233] *cf* ibid.

[234] See above chapter 3, section II.B.ii.

[235] These are the consultations conducted by the Commission in the first attempt to revise the Novel Food Regulation, in the preparation of its recommendation for a definition of the term 'nanomaterial', EFSA's public consultation and that of SCENIHR on its draft opinion on the scientific basis for a definition of the term 'nanomaterial'.

competent authorities and stakeholders' were furthermore performed for the impact assessment of the Food Additives Regulation.[236]

In the four online consultations, all affected actors could theoretically submit their comments on an electronic template. The threshold to access these consultations was hence very low.[237] These consultations were publicised generally with a press release on the day of their launch.[238] Actors thus had the opportunity to identify themselves as affected (subjective actor identification). Whether and, if so, based on which criteria targeted actors were additionally invited by the regulator to participate in the consultation is not disclosed (objective actor identification).[239] A former EFSA staff member stated, however, that emails are commonly sent out to 'relevant stakeholders'.[240]

Documentation regarding these online consultations was published in all four cases on the home pages of the responsible Directorate-General[241] and EFSA's website respectively. Only two of the online consultations[242] were additionally advertised on the Commission's 'single access point' *Your Voice in Europe*, where, pursuant to the Commission's minimum standards, open public consultations should be published for the sake of transparency and broader publicity.[243] Distinct formats were then used for the submission of comments. EFSA and DG Environment did not pose any particular questions to the participants but invited comments on the draft guidance and draft recommendation in general, thereby leaving room for participants to bring forward their own proposals. However, in the consultation that was conducted as part of the impact assessment for the first revision of the Novel Food Regulation the Commission requested comments

[236] 'Annex to the Proposal for a European Parliament and Council Regulation on Food Additives' SEC (2006) 1040 (n 173) 10.

[237] See also C Quittkat, 'Consultation in Daily Practice: An In-Depth Analysis' in B Kohler-Koch and C Quittkat (eds), *De-Mystification of Participatory Democracy: EU Governance and Civil Society* (Oxford, Oxford University Press, 2013) 64.

[238] See European Food Security Authority, 'EFSA launches public consultation on guidance for the risk assessment of nanomaterials in food and feed' (Press Release, 14 January 2011) www.efsa.europa.eu/en/press/news/scaf110114.htm. Similar to EFSA, also SCENIHR announced the public consultation in a press release only on the day the process was launched, see 'Public consultation: Definition of "nanomaterial"' (Press Release, 12 July 2010) www.ec.europa.eu/dgs/health_consumer/dyna/enews/enews.cfm?al_id=1039.

[239] That certain actors received an email calling to their attention the launch of a public consultation is however highly probable. This author eg received an email from EFSA after the launch of its public consultation on a draft version of its nano guidance document on 17 January.

[240] Interview with a former EFSA staff member (Brussels, 28 November 2013), notes on file with the author.

[241] DG Sanco for the consultations conducted in the context of the Novel Food Regulation and in the context of SCENIHR's opinion on the definition of the term 'nanomaterial' and DG Environment for the consultation conducted on a draft version of the Commission's recommendation on the definition of the term 'nanomaterial'. EFSA maintains a dedicated website for public consultations where it also published documentation related to the public consultation conducted on a draft version of the nano guidance document.

[242] SCENIHR's consultation and the Commission's consultation on its recommendation for a definition of 'nanomaterial'.

[243] 'Towards a reinforced culture of consultation and dialogue' COM (2002) 704 final (n 216) 20.

on a questionnaire that was framed along four main issues.[244] Most importantly, participants were not explicitly invited to discuss the proposal's substance with respect to nanotechnologies. Similarly, SCENIHR 'abstracted' 11 sections of the draft opinion and requested comments specifically on those issues.[245] In these consultations, the participants' agenda-setting power was arguably restricted. Other problems surfaced as regards the publication of the results of the online consultations. Although the Commission's minimum standards require the results of consultations to be displayed online,[246] the individual responses were published for only three of the four consultations.[247]

Overall, the four online consultations exhibited several shortcomings, if compared to the Habermasian ideal, but also if contrasted with the Commission's own minimum consultation standards. These are:

— Insufficiently transparent criteria for the launch of objective actor identification processes;
— Inconsistent publication of consultations on the dedicated website *Your Voice in Europe*;
— Narrowly framed consultation questions restricting the participants' agenda-setting power; and
— Publication of individual comments in only three of the four consultations.

Targeted consultations with Member States and stakeholders took place in the preparation of the legislative proposal for a new Food Additives Regulation.[248] The impact assessment lists 'some of the stakeholder organisations involved' in the consultations,[249] and the dates of several meetings at which the 'abovementioned

[244] European Commission, 'Explanatory document—Revision of Regulation (EC) No 258/97 of the European Parliament and of the Council of 27 January 1997 concerning Novel Foods and Novel Food Ingredients' (2006).

[245] The 11 sections are annexed to the explanatory note, 'Explanatory Note on how the Comments received during the Public Consultation were taken into Account for the final SCENIHR Opinion on the Scientific Basis for the Definition of the Term Nanomaterial' (n 196). The committee explained that 'this approach was undertaken to guide the responders to address key questions, in what is a very complex matter, thus providing more focussed feedback' (2).

[246] 'Towards a reinforced culture of consultation and dialogue' COM (2002) 704 final (n 216) 21–22.

[247] For the consultation conducted for the impact assessment of the Novel Food Revision, see www.ec.europa.eu/food/food/biotechnology/novelfood/resp_consult_258_97_en.htm; for EFSA's consultation on a draft of its nano guidance document, see www.efsa.europa.eu/en/consultationsclosed/call/scaf110114.htm; for the consultation conducted by DG Environment on a draft version of its recommendation for a definition of the term 'nanomaterial', see www.ec.europa.eu/environment/consultations/pdf/Nano_Consultation%20comments.pdf.

[248] Annex to the Proposal for a European Parliament and Council Regulation on Food Additives' SEC (2006) 1040 (n 173) 10.

[249] These are BEUC (the European Consumers' Organisation), CIAA (Confederation of the Food and Drink Industries of the EU), ISA (International Sweeteners Association), Cefic (European Chemical Industry Council), AMFEP (Association of Manufacturers and Formulations of Enzyme Products), ELC (Federation of European Food Additives and Food Enzymes Industries), FEDIMA (Federation of the Intermediate Products Industries for the Bakery and Confectionary Trades in the EEA) and CAOBISCO (Association of the Chocolate, Biscuit and Confectionary Industries of the EU), see Annex to the Proposal for a European Parliament and Council Regulation on Food Additives' SEC (2006) 1040 (n 173) 24.

stakeholders and governmental experts from Member States were consulted'.[250] No subjective actor identification process took place. The impact assessment then summarises on three pages the general preferences of the consulted parties.[251] There is no disclosure as to who participated in which of the scheduled meetings. The announcement, content and results (besides the summary in the impact assessment) of the consultation(s) are not available on the Commission's website *Your Voice in Europe* or on DG SANTE's own home page.[252]

With regards to participation and representation, the minimum consultation standards require the Commission to take into account 'the need for a proper balance, where relevant, between the representatives of social and economic bodies, large and small organisations or companies, wider constituencies … and specific target groups'.[253] Closer scrutiny of the consultations conducted by the Commission, SCENIHR and EFSA reveals an imbalance in participants' representation.

The imbalance can be seen between participants representing the economic rationality, on the one hand, and participants representing environmental, health and safety interests, on the other.[254] Industry and trade associations clearly dominate. This discrepancy proved to be the leitmotif throughout the consultations analysed. It is interesting to note that the imbalance occurs independently of whether or not the Commission's minimum consultation standards were applicable. The results are summarised in Table 4.

To establish whether comments were incorporated into the final decision requires a high level of technical understanding. This exercise is considerably facilitated by follow-up reports that explain how the final version of the regulatory measure was amended after the consultation. Only the scientific committee SCENIHR, however, published such an 'explanatory note'.[255] While this makes it difficult to put forward any general remarks, there are some indications that comments were not always taken into account.

[250] ibid.

[251] ibid 10–14. The problem with such 'summary reports' has been convincingly demonstrated by Quittkat: 'case studies show that these reports are also far from providing a differentiated and balanced summary of the submissions', see C Quittkat, 'New Instruments Serving Democracy: Do Online Consultations Benefit Society?' in B Kohler-Koch and C Quittkat (eds), *De-Mystification of Participatory Democracy: EU Governance and Civil Society* (n 237) 99.

[252] Upon request, the Commission made available the questionnaire sent to the targeted participants (on file with the author).

[253] 'Towards a reinforced culture of consultation and dialogue' COM (2002) 704 final (n 216) 20.

[254] This, of course, can only be concluded for those consultations for which relevant data is available, hence excluding the consultation conducted by the Commission in the drafting of the Food Additives Regulation. It is possible that it is partly biased, due to the fact that the individual submissions are not always available. Here, I had to rely on the summary analysis prepared the Commission (and SCENIHR).

[255] 'Explanatory Note on how the Comments received during the Public Consultation were taken into Account for the final SCENIHR Opinion on the Scientific Basis for the Definition of the Term Nanomaterial' (n 245).

Table 4: Imbalance in the Representation of Affected Societal Actors

Consultations		**Number of participants**	**Overview of replies according to participant profile**	**Economic *v.* environmental/ safety/health rationalities**
Legislative Acts	Food Additives Regulation	n/a	n/a	n/a
	Novel Food Regulation[256] (first attempt to revise in 2008)	65	17 public authorities 2 consumer org. 38 industry 8 others	60% *v.* 3%
EFSA Nano Guidance[257]		35	9 public authorities 1 consumer org. 1 environmental NGO 3 animal rights groups 13 industry 7 academia	37% *v.* 14%
Commission Recommendation for a Definition of the Term 'Nanomaterial'	SCENIHR[258]	94	7 public authorities 14 NGOs 39 businesses 7 trade associations 4 academia 8 individuals 15 others	49% *v.* 15%
	Commission[259]	168	20 public authorities 2 consumer org. 3 environmental NGOs 105 industry 20 academia 6 standard. bodies 2 trade unions 10 others	63% *v.* 4%

[256] See for the individual replies to the Novel Food consultation www.ec.europa.eu/food/food/biotechnology/novelfood/resp_consult_258_97_en.htm.

[257] See European Food Safety Authority, 'Technical Report of EFSA—Outcome of the public consultation on the draft scientific opinion on Guidance on risk assessment concerning potential risks arising from applications of nanoscience and nanotechnologies to food and feed' (Supporting Publications 2011) 126, 1 www.efsa.europa.eu/en/supporting/doc/126e.pdf, 1.

[258] See European Commission, 'Explanatory Note how the Comments received during the Public Consultation were taken into Account for the final SCENIHR Opinion on the Scientific Basis for the Definition of the Term Nanomaterial' (SANCO C7, no date indicated) www.ec.europa.eu/health/scientific_committees/emerging/docs/scenihr_o_032_note.pdf.

[259] See for the individual replies to DG Environment's publication consultation on a draft of the recommendation for a definition of the term 'nanomaterial', www.ec.europa.eu/environment/consultations/pdf/Nano_Consultation%20comments.pdf.

In the first attempt to revise the Novel Food Regulation, for instance, it was noted above that participants to the consultation were not explicitly invited to discuss the proposal's substance with respect to nanotechnologies. One of the participants, the European Consumers' Organisation BEUC, nevertheless mentioned concerns regarding nanotechnologies in its submission: 'we ask the Commission to … fully consider, in the review, whether the new legislation would guarantee adequate protection for consumers from future developments in food technologies (eg nanotechnologies, cloning)'.[260] BEUC's comment, however, was not reflected in the summary of the public consultation in the impact assessment.

Troublesome too is the fate of the submissions that SCENIHR received on a draft version of its scientific opinion on a definition of the term nanomaterial. It will be remembered that the Commission mandated SCENIHR to prepare this opinion as a basis for its recommendation. Surprisingly, however, the Commission published its draft recommendation before SCENIHR adopted the final opinion. This means that none of the comments that SCENIHR incorporated based on its public consultation are hence reflected in the Commission's draft recommendation. Arguably, this fact substantially reduced, if not nullified, the participants' influence on the final Commission recommendation.

Second Criterion: Equality

The second criterion derived from the ideal speech situation requires each actor to participate equally in the discourse.[261] To this end, all participants should be given access to information about the regulatory measure as well as sufficient time to contribute to a consultation.

The Commission's minimum standards require communication related to a consultation to 'include all necessary information to facilitate responses', including 'a summary of the context, scope and objectives of consultation, including a description of the specific issues open for discussion or questions with particular importance for the Commission'.[262] Also, in practice, prior to all four online consultations, the Commission, SCENIHR and EFSA made information available on their websites. This could be in form of an explanatory document[263] or a draft version of the measure.[264] Also in case of the targeted consultations performed by the Commission in the preparation of its impact assessment for the new Food Additives Regulation, 'a working document for a proposal on food additives and

[260] European Consumers's Organisation's (BEUC) contribution www.ec.europa.eu/food/food/biotechnology/novelfood/documents/beuc.pdf.

[261] See above chapter 3, section II.B.ii.

[262] 'Towards a reinforced culture of consultation and dialogue' COM (2002) 704 final (n 216) 19.

[263] 'Explanatory Document—Revision of Regulation (EC) No 258/97' (n 244).

[264] EFSA made the draft guidance document available, see www.efsa.europa.eu/en/consultationsclosed/call/scaf110114.htm; DG Sanco published SCENIHR's preliminary opinion, see www.ec.europa.eu/health/scientific_committees/consultations/index_en.htm; DG Environment published the draft recommendation for a definition of the term 'nanomaterial', see ww.ec.europa.eu/environment/consultations/nanomaterials.htm.

a relevant questionnaire was circulated to the Member States and the different stakeholders'.[265]

According to the minimum standards, the Commission should grant affected actors at least eight weeks to reply to a consultation; these eight weeks should be extended in certain circumstances, inter alia in order to take account of 'main holiday periods'.[266] Since 2012, the minimum period has been extended to 12 weeks.[267] The information required to evaluate the length of the period is only available for the four online consultations (see Table 5).[268]

Table 5: Consultation Periods

Consultations		**Date**	**Time Period**	**Remarks**
Legislative Acts	Food Additives Regulation	n/a	n/a	n/a
	Novel Food Regulation (first revision)	2 June 2006 to 1 August 2006	8 weeks	Summer holidays
EFSA Nano Guidance		14 January 2011 to 25 February 2011	6 weeks	
Commission Recommendation for a Definition of the Term 'Nanomaterial'	SCENIHR	12 July 2010 to 15 September 2010	8 weeks	Summer holidays
	Commission	21 October 2010 to 19 November 2010	4 weeks	Justification: 'the SCENIHR pre-consultation opinion on the scientific basis for the definition of the term "nanomaterial" was closed after 8 weeks of consultation on 15 September 2010. This draft proposal for the term "nanomaterial" builds on the scientific opinion.'[269]

[265] 'Annex to the Proposal for a European Parliament and Council Regulation on Food Additives' SEC (2006) 1040 (n 173) 10.

[266] 'Towards a reinforced culture of consultation and dialogue' COM (2002) 704 final (n 216) 21.

[267] European Commission, 'Smart regulation in the European Union' (Communication) COM (2010) 543, 10 and 'Better regulation guidelines' SWD (2015) 111 final (n 216) 77.

[268] It is unclear how much time targeted actors were given to reply to the food additives questionnaire or to EFSA's presentation of the draft nano guidance to the 'Scientific Network for Risk Assessment of Nanotechnologies in Food and Feed'.

[269] See www.ec.europa.eu/environment/consultations/nanomaterials.htm.

Table 5 shows, first, that the six weeks which EFSA granted to participants to reply to its consultation contradict the Commission's minimum timeframe of (then) eight weeks. EFSA's own consultation standards, it must be recalled, do not prescribe a minimum period. The six-week period is indeed short, especially since the Commission's eight-week period had already been subject to severe criticism, most notably by the European Parliament, for constituting an obstacle to 'equal access'.[270] These concerns are reflected in the extension of the minimum period to 12 weeks.[271] The Commission's consultation on its draft recommendation for a definition of nanomaterial, which closed after only four weeks, appears to be even more problematic. The Commission justifies this short period by pointing out that SCENIHR had already submitted its draft opinion for a public consultation. Since the draft recommendation builds on SCENIHR's opinion, according to the Commission, the repetition of an extensive consultation was not necessary.[272] Beyond doubt, this reasoning is problematic, above all because the results of SCENIHR's public consultation were not considered by the Commission in its draft recommendation (as the Commission adopted its draft recommendation before SCENIHR adopted its final scientific opinion). Furthermore, it was shown above that SCENIHR's consultation standards are considerably less demanding than those of the Commission. Finally, the Commission launched two of the consultations during major holiday periods, without prolonging the consultation period accordingly, as recommended by the minimum standards. This fact might have constrained societal actors with relatively less (human or financial) resources to prepare their responses, thereby reinforcing the observed imbalance in participation between industry and NGOs.

iii. Synthesis: Participation in Nano Practice

The focus on executive rule making in the regulation of nanotechnologies in food implies a restricted role for the European Parliament. It is remarkable, however, that also in the case of comitology, where the Parliament is formally granted a veto right under the regulatory procedure with scrutiny, the Parliament did not (or could not) make use of this right in practice.

At the same time, the preceding analysis leaves little doubt that the administrative participation of affected actors, in its current form, is unable to compensate for the weak parliamentary involvement. The result is a deficit in input legitimacy, which stands in sharp contrast to the assumptions made in chapter three that the inherently controversial questions characterising the regulation of nanotechnologies should be exposed to a political public debate.

[270] The European Parliament, for instance, requested an extension of this period to 12 weeks in order to ensure 'equal access', see 'Resolution of 8 June 2011 on guaranteeing independent impact assessments' (n 177) para 8.

[271] 'Smart regulation in the European Union' COM (2010) 543 (n 263) 10.

[272] See European Commission, Environment—Consultation on the term of nanomaterials (2010) www.ec.europa.eu/environment/consultations/nanomaterials.htm.

On the one hand, administrative participation was shown to suffer from the fact that the Commission's minimum standards are only applicable to consultations performed in the drafting of legislative acts. This is almost paradoxical since the 'proper' participation of affected actors should be ensured in particular when the Parliament is not involved. The public consultation conducted by EFSA, albeit not falling within the scope of the Commission's minimum standards, was subject to the Agency's own procedural rules. Here, however, there was substantial room for review of EFSA's standards, in order to align them with those of the Commission. Arguably, the standards EFSA uses are ill-suited to the (political) contents of the guidance, illustrating the fundamental tension between the Agency's formal mandate and regulatory practice. SCENIHR's rules of procedure, instead of offering safeguards for affected actors, were found to rather give a *carte blanche* to the committee to proceed freely in its stakeholder contacts.

On the other hand, apart from lenient or inapplicable consultation standards, when turning to practice, all public consultations that were examined exhibited some major shortcomings when compared to the criteria derived from the ideal speech situation. Deficits ranged from merely summarised consultation results, an imbalanced representation of the different affected actors, narrowly framed questions restricting the participants' agenda setting powers, to insufficiently transparent actor identification processes and too short (or unfavourable) consultation periods.[273] These findings are summarised in Table 6.

C. Accountability

This section delves into the accountability question. It will analyse the extent to which the EU regulator could be held to account ex post (1) for how it has been pooling knowledge, and (2) for how it has included (or not) affected actors in the regulatory process. Chapter three introduced four different accountability mechanisms; accountability via the political, the legal, the administrative and the social fora.[274] Their applicability and operation is analysed below.

i. Political Accountability vis-à-vis the European Parliament

Political accountability and input legitimacy through political participation are intrinsically linked.[275] The political forum ultimately consists of societal actors

[273] These findings are confirmed by more general studies on the Commission's regime of online consultations, see C Quittkat, 'New Instruments Serving Democracy' (n 251) 99; C Marxsen, 'Open Stakeholder Consultations at the European Level—Voice of the Citizens?' (2015) 21 *European Law Journal* 257. Neyer refers to the Commission's consultation practices as 'elite pluralism', see J Neyer, *The Justification of Europe: A Political Theory of Supranational Integration* (Oxford, Oxford University Press, 2012) 145.

[274] See above chapter 3, section II.B.iii.

[275] See above chapter 3, section II.B.iii.a.

Table 6: Administrative Participation in Nano Practice

		Legislative review			Non-legally binding regulation		
		Legislative acts		Implementing acts FCM Regulation	EFSA Nano Guidance	Nano Definition	
		Food Additives Regulation	**Novel Food Regulation**			**SCENIHR public consultation**	**COM public consultation**
Was a consultation performed?		**Yes**	**Yes**	**No**	**Yes**	**Yes**	**Yes**
Participation standards	Were the Commission's minimum consultation standards applicable?	**Yes**	**Yes**	**No**	**No**	**No**	**No**
	If not, were other standards set in place?	—	—	—	**Yes** (EFSA standards)	**Yes** (SCENIHR rules of procedure)	**No**
1. 'Full inclusion' of 'all affected actors'	Online consultation?	**n/a**	**Yes**	—	**Yes**	**Yes**	**Yes**
	Publication of results?	Summary in impact assessment	**Yes** (individual submissions)	—	**Yes** (individual submissions)	Summary by DG Sanco	**Yes** (individual submissions)
	Number of Participants?	**n/a**	65	—	35	94	168
	Balanced representation?	**n/a**	60% industry v. 3% NGOs; 2 of 17 from new MS	—	37% industry v. 14% NGOs; 0 of 9 from new MS	49% industry v. 15% NGOs; n/a	63% industry v. 4% NGOs; 0 of 20 from new MS
	Subjective actor identification process?	**No**	**Yes**	—	**Yes**	**Yes**	**Yes**

(continued)

Table 6: *(Continued)*

		Legislative review			**Non-legally binding regulation**		
		Legislative acts		**Implementing acts FCM Regulation**	**EFSA Nano Guidance**	**Nano Definition**	
		Food Additives Regulation	**Novel Food Regulation**			**SCENIHR public consultation**	**COM public consultation**
	Objective actor identification process?	**Yes** (criteria unclear)	**n/a**	—	**Yes** (criteria unclear)	**n/a**	**n/a**
	Agenda—setting powers?	**Narrowly framed questions** (nano not mentioned)	**Narrowly framed questions** (nano not mentioned)	—	**Yes**	**Request of comments on selected issues**	**Yes**
	Influence on final decision?	**n/a**	**Debatable** (only nano response not mentioned in IA)	—	**n/a**	**Nullified** (COM draft recommendation adopted *before* final SCENIHR opinion)	**n/a**
2. Equality	Background information?	**Yes**	**Yes**	—	**Yes**	**Yes**	**Yes**
	Length of consultation period?	**n/a**	**8 weeks** (in summer holidays)	—	**6 weeks**	**8 weeks** (in summer holidays)	**4 weeks**

who not only choose their representatives in elections but who also hold the latter to account for their conduct during previous legislative periods. Where societal actors are represented in the ordinary legislative procedure due to the co-legislative function of the European Parliament, political accountability is assumed to be given. The situation is more complex in executive rule making, where the Parliament is generally not involved in the drafting process. The question that arises here is the extent to which the Parliament has the opportunity to scrutinise the (adoption process of these) measures ex post. Does the Parliament possess (1) a right to receive information about the Commission and EFSA's regulatory activities; (2) is it able to question this information; and (3) can it make judgements about the regulator's conduct?

In addition to the 'grand supervisory powers'[276] that the Parliament possesses—including its budgetary control, the right to ask parliamentary questions or its right to approve and dismiss the college of Commissioners—its ability to hold the Commission to account for its day-to-day executive functions is limited.[277] In comitology, this role is still to a large extent reserved for national representatives in comitology committees.[278] The Parliament's rights are restricted to receiving information (such as agendas of the comitology meetings and draft acts).[279] Nevertheless, the Parliament retains the possibility, as co-author of the FCM Regulation, to revoke the delegation to the Commission altogether. However, as will be seen further below, the Parliament only uses this sanction power in exceptional circumstances.

There is no particular parliamentary scrutiny over Commission recommendations. The Parliament is informed about such measures mainly via the Commission's annual activity report. Thus the relevant report informs the Parliament that 'the Commission took an important step towards greater protection for citizens by recommending a definition of "nanomaterials" which will help determine which materials need special treatment in specific legislation'.[280] The Parliament did not use its supervisory powers to further investigate (the adoption process of) the recommendation; the MEPs did not address questions to the Commission[281] nor was the content of the recommendation subject to a discussion in a parliamentary committee.[282]

[276] ibid.

[277] HCH Hofmann et al, *EU Administrative Law and Policy* (n 217) 777.

[278] For an analysis of political accountability via the national representatives in the comitology committees, see GJ Brandsma, 'Accountable Comitology?' in M Bovens, D Curtin and P't Hart (eds), *The Real World of EU Accountability: What Deficit?* (Oxford, Oxford University Press, 2010).

[279] Council Decision 1999/468/EC of 28 June 1999 (n 219), Art 7(3); Regulation (EU) 182/2011 of the European Parliament and of the Council of 16 February 2011 laying down the rules and general principles concerning mechanisms for control by Member States of the Commission's exercise of implementing powers [2011] OJ HR L55/13, Art 10(4).

[280] European Commission, '2011 Annual Activity Report' (DG Environment, 2011) 16 www.ec.europa.eu/atwork/synthesis/aar/doc/env_aar_2011.pdf.

[281] See www.europarl.europa.eu/portal/en.

[282] According to a search of documents of the parliamentary committees, see www.europarl.europa.eu/committees/en/search-in-documents.html.

As part of the EU's executive, the political accountability of EU agencies has increasingly come under the spotlight of scholarly attention.[283] In the case of EFSA too, the Parliament enjoys a general right to be informed about the Agency's activities through the submission of annual reports.[284] The 2011 Annual Report explains that EFSA adopted guidance which was 'the first of its kind to give practical advice on the assessment of potential risks arising from applications of nanotechnologies in the food and feed chain'.[285] If the Parliament wanted to question the content of the report (or receive further information on it), there is no legal provision in the General Food Law that would provide for a 'debate' on the report.[286] Yet, there exists a practical arrangement between the Parliament and EFSA, which foresees an annual hearing of the Agency's Executive Director in front of EFSA's 'partner' parliamentary committee, the Committee on Environment, Public Health and Food Safety.[287] In the hearing that took place five months after the publication of the nano guidance, however, the document was not picked up for discussion by the MEPs in attendance.[288]

In theory, if the parliamentary examination of the annual report (or hearing) turned out to be negative, the Parliament could sanction EFSA, in the same way that it could sanction the Commission, via its budgetary powers.[289] The Parliament used this power against EFSA for the first time in 2012, when it suspended the approval of the Agency's budget for 2010.[290] The Parliament's main concern at that time focused on (the application of) EFSA's procedures on conflict of interests, severe problems with which were revealed by an investigation of the European Ombudsman (see further section III.C.iii on administrative accountability). Beyond its budgetary powers, the Parliament, again as co-author of the General Food Law, maintains, as part of its ultimate power, the possibility to prescribe EFSA's tasks and revoke the mandate to carry out those tasks in the case of underperformance.[291]

283 See eg M Busuioc, 'European Agencies: Pockets of Accountability' in M Bovens, D Curtin and P't Hart (eds), *The Real World of EU Accountability: What Deficit?* (n 273); F Jacobs, 'EU Agencies and the European Parliament' in M Everson, C Monda and E Vos (eds), *European Agencies in Between Institutions and Member States*, European Monographs no 85 (Alphen aan den Rijn, Wolters Kluwer Law & Business, 2014).

284 Art 26(3) GFL.

285 European Food Safety Authority, *Annual Report 2011* (EFSA, Parma, 2012) 13 www.efsa.europa.eu/en/corporate/doc/ar11en.pdf.

286 M Busuioc, 'European Agencies' (n 278) 101.

287 European Food Safety Authority, *Annual Report 2012* (EFSA, Parma, 2013) 25 www.efsa.europa.eu/en/corporate/doc/aar12.pdf.

288 European Parliament, Committee on the Environment, Public Health and Food Safety (ENVI), Committee Meeting of 7 November 2011, record available www.europarl.europa.eu/ep-live/en/committees/video?event=20111107-1500-COMMITTEE-ENVI.

289 This is because EFSA is an Agency funded by the EU budget, see Art 44(4) GFL.

290 European Parliament, 'Resolution of 10 May 2012 on discharge in respect of the implementation of the budget of the European Union Agencies for the financial year 2010: performance, financial management and control of European Union Agencies' (P7_TA(2012)0164) paras 52–60.

291 M Busuioc, 'European Agencies' (n 278) 107.

Having said that, both sanction mechanisms are unlikely to be used in the ex post scrutiny of individual regulatory output. Rather, these mechanisms are triggered by systemic problems in the Agency's (or the Commission's) overall performance or by topics that carry a particular political (and media) salience.[292] In practice, the Parliament did not further inquire into (the adoption of) EFSA's guidance, nor, as was seen above, did it query the adoption of the two implementing acts under the FCM Regulation or of the Commission's recommendation for a definition of nanomaterial.

ii. Legal Accountability: The Role of the EU Courts

a. 'Reviewable Act' as Gatekeeper to Judicial Review

The Straightforward Case of Binding Acts

Pursuant to Article 288 TFEU, regulations are of a binding nature.[293] The two legislative acts, namely, the new Novel Food Regulation and the Food Additives Regulation, as well as the two implementing acts adopted under the FCM Regulation, therefore qualify as 'reviewable acts' under Article 263 TFEU and would hence be admissible for review by the EU courts. This is the easy answer to the question of the legal accountability of binding acts. The reality emerges as somewhat more intricate. Zooming in on the issue of judicial review of binding acts, two important limitations arise. The first limitation concerns the long-debated question of locus standi of affected actors before the EU courts, that is, the question of *who* can hold the EU regulator to account, which will be further discussed in section III.C.ii.b. The second limitation focuses on the intensity of review under Article 263 TFEU, that is, the question *for what* can the EU regulator be held to account, which is examined in section III.C.ii.c. These limitations are exemplified by concerns that arose earlier in the discussions on pooling knowledge and participation. For instance, could the producer of a food additive in nanoform challenge the Food Additives Regulation because of the Parliament and Council's insufficiently transparent knowledge collection? Could a producer challenge the Commission Regulation on plastics because it contains a separate authorisation requirement for substances in nanoform although no impact assessment was performed? Or could an environmental NGO take action based on the fact that the Commission launched the public consultation in the middle of the summer holidays, effectively preventing the submission of a well-researched reply? Before engaging with these questions, a more fundamental issue needs to be confronted first: non-binding regulation is generally excluded from review by the EU courts.

[292] See ibid 105.

[293] See on the legal effect of EU instruments, above chapter 3, section I.C.ii.

The Reviewability of Non-binding Acts

Legal accountability in the case of the Commission's recommendation for a definition of nanomaterial appears to be inherently problematic. Recommendations are explicitly of a non-binding character.[294] Accordingly, Article 263(1) TFEU states that the Court of Justice shall review the legality of 'acts of the Council, of the Commission and of the European Central Bank, *other than recommendations and opinions*'.[295] Following the Court's substantive approach in determining whether an act produces legal effects,[296] however, even recommendations could undergo an examination before the Court excludes 'legal effects' in exceptional situations.[297] The challenge is to prove that the recommendation de facto affects the legal position of third parties. There are two aspects that must be considered.

First, there is room to argue that the Commission's recommended definition merely constitutes a 'preparatory act', which only creates legal effects vis-a-vis third parties once inserted into the legislative framework via a legislative or non-legislative procedure. Here, reasoning similar to the Court's argumentation in *Olivieri* is conceivable, according to which preparatory measures are incapable of directly affecting the legal position of those being regulated.[298] However, the situation becomes tricky when the nano definition is not only used to 'prepare' legally binding regulation but also 'unidentified legal objects', such as agency guidance documents. This, as will be seen in chapter five, is the case in the chemicals sector.[299] The *Olivieri* reasoning would no longer hold, since the legal effects of the subsequent instrument, which is prepared by the nano definition, are also uncertain. Only binding decisions, which are adopted based on the guidance documents, could then be judicially challenged, rendering it more and more difficult to retrace the proper preparatory act from the emerging 'soft law construct' underlying the final decision. Moreover, treating the recommendation as a 'preparatory act' would ignore the practical effects that the definition exerts on the behaviour of affected actors—without resulting in a (binding) act at all.

Secondly, in determining whether a recommendation could de facto affect the legal position of third parties, in the past the courts have first looked at a measure's wording.[300] This is important since, in the recommendation laying down

[294] Pursuant to Art 288 TFEU.

[295] Emphasis added.

[296] See for a discussion above chapter 3, section I.C.ii.

[297] This approach was pursued by the Court in *Grimaldi*. For a more detailed discussion of this case, see above chapter 3, section I.C.ii.

[298] Case T-326/99 *Nancy Fern Olivieri v Commission of the European Communities and European Agency for the Evaluation of Medicinal Products* [2003] ECR II-6053, para 53; Case C-60/81 *International Business Machines Cooperation v Commission of the European Communities* [1981] ECR 2639, para 12.

[299] See below chapter 5, section II.B.iii.

[300] See J Scott, 'In Legal Limbo: Post-Legislative Guidance as a Challenge for European Administrative Law' (2011) 48 *Common Market Law Review* 329, 340.

a definition of nanomaterial, the Commission merely 'invites'—as opposed to 'requires'—its addressees to follow the proposed definition.[301] The wording is thus far from imperative.[302] It is therefore improbable that the Court would not consider the nano definition, in the Court's words in *Grimaldi*, to be a 'true recommendation'.[303]

It is also doubtful whether EFSA could be legally held to account for (the adoption of) its guidance document. This is despite the fact that the Treaty of Lisbon explicitly included agency acts within the scope of Article 263(1) TFEU. Contrary to the Commission recommendation, however, guidance documents are not listed in Article 288 TFEU. They are truly 'unidentified legal objects'.[304] Earlier research found that guidance documents often escaped the courts' scrutiny.[305] The fact that EFSA's guidance document was adopted in the form of a scientific opinion further obstructs the determination of its legal effects. Although there are four distinct instances in which EFSA may adopt a scientific opinion—on its own initiative,[306] at request of the Parliament or a Member State,[307] at request of the Commission,[308] and 'in all cases where Community legislation makes provision for the Authority to be consulted'[309]—most opinions are adopted under the last instance. Such classic scientific opinions generally constitute an intermediate stage of a Commission pre-market approval decision.

This is also reflected in existing case law, which has predominantly dealt with scientific opinions adopted as part of an authorisation procedure.[310] In the above-mentioned *Olivieri* judgment, for instance, the then Court of First Instance (now General Court) declared the request for an annulment of a scientific opinion of the European Medicines Agency inadmissible, as the opinion constituted only an 'intermediate measure whose purpose is to prepare for the marketing

[301] Commission Recommendation 2011/696/EU (n 135) paras 1 and 7.

[302] See, for instance, Case C-325/91 *French Republic v Commission of the European Communities* [1993] ECR I-3283, in which the Court was confronted with a Commission Communication that 'required' Member States to report to the Commission, or Case C-303/90 *French Republic v Commission of the European Communities* [1991] ECR I-5315. See for a more detailed discussion of these cases, J Scott, 'Post-Legislative Guidance as a Challenge for European Administrative Law' (2011) 48 *Common Market Law Review* 329, 339–41.

[303] In the landmark *Grimaldi* case, the Court first established whether the recommendation it was confronted with—a Commission recommendation laying down a European schedule for occupational diseases—was a 'true recommendation, that is to say a measure which, even as regards the persons to whom they are addressed, are not intended to produce binding effects', see Case C-322/88 *Salvatore Grimaldi v Fonds des maladies professionnelles* [1989] ECR 04407, para 16.

[304] For the concept of 'unidentified legal objects', see above chapter 3, section I.C.ii.

[305] J Scott, 'In Legal Limbo' (n 295) 329.

[306] Art 29(1b) GFL.

[307] ibid.

[308] Art 29(1a) GFL.

[309] ibid.

[310] See for instance Case T-326/99 *Nancy Fern Olivieri v Commission* (n 293); Case T-311/06 *FMC Chemical and Arysta Lifesciences v EFSA* [2008] ECR II-00088*.

authorisation decision'.[311] The reasoning should however be distinct for EFSA's nano guidance. On the one hand, it is difficult to see the guidance document as a mere preparatory act. The adoption of the guidance concludes an administrative procedure. No further act, such as an implementing act by the Commission, will necessarily follow. On the other hand, precisely because there may not be a subsequent Commission decision 'rubber-stamping'[312] EFSA's guidelines, it is also more difficult to review the legality of the document indirectly[313] by treating it as an 'essential procedural requirement' of the Commission decision.[314]

Nevertheless, it seems unlikely that the Court would consider EFSA's guidance as an act producing legal effects vis-a-vis third parties. First, in *Schering-Plough* the then Court of First Instance broadened its argument to refuse the admissibility of an agency measure, in the context of the European Medicines Agency, by looking more widely at the Agency's overall mandate in its founding regulation, which merely provided for the competence to give 'scientific *advice*' (emphasis added).[315] The Court then used a perilous circular reasoning. It concluded that the action for annulment cannot be directed against the European Medicines Agency because of its strict advisory function and must instead be addressed to the Commission.[316] Such argumentation would be transferrable to EFSA's nano guidance, since the General Food Law also restricts EFSA's mission to the provision of 'scientific *advice* and scientific and technical *support* for the Community's legislation and policies' (emphasis added).[317] Any de facto legal effects EFSA's acts might have would be shielded behind its formal mandate of a source of knowledge, while, in practice, the Agency has assumed regulatory functions.

Thirdly, while a guidance document of an EU agency has not yet been challenged before the EU courts, in the case law on Commission guidance documents, the EU courts have been largely reluctant to acknowledge legal effects of the latter. In *Chemische Fabrik Kreussler*,[318] for example, the Court stated, without further ado, that a guidance document adopted by DG Enterprise on the implementation of the directive on medical devices 'cannot be of a legally binding nature or enforceable against individuals' as it 'is not one of the legal acts of the European

[311] Case T-326/99 *Nancy Fern Olivieri v Commission* (n 293), para 53. The Court referred to its *IBM* judgment, pursuant to which preparatory acts are unable to affect the legal position of an applicant, see Case T-326/99 *Nancy Fern Olivieri v Commission* (n 293) para 51; Case C-60/81 *International Business Machines Cooperation v Commission* (n 293) para 12. See also Case T-311/06 *FMC Chemical and Arysta Lifesciences v EFSA* (n 305).

[312] Dehousse used the term 'rubber-stamped' in the context of scientific opinions of the European Medicines Agency, see R Dehousse, 'Delegation of Powers in the European Union: The Need for a Multi-principals Model' (2008) 31 *West European Politics* 789, 799.

[313] Case T-123/00 *Dr. Karl Thomae GmbH v Commission of the European Communities* [2002] ECR II-5193.

[314] Joint Cases T-74/00, 76, 83, 85, 132, 137, 141 *Artegodan GmbH and Others v Commission of the European Communities* [2002] ECR II-4945, para 197.

[315] Case T-133/03 *Schering-Plough Ltd v Commission and EMEA* [2008] not published, para 18.

[316] ibid para 23.

[317] Art 22(2) GFL.

[318] See above chapter 3, section I.C.ii.

Union referred to in Article 288 TFEU'.[319] The challenge would be to prove that EFSA's nano guidance was de facto intended to produce legal effects and furthermore affects the legal position of the food industry. In principle, this means that the guidance must introduce a new obligation or add to the legal text.[320] Again, the wording of the measure is decisive.[321] EFSA's nano guidance however states that 'the test requirements stipulated in current EFSA guidance documents … *should* be applied for [engineered nanomaterials] according to its intended use and *should* be followed' (emphasis added).[322] The choice of the word 'should' seems to indicate that EFSA 'recommends' that regulatees apply the guidance, instead of 'requiring' them to do so by choosing the word 'shall' or 'must'. This is supported by the Commission's request to draft the scientific opinion, which restricts the Agency's mandate to the provision of 'practical recommendations'.[323]

Both EFSA's nano guidance and the Commission's recommendation are thus unlikely to be admissible before the EU courts. Overall, this leaves one to wonder how effective the EU courts' 'substantive approach' to the determination of legal effects really is, given the opportunity it allowed two measures, which were clearly shown to impact on the (legal) interests of affected actors, to escape the possibility of a judicial review.

b. Legal Standing as a First Hurdle

Hurdles to an effective review also exist for reviewable acts. The first limitation concerns the issue of the restricted standing of natural or legal persons before the EU courts which is well-known and therefore only briefly touched upon here.[324] Individuals who want to challenge a legislative act in the form of a generally applicable regulation need to prove their direct and individual concern.[325] In line with the restrictive *Plaumann* doctrine,[326] it is therefore virtually impossible for an NGO or food producer to claim individual concern in the hypothetical case of a challenge of the Novel Food and Food Additives Regulations.[327]

[319] Case C-308/11 *Chemische Fabrik Kreussler & Co. GmbH v Sunstar Deutschland GmbH* [2012] not published, para 23.

[320] See for an analysis of Cases C-366/88 *French Republic v Commission of the European Communities* [1990] ECR I-03571, para 23; C-303/90 *France v Commission* (n 297) para 24 and C-325/91 *French Republic v Commission of the European Communities* (n 297) para 14; J Scott, 'In Legal Limbo' (n 295).

[321] J Scott, 'In Legal Limbo' (n 295) 340.

[322] European Food Safety Authority, 'Scientific Opinion' (n 109) 2140.

[323] ibid.

[324] See for an overview, HCH Hofmann et al, *EU Administrative Law and Policy* (n 217) 812ff.

[325] According to Art 263(4) TFEU, 'any natural or legal person may … institute proceedings against an act addressed to that person or which is of direct and individual concern to them, and against a regulatory act which is of direct concern to them and does not entail implementing measures'.

[326] Case C-25/62 *Plaumann & Co. v Commission of the European Economic Community* [1963] ECR 00095.

[327] The direct action would have to be brought by a Member State, the Commission, European Parliament or Council, or indirectly by the individual through a preliminary reference under Art 267 TFEU.

However, the two implementing acts adopted under the FCM Regulation should follow the more flexible variant of judicial review under Article 263(4) TFEU,[328] in line with the Court of Justice's definition of 'regulatory act'.[329] Whether the conditions of direct concern and the absence of implementing measures would be fulfilled, however, is questionable. For instance, it may be doubted whether the two Commission Regulations at issue, which establish specific requirements for the marketing of intelligent packaging and plastic packaging respectively, would be considered to directly affect the legal situation of a producer of nanoform substances or whether it is rather the subsequent Commission decision that, based on these requirements, adds or removes substances from the positive list.[330]

c. Intensity of Review as a Second Hurdle

The second limitation refers to the extent to which the EU courts are willing to review acts (a) based on the factual findings made by the EU institutions, including their collection of knowledge, (b) based on (the absence of) affected actors' administrative participation in the regulatory process and (c) based on potential infringements of self-imposed procedures established for these purposes, such as the 2009 Impact Assessment Guidelines or the Commission's minimum consultation standards.

... Based on the Factual Findings of the EU Institutions, Including Their Collection of Knowledge

Since its early case law, the Court of Justice has stressed that it would limit its review of factual findings and complex assessments in order to not substitute its own judgment with that of the decision maker. Instead, the Court would intervene only in cases of a 'manifest error'.[331] While this criterion of a manifest

[328] For further discussion, see J Bast, 'New Categories of Acts After the Lisbon Reform: Dynamics of Parliamentarization in EU Law' (2012) 49 *Common Market Law Review* 885; S Peers and M Costa, 'Court of Justice of the European Union (General Chamber), Judicial Review of EU Acts After the Treaty of Lisbon; Order of 6 September 2011, Case T-18/10 Inuit Tapiriit Kanatami and Others v Commission & Judgment of 25 October 2011, Case T-262/10 Microban v Commission' (2012) 8 *European Constitutional Law Review* 82.

[329] In *Inuit*, the General Court clarified that a 'regulatory act' 'must be understood as covering all acts of general application apart from legislative acts', see Case T-18/10 *Inuit Tapiriit Kanatami and Others v European Parliament and Council of the European Union* [2011] ECR II-5599, para 56. The Court of Justice confirmed the General Court's definition in Case C-583/11 P *Inuit Tapiriit Kanatami and Others v Parliament and Council* [2013] not published.

[330] *cf* Case T-262/10 *Microban International Ltd and Microban (Europe) Ltd v European Commission* [2011] ECR II-07697.

[331] eg Case C-57/72 *Westzucker GmbH v Einfuhr- und Vorratsstelle für Zucker* [1973] ECR 321. See also P Craig, *EU Administrative Law*, Collected Courses of the Academy of European Law XVI/1, 2nd edn (Oxford, Oxford University Press, 2012) 408.

error has persisted over time, the General Court in particular has been applying the test with greater intensity more recently.[332] In the area of risk regulation, this shift became most apparent in *Pfizer*.[333] In this case, the then Court of First Instance, by referring to the importance of procedural guarantees, most notably the duty to examine carefully and impartially all relevant aspects of an individual case,[334] engaged in a thorough procedural review, first, of the factual basis of the measure and, then, of the EU institutions' assessment thereof.[335] This thorough scrutiny has, however, not been conducted by the EU courts in a consistent manner. While in some later cases the court reverted again to a more deferential approach,[336] in others it went into remarkable detail as to how information was being generated, including by the Parliament and Council.[337] Before the EU courts, the EU regulator may thus be asked to justify itself by exposing the information basis of its choices. This function of the Court is of great interest for the two Regulations under scrutiny in this chapter, for which neither the Commission nor Council and Parliament conducted impact assessments of their nano-specific amendments. Yet, the standard of judicial review that the EU courts apply differs from case to case.[338] This variation is regrettable, not least due to its lack of a principled basis.[339]

... Based on (the Absence of) Societal Actors' Administrative Participation in the Regulatory Process

In the past, the EU courts have consistently denied a general consultation right for affected societal actors.[340] Where participation rights are not explicitly granted in the Treaties or in secondary legislation, it is at the discretion of the EU institutions to open the door to administrative participation in their regulatory process.

[332] P Craig, *EU Administrative Law* (n 326) 416.

[333] Case T-13/99 *Pfizer Animal Health SA v Council of the European Union* [2002] ECR II-3305.

[334] ibid para 171. The Court refers here to the ECJ judgment in Case C-269/90 *Technische Universität München v Hauptzollamt München-Mitte* [1991] ECR I-5469, para 14.

[335] See for a discussion, P Craig, *EU Administrative Law* (n 326) 417–19.

[336] See eg Case C-120/99 *Italian Republic v Council of the European Union* [2001] ECR I-7997; Joined Cases C-27/00 and Joined Cases C-27/00 and C-122/00 *The Queen v Secretary of State for the Environment, Transport and the Regions, ex parte Omega Air Ltd and Omega Air Ltd, Aero Engines Ireland Ltd and Omega Aviation Services Ltd v Irish Aviation Authority* [2002] ECR I-2569; Case C-14/01 *Molkerei Wagenfeld Karl Niemann GmbH & Co. KG v Bezirksregierung Hannover* [2003] ECR I-2279.

[337] See eg Case-343/09 *Afton Chemical Ltd v Secretary of State for Transport* [2010] ECR I-7027.

[338] See eg M Lee, *EU Environmental Law, Governance and Decision-Making*, Modern Studies in European Law vol 43, 2nd edn (Oxford, Hart Publishing, 2014) 41.

[339] P Craig, *EU Administrative Law* (n 326) 437; AH Türk, 'Oversight of Administrative Rule-Making: Judicial Review' (2013) 19 *European Law Journal* (2013) 126, 140.

[340] P Craig, *EU Administrative Law* (n 326) 292. The leading authority is the *Atlanta* case, Case C-104/97 P *Atlanta AG and Others v Commission of the European Communities and Council of the European Union* [1999] ECR I-6983.

... Based on Potential Infringements of Self-imposed Procedures by the EU Institutions

Finally, one might wonder whether the adoption of the post-'governance debate' self-imposed procedures, on the one hand, facilitated the Court's review of knowledge collected by the EU institutions and, on the other, enhanced the meaningful participation of affected actors in their decision-making process. In other words, have procedures, such as the impact assessment procedure and the Commission's minimum consultation standards, narrowed the broad discretion of the EU regulator?

Signs have surfaced in the case law that the EU courts are increasingly interested in these self-imposed rules.[341] Already in *Pfizer*, in the context of the Commission's guidelines on the application of the precautionary principle, the then Court of First Instance remarked that:

> [T]he Community institutions may lay down for themselves guidelines for the exercise of their discretionary powers by way of measures not provided for in Article 189 of the EC Treaty [now Article 288 TFEU], ... In such circumstances, the Community judicature ascertains, applying the principle of equal treatment, whether the disputed measure is consistent with the guidelines that the institutions have laid down for themselves by adopting and publishing such communications.[342]

Alemanno deduces that 'the EC courts seem increasingly willing to consider the Commission under a duty to act in a consistent and non-arbitrary manner, which entails a duty to apply the rules that it has established for itself'.[343] Following this logic, the adherence to the Commission's self-imposed requirement to conduct an impact assessment or to stick to its minimum consultation standards should be considered by the EU courts as an essential procedural requirement in an act's adoption process, non-compliance with which constitutes an infringement of the latter and, by implication, a ground for judicial review under Article 263 TFEU.[344] Yet, to what extent is this really the case?

The degree to which the impact assessment guidelines or consultation standards could indeed be self-binding upon the Commission seems to depend first and foremost on the nature of these rules, especially their clarity and room for institutional discretion.[345] For the two implementing acts under the FCM Regulation, the first hurdle is the 2009 Impact Assessment Guidelines' (and hence the consultation

[341] A Alemanno, 'The Better Regulation Initiative at the Judicial Gate: A Trojan Horse within the Commission's Walls or the Way Forward?' (2009) 15 *European Law Journal* 382, 394; A Meuwese, *Impact Assessment in EU Law-Making* (n 177) 157.

[342] See Case T-13/99 *Pfizer Animal Health v Council* (n 328) para 119.

[343] A Alemanno, 'The Better Regulation Initiative at the Judicial Gate' (n 336) 394. See also a review of competition law and state aid cases by O Ştefan, *Soft Law in Court*, European Monographs no 81 (Alphen aan den Rijn, Wolters Kluwer Law International, 2013) 168.

[344] A Alemanno, 'The Better Regulation Initiative at the Judicial Gate' (n 336) 394.

[345] ibid 393.

standards') ambiguous scope of application (what is a 'significant impact'?). But even when the 2009 Impact Assessment Guidelines are clearly applicable, as they were in the revision of the Novel Food and Food Additives Regulations, they are vague in their requirements, as the determination of scope and level of knowledge collection, stakeholder consultation and the consequent quantification of impacts rests largely at the discretion of the Commission due to the underlying principle of 'proportionate level of analysis'.[346] Similarly, the minimum consultation standards hardly lay down concrete rules: 'all necessary information' needs to be communicated 'where relevant' or 'where applicable' to the participants, the Commission should ensure that 'relevant parties have an opportunity to express their opinions' and that 'adequate awareness-raising publicity' is given.[347] It thus appears that much discretion is left to the Commission to determine the proportionality, adequateness, relevance, applicability or necessity of its self-imposed rules on a case-by-case basis.[348] Similarly, the Council and Parliament are only required, pursuant to their respective guidelines, to conduct their own impact assessment when they introduce a 'substantial amendment', a concept which is not further defined.

In order to review the EU institutions' compliance with their self-imposed procedures, the court would hence need to plunge into the factual findings and related assessments of the Commission (and Parliament and Council) and define, not only the 'significant impact' trigger for implementing acts, but also the underlying principles applied to the procedures, such as a 'proportionate level of analysis' and terms including 'adequate feedback' and 'all necessary information' on a case-by-case basis. In view of the Court's 'manifest error' approach, this seems unlikely. One might therefore wonder whether these guidelines are indeed limiting the discretion left to the EU institutions in their fact-finding process/assessment and in conducting their public consultations—at least before the EU courts. To challenge the two implementing acts because no impact assessment (and public consultation) was performed or to challenge the Novel Food Regulation on the ground that the eight-week period fell into a major holiday period is therefore extremely difficult. Also, the fact that the nano provisions were not subject to an impact assessment in the revision processes of the Novel Food and Food Additives Regulations hardly seems to be sufficient to establish a ground for review.

[346] See above section III.A.i.a.

[347] 'Towards a reinforced culture of consultation and dialogue' COM (2002) 704 final (n 216) 21 and 22.

[348] In fact, the Commission even mentions in its minimum consultation standards that 'a situation must be avoided in which a Commission proposal could be challenged in the Court on the grounds of alleged lack of consultation of interested parties. Such an over-legalistic approach would be incompatible with the need for timely delivery of policy', see 'Towards a reinforced culture of consultation and dialogue' COM (2002) 704 final (n 216) 10.

The situation seems different where the Commission completely omits either the impact assessment or public consultation in the drafting of legislative acts. A first indication of this direction was given by Advocate General Sharpston in *Spain v Council*.[349] In this case, Spain attempted to annul Council Regulation 864/2003 that established a new cotton support system, inter alia, on the basis that the Commission and Council had failed to take into account labour costs, resulting in the unprofitability of cotton production in Spain and thus in a disproportionate outcome of the regulation. An impact assessment had not been performed by the Commission. In her analysis, AG Sharpston established a breach of the principle of proportionality based on two aspects, one of them being the missing impact assessment: 'In the absence of any impact study, certain choices made by the Commission and the Council appear arbitrary'.[350] The Court followed the AG's conclusions regarding the breach of the principle of proportionality without, however, mentioning the absence of the impact assessment.

In the subsequent *Vodafone* case,[351] the Court explicitly considered the impact assessment as part of its proportionality analysis. The operators of public mobile telephone networks indirectly challenged the validity of Roaming Regulation 717/2007 in a preliminary reference. One of the main arguments of the plaintiffs was a breach of the principle of proportionality, as the Regulation imposes not only a ceiling for wholesale charges per minute but also for retail charges and that it imposes an obligation to provide information about those charges to roaming customers. In its judgment, the Court rejected the argument as unfounded based on the fact that the Commission conducted a prior impact assessment in which it evaluated the effects of the various available options.[352]

There are two remarks that may be made on this case law. First, in *Vodafone*, the Court did not question the accuracy of the impact assessment's contents or analyse the procedure according to which the assessment was performed. This confirms the suspicion that the Court remains wary of interfering with the Commission's discretion in conducting 'complex assessments', including impact assessments. Indeed, the Court did not touch upon the interpretation of the principle of a 'proportionate level of analysis'. Secondly, so far the Court seems reluctant to embrace the impact assessment framework as a formal (essential) procedural requirement in the legislative process, such as under the duty to give

[349] Case C-310/04 *Kingdom of Spain v Council of the European Union* [2006] ECR I-7285, Opinion of AG Sharpston.

[350] ibid para 94.

[351] Case C-58/8 *The Queen, on the application of Vodafone Ltd v Secretary of State for Business, Enterprise and Regulatory Reform* [2010] ECR I-4999.

[352] ibid para 55. In a similar vein, the ECJ used the impact assessment in establishing the absence of a breach of the proportionality principle in *Luxembourg v Parliament and Council*, Case C-176/09 *Grand Duchy of Luxembourg v European Parliament and Council of the European Union* [2011] ECR I-3727, paras 62–72.

reasons or impartial evaluation,[353] but instead considers its existence (or absence) as an element of the proportionality analysis.[354]

In view of the preceding discussion it is, therefore, improbable that the EU institutions would be legally held to account by the EU courts for the way they (1) have collected knowledge and (2) have included affected societal actors in the legislative procedure—as long as *an* impact assessment is available and *a* public consultation was performed. The hesitant approach of the EU courts leaves the EU regulator with a broad discretion, enabling political choices and incomplete analyses to hide behind the vague notion of 'complex assessments'.

iii. Administrative Accountability: Making Way for the EU Ombudsman

In view of the gap in legal accountability, the administrative forum, in particular the European Ombudsman, emerges as an important (potential) remedy. The Ombudsman investigates cases of maladministration which 'occur if an institution fails to act in accordance with the law, fails to respect the principles of good administration, or violates human rights'.[355] On the one hand, the Ombudsman could hence assume an important function in compensating for the lack of judicial review of non-binding acts or indeed 'unidentified legal objects'. On the other hand, the Ombudsman's understanding of maladministration seems broad enough also to embrace a closer scrutiny of the EU institutions' compliance with self-imposed rules, such as the impact assessment procedure or the Commission's minimum consultation standards.

[353] In *Spain v Council*, despite the absence of an impact assessment AG Sharpston could not find a breach of the duty to give reasons, since, as she argued, 'it is settled case-law that the extent of the requirement to state reasons depends on the nature of the measure in question and … in the case of measures intended to have general application the preamble may be limited to indicating the general situation which led to its adoption, on the one hand, and the general objectives which it is intended to achieve, on the other. Moreover, if the contested measure clearly discloses the essential objective pursued by the institution, it would be excessive to require a specific statement of reasons for the various technical choices made'. The explanations given in the preamble were, in her opinion, sufficient to satisfy the administrative duty to give reasons. This refutes arguments put forward in the literature that 'impact assessments at least make laws more accountable by reinforcing the duty to give reasons', see P Popelier, 'Governance and Better Regulation: Dealing with the Legitimacy Paradox' (2011) 17 *European Public Law* 555, 562.

[354] Following this logic, Lenaerts argued that the Court in *Vodafone* 'applie[d] the principle of proportionality in a procedural fashion. Instead of second-guessing the merits of the substantive choices made by the EU legislator, the ECJ preferred to make sure that lawmakers had done their work properly', see K Lenearts, 'The European Court of Justice and Process-oriented Review' (2012) College of Europe Research Paper in Law 01/2012, 7.

[355] See www.ombudsman.europa.eu/media/en/default.htm#hl1. To establish what the Ombudsman captures under the notion of 'good administration', it adopted the *European Code of Good Administrative Behaviour* in 2001. This Code, according to the Ombudsman, shall 'help citizens to know what administrative standards they are entitled to expect from the EU institutions. It also serves as a useful guide for civil servants in their relations with the public. By making the principle of good administration more concrete, the Code helps to encourage the highest standards of administration', European Ombudsman, *The European Code of Good Administrative Behaviour* (2013) 4 www.ombudsman.europa.eu/resources/code.faces#/page/1.

a. Non-Compliance with Self-Imposed Rules as 'Maladministration'

In previous cases, the EU Ombudsman has considered failures to comply with the Commission's minimum consultation standards and Impact Assessment Guidelines as 'maladministration' and thus within the scope of its investigative mandate. An interesting complaint was lodged to the Ombudsman in this respect in 2006. In this case, the complainant alleged that, in the adoption process of the draft Regulation on tariffs for international roaming services (the same Regulation that was later at stake in the above-discussed *Vodafone* case), the Commission failed to comply, first, with its own consultation standards and, secondly, with its own Impact Assessment Guidelines.[356] Above it was concluded that, due to the vague formulation of these self-imposed rules, it is unlikely that the Court would consider them to significantly limit the Commission's discretion in collecting knowledge and involving affected actors in the regulatory process. Also, the Ombudsman clarified in the preliminary remarks to its decision that it would follow the Court's 'manifest error' test and, therefore, would refrain from engaging in any substantive review of the Commission's factual findings and assessment thereof.[357] Thereafter, however, unlike the Court, the Ombudsman engaged in a careful comparison of the Commission's self-imposed rules with its conduct in the case concerned. Among other things, the complainant submitted that the consultation period was considerably below the then eight weeks laid down in the minimum standards. The Commission argued that since an earlier survey had been sent to 'interested parties', a full public consultation had no longer been necessary. The Ombudsman, however, was sceptical; it was 'not convinced that all interested parties had the opportunity to express their views'[358] and therefore found that there was a case of maladministration.

As regards the breach of the Commission's Impact Assessment Guidelines, the complainant alleged that the impact assessment of the Commission was 'incomplete' as it did not cover certain issues, such as the 'implications arising from a decision to depart from the flexibility afforded to NRAs [National Regulatory Authorities]'. The Commission justified its scope of analysis with the fact that 'the Impact Assessment Guidelines do not require any 'minimum list' for the scope of an Impact Assessment'. In other words, the Commission relied on the Guidelines' principle of a 'proportionate level of analysis'. While, so far, the EU courts have refrained from touching this principle, the Ombudsman stressed that it was aware of the problems caused by the wide discretion that the principle concedes to the Commission in the effective operation of the impact assessment framework. However, it ultimately concluded that 'it does not appear that the approach used by the Commission is manifestly incorrect'. The Ombudsman eventually found

356 European Ombudsman Decision 3617/2006/JF of 3 July 2008, para 1.1.
357 ibid para 1.2.
358 ibid.

no instance of maladministration. What does this decision tell us? Could the producer of a food additive in nanoform bring to the Ombudsman a complaint that the Commission's impact assessment did not address the implications arising from a separate authorisation requirement for 'changes in particle size'? The answer is most likely 'no'. Although the Ombudsman went into far more detail as to the execution of the impact assessment than the Court, it was ultimately hesitant to interfere with the Commission's discretion conceded by the principle of a 'proportionate level of analysis'.

b. A Remedy to the Lack of Judicial Review? From Ombudsmanian Activism and Firm Bites of a Toothless Tiger

Recourse to the EU Ombudsman also constitutes a potential remedy for the absence of judicial review for non-binding measures and their adoption processes. In contrast to the EU courts, the Ombudsman scrutinises the administration's behaviour independent of whether it leads to a binding or non-binding act. There is consequently no 'reviewable act' gatekeeper. Also, while access to the EU courts is highly restricted, especially for individuals, every citizen residing in an EU Member State could complain to the Ombudsman.[359]

In recent years the Ombudsman has started to pay close attention to the internal procedures of EU agencies, including EFSA's administration. The first case that the Ombudsman opened against EFSA in May 2010 was brought by a German NGO. The case arose when the head of EFSA's GMO Unit moved to a Swiss biotechnology company to take up the post of Head of Biotech Regulatory Affairs, less than two months after her departure from the Agency.[360] The Ombudsman was asked to investigate whether EFSA had properly handled the potential conflict of interest arising from the move of the former staff member.[361] To this end, the Ombudsman not only scrutinised the operation of procedures set in place by EFSA to avoid 'revolving door' practices in this case, but the Ombudsman also analysed the very adequacy of these procedures. In its draft recommendations to EFSA, the Ombudsman demanded a strengthening of the Agency's rules on conflicts of interests. The Ombudsman's investigation of EFSA attracted quite some media attention.[362] As a result, the European Parliament suspended the approval of the Agency's budget for 2010, among other reasons, for reasons of conflict of

[359] See www.ombudsman.europa.eu/media/en/default.htm. See also EM Busuioc, *European Agencies: Law and Practices of Accountability*, Oxford Studies in European law (Oxford, Oxford University Press, 2013) 223.

[360] European Ombudsman, Draft Recommendation 0775/2010/ANA of 7 December 2011, para 2.

[361] ibid para 42.

[362] See, for instance, EU Observer, 'EU food agency criticised over GMO lobbying' *EU Observer* (Brussels, 14 December 2011) https://euobserver.com/tickers/114634.

interest (see also section III.B.ii.a on political accountability).[363] The findings of the Ombudsman thus served as the basis for a further accountability forum, the European Parliament, to exercise its budgetary control powers. In the aftermath of the Ombudsman's draft recommendations (and the subsequent 'noise' by the political forum and the Court of Auditors) EFSA adopted, among other rules, new rules on independence.[364] This shows that the Ombudsman has the potential to constitute an important accountability forum with a de facto capacity to impose consequences on the regulator's conduct. Despite its image as a toothless tiger, the Ombudsman may indeed be capable of taking firm bites.

In view of this analysis, the Ombudsman could play a role in reviewing the adoption process of non-binding regulation or 'unidentified legal objects', such as EFSA's nano guidance, taking as a standard general administrative principles, but also their compliance with EFSA's own procedural rules. What is more, the 2010 'revolving doors' case shows that the Ombudsman is willing to function as a platform for debate on the adequacy of rules established by EU agencies and to bring these issues up for discussion in further accountability fora. By analogy, the Ombudsman could assess (and compare) further trends of proceduralisation in EU agencies, such as the adoption of consultation standards or the workflow in the adoption of scientific opinions. So far, however, these procedures have not been subject to the Ombudsman's investigation.

iv. Social Accountability: A Transparent Regulatory Process?

Social accountability refers to affected actors' ex post scrutiny over regulatory conduct. A prerequisite for this scrutiny is the existence of a transparent regulatory process.[365] Two elements were identified in chapter three to foster transparency: access to documents and reason giving. A further condition for a transparent regulatory process is arguably an institution's language regime, that is, whether it requires the regulatory measure and its preparatory documents to be translated into the official languages of the EU. Finally, the application and operation of the procedures for pooling knowledge were found to further increase (or decrease) transparency. The repeated emptiness of these procedures in practice[366] is hence problematic. The elements of access to documents (below section a), reason giving (below section b) and the availability of regulatory output in the official languages of the EU (below section c), as well as their applicability to the different regulatory measures, are analysed in turn.

[363] 'Resolution of 10 May 2012 on discharge in respect of the implementation of the budget of the European Union Agencies for the financial year 2010' (n 285) paras 52–60.

[364] European Ombudsman, Decision 0775/2010/ANA of 23 May 2013, para 74.

[365] See above chapter 3, section II.B.iii.d.

[366] See above section III.A.i.c.

a. Access to Documents

Regulation 1049/2001 on public access to documents applies to documents held by the European Parliament, Council and Commission.[367] By implication, EU agencies, including EFSA, are not covered by its scope. However, the Regulation recommends in its Recitals that 'all agencies established by the institutions should apply the principles laid down in this Regulation'.[368] Pursuant to the General Food Law, EFSA's Management Board shall thus adopt a respective implementing decision,[369] which the Board did in 2003.[370] Thus, affected actors are able to request access to documents held by the EU institutions and EFSA for all regulatory measures that were identified above in section II.[371]

However, only those documents 'drawn up or received in the course of procedures for the adoption of acts which are legally binding' must, according to Regulation 1049/2001, also be made directly accessible, meaning that these documents should be readily available in electronic form or through a register.[372] There is therefore no need to actively request these documents. By inference, documents that were drawn up or received in the drafting of non-binding acts, such as the Commission's recommended nano definition, need to be directly accessible only 'where possible'.[373] This means that affected actors are required to request documents explicitly, which arguably requires a deep knowledge of the EU's decision-making process.[374] In practice, this might constitute a real hurdle to effective access to documents.

To allow for the direct access to documents drawn up in comitology, an online 'Comitology Register' was established in 2003.[375] When examining the 'directly accessible documents' for the two implementing acts adopted under the FCM Regulation, however, a further problem arises. While all documentation is available, these documents are not necessarily informative. For instance, from a summary record of the meeting of the Standing Committee on the Food Chain and Animal Health (SCFCAH), at which the draft regulation on intelligent packaging was discussed, the reader only gets to know that 'the Standing Committee voted

[367] Regulation of the European Parliament and of the Council (EC) 1049/2001 of 30 May 2001 regarding public access to European Parliament, Council and Commission documents [2001] OJ L145/43, Art 1(a).

[368] ibid Recital 8.

[369] Art 41 GFL.

[370] European Food Safety Authority, 'Decision concerning Access to Documents' (Decision of Management Board, MB 16.09.2003). Art 7 adopted pursuant to Art 41 GFL.

[371] Subject, of course, to the exceptions in Regulation 1049/2001 (n 362) Art 4.

[372] Regulation 1049/2001 (n 362) Art 12(2).

[373] ibid Art 12(3).

[374] See also M Lee, *EU Environmental Law* (n 333) 105.

[375] Council Decision 1999/468/EC (n 274) Art 7(5) and Regulation (EC) 182/2011 (n 274) Art 10(5). See also GJ Brandsma, D Curtin and A Meijer, 'How Transparent are EU "Comitology" Committees in Practice?' (2008) 14 *European Law Journal* 819, 826. The documents to be made available in the register are now listed in Regulation (EC) 182/2011 (n 274) Art 10(1).

in favour of the draft Regulation on active and intelligent materials'[376] but not the reasons for the favourable vote.[377] Similar reservations arise with regard to the draft regulation on plastics. The minutes of the Standing Committee note that national representatives had comments on a first draft of this measure.[378] Yet, this first draft[379] is not available in the Register but can be requested via Regulation 1049/2001.[380] Comparing this first draft to the final regulation, it becomes clear that the national representatives had indeed demanded a more stringent approach towards substances in nanoform. These discussions, however, are not reflected in the minutes of the Standing Committee.[381] The distinction between the documents' formal availability and their actual content—or the 'reality of access'—is therefore problematic.[382]

b. Reason Giving

According to Article 296 TFEU, 'legal acts shall state the reasons on which they are based'. 'Legal acts', according to Craig and de Búrca, do not only refer to 'administrative decisions' but to 'all legal acts, including legislative, delegated, and implementing acts'.[383] However, are acts of EU institutions and agencies that are of non-binding or even unidentified legal nature also subject to the duty to state reasons? This question has attracted little attention so far.[384] It relates, however, back to the rationale of the duty to state reasons, whether it is mainly aimed at facilitating the judicial review of 'reviewable acts'[385] or whether it has the further, and broader, function of ensuring the transparency of the regulatory process. Following the latter logic, non-binding acts, which carry important practical

[376] European Commission, 'Summary Record of the Standing Committee on the Food Chain and Animal Health, Section Toxicological Safety of the Food Chain' (SANCO—D1 (2009)410249, 12 February 2009) para 2.

[377] This observation is also reflected in a much more detailed research on the transparency of comitology committees, see GJ Brandsma et al, 'How Transparent are EU "Comitology" Committees in Practice?' (n 370) 832.

[378] European Commission, 'Summary Record of the Standing Committee on the Food Chain and Animal Health, Section Toxicological Safety of the Food Chain' (SANCO—D1(2009)D/411905, 8 December 2009) para 3.

[379] ibid.

[380] The Commission's first draft does not exclude nanoplastics from the scope of the exemption of the general authorisation requirement. The received document (no: SANCO//2009 (POOL/E3/2009/xxxx/xxx-EN.doc)) is on file with the author.

[381] 'Summary Record of the Standing Committee on the Food Chain and Animal Health, Section Toxicological Safety of the Food Chain' (n 373) para 3.

[382] P Craig, *EU Administrative Law* (n 326) 362.

[383] P Craig and G De Búrca, *EU Law: Texts, Cases and Materials*, 5th edn (Oxford, Oxford University Press, 2011) 522 and 523.

[384] An exception is Linda Senden, see L Senden, *Soft Law in European Community Law: Its Relationship to Legislation* (Nijmegen, Wolf Legal Publishers, 2003) 95.

[385] According to Paul Craig, the duty to state reasons is a process right, see P Craig, *EU Administrative Law* (n 326) 340.

effects for affected societal actors, such as EFSA's guidance document, should also state the reasons on which they are based.

A further factor compromising the transparency-generating effect of reason giving is arguably the narrow scope of this duty. When discussing the legal accountability of legislative acts, it was noted that the absence of an impact assessment has so far not resulted in a breach of the duty to state reasons. As AG Sharpston explained in the above-noted *Spain v Council* case, 'it is settled case-law that the extent of the requirement to state reasons depends on the nature of the measure in question and … in the case of measures intended to have general application the preamble may be limited to indicating the general situation which led to its adoption, on the one hand, and the general objectives which it is intended to achieve, on the other'.[386] The brief explanations given in the preamble were therefore, in her opinion, sufficient to satisfy the duty to give reasons.

c. Language Regime

Pursuant to Article 297 TFEU, legislative acts[387] and non-legislative acts in the form of regulations, directives and decisions[388] must be published in the Official Journal of the EU. The Official Journal, in turn, is translated into the official languages of the Union.[389] This means that legislative acts and the two implementing acts adopted under the FCM Regulation are available in all languages. Also, the Commission's recommendation for a definition of nanomaterial, while not explicitly required by Article 297 TFEU, was published in the L-series of the Official Journal and has been translated accordingly.[390] Agency acts, on the contrary, are not published in the Official Journal. While the General Food Law requires EFSA to publish its scientific outputs,[391] and the Agency launched the 'EFSA Journal' for this purpose,[392] the Journal is not translated. Affected actors, who are unable to read English, will effectively not be able to access the nano guidance. Another problem arises with regard to the availability of preparatory documents drawn up in the regulatory process, including impact assessments or indeed public consultations. All these documents are generally only available in English.[393] This

[386] Case C-310/04 *Spain v Council*, Opinion of AG Sharpston (n 344) para 49.

[387] Art 297(1) TFEU.

[388] Art 297(2) TFEU.

[389] Council Regulation (EEC) 1 of 15 April 1958 determining the languages to be used by the European Economic Community [1958] OJ Series I Volume 1952-1958/59, Art 5.

[390] Senden confirmed that when '[l]ooking at institutional practice, however, the Commission often publishes interpretative and decisional acts in the OJ', see L Senden, 'Soft Post-Legislative Rulemaking: A Time for More Stringent Control' (2013) 19 *European Law Journal* 57, 68.

[391] Art 38(1)(f) GFL.

[392] See www.efsa.europa.eu/fr/efsajournal/about.htm.

[393] See for more general observations, B Kohler-Koch, 'Civil Society Participation: More Democracy or Pluralisation of the European Lobby?' in B Kohler-Koch and C Quittkat (eds), *De-Mystification of Participatory Democracy: EU Governance and Civil Society* (n 237) 179. This point has also already

may not only render it more difficult for certain affected actors to scrutinise the adoption process ex post, it may also prevent them from actively participating in the process, contributing to the imbalances in representation described in section III.B.ii.c.

v. Synthesis: Holding the EU Regulator to Account

The aim of this section was to gain a clear picture of how the identified accountability mechanisms apply and operate in practice. The analysis revealed that ex post scrutiny of executive rule making is clearly restricted. The Parliament uses its supervisory powers in practice only for systemic deficiencies or highly politicised issues. The Parliament did not inquire into (the adoption processes of) any of the regulatory options adopted by the EU executive. At the same time, non-binding regulation is generally barred from judicial review, except where it can be demonstrated that these measures are intended to produce legal effects. EFSA's guidance document and the Commission's recommendation for a definition of nanomaterial were found unlikely to be considered 'reviewable acts', most notably due to their cautious wording. The result is paradoxical. While the regulatee will most likely be unsuccessful in legally challenging the contents of EFSA's guidance document, the very same document might have critical indirect legal effects on the regulatee, for instance when being relied upon by a national or EU court in interpreting the legal text, such as the Novel Food or Food Additives Regulations.[394] The same is true for the Commission's recommendation for a definition of nanomaterial, which already has important practical implications, for instance in deciding whether or not a producer has to separately authorise a nanofood.

These concerns are fostered by further findings that emerged when analysing the transparency of the adoption processes of these measures. More legal paradoxes arise if one recognises that non-binding acts play an important role in the EU risk regulation of nanotechnologies in food. For instance, why would the duty to state reasons in Article 296 TFEU only apply to 'legal acts'? Why is there no obligation to translate documents not published in the Official Journal, such as EFSA's guidance document, into the 24 official languages of the EU?[395]

been remarked upon critically by the office of the European Ombudsman, see presentations given by I Harden, 'Legal implications: non-representative rulemaking procedures' and B Kohler-Koch, 'Colliding Visions of Representation and Participation' (both at the 3rd ACELG Annual Conference on 'Postnational Democracy: Beyond Representation in the EU', University of Amsterdam, 22 November 2013).

[394] See discussion of Case C-308/11 *Chemische Fabrik Kreussler & Co. GmbH v Sunstar Deutschland GmbH* [2012] not published. See also above chapter 3, section I.C.ii.

[395] In their case law, the EU courts have also upheld such language practices in the context of OHIM trademarks, (Case C-361/01 *Christina Kik v Office for Harmonisation in the Internal Market (Trade Marks and Designs) (OHIM)* [2003] ECR I-8283) and Commission Guidelines on electronic communications

Why should only 'documents drawn up or received in the course of procedures for the adoption of acts which are legally binding … be made directly accessible' in public registers?

As regards binding regulation, different problems have arisen. Although legal accountability is provided, in principle, in this context the question appeared problematic as to what extent legislative or non-legislative acts could be reviewed based on the collection of knowledge by EU institutions, the involvement of affected actors and their (non-)compliance with self-imposed standards, such as the impact assessment procedure or the Commission's minimum consultation standards. The answer to the latter question was found to depend largely on the clarity and institutional discretion left by these (self-imposed) rules. Their vague nature and scope of application renders it difficult, if not impossible, to establish an infringement of the self-imposed rules. This is especially troublesome in view of the many instances of non-compliance that may be observed in practice. The EU Ombudsman appears in this respect to be a valuable administrative remedy. Especially with regard to the adoption of legislative acts, the European Ombudsman handles complaints by EU citizens on the institutions' non-compliance with self-imposed procedural rules. Yet, both the EU courts and the Ombudsman have so far largely refrained from reviewing the EU institutions' factual findings, including their collection of knowledge. Instead, the two accountability fora only interfere in the case of a 'manifest error' on the part of the institutions. This cautious approach has also prevented the courts and the Ombudsman from further clarifying the scope of application (and trigger) for the impact assessment procedure.

IV. CONCLUSION

Nanotechnologies have reached our plates. Various applications are already available on the EU market—with as yet uncertain environmental, health and safety implications. To confront these challenges, this chapter showed that the Commission, instead of exercising its right of legislative initiative, has focused its attention on regulatory options in the executive sphere. The result is a slowly progressing legislative review, which is characterised by inconsistencies between the different legislative frameworks as regards their nano-specific provisions. It was shown that the European Parliament in particular has expressed its strong disagreement with the approach taken by the Commission and has tried to push the topic of

markets (Case C-410/09 *Polska Telefonia Cyfrowa sp. z o.o. v Prezes Urzędu Komunikacji Elektronicznej* [2011] ECR I-3853). For an analysis of the judgment, see O Ştefan, 'European Union Soft Law: New Developments Concerning the Divide Between Legally Binding Force and Legal Effects' (2012) 75 *The Modern Law Review* 879.

nanotechnologies, where possible, back onto the political agenda and into the legislative framework for food. At the same time, the chapter illustrated that executive rule making, in an area torn between nanomania and nanophobia, is more than technical specifications. The implementing acts under the FCM Regulation, EFSA's nano guidance, as well as the Commission's recommendation for a definition of nanomaterial were shown to accommodate sensitive political choices and a balancing of distinct (and conflicting) rationalities. In addition, these measures, independent of their formal (non-)bindingness, result in important practical and (indirect) legal effects for affected actors. In the case of EFSA, this led to the question of whether the Agency is overstepping its legislative mandate. It seems that EFSA has outgrown its formal role as a neutral source of knowledge and has turned into a regulator in its own right.

This chapter therefore asked: How is the EU regulator organising its knowledge collection? How does it ensure the legitimacy of its regulatory activities? To this end, the applicability and practical operation of the procedures established by the EU regulator for these purposes in the aftermath of the European governance debate were tested, with sobering results.

First, the impact assessment procedure—a flagship tool of the European governance debate—proved largely empty in practice. On the one hand, this is because of the procedure's ambiguous application to executive rule making. In practice, the Commission neither conducted an impact assessment for the implementing acts nor for its recommended nano definition. On the other hand, even where the impact assessment procedure was clearly applicable, that is, in the preparation of legislative proposals, the underlying principle of a 'proportionate level of analysis' was found to supply the Commission with a *carte blanche* in its operation. Thus, in practice, the two impact assessments did not assess the inclusion, or rather non-inclusion, of nano-specific requirements in the revisions of the novel food and food additives regulations.

Secondly, the increasing reliance on regulatory measures in the executive sphere resulted in a depoliticisation of the inherently controversial, thus political, nano debate. The Parliament's absence in executive rule making could not be substituted by the administrative participation of affected actors in the regulatory process—notwithstanding a clear trend towards public consultations. In the executive setting, these consultations were found to be launched in the absence of consultation standards or, in the case of EFSA, based on consultation standards which are considerably less demanding than those of the Commission. The tension between the Agency's formal mandate as a scientific advisor and its de facto assumption of regulatory tasks became particularly evident here. The picture became even bleaker when looking at the practical operation of the various consultations, especially their approximation to the criteria derived from the Habermasian ideal speech situation. To be clear, these public consultations showed little potential to stimulate a European public debate, which is a precondition for a participatory discourse as envisaged by Habermas and, hence, for input legitimate regulation.

Finally, the insufficiently transparent collection of knowledge and the lack of participation by affected actors could not be remedied by a solid ex post scrutiny of the EU executive's conduct by the different accountability fora.

Overall, this chapter revealed a mismatch between the raison d'etre of the legal procedures established for pooling knowledge and ensuring legitimacy, on the one hand, and the empirical reality of their operation in practice, on the other. In the next chapter, these findings will be compared to the regulatory developments in the chemicals sector.

5

Nanotechnologies in Chemicals

THIS CHAPTER DELVES into the second case study and analyses the EU's regulation of nanotechnologies in chemicals. The chemicals sector will prove to be an instructive case to compare to the regulatory developments in the food sector. Not only are the two sectors characterised by a similar institutional set-up, due to the creation of an independent EU agency, they also constitute key industries of the EU economy. The comparison will moreover benefit from a time dimension. While the legislative frameworks for food additives and novel foods were among the first to be revised after the launch of the Commission's 'incremental approach' in 2004, the developments in the chemicals sector are much more recent and are still ongoing. This also implies that some of the conclusions in this chapter remain preliminary.

To facilitate a comparison, the structure of the second case study will resemble that of the first one. Accordingly, this chapter will first introduce the application of nanotechnologies in chemicals (section I). Thereafter, the EU regulatory framework for chemicals, and its coverage of nanotechnologies, will be identified (section II). The chapter will then turn to the critical analysis of the current regulatory developments through the lenses of regulatory capacity. How has the EU regulator confronted the increasing fragmentation of knowledge (section III.A) and how does it ensure the regulation's legitimacy (sections III.B and III.C)? To answer these questions, this second case study will also analyse the applicability and operation of the legal procedures established by the EU institutions in the aftermath of the governance debate. Comparisons with the foregoing analysis in the food sector are drawn wherever possible.

I. NANOTECHNOLOGIES IN CHEMICALS

A. Innovating Chemicals

Globalisation and the increasing pace of scientific and technological innovation have transformed the chemicals sector into a high-tech industry operating on a transnational scale.[1] World trade in chemicals more than tripled within the last

[1] Centre for Strategy & Evaluation Services, 'Interim Evaluation: Impact of the REACH Regulation on the Innovativeness of the EU Chemical Industry' (Final report, June 2012) 4; High-Level Group on the Competitiveness of the European Chemicals Industry, 'European Chemicals Industry: Enabler of a Sustainable Future' (Final Report, European Commission DG Enterprise and Industry, 2009) 17.

decade.[2] While only a small portion of chemical products is directly sold to households or other end-users,[3] its majority forms the base for a broad range of industrial sectors, such as agriculture, food, construction, textiles, clothing, automobiles, healthcare and electronics.[4] Food ingredients too, as was seen in the preceding chapter,[5] are chemical substances. The chemicals industry therefore occupies a key position in the industrial value chain.[6]

The chemicals industry is, however, not only renowned for its strategic economic position. The undesired side effects of its innovations have also attracted at least as much attention as its advances. Since the beginning of the industrialisation process, the sector has manufactured numerous products which later proved to have severe adverse effects for public health and the environment. Despite rising safety standards, such incidents have continued to occur. A famous illustration is the asbestos case. Since the late-nineteenth century, asbestos fibres were used in insulating materials, fireproof textiles and cement products, as they proved to be extremely heat resistant, and strong as well as affordable. Only after decades of use was it recognised that their prolonged inhalation poses a risk to health and may induce several forms of cancer.[7] In view of such past experiences, the chemicals sector has been subject to attempts of regulatory intervention at the national, European and international level.[8]

B. Applications of Nanotechnologies in the Chemicals Sector

Nanomaterials are not new to the chemicals industry. For instance, 'nanoscale structures have been important to the catalyst industry for over 100 years'.[9] A breakthrough, however, occurred in the last decade with the discovery of novel tools to observe, manipulate and measure properties at the nanoscale.[10] Forming

[2] Centre for Strategy & Evaluation Services, 'Interim Evaluation' (n 1) 4.

[3] High-Level Group on the Competitiveness of the European Chemicals Industry, 'European Chemicals Industry' (n 1) 6.

[4] ibid 5.

[5] See above chapter 4, section I.B.i. Food additives and novel food ingredients falling within the scope of the respective EU legislative frameworks, however, are exempt from the EU chemicals legislation REACH, see below section II.A.i.d.

[6] Centre for Strategy & Evaluation Services, 'Interim Evaluation' (n 1) 4; European Chemical Industry Council, 'Facts and Figures 2012: The European Chemicals Industry in a Worldwide Perspective' (Cefic, June 2012) 12 www.cefic.org/Documents/FactsAndFigures/2012/Facts-and-Figures-2012-The-Brochure.pdf.

[7] Institute of Technology Assessment of the Austrian Academy of Sciences, 'NanoTrust Dossiers: Carbon Nanotubes—Part II: Risks and Regulation' (No.024en, February 2012) 1.

[8] See for an overview, eg, G Bengtsson, 'Global Trends in Chemicals Management' in J Eriksson, M Gilek and C Rudén (eds), *Regulating Chemical Risks: European and Global Challenges* (Dordrecht, Springer, 2010).

[9] Royal Society & The Royal Academy of Engineering, *Nanoscience and Nanotechnologies: Opportunities and Uncertainties* (London, The Royal Society, 2004) 25.

[10] ibid.

the basis for many other industrial sectors, nanotechnological advancements in the chemicals industry are projected to lead to innovation and growth in vast parts of the global economy. At the same time, the chemical industry, precisely because of its gatekeeper position, is also the first contact point for the spreading symptoms of nanophobia.

i. Nanomania

The novel properties and functionalities of substances in nanoform have created great expectations in the chemicals sector. In 2012, the European Chemical Industry's Council (Cefic) announced that 'nanomaterials and nanotechnologies can contribute to solving issues of global concern, such as improved healthcare, clear water, mobility, and energy generation and storage'.[11] Since theoretically every conventional chemical substance also exists at the nanoscale, there are innumerable potential materials and fields of application.[12] Two of the most prominent (and controversial) nanomaterials are carbon nanotubes (CNTs) and nanosilver.[13]

CNTs are extended rolls of carbon, measuring a couple of nanometres in width and up to a few centimetres in length.[14] While the first CNT products are ready for commercialisation, they are currently sold only in limited quantities.[15] The most marketed CNTs are found in lifestyle and sports products, such as in tennis rackets, but also in coatings and paints.[16] In the future, they are expected to be used especially in the transport and energy sectors, in order to enhance the performance of wind power plants and to reduce the weight of cars, ships and airplanes.[17]

The nanoform of silver is already present in a broad range of products.[18] Currently, nanosilver is mostly exploited for its antibacterial and antifungal characteristics in medicine, textile engineering, water treatment, and in diverse consumer products. In the preceding chapter on food, it was noted that nanosilver is also used to inhibit microbial growth in materials coming into contact with food,

[11] See European Chimical Industry Council (Cefic) Q&As on nanotechnologies www.cefic.org/Documents/RESOURCES/QandA/Cefic%20Nano%20QAs%20for%20public%203%20October%202012_FINAL.pdf.

[12] ObservatoryNano, 'General Sector Reports: Chemistry & Materials' (FP7 Report, June 2009) s 3.1.

[13] The European Commission lists these two nanomaterials as part of the 'group of materials currently attracting most attention', see European Commission, 'Second regulatory review on nanomaterials' (Communication) COM (2012) 572 final, 3.

[14] Royal Society & The Royal Academy of Engineering, *Nanoscience and Nanotechnologies* (n 9) viii and 8.

[15] ObservatoryNano, 'General Sector Reports' (n 12) s 3.1.

[16] ObservatoryNano, 'Focus Report 2010: CNT and Nanodiamond' (FP7 Report, June 2009) 3.

[17] Institute of Technology Assessment of the Austrian Academy of Sciences, 'NanoTrust Dossiers' (n 7) 1.

[18] Scientific Committee on Emerging and Newly Identified Health Risks (SCENIHR), 'Risk Assessment of Products of Nanotechnologies' (Scientific Opinion, 19 January 2009) 14 www.ec.europa.eu/health/ph_risk/committees/04_scenihr/docs/scenihr_o_023.pdf.

such as refrigerator surfaces, storage bags, or kitchenware.[19] Nanosilver belongs to the most promising nanomaterials in the upcoming years.[20]

ii. Nanophobia

At the same time, both nanomaterials have stirred public anxieties. In 2008, a toxicological mice study confirmed long-harboured fears that the use of certain CNTs may lead to lung cancer.[21] This is due to the fact that some CNTs have characteristics similar to those of the hazardous asbestos fibres.[22] The available data, however, is yet preliminary and the results demonstrate short-term effects only.[23]

With respect to nanosilver too, studies indicate gaps in the available data on both exposure and hazard, which preclude conclusions as to the substance's health and environmental risks.[24] Early results show that repeated inhalation of nanosilver might result in health risks.[25] The German Federal Institute for Risk Assessment therefore advised producers to abstain from the use of nanosilver in consumer products as long as the safety of the substance has not been confirmed conclusively.[26] In 2012, the European Consumers Organisation, BEUC, together with the Consumer's Voice in Standardisation, ANEC, published a dossier entitled *NANO Very Small and Everywhere: A Technological Magic Silver Bullet or a Serious Safety Risk?*, in which they expressed their concerns regarding the 'steeply rising number of products and services' containing nanosilver, whilst at the same time this substance is 'insufficiently assessed regarding its safety for consumers and the environment'.[27]

[19] See above chapter 4, section I.B.i. Q Chaudhry, M Scotter, J Blackburn, B Toss, A Boxall, L Castle, R Aitken and R Watkins, 'Applications and Implications of Nanotechnologies for the Food Sector' (2008) 25 *Food Additives and Contaminants* 241, 246.

[20] ObservatoryNano, 'General Sector Reports' (n 12) s 3.1.

[21] CA Poland, R Duffin, I Kinloch, A Maynard, WA Wallace, A Seaton, V Stone, S Brown, W MacNee and K Donaldson, 'Carbon Nanotubes Introduced into the Abdominal Cavity of Mice Show Asbestos-like Pathogenicity in a Pilot Study' (2008) 3 *Nature Nanotechnology* 423, 423. SCENIHR also concluded that for specific CNTs 'a risk for mesothelioma … cannot be excluded', see (SCENIHR), 'Risk Assessment of Products of Nanotechnologies' (n 18) 9.

[22] (SCENIHR), 'Risk Assessment of Products of Nanotechnologies' (n 18) 9; Institute of Technology Assessment of the Austrian Academy of Sciences, 'NanoTrust Dossiers' (n 7) 2.

[23] Institute of Technology Assessment of the Austrian Academy of Sciences, 'NanoTrust Dossiers' (n 7) 2.

[24] FM Christensen, 'Nano–silver—Feasibility and Challenges for Human Health Risk Assessment Based on Open Literature' (2010) 4 *Nanotoxicology* 284.

[25] SCENIHR reports that an oral toxicity study conducted on rats demonstrates that silver nanoparticles accumulate in all organs that were examined—in blood, brain, kidneys, liver, lungs, stomach and testes. See (SCENIHR), 'Risk Assessment of Products of Nanotechnologies' (n 18) 26.

[26] German Federal Institute for Risk Assessment, 'BfR rät von Nanosilber in Lebensmitteln und Produkten des täglichen Bedarfs ab' (BfR discourages nanosilver in food and everyday products) (Stellungnahme No 024/2010 des BfR vom 28 Dezember 2009).

[27] European Consumer Voice in Standardisation (ANEC) and European Consumer Organisation (BEUC), 'NANO Very Small and Everywhere: A Technological Magic Silver Bullet or a Serious Safety Risk?' (2012) 3, www.anec.eu/attachments/ANEC_BEUC%20nano-silver%20brochure%20updated.pdf.

C. The EU Chemicals Sector and Nanotechnologies

The limited overview of the huge amount of nanomaterials on the market illustrates the deep contradictions that accompany their emergence. However, the EU chemicals industry, in comparison to the food industry,[28] approaches its activities in the field of nanotechnologies in a more open manner. Major European chemical companies, such as BASF and Evonik, have launched dedicated websites through which they inform customers and interested parties about their nano-related activities.[29]

In the current absence of a mandatory EU-wide register for nanomaterials,[30] it remains, nevertheless, difficult to determine their exact presence on the EU market. Already in 2008, the German Ministry of Education and Research signalled that 'nearly all major chemical companies are involved in the production of nanoscale materials'.[31] The Commission estimates the total number of EU nanomaterial manufacturers in the range of 200 to 400.[32] The chemicals industry, like the food sector, forms a cornerstone of the EU economy with about 29,000 chemical companies and a total staff of 1.2 million.[33] The European Commission assumes that the future competitiveness of the (EU) chemicals industry will depend to an important degree on its potential to exploit nanotechnologies.[34]

II. THE EU REGULATORY FRAMEWORK FOR NANOTECHNOLOGIES IN CHEMICALS

A. Reforming the EU Chemicals Policy

Upheavals in other areas in the late 1990s, most notably in the food sector,[35] also reinforced public concerns for chemical risks.[36] A fundamental review of the EU

[28] See above chapter 4, section I.C.

[29] See for BASF, Nanotechnologies, www.basf.com/group/corporate/nanotechnology/en/microsites/nanotechnology/what-is-nano/index; for Evonik Industries, Nanotechnology, www.nano.evonik.com/sites/nanotechnology/en/Pages/default.aspx.

[30] See, on the current absence of a mandatory register, above chapter 1, section IV.C.

[31] German Federal Ministry for Education and Research, 'Welcome to Nanotech Germany: Seven Reasons Why Germany is a Strong Partner in Nanotechnology' (2008) 27 www.internationales-buero.de/en/nanotechnology.php.

[32] European Commission, 'Possible Amendments of Annexes to REACH for Registration of Nanomaterials' (Inception Impact Assessment, 6 February 2016) 3.

[33] High-Level Group on the Competitiveness of the European Chemicals Industry, 'European Chemicals Industry' (n 1) 7.

[34] 'Second Regulatory Review on Nanomaterials' COM (2012) 572 final (n 13) 3.

[35] D Pesendorfer, 'EU Environmental Policy under Pressure: Chemicals Policy Change Between Antagonistic Goals' (2006) 15 *Environmental Politics* 95, 104.

[36] V Heyvaert, 'Regulating Chemical Risk: REACH in a Global Governance Perspective' in J Eriksson, M Gilek and C Rudén (eds), *Regulating Chemical Risks: European and Global Challenges* (n 8) 220.

chemicals policy was announced, with health and environmental protection to be put on an equal footing with economic aspirations.[37] The most perilous gap that had unfolded was the distinction between 'existing' chemicals and 'new' (introduced onto the European market after 1981) chemicals, on which the old policy was based.[38] Whereas all new substances entering the EU market were subject to a notification and risk assessment requirement, such requirements were absent for existing substances, which amounted to 99 per cent of the total volume of substances on the EU market.[39] The result was a tremendous gap in knowledge about existing substances with potential adverse consequences not only for human health and the environment but also for innovation by discouraging the search for new, less harmful chemicals.[40]

Prior attempts at reforming the old EU chemicals policy proved deficient. The adoption of Regulation 793/93 on existing substances[41] obliged manufacturers and importers to report all available information about existing chemicals to the European Chemicals Bureau.[42] According to priority lists, substances were assigned to different national authorities for further assessment. The national authorities then reported their findings to the Commission, which drafted a legislative proposal for risk reduction.[43] Most problematic was that the system did not offer any incentives for producers and importers to report information to the Commission. On the one hand, penalties in the case of failing to report hardly served as a deterrent.[44] Compliance, on the contrary, bore the risk of the (potentially) dangerous chemical being restricted or completely prohibited, hence implying high economic losses for the producer.[45] On the other hand, the responsibility for risk assessment rested primarily with national public authorities, which barely had the resources to produce the relevant information[46] and instead had to request the information from industry, resulting in high administrative costs and temporal delays.[47]

[37] E Fisher, 'The "Perfect Storm" of REACH: Charting Regulatory Controversy in the Age of Information, Sustainable Development, and Globalisation' (2008) 11 *Journal of Risk Research* 541, 551.

[38] V Heyvaert, 'The EU Chemicals Policy: Towards Inclusive Governance?' in E Vos (ed), *European Risk Governance—Its Science, its Inclusiveness and its Effectiveness* (Mannheim, CONNEX Report Series, 2008) 4.

[39] European Commission, 'White Paper—Strategy for a Future European Chemicals Policy' COM (2001) 88 final, 6.

[40] J Scott, 'REACH: Combining Harmonisation and Dynamism in the Regulation of Chemicals' in J Scott (ed), *Environmental Protection: European Law and Governance*, Collected Courses of the Academy of European Law XVIII/3 (Oxford, Oxford University Press, 2009) 57.

[41] Council Regulation (EEC) 793/93 of 23 March 1993 on the evaluation and control of the risks of existing substances [1993] OJ L84/1.

[42] The European Chemicals Bureau, today referred to as the Consumer Product Safety and Quality (CPS&Q) Unit, operates as a scientific committee within the Joint Research Centre and was (and still is) directly dependent on the European Commission.

[43] V Heyvaert, 'The EU Chemicals Policy' (n 38) 4.

[44] ibid 5.

[45] C Calliess and M Lais, 'REACH Revisited—Der Verordnungsvorschlag zur Reform des Chemikalienrechts als Beispiel einer neuen europäischen Vorsorgestrategie' (2005) 5 *Natur und Recht* 290, 291.

[46] E Fisher, 'The "Perfect Storm" of REACH' (n 37) 547.

[47] In more than 15 years, only 141 of the more than 100,000 registered substances were risk assessed, see K Malkiewicz, M Pettitt, KA Dawson, A Toikka, SO Hansson, J Hukkinen, I Lynch and J Lead, 'Nanomaterials in REACH' (Project Report, SKEP ERA-NET, August 2011) 26.

i. REACH and Its Main Pillars

The Commission proposed a fundamental reform of its chemicals policy in the 2001 White Paper on a 'Strategy for a Future Chemicals Policy'[48] by establishing a uniform system applicable to all chemicals, including existing and new substances, called the Registration, Evaluation and Authorisation of Chemicals (REACH).[49] In 2003, the Commission presented a legislative proposal to Council and European Parliament.[50] After three years of negotiations, REACH went down in the history of EU law making as 'one of the most controversial legislative proposals' ever adopted.[51] Regulation 1907/2006[52] (hereafter 'REACH') entered into force on 1 June 2007. Three introductory points should be made before we go into the Regulation's details.

First, REACH shifts the primary responsibility for the safety and assessment of chemical substances from national authorities to industry.[53] While REACH has a 'traditional regulatory core',[54] in the sense that it stipulates the obligatory requirements for data delivery, the registration, evaluation, authorisation and restriction of chemical substances, it delegates the duty to produce, assess, publicise and communicate the information to private actors.[55] Furthermore, the norms stipulated in REACH are often indefinite.[56] Technical specifications are destined to flow from the elaboration of details in implementing acts by the Commission and in 'technical and scientific guidance' prepared by the newly established European Chemicals Agency (ECHA).

Secondly, like the European Food Safety Authority (EFSA), ECHA is also formally barred from political risk management decisions. The Agency 'is established for the purposes of managing and in some cases carrying out the technical, scientific and administrative aspects' of REACH,[57] thereby acting as the Union's risk assessor, 'chief administrator of the scheme'[58] at the 'centre of the institutional

[48] For a review of the White Paper, see MD Rogers, 'The European Commission's White Paper 'Strategy for a Future Chemicals Policy': A Review' (2003) 23 *Risk Analysis* 381.

[49] ibid 384.

[50] European Commission, 'Proposal for a regulation of the European Parliament and of the Council concerning the registration, evaluation, authorisation and restriction of Chemicals, establishing a European Chemicals Agency and amending Directive 1999/45/EC and Regulation (EC) {on Persistent Organic Pollutants}' COM/2003/0644 final.

[51] E Fisher, 'The "Perfect Storm" of REACH' (n 37) 541.

[52] Regulation of the European Parliament and of the Council (EC) 1907/2006 of 18 December 2006 concerning the Registration, Evaluation, Authorisation and Restriction of Chemicals (REACH) [2006] OJ L396 (hereafter 'REACH Regulation' or 'REACH').

[53] Art 1(3) REACH.

[54] C Hey, K Jacob and A Volkery, 'Better Regulation by New Governance Hybrids? Governance Models and the Reform of the European Chemicals Policy' (FFU-Report 02/2006, Environmental Policy Research Centre, Freie Universität Berlin, 2006) 12, www.polsoz.fu-berlin.de/polwiss/forschung/systeme/ffu/publikationen/2006/hey_christian_jacob_klaus_volkery_axel_2006/rep_2006_02.pdf.

[55] E Fisher, 'The "Perfect Storm" of REACH' (n 37) 548.

[56] E Korkea-aho, 'Laws in Progress? Reconceptualizing Accountability Strategies in the Era of Framework Norms' (2013) 2 *Transnational Environmental Law* 363, 367.

[57] Art 75(1) REACH.

[58] V Heyvaert, 'The EU Chemicals Policy' (n 38) 8.

design'.[59] ECHA furthermore, as alluded to under the previous point, plays a key role with regard to the implementation of REACH by issuing guidance documents[60] that fill in the blanks left by the Regulation's framework character.

Finally, the REACH system operates according to three separate stages, which comprise the registration (below section a), evaluation (below section b) and authorisation (below section c) of chemical substances. It will be seen that not every chemical has to pass through each of these stages. Whether a chemical must do so depends on its production volume, dangerousness, its purpose of use and exposure to humans and the environment.[61]

a. Registration

Title II of REACH lays down the registration requirement.[62] Following the 'no data, no market' principle,[63] no chemical substance exceeding an annual production volume of one tonne shall be marketed in the EU without prior registration.[64] The information needed for registration depends mainly on the volume in which the substance is manufactured or imported.[65] While all substances subject to registration have to comply with basic information requirements,[66] staggered information requirements apply to substances produced in more than one tonne, more than 10 tonnes, more than 100 tonnes or more than 1,000 tonnes per year.

For substances produced in volumes between one and 10 tonnes, Article 12(1) of REACH refers to Annex VII, which requires the provision of basic information on the substance's physicochemical properties, toxicological and ecotoxicological information, in the form of a 'technical dossier'. A further distinction is made here between phase-in ('existing') and non-phase-in ('new') substances. Whereas for non-phase-in substances a technical dossier always has to be submitted, this information must only be provided for phase-in substances in cases where they are particularly hazardous.[67] Substances manufactured or imported in volumes of more than 10 tonnes per year additionally require the submission of a Chemical Safety Report (CSR) containing a chemical safety assessment.[68] It is only for these substances that a risk assessment becomes necessary. In addition to the CSR,

[59] FM Fleurke and H Somsen, 'Precautionary Regulation of Chemical Risk: How REACH Confronts the Regulatory Challenges of Scale, Uncertainty, Complexity and Innovation' (2011) 48 *Common Market Law Review* 357, 363.

[60] Art 77(2) REACH.

[61] C Calliess and M Lais, 'REACH Revisited' (n 45) 293.

[62] K Malkiewicz et al, 'Nanomaterials in REACH' (n 47) 34.

[63] Art 5 REACH.

[64] Art 6(1) REACH.

[65] Art 12(1) REACH.

[66] eg providing the identity of manufacturer and substance, see Art 10(1) REACH.

[67] See criteria in Annex III REACH.

[68] Art 14(1) REACH. The CSA is conducted pursuant to Annex I REACH.

for substances produced in tonnages above 100 tonnes and 1,000 tonnes per year respectively, supplementary information on their physicochemical properties and (eco)toxicology must be submitted.[69]

While the tonnage triggers are laid down in the articles of REACH itself, most notably in Article 12, the Regulation's annexes contain the specific information to be included in the respective technical dossier (and CSR). The rationale behind the volume-based information and assessment triggers is the assumption of a correlation between production volume, on the one hand, and dangers to humans and environment, on the other.[70] This implies that for substances produced in volumes between one and 10 tonnes per year 'no genuine risk assessment needs to be carried out'.[71] Substances produced below the one tonne threshold completely escape the registration duty.

In addition to the staggered registration requirements, there are also transitional provisions in place for phase-in substances. If pre-registered,[72] delayed registration deadlines apply for phase-in substances. Depending on the production volume, the deadline was December 2010 for substances produced in the 1,000 tonnage band, June 2013 for substances produced in quantities of more than 100 tonnes per year and the deadline is June 2018 for those substances produced in volumes below 100 tonnes.[73]

b. Evaluation

Title VI of REACH lays down the evaluation stage. After the completeness check,[74] ECHA performs a compliance check of 5 per cent of the registration dossiers in each tonnage band.[75] To this end, the Agency examines whether the information provided in the technical dossier and, if applicable, in the CSR corresponds to the requirements set out in the relevant articles and annexes of REACH. Based on this compliance check, the Agency may request further information from the registrant[76] and/or include a substance in the 'Community rolling action plan' according to which a so-called 'substance evaluation' is carried out.[77] Substance evaluations shall be conducted in case there are grounds for considering that a given substance constitutes a risk to human health or the environment, taking

[69] See Annexes IX and X REACH.

[70] FM Fleurke and H Somsen, 'Precautionary Regulation of Chemical Risk' (n 59) 372.

[71] ibid 373.

[72] Pre-registration pursuant to Art 28 REACH was possible until December 2008.

[73] Art 23 REACH.

[74] The Agency undertakes a completeness check of each registration dossier—without however conducting an assessment of the quality or adequacy of the data submitted—and assigns the dossier a registration number, Art 20 REACH.

[75] Art 41 REACH. See also BG Hansen and M Blainey, 'REACH: A Step Change in the Management of Chemicals' (2006) 15 *Review of European, Comparative & International Environmental Law* 270, 276.

[76] Art 41(3) REACH.

[77] Art 44(2) REACH.

into consideration two prioritising criteria: 'hazard information' and 'tonnage'.[78] Based on the rolling action plan, these substances are then assigned to national competent authorities for further evaluation.[79] The respective national competent authority circulates its draft decision to the Agency and to the other competent authorities.[80] ECHA may then adopt the decision, if no other Member State proposes amendments.[81] If amendments are proposed, the draft decision is forwarded to the Agency's Member State Committee. If the Member State Committee reaches a unanimous agreement on the draft decision, the Agency can still adopt the decision. If not, the decision is taken by the Commission following the examination procedure for implementing acts.[82]

c. Authorisation

Independent of volume, Substances of Very High Concern (SVHC) can only be placed on the market if authorised in accordance with Title VII of REACH. In its simplified form, the authorisation procedure comprises three steps. First, ECHA, on request of the Commission or based on a dossier prepared by a Member State, establishes a candidate list of SVHC.[83] Secondly, substances on the candidate list may be included by the Commission in Annex XIV of REACH, which comprises the list of substances subject to authorisation, pursuant to the regulatory procedure with scrutiny.[84] Article 57 of REACH defines the substances which meet the criteria for SVHC. There are three categories: first, substances that are classified as carcinogenic, mutagenic or toxic for reproduction (CMR 1 or 2);[85] and, secondly, substances that are classified as persistent, bioaccumulative and toxic (PBT) or very persistent and very bioaccumulative (vPvB).[86] In addition to these rather narrow categories, a third category comprises substances which do not meet the criteria of the other categories but 'for which there is scientific evidence of probable serious effects to human health or the environment which give rise to an equivalent level of concern to those of other substances'.[87] Once on the list, SVHC can only be marketed if authorised following a procedure laid down in Article 60 of REACH.[88] It is the Commission that takes the authorisation decision,[89] after having received the opinions of ECHA's Committees on Risk Assessment (RAC)

[78] Art 44(1) REACH.
[79] Art 45 REACH.
[80] Art 52(1) REACH.
[81] Art 51 REACH.
[82] See procedure in Art 51 REACH.
[83] Art 59 REACH.
[84] Art 58(1) REACH.
[85] Art 57(a–c) REACH.
[86] Art 57(d and e) REACH.
[87] Art 57(f) REACH.
[88] Art 56(1) REACH.
[89] Art 60(1) REACH.

and Socio-Economic Analysis (SEAC), in line with the examination procedure for implementing acts.[90]

An alternative to the authorisation procedure is the EU-wide restriction of dangerous substances, which can be imposed, like authorisations, independent of the production volume.[91] Such substances can then only be manufactured, placed on the market or used if they comply with the conditions (eg their allowed uses or existence in certain products) set out in Annex XVII of REACH.[92]

d. Scope of Application: Chemicals in Food

REACH applies to all chemicals falling within its broad definition of 'substance' in Article 3(1). Theoretically, every chemical substance used in food is therefore also subject to REACH. Most of these substances are, however, relieved from the requirements under Title II (Registration), Title VI (Evaluation) and Title VII (Authorisation) of REACH to the extent that they are used in food or feedingstuffs in accordance with the General Food Law (GFL).[93] Whereas food additives are explicitly exempt from these provisions of REACH, also 'novel foods and ingredients' falling within the scope of the Novel Food Regulation are freed from their obligations.[94]

ii. REACH and Nano

REACH was proposed in 2003 shortly before the Commission launched its *European Strategy on Nanotechnology* in 2004.[95] In the course of the three-year negotiation on REACH, discussions on the regulatory implications of nanotechnologies took place, but knowledge of nanomaterials was considered insufficient to propose any specific provisions.[96] REACH therefore does not make any explicit reference to nanomaterials. Nevertheless, its provisions apply to all 'substances' within the broad scope of its definition.[97] Substances in nanoform are therefore also covered by REACH in principle.[98]

[90] Art 64 REACH.

[91] Title VIII REACH. See also BG Hansen and M Blainey, 'REACH' (n 75) 272.

[92] Art 67(1) REACH. Like proposals for authorisations, proposals for restrictions are also prepared by ECHA on request of the Commission or a Member State, Art 69 REACH. Based on the Agency's opinions, the Commission prepares an amendment of Annex XVII, adopting it following the regulatory procedure with scrutiny, see Art 73(2) REACH.

[93] Art 2(5)(b) REACH.

[94] Milieu Ltd, 'Technical Assistance Related to the Scope of REACH and Other Relevant EU Legislation to Assess Overlaps' (Final Report (revised), European Commission, DG Environment, 2012) 306 www.ec.europa.eu/environment/chemicals/reach/pdf/studies_review2012/report_study8.pdf.

[95] See above chapter 1, section IV.

[96] K Malkiewicz et al, 'Nanomaterials in REACH' (n 47) 27.

[97] Art 3(1) REACH.

[98] K Malkiewicz et al, 'Nanomaterials in REACH' (n 47) 36.

There are, however, concerns regarding the effective implementation of REACH with regard to nanomaterials. These concerns have mostly centred on the question of whether nanomaterials are to be considered the same substance as the respective bulkform material, or a different substance.[99] This question touches upon the criteria employed by REACH to identify a substance and to establish the sameness of the substances. Currently, the substance identification criteria mentioned in Annex VI(2) of REACH make no distinction as to size.[100] It has therefore been argued that 'the list of parameters required for substance identification is neither adequate for distinguishing between the bulk and nanoforms of certain substances, nor for distinguishing between different nanoforms'.[101] The responsibility to decide on the sameness of nanomaterials rests with industry.[102] In this context, the absence of a definition of nanomaterial in REACH has also been criticised.[103] It is feared that the nano-specific characteristics of substances are not sufficiently taken into account in the different stages of registration, evaluation and authorisation.[104]

The issue of substance identification is especially problematic at the *registration* stage. It was explained earlier that registration and data requirements are dependent upon the annual production volume of the substance, its status as a phase-in or non-phase in substance and its hazardousness.[105]

If substances in nanoform are considered the 'same' substance as their bulkform equivalent, the two forms are registered together in one dossier. This begs the question as to how nano-specific information can be collected. In essence, 'there is no legal obligation to provide information on nanoforms'.[106] The Commission, in 2008, however, perceived this question as unproblematic, as it considered that REACH 'requires that macromaterial registration dossiers that also encompass nanomaterials should include, at a minimum, nanomaterial information concerning the following: properties, uses, effects, relevant classifications, safety

[99] ibid 52.

[100] C Calliess and H Stockhaus, 'Precautionary Principle and Nanomaterials: REACH Revisited' (2012) 9 *Journal for European Environmental & Planning Law* 113, 121.

[101] K Malkiewicz et al, 'Nanomaterials in REACH' (n 47) 53.

[102] European Commission, 'Summary Record of the 2nd Meeting of the REACH Competent Authorities subgroup on nanomaterials, 10–11 November 2008, CASG Nano/15/2008' (Comment by the Netherlands, 2009) 5 (document on file with the author).

[103] C Calliess and H Stockhaus, 'Precautionary Principle and Nanomaterials' (n 100) 133.

[104] Landesanstalt für Umwelt, Messungen und Naturschutz Baden Württemberg, 'Nanomaterialien: Regulierungen national-international' (Bericht, June 2012) 12 www.lubw.baden-wuerttemberg.de/servlet/is/219885/nanomaterialien_regulierungen.pdf?command=downloadContent&filename=nanomaterialien_regulierungen.pdf; K Malkiewicz et al, 'Nanomaterials in REACH' (n 47); RIVM, 'Nanomaterials under REACH: Nanosilver as a Case Study' (Report 601780003/2009, 2009); E Vogelezang-Stoute, 'Regulating Nanomaterials: Bottlenecks and Perspectives in EU Legislation on Chemicals and Products' (2012) 21 *European Energy and Environmental Law Review* 41, 43.

[105] K Malkiewicz et al, 'Nanomaterials in REACH' (n 47) 37.

[106] 'Summary Record of the 2nd Meeting of the REACH Competent Authorities subgroup on nanomaterials' (n 102) 5.

assessment and relevant exposure scenarios'.[107] First analyses, however, identified important deficiencies in the information included in a selected number of REACH registration dossiers following the first deadlines in 2010[108] and 2013.[109] The Commission observed that 'many registrations for substances known to have nanomaterial forms do not mention clearly which forms are covered or how information relates to the nanoform. Only little information is specifically addressing safe use of the specific nanomaterials supposed to be covered by the registration dossiers'.[110] A mere four of the thousands of dossiers submitted by the second registration deadline in 2013 indicated that they covered nanomaterials.[111]

There are two further implications flowing from a common nano/bulkform registration. First, the total volume of production of the substance would be taken into account when applying the tonnage triggers under REACH.[112] In principle, this would mean that increased information requirements are applicable compared to the situation in which only the volume of the nanosubstance was considered. Secondly, if the bulkform of the nanomaterial counts as an existing 'phase-in' substance under REACH, the nanoform is also considered as 'phase-in' instead of as a new or 'non-phase-in' substance.[113] On the one hand, the nanoform substance would then also benefit from the delayed registration deadlines, possibly until 2018, before information on the nanomaterial is submitted to ECHA.[114] On the other hand, the basic data requirements (the compilation of the technical dossier) only apply to phase-in substances if they are predicted to be particularly hazardous or if they are produced in volumes of more than 10 tonnes per year.[115] Substantially less information may thus be collected for phase-in substances than for 'new' ones. It was therefore recommended that nanoforms of substances are treated as different from their bulkform,[116] so that they require a separate registration dossier,[117] and that the 'application of the transitional periods to nanomaterials [can] be excluded'.[118]

[107] See European Commission, 'Nanomaterials in REACH' (Follow-up to the 6th Meeting of the REACH Competent Authorities for the implementation of Regulation (EC) 1907/2006, CA/59/2008 rev. 1, 16 December 2008) 6.

[108] European Commission, 'Scientific technical support on assessment of nanomaterials in REACH registration dossiers and adequacy of available information' (Final Report Nano Support Project Task I, 2012).

[109] 'Possible amendments of annexes to REACH for registration of nanomaterials' (n 32) 3.

[110] 'Second Regulatory Review on Nanomaterials' COM (2012) 572 final (n 13) 6.

[111] 'Possible amendments of annexes to REACH for registration of nanomaterials' (n 32) 3.

[112] 'Nanomaterials in REACH' (n 107) 6.

[113] K Malkiewicz et al, 'Nanomaterials in REACH' (n 47) 45; see European Commission, 'Nanomaterials in REACH' (n 107) 7.

[114] K Malkiewicz et al, 'Nanomaterials in REACH' (n 47) 45.

[115] See above section II.A.i.a.

[116] European Parliament, 'Resolution of 24 April 2009 on regulatory aspects of nanomaterials' (P6_TA(2009)03287), para 11; K Malkiewicz et al, 'Nanomaterials in REACH' (n 47) 46.

[117] 'Nanomaterialien: Regulierungen national-international' (n 104) 12.

[118] C Calliess and H Stockhaus, 'Precautionary Principle and Nanomaterials' (n 100) 125.

If, however, the nanoform of a substance is indeed treated as different from its bulkform, further problems occur. The most debated problem relates to the applicability of REACH's tonnage thresholds. Surveys suggest that nanomaterials are produced or imported in small volumes.[119] According to a 2012 study commissioned by DG Enterprise, '39% of cases involved manufacture or import of less than 10 kg per year of nanomaterials, and only 19% of cases were over 100 tonnes per year, 32% were over 1 tonne per year'.[120] Given the current tonnage triggers, this would mean that many nanomaterials would not reach the thresholds triggering data requirements that allow for a risk assessment, that is, the preparation of a CSR, to take place.[121] Thirty-nine per cent of nanomaterials would even fall below the one tonne trigger for registration.[122] Eventually, 'the current tonnage triggers system would result in an ongoing scarcity of data—no assessment of fate in the environment, chronic effects, or toxicokinetic studies would be required for [nanomaterials], thereby perpetuating the current lack of data for meaningful hazard assessment even for nanoproducts already on the market; additionally, no sources of exposure could be predicted'.[123] Critics, among them the European Parliament, have therefore argued that the current tonnage thresholds and standard information requirements are inadequate for nanomaterials.[124] Several proposals have been made to this end which range from adjusted thresholds for nanoform substances[125] to 'a base set information requirements … for all nanomaterials to be registered, independent of their production/imported volume', including a CSR.[126]

The dependency of the *evaluation* stage upon the registration of a substance might furthermore prevent a non-registered nanoform substance from undergoing a 'substance evaluation'.[127] Yet, even if registered, the current criteria for prioritisation—'hazard information' and 'tonnage'[128]—are arguably not tailored

[119] 'Nanomaterialien: Regulierungen national-international' (n 104) 12; K Malkiewicz et al, 'Nanomaterials in REACH' (n 47) 42.

[120] GAIA, 'Study on REACH Contribution to the Development of Emerging Technologies' (Final Report, DG Enterprise and Industry, 2012) 62.

[121] 'Nanomaterialien: Regulierungen national-international' (n 104) 12.

[122] K Malkiewicz et al, 'Nanomaterials in REACH' (n 47) 42.

[123] ibid 43.

[124] European Parliament, 'Resolution of 24 April 2009' (n 116) para 11; 'Nanomaterialien: Regulierungen national-international' (n 104) 13; see also RIVM, 'Nanomaterials under REACH: Nanosilver as a Case Study' (n 104) 12 and 58, K Malkiewicz et al, 'Nanomaterials in REACH' (n 47) 43; JP Montfort, G Indirli, D Georgieva and CM Carrega, 'Nanomaterials under REACH: Legal Aspects' (2010) 1 *European Journal of Risk Regulation* 51, 55.

[125] See, for instance, K Malkiewicz et al, 'Nanomaterials in REACH' (n 47) 44; 'Nanomaterialien: Regulierungen national-international' (n 104) 13.

[126] RIVM, 'Nanomaterials under REACH: Nanosilver as a Case Study' (n 104) 12 and 58.

[127] S Heselhaus, 'Risk Management of Nanomaterials: Environmental and Consumer Protection under Existing EC Legislation on Chemicals, Pesticides and Biocides' (2010) 12 *Environmental Law Review* 115.

[128] Art 44(1) REACH.

to nano-specific properties. It appears to be especially problematic that the production volume of a substance is again a decisive criterion.[129]

A further wave of criticism focuses on the implementation of the *authorisation* provisions of REACH. While authorisation obligations for SVHC arise independent of a substance's production volume, it has been argued that the criteria for SVHC are also ill-suited to the particular characteristics of nanomaterials. This is because all three categories of SVHC 'refer to substances with well known risks, such as carcinogenic or persistent substances, but not to nanomaterials with uncertain risks'.[130] Even the more open-ended third category requires 'scientific evidence of probable serious effects to human health or the environment'.[131] Commentators have therefore advocated the insertion of a general clause that 'stipulates an authorisation requirement for substances for which there is a *possibility* of serious effects to human health or the environment' (emphasis added).[132] Similar criticism has been expressed in the context of the restriction procedure.[133]

Based on the foregoing analysis, the current discussion on the applicability of REACH to nanomaterials can be summarised as focusing on five main uncertainties:

1. The applicability of the current parameters for substance identification, coupled with the absence of a definition of 'nanomaterial' in the REACH Regulation.
2. The applicability of current tonnage thresholds and data requirements for registration.
3. The applicability of the current criteria for prioritisation under substance evaluation.
4. The applicability of the current criteria for the identification of SVHC.
5. The applicability of current risk assessment methods to nanomaterials.

iii. Revising REACH? No But Yes

In its *Second Regulatory Review on Nanomaterials* of October 2012, the Commission lastly revealed that it does not intend to propose amendments to the legal text of REACH. Instead, it found that 'REACH sets the best possible framework for the risk management of nanomaterials when they occur as substances or mixtures but more specific requirements for nanomaterials within the framework have proven necessary. *The Commission envisages modifications in some of the REACH Annexes and encourages ECHA to further develop guidance for registrations after*

129 S Heselhaus, 'Risk Management of Nanomaterials' (n 127).
130 E Vogelezang-Stoute, 'Regulating Nanomaterials' (n 104) 44.
131 Art 57(f) REACH.
132 C Calliess and H Stockhaus, 'Precautionary Principle and Nanomaterials' (n 100) 129.
133 ibid 131.

2013' (emphasis added).[134] This position was confirmed in the Commission's first review of REACH, which was published a few months later in February 2013.[135] In that review, the Commission justified its decision not to change the enacting terms of REACH with reference to 'legislative stability and predictability'.[136] The decision was taken based on several thematic studies. For nanomaterials, the Commission referred to the Joint Research Centre's Nano Support Project. While this project analysed the adequacy of current information requirements for nanomaterials in the REACH annexes,[137] other long-debated uncertainties, including the adequacy of tonnage triggers, the criteria for substance evaluation or authorisation, were not subject to an assessment by the Commission.

The Commission's decision not to open the legal text of REACH met with fierce resistance—from the European Parliament, a group of Member States and several stakeholders. As a first reaction, Member States, in a meeting of the competent authorities for REACH, 'questioned the comprehensiveness of the Communication in terms of taking into account input from Member States and addressing explicit questions, requests etc. by EP, Member States and NGOs in 2008–2012'.[138] At a subsequent workshop organised by the Commission in Brussels, an MEP bemoaned that the 'Commission's second review has failed to adequately act upon the requests of Parliament'.[139] She expressly criticised the absence of commitment on the part of the Commission to introduce nano-specific provisions into the individual legislative frameworks and stated that a mere update of REACH's annexes and ECHA's guidance documents would not address the fundamental shortcomings.[140] Similar reactions were put forward by various stakeholders. Illustrative of the dissatisfaction is an open letter sent to the Commission by nine environmental

[134] 'Second Regulatory Review on Nanomaterials' COM (2012) 572 final (n 13).

[135] The Commission announced that it 'will make an impact assessment of relevant regulatory options, in particular possible amendments of REACH Annexes, to ensure further clarity on how nanomaterials are addressed and safety demonstrated in registration dossiers. If appropriate the Commission will come forward with a draft implementing act by December 2013. … changes to the enacting terms of REACH will not be proposed', see European Commission, 'General report on REACH' COM (2013) 49 final, 13.

[136] ibid.

[137] 'Scientific technical support on assessment of nanomaterials in REACH registration dosssiers and adequacy of available information' (n 108); European Commission, 'Examination and Assessment of Consequences for Industry, Consumers, Human Health and the Environment of Possible Options for Changing the REACH Requirements for Nanomaterials' (Final Report Nano Support Project Task II, 2013).

[138] European Commission, 'Summary Record 9th Meeting of the REACH Competent Authorities Sub-Group on Nanomaterials 20 November 2012, CASG Nano/02/2013' 2 (document on file with the author).

[139] S Hassi, 'Towards an Effective Governance of Nanomaterials: First Reaction to the Second Regulatory Review on Nanomaterials' (Workshop 'Second Regulatory Review of Nanomaterials', European Commission, Brussels, 30 January 2013).

[140] ibid.

NGOs, consumer organisations, trade union confederations and a women's rights organisation, in which they:

> express[ed] [their] extreme disappointment and deep concerns with the Commission's Second Regulatory Review on Nanomaterials ... In contradiction with these [the Commission's own] conclusions, the Commission only considers a limited amendment to the REACH annexes, which is insufficient to close existing loopholes, and manifestly insufficient to overcome the current lack of information on nanomaterials in products.[141]

B. Addressing Nanotechnologies via Comitology

Pursuant to its commitment in the REACH review of 2013, the Commission is presently drafting one or more implementing act(s) with a view to further 'clarifying' the information requirements in the REACH annexes.[142] To this end, the Commission launched an impact assessment and a linked public consultation in 2013.[143] Originally, the Commission envisaged the draft act(s) to be adopted in spring 2014.[144] In February 2016, the Commission published a draft ('inception') impact assessment, pursuant to the amended 2015 Impact Assessment Guidelines, which still has to be approved by the newly established Regulatory Scrutiny Board.[145]

C. Addressing Nanotechnologies via ECHA Guidance Documents

In the meantime, the Commission 'encouraged' ECHA to adopt guidance documents in order to make REACH fit for nanomaterials.[146] As was seen earlier, the European Chemicals Agency has been delegated the task of providing 'technical and scientific guidance' on the functioning of REACH and its main pillars—to Member States, stakeholders, manufacturers, and importers of substances[147]—in order to flesh out the often vague terms of the legal text.[148]

[141] The letter was signed by the European Environmental Bureau (EEC), the European Consumers' Organisation (BEUC), the Centre for International Environmental Law (CIEL), the European Trade Union Confederation (ETUC), the European Environmental Citizens' Organisation for Standardisation (ECOS), the European Consumer Voice in Standardisation (ANEC), Women in Europe for a Common Future (WECF), ClientEarth, BUND e.V. (Friends of the Earth Germany), and by Friends of the Earth Europe on 23 October 2012 www.ciel.org/Publications/Nano_EC_23Oct2012.pdf.

[142] 'General Report on REACH' (n 135) 13.

[143] ibid.

[144] According to the time schedule envisaged by the Commission, the draft proposal(s) should have been submitted to the respective comitology committee on 30 April 2014, see European Commission, 'Impact Assessment of Modifications of the REACH Annexes for Nanomaterials' (13th Meeting of Competent Authorities for REACH and CLP (CARACAL), CA/36/2013, 11 November 2013) 3.

[145] 'Possible amendments of annexes to REACH for registration of nanomaterials' (n 32).

[146] 'Second Regulatory Review on Nanomaterials' COM (2012) 572 final (n 13) 11.

[147] Art 77(2) REACH.

[148] E Korkea-aho, 'Laws in Progress?' (n 56) 380.

In contrast to the General Food Law then, REACH foresees the adoption of a distinct category of guidance documents by ECHA, co-existent to that of scientific opinions. To date, 21 of these documents exist, forming a paper jungle of several thousand pages. These documents, albeit formally of a non-binding nature, occupy a central role in REACH's day-to-day operation.[149] Their significance is illustrated by a search of ECHA's frequently asked questions database,[150] which features 175 Q&As on REACH, 62 of which are answered by reference to a REACH guidance document. An ECHA staff member confirmed that, in communicating with stakeholders, guidance documents are constantly pointed to.[151] In view of their practical weight, Korkea-aho argued that these guidance documents should also function as 'an aid' to the EU courts, as a way to ensure that REACH 'delivers the intended benefits, providing the courts with the requisite (technical) information'.[152] And indeed, the significance of REACH guidance documents seems to have surpassed a pure practical effect. In their, as yet, short lifetime, the REACH guidance documents have been evoked at least once before the EU courts.[153] In her opinion to a preliminary reference, Advocate General Kokott relied on the REACH guidance for monomers and polymers to support her conclusions that an obligation to register reacted monomer substances entailed in polymers is not disproportionate—a question which was posed to the Court of Justice of the EU by the High Court of Justice of England and Wales.[154]

Coming back to the question of nanomaterials, the Agency responded to the Commission's request by confirming in its multi-annual work programme for 2014–18 that it will develop further guidance especially on the registration of substances in nanoform.[155] So far, ECHA has aligned one of its REACH guidance documents to the specific characteristics of nanomaterials, the *Guidance on Information Requirements and Chemical Safety Assessment*. Additionally, ECHA adopted a guidance document instructing registrants on how to prepare registration dossiers for nanomaterials using the data submission tool IUCLID (International Uniform ChemicaL Information Database) entitled *Nanomaterials in IUCLID 5*. These two documents are introduced below with particular focus on the content seeking to address (some of) the uncertainties of REACH's coverage of nanomaterials that were described above.

[149] ibid 380; L Bergkamp and M Penman, 'Conclusions' in L Bergkamp (ed), *The European Union REACH Regulation for Chemicals: Law and Practice* (Oxford, Oxford University Press, 2013) 412.

[150] See European Chemicals Agency, FAQs, www.echa.europa.eu/support/qas-support/browse/-/qa/70Qx/view/topic/REACH.

[151] Interview with an ECHA staff member (Helsinki, 25 November 2013) notes on file with the author.

[152] E Korkea-aho, 'Better Judicial Review? EU Courts and the Smart Regulation Agenda in Implementing Chemicals Regulation' (2012) 6 *Legisprudence* 397, 424 and 422.

[153] See also E Korkea-aho, 'Laws in Progress?' (n 56) 380.

[154] Case C-558/07 *The Queen, on the application of S.P.C.M. SA C.H. Erbslöh KG Lake Chemicals and Minerals Ltd Hercules Inc. v Secretary of State for the Environment, Food and Rural Affairs* [2009] ECR I-5783, Opinion of AG Kokott, paras 127 and 131.

[155] European Chemicals Agency, *Multi-Annual Work Programme 2014–2018* (2013) 24.

i. ECHA Guidance on Information Requirements and Chemical Safety Assessment

In its REACH Guidance on Information Requirements and Chemical Safety Assessment (hereafter 'Guidance on IR and CSA') the European Chemicals Agency details the information requirements laid down in the annexes to REACH. The document thereby aims to assist registrants, ECHA staff and Member States in the completion and evaluation of registration dossiers.[156] The Guidance consists of more than 300 pages, excluding a list of updates, which currently amounts to 21 additional documents.[157] In April 2012, ECHA updated this guidance document via the adoption of six appendices.[158] These appendices clarify the information requirements for substances in nanoform. All six appendices have at their roots the Commission's definition of 'nanomaterial' which is laid down in its recommendation of October 2011.[159]

To illustrate the contents of the appendices, an example is helpful. Annex VII of REACH requires registrants to provide information on the endpoint 'granulometry'—without further specification. Granulometry, according to the Oxford English Dictionary, refers to the 'distribution or measurement of grain sizes in sand, rock, or other deposits'. The respective nano appendix now explains that:

> Granulometry is, as expected, the central issue for nanomaterials. For that reason it is the endpoint requiring most recommendations to cover nanomaterials. The need for

[156] European Chemicals Agency, 'Guidance on Information Requirements and Chemical Safety Assessment Part A: Introduction to the Guidance', Version 1.1 (2011) 8.

[157] The Guidance on IR and CSA as well as its various updates are accessible through ECHA's website.

[158] Three of these appendices hence formulate nano-specific recommendations for physicochemical properties (ECHA, 'Guidance on Information Requirements and Chemical Safety Assessment: Appendix R7-1 Recommendations for Nanomaterials Applicable to Chapter R7a Endpoint Specific Guidance' (2012) www.echa.europa.eu/documents/10162/13632/appendix_r7a_nanomaterials_en.pdf), toxicological information requirements (ECHA, 'Guidance on Information Requirements and Chemical Safety Assessment: Appendix R7-1 Recommendations for Nanomaterials Applicable to Chapter R7b Endpoint Specific Guidance' (2012) www.echa.europa.eu/documents/10162/13632/appendix_r7b_nanomaterials_en.pdf) and ecotoxicological endpoints (ECHA, 'Guidance on Information Requirements and Chemical Safety Assessment: Appendix R7-1 Recommendations for Nanomaterials Applicable to Chapter R7c Endpoint Specific Guidance' www.echa.europa.eu/documents/10162/13632/appendix_r7c_nanomaterials_en.pdf). Two further appendices provide recommendations for nanomaterials in the characterisation of hazards, as regards human health (ECHA, 'Guidance on Information Requirements and Chemical Safety Assessment: Appendix R8-15 Recommendations for Nanomaterials Applicable to Chapter R8 Characterisation of Dose [Concentration]—Response for Human Health' (2012) www.echa.europa.eu/documents/10162/13643/appendix_r8_05-2012_en.pdf) and the environment (ECHA, 'Guidance on Information Requirements and Chemical Safety Assessment: Appendix R10-2 Recommendations for Nanomaterials Applicable to Chapter R10 Characterisation of Dose [Concentration]—Response for Environment' (2012) www.echa.europa.eu/documents/10162/13643/appendix_r10_05-2012_en.pdf). The last appendix contains recommendations on occupational exposure estimation for nanomaterials (ECHA, 'Guidance on Information Requirements and Chemical Safety Assessment: Appendix R14-4 Recommendations for Nanomaterials Applicable to Chapter R14 Occupational Exposure Estimation' (2012) www.echa.europa.eu/documents/10162/13643/appendix_r14_05-2012_en.pdf).

[159] See above chapter 4, section II.B.iii.

> modifications starts already with the definition of what is considered to be covered by the term 'granulometry'.[160]

The appendix hence proposes two possible definitions: Either 'granulometry refers only to particle size distribution' or 'granulometry includes shape and surface area in addition to particle size distribution'.[161] The appendix comes to the conclusion that 'shape and surface area are parameters that need to be taken into account (for instance because of the impact on toxicology), so either they are considered together with the granulometry or proposed to be new endpoints'.[162] It then opts for the second possibility:

> For the purpose of structuring the granulometry section within this appendix it has been considered to be clearer and more helpful to the reader to restrict the scope of text concerning granulometry to consider only particle size distribution and to add two additional sections for discussion of shape and surface area.[163]

In short, in order to make the endpoint 'granulometry' fit for nanomaterials, the guidance update interpreted the term to include two additional endpoints, those of shape and surface area, which do not currently exist in the standard REACH information requirements. Arguably, the nano appendix thereby supplements the requirements in the REACH annexes. Moreover, the drafting history of the guidance update (see for an in-depth analysis section III below) shows that this interpretation of the term 'granulometry' was by no means uncontroversial. On the one hand, stakeholders expressed fundamental concerns as to whether 'surface area' as an endpoint should at all be recommended for inclusion in REACH.[164] On the other hand, the 'Stakeholder Consultation Group'[165] warned that this interpretation would go beyond the current legal requirements of REACH; it found that 'it's a legal issue to decide whether the sub-set parameters of granulometry can be accepted and enforced as an information requirement'.[166]

The distinction between political choice and technical specification emerges here as a particularly fine line. In view of the existing scientific uncertainty, it is reasonable to assume that the identification of additional endpoints does entail political choices. With this interpretation, the guidance update thus addresses uncertainties or ambiguities expounded in the preceding section regarding the adequacy of the standard information requirements for nanomaterials in REACH and its annexes.

[160] ECHA, 'Guidance on Information Requirements and Chemical Safety Assessment: Appendix R7-1' (n 178) 9.
[161] ibid.
[162] ibid.
[163] ibid.
[164] Notes from the 3rd Meeting of the Stakeholder Expert Consultation Group (Brussels, 15 and 16 December 2010) 3 (document on file with the author).
[165] For an in-depth analysis see below section III.
[166] Notes from the 3rd Meeting of the Stakeholder Expert Consultation Group (n 164).

In addition to the practical and indirect legal effects ECHA's guidance documents generally carry in the implementation of REACH (see above section II.C), the update of the Guidance on IR and CSA now seems to have its first concrete impacts for registrants. Within the scope of the REACH compliance check,[167] ECHA issued decisions on three substances that include nanoforms. These decisions require the registrants to submit further information on 'granulometry' before compliance with the REACH information requirements can be established.[168] If the additional information is not provided within the deadline set by the Agency, the concerned substances can no longer be marketed in the European Union. It appears that these decisions draw on the additional information requirements for granulometry as recommended in the nano appendices.[169]

ii. ECHA Guidance on Nanomaterials in IUCLID 5

ECHA adopted a first version of the guidance document *Nanomaterials in IUCLID 5* in June 2010 and updated it three years later in February 2013.[170] Its aim is to provide registrants with directions on how to prepare registration dossiers for nanomaterials using the online submission tool IUCLID. While this document stresses that '[i]t is the responsibility of the registrant to identify the substance and this document does not provide any information that will aid the registrant deciding when a nanomaterial can be considered to be a distinct substance or a nanoform',[171] the 2013 update of the guidance advises registrants to consider the Commission's recommendation for a definition of nanomaterial when making this decision.[172]

The guidance gives instructions on how to include nano-specific information in the IUCLID dossier if the registrant identifies the nanomaterial either as a distinct substance or as a form of the bulk material.[173] If the registrant identifies the nanomaterial as a distinct substance, 'the registrant can complete the IUCLID dossier as for any other substance'.[174] The guidance indicates when additional information about the nanomaterial, such as the information identified in ECHA's update of the Guidance on IR and CSA, can be included in the dossier.[175] If the registrant, to the contrary, considers the substance in nanoform the 'same' substance as its bulk-form equivalent and registers the different forms of the substance together in one

[167] See above section II.A.i.b.

[168] European Chemicals Agency, Newsletter October 2013, Issue 5, 8 www.newsletter.echa.europa.eu/documents/6362380/8854846/newsletter_2013_issue_5_october_en.pdf.

[169] Interview with an ECHA staff member (Helsinki, 25 November 2013) notes on file with the author.

[170] European Chemicals Agency, 'Nanomaterials in IUCLID 5' (Guidance and Support, Version 2.0, February 2013) www.iuclid.eu/index.php?fuseaction=home.documentation&type=public#bprmanual.

[171] ibid 4.

[172] ibid. For a discussion of the Commission's recommendation on a definition of 'nanomaterial' see above Chapter 4, section II.B.iii.

[173] European Chemicals Agency, 'Nanomaterials in IUCLID 5' (n 170) 10.

[174] ibid.

[175] ibid 11.

dossier, 'the registrant is recommended to use labels for each form to enable tracking of specific forms throughout the dossier'.[176] The guidance document explains how this should be done and where the registrant can include information on nanoform-specific physicochemical properties (again with a reference to the nano update of the Guidance on IR and CSA).[177]

In this guidance document ECHA attempted to address the above-identified uncertainty as to how to collect nano-specific information in registration dossiers, especially when the registrant considers the nanoform to be the 'same' substance as the bulkform equivalent. The guidance document was originally adopted shortly before the first REACH registration deadline in December 2010. Significant deficiencies in the nano-specific information provided in the REACH registration dossiers submitted for the 2010 deadline were, however, identified (see also section II.A.ii). The guidance was eventually updated roughly half a year before the second registration deadline in June 2013 and complements the nano appendices to the Guidance on IR and CSA as discussed above.

D. The State of Play: Spotlight on the EU Executive

The preceding analysis showed that the European Commission addresses the presence of chemical substances in nanoform, first, through the (prospective) adoption of implementing acts under REACH and, secondly, by asking the European Chemicals Agency to adjust its existing REACH guidance documents to the particularities of nanomaterials. Consequently, similar to what was witnessed in the food sector in chapter four, the Commission seems wary of instigating a legislative procedure to confront the emergence of nanomaterials and, in its place, explores regulatory options in the executive setting.

First, the path chosen by the Commission implies that three out of the five identified uncertainties regarding the applicability of REACH to nanomaterials[178] remain unaddressed.[179] Those uncertainties—the applicability of the existing tonnage thresholds, the criteria for prioritisation under substance evaluation and the criteria for the identification of SVHC—are enshrined in the legal text of REACH and would require a legislative amendment.[180] The decision of the Commission

[176] ibid 10.

[177] ibid 21.

[178] See above section II.A.ii.

[179] See also E Vogelezang-Stoute, 'Regulating Uncertain Risks of New Technologies: Nanomaterials as a Challenge for the Regulator' in M Peeters and R Uylenburg (eds), *EU Environmental Legislation: Legal Perspectives on Regulatory Strategies*, New Horizons in Environmental and Energy Law (Cheltenham, Edward Elgar Publishing, 2014) 223.

[180] See also J-P Montfort et al, 'Nanomaterials under REACH' (n 124) 55; C Calliess and H Stockhaus, 'Precautionary Principle and Nanomaterials' (n 100) 134. See also 'Summary Record 9th Meeting of the REACH Competent Authorities Sub-Group on Nanomaterials' (n 138) according to which '[s]ome MS questioned the conclusions of COM that amending only REACH annexes would suffice to make REACH more effective for nanomaterials. A MS and an observer expressed doubts whether the legal limits of comitology would enable solutions (eg ability to address phase-in status of new nanoforms of phase-in substances)'.

not to propose changes to its enacting terms was hence in itself of a highly political nature, inciting vehement criticism by the European Parliament, several Member States and stakeholders.

Secondly, the EU executive moved again into the spotlight of regulating nanotechnologies. REACH is constructed in such a way that 'technical and scientific' questions are delegated to the resolution in expert fora at a 'post-legislative' stage.[181] The devil lies in the detail. The nature of the blanks to be filled in is crucial: What if value judgements infiltrate the supposedly technical or scientific process, value judgements that seem intrinsic to the regulation of nanotechnologies? This question arises especially when considering the drafting history of the nano appendices to the Guidance on IR and CSA. The choices contained therein no longer seem to fit into the 'drawer of technical specification', as it was called in the preceding food case study. Here, policy choices appear to be cloaked in scientific or technical language. At the same time, the nano appendices seem de facto to supplement the information requirements of the annexes of REACH. This, coupled with the practical and indirect legal effects of REACH guidance documents, conveys the impression that the nano appendices were used to substitute (at least temporarily) a formal non-legislative procedure.

A lot of (political) responsibility hence rests on the shoulders of ECHA. To recall, according to REACH, the Agency was established 'for the purposes of managing and in some cases carrying out the technical, scientific and administrative aspects of this Regulation'.[182] Like EFSA, ECHA is hence formally precluded from taking political risk management decisions—in line with the principle of risk analysis and, arguably, the non-delegation doctrine of *Meroni*.[183] In view of the preceding analysis, however, there is room to argue that ECHA, like EFSA, developed in practice beyond the legislative mandate. ECHA's guidance documents and their adoption procedure therefore require closer scrutiny, which will be undertaken in the subsequent sections of this chapter when analysing the current developments through the lenses of regulatory capacity.

III. ANALYSING THE EU'S REGULATION OF NANOCHEMICALS THROUGH THE LENSES OF REGULATORY CAPACITY

The examination of the status quo of the EU regulatory framework for chemicals revealed that the European Commission has been addressing the rise of nanotechnologies not via a legislative amendment of REACH but via ECHA guidance

[181] See for the term 'post-legislative', J Scott, 'In Legal Limbo: Post-Legislative Guidance as a Challenge for European Administrative Law' (2011) 48 *Common Market Law Review* 329.

[182] Art 75(1) REACH.

[183] On the principle of risk analysis, see above chapter 2, section III.B.i. On the *Meroni* doctrine, see above chapter 3, section II.B.iii.a.

documents and, prospectively, Commission implementing act(s). This section scrutinises the applicability and operation of the procedures instigated by the EU regulator, introduced in chapter three, for pooling knowledge (below section A) and ensuring the input (below section B) and output (below section C) legitimacy of its regulatory activities. Since the Commission's implementing act(s) is (are) still on the drawing board, the ensuing analysis thereof is preliminary and limited to the information already available.

A. Pooling Knowledge

The main tool instigated by the EU regulator in the aftermath of the European governance debate to bring together the societally dispersed knowledge in the drafting of policy and legislative initiatives is the impact assessment procedure.[184] Furthermore, the sources of scientific and technical knowledge were reformed by putting in place (new) procedural frameworks for the creation and operation of Commission expert groups and EU agencies.[185] In line with the previous food case study, this section turns to the analysis of the application and practical operation of these procedures, first, in the current drafting process of the REACH implementing acts and, secondly, in the drafting of ECHA's guidance documents.

i. Pooling Knowledge in the Drafting of the REACH Implementing Act(s)

a. The Commission's Impact Assessment?

The food case study illustrated the ambiguous scope of application of the Commission's 2009 Impact Assessment Guidelines.[186] There, it was found that the 2009 Guidelines were clearly applicable only to legislative acts. Implementing acts, by inference, escaped the commitment except where they carried 'significant

[184] European Commission, 'Impact Assessment Guidelines' SEC (2009) 92. Furthermore, Parliament and Council agreed to conduct its own impact assessments in case of 'substantive amendments', see European Commission, European Parliament and Council of Ministers, 'Interinstitutional Common Approach to Impact Assessment' (2005) www.ec.europa.eu/smart-regulation/impact/key_docs/docs/ii_common_approach_to_ia_en.pdf. For an introduction to and discussion of these procedures, see above chapter 3, sections II.A.ii and II.A.iii.

[185] The procedural framework for Commission expert groups is laid down in European Commission, 'Framework for Commisison's Expert Groups: Horizontal Rules and Public Register' (Communication) C(2010) 7649 final, revised in 2016 by European Commission, 'Commission decision of 30.5.2016 establishing horizontal rules on the creation and operation of Commission expert groups' C(2016) 3301 final. The procedural framework for decentralised EU agencies is established by the Joint Statement of the European Parliament, the Council of the EU and the European Commission on decentralised agencies www.europa.eu/european-union/sites/europaeu/files/docs/body/joint_statement_and_common_approach_2012_en.pdf. For an introduction to and discussion of these frameworks, see above chapter 3, sections II.A.ii.a and II.A.ii.b.

[186] See above chapter 4, section III.A.i.a.

impacts'.[187] The absence of a definition of 'significant impacts', in turn, opened up a grey zone and, consequently, left broad discretion to the Commission in deciding on the applicability of the Guidelines on a case-by-case basis. The preceding chapter thus criticised the fact that the two implementing acts under the Food Contact Materials Regulation[188] were adopted without a prior impact assessment being performed—despite the important ('significant') impacts their nano provisions entail for affected actors.

For the forthcoming implementing act(s) under REACH, the Commission decided differently. Although the Commission's Joint Research Centre had already conducted the Nano Support Project for the REACH revision of 2013, which entailed an evaluation of the adequacy of the information requirements for nanomaterials,[189] the Commission still considered it necessary to launch a formal impact assessment, including the integrated public consultation. While the final impact assessment is yet to be adopted, the Commission presented an early analysis of the consultation's results in a discussion paper in November 2013[190] and published a draft ('inception') impact assessment in February 2016.[191] Given the broad resistance that the Commission faced with its decision not to revise the enacting terms of REACH, the decision for an impact assessment certainly has a political dimension in order to achieve a greater acceptability of the forthcoming draft proposal(s).[192] Indeed, the highly politicised debate around the REACH revision and especially the question of the treatment of nanomaterials therein must be contrasted with the relatively unnoticed amendment of the implementing acts for plastics and intelligent food packaging discussed in the preceding chapter four. At the time, parliamentary attention mainly focused on the parallel legislative procedure and the coverage of nanomaterials under the Novel Food Regulation.

b. Consulting the 'Competent Authorities for REACH and CLP'

The 'Competent Authorities for REACH and CLP' (CARACAL) are an integral part of the impact assessment process, as well as for the drafting of the

[187] ibid.

[188] For a discussion of the two implementing acts under the Food Contact Materials Regulation, see above Chapter 4, section II.B.i.

[189] See above section II.A.i.

[190] 'Impact Assessment of Modifications of the REACH Annexes for Nanomaterials' (n 144) 4–8. According to this document, the Commission received a total of 142 submissions.

[191] 'Possible amendments of annexes to REACH for registration of nanomaterials' (n 32).

[192] Radaelli and Meuwese describe this use of impact assessments as 'bracket[ing] disagreement', see CM Radaelli and A Meuwese, 'Hard Questions, Hard Solutions: Proceduralisation through Impact Assessment in the EU' (2010) 33 *West European Politics* 136, 143.

implementing act(s) more generally.[193] The CARACAL, in line with the Horizontal Rules on Expert Groups,[194] is an expert group of the Commission, which assists in the implementation of REACH. The group consists of representatives from all Member States as well as 30 observers, including third country authorities, NGOs, international organisations, trade unions and industry associations.[195] It is important to note that the Member States in the CARACAL are mostly the same national representatives that also sit in the respective comitology committee, the 'Committee established under the Regulation concerning the Registration, Evaluation, Authorisation and Restriction of Chemicals (REACH)'.

According to the CARACAL's rules of procedure, the Commission shall publish all relevant documents, such as agendas, minutes and participants' submissions, in the Register of Expert Groups.[196] Accordingly, for the CARACAL's meeting of November 2013, the Commission circulated two discussion papers on the modification of the REACH annexes for nanomaterials.[197] The comments Member States and observers submitted prior to the meeting (if any) are, however, not publicly available. In the discussion papers, Member State representatives were invited to consider several questions regarding the testing needs of nanomaterials, related costs, as well as 'how to balance between "need to know", "nice to know", and the associated additional costs'.[198] Overall, the CARACAL seems very closely involved in the ongoing drafting process of the implementing act(s). A reason therefore could also be that it is composed of the same Member States representatives who eventually approve the measure(s) in the comitology procedure. The group's impact thus cannot be compared to the role of the Advisory Group on the Food Chain in the drafting of the plastics measure under the Food Contact Materials Regulation.[199] Only in one aspect may the two groups be paralleled: in the difficulty of tracing their members' input.

[193] More information about the expert group CARACAL can be found in the Commission register of expert groups, www.ec.europa.eu/transparency/regexpert/index.cfm?do=groupDetail.groupDetail&groupID=2385.

[194] 'Framework for Commission's expert groups' C(2010) 7649 final (n 185), revised in May 2016 by 'Commission decision of 30.5.2016 establishing horizontal rules on the creation and operation of Commission expert groups' C(2016) 3301 final (n 185), see above chapter 3, section II.A.ii.a.

[195] For a complete list of members, see www.ec.europa.eu/transparency/regexpert/index.cfm?do=groupDetail.groupDetail&groupID=2385. The Commission appoints stakeholder organisations to become observers to the group, see European Commission 'Revised Rules of Procedure for the Competent Authorities for REACH and CLP (CARACAL)' (CA/03/2009-Rev. 1, 9 November 2012) Art 2(e).

[196] ibid Art 13.

[197] 'Impact Assessment of Modifications of the REACH Annexes for Nanomaterials' (n 144); European Commission, 'Modifications of the REACH Annexes for Nanomaterials' (13th Meeting of Competent Authorities for REACH and CLP (CARACAL), CA/53/2013, 14 November 2013).

[198] 'Impact Assessment of Modifications of the REACH Annexes for Nanomaterials' (n 144) 3.

[199] See above chapter 4, section III.A.ii.

ii. Pooling Knowledge in the Drafting of ECHA's Guidance Documents

Since the Commission's impact assessment commitment is restricted to 'Commission initiatives',[200] ECHA, like EFSA, is not obliged to conduct impact assessments of its regulatory output. At the same time, the European Chemicals Agency has assumed a key role in the regulation of nanotechnologies in chemicals through the adoption of its guidance documents. It is pertinent therefore to ask: how is ECHA drafting these documents? In the subsequent paragraphs, the procedure established by ECHA for the adoption of guidance documents is sketched first. Afterwards, the operation of this procedure is examined in practice for both of the guidance documents under scrutiny in this chapter. The results are then assessed and compared to the procedure according to which EFSA adopted its nano guidance in the food sector.

a. ECHA's Procedure for the Adoption of Guidance Documents

REACH, like the General Food Law, does not prescribe a specific procedure for the adoption of ECHA guidance documents. This task has been delegated to ECHA's Management Board,[201] which adopted a 'Consultation Procedure for Guidance' in 2008.[202] The procedure applies to 'technical and scientific guidance' referred to in Article 77(2)(g) and (h) of REACH.[203]

In the first step of this procedure, the ECHA Secretariat[204] identifies the need to draft new or to update existing guidance documents.[205] Once such a need is identified, the Secretariat prepares an initial draft. External experts and the Commission may be involved at the Agency's discretion. The ECHA Secretariat subsequently launches a consultation process with affected societal actors. First, the draft guidance is presented to the so-called Partner Expert Group (PEG), which consists of 'experts from the various stakeholders and institutional interested parties'.[206] The PEG members are nominated by the 'institutional interested parties', which

[200] 'Impact Assessment Guidelines' SEC (2009) 92 (n 184) 6.

[201] The Management Board 'shall adopt the internal rules and procedures of the Agency. These rules shall be made public', see Art 78 REACH.

[202] European Chemicals Agency, '(Revised) Consultation Procedure on Guidance' (Document endorsed by the Management Board, MB/14/2011 final, Helsinki, 25 March 2011); updated by European Chemicals Agency, 'Second Revision to the Consultation Procedure for Guidance' (MB/63/2013 (final), Helsinki, 18 December 2013).

[203] '(Revised) Consultation Procedure on Guidance' (n 202) 2 (fn 2).

[204] ECHA has a Unit A.2 'Guidance and Forum Secretariat', whose task is, among others, to 'coordinate the development of new guidance and update existing ECHA guidance documents on REACH, CLP and other EU legislation', see www.echa.europa.eu/de/about-us/who-we-are/directorates-and-units/directorate-a.

[205] For these purposes, the Secretariat gathers information from industry via the REACH helpdesks, MS Competent Authorities (MSCAs) and from the general public via online feedback forms available on ECHA's website.

[206] '(Revised) Consultation Procedure on Guidance' (n 202) 5.

include ECHA, Member States, the Commission and third country representatives, and by 'Accredited Stakeholder Organisations' that are selected by ECHA according to eligibility criteria approved by its Management Board.[207] The eligibility criteria comprise (1) the organisation's legal establishment in the EU/EEA with activities at the EU level; (2) the organisation's legitimate interest in ECHA's work;[208] (3) the organisation's representative function in its field of competence; and (4) the organisation's non-profit making nature.[209] Organisations that meet these criteria can apply to the Agency via an open call for expressions of interest.[210] The nominees appointed by the Accredited Stakeholder Organisations and by the institutional interested parties then become the members of the PEG who are invited to discuss the draft guidance. Based on their comments, the ECHA Secretariat may modify the draft.

It is at the discretion of ECHA's Secretariat additionally to consult the Agency's committees (the Risk Assessment Committee, the Committee for Socio-Economic Analysis or the Member State Committee) and/or the Agency's Enforcement Forum. This decision is taken by the Agency on a case-by-case basis.[211] The 2011 version of the consultation procedure provided furthermore that '[i]n certain cases, in particular for entirely new guidance, it may be decided to launch a general Internet consultation'.[212] Such a general Internet consultation is no longer foreseen in the latest revision of the procedure in December 2013.[213] Finally, the Commission and Member State competent authorities are consulted as a mandatory step 'to ensure that the amendment, revision or new guidance will find as wide as possible support and harmonised implementation by all authorities'.[214] Based on the outcome of this last consultation, the ECHA Secretariat produces the final text. The procedure is summarised in Figure 2.

[207] European Chemicals Agency, 'ECHA's approach to engagement with its Accredited Stakeholder Organisations' (Document endorsed by the Management Board, MB/69/2011, Helsinki, 16 December 2011). Pursuant to Article 108 REACH, 'the Management Board shall … develop appropriate contacts between the Agency and relevant stakeholder organisations'.

[208] A stakeholder organisation may have a legitimate interest either because it represents a sector affected by EU chemicals legislation or because it represents a sector that is indirectly affected, such as NGOs.

[209] '(Revised) Consultation Procedure on Guidance' (n 202).

[210] ibid 7. An updated list of ASOs is available on ECHA's website, see www.echa.europa.eu/about-us/partners-and-networks/stakeholders/echas-accredited-stakeholder-organisations. Around 70 ASOs are currently listed. ASOs, after having signed a declaration of interest, a code of conduct and a declaration of confidentiality (see 'ECHA's approach to engagement with its Accredited Stakeholder Organisations' (n 207) 3) may be invited to participate in the meetings of the Agency's committees, the forum, may be consulted on scientific/technical issues for instance via the PEG, and are encouraged to participate in public consultations.

[211] '(Revised) Consultation Procedure on Guidance' (n 202) 4.

[212] ibid.

[213] 'Second Revision to the Consultation Procedure for Guidance' (n 202).

[214] '(Revised) Consultation Procedure on Guidance' (n 202) 5.

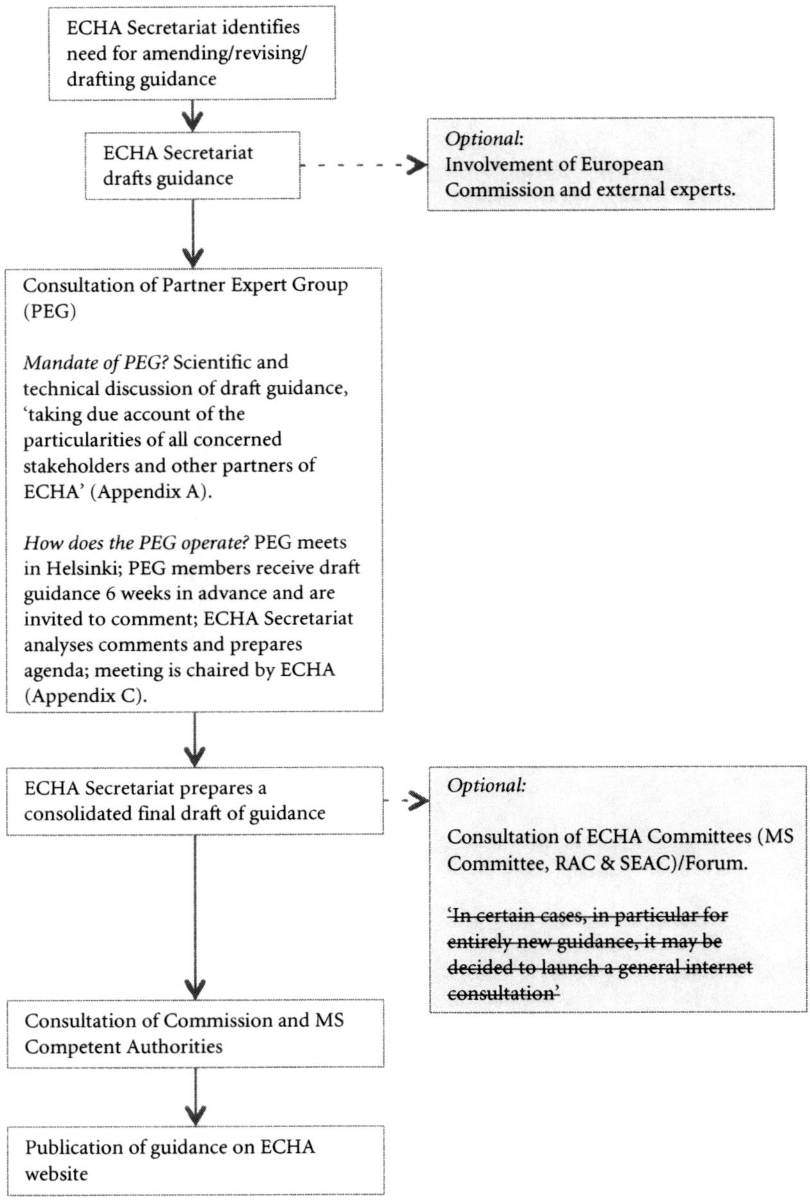

Figure 2: ECHA Procedure for the Drafting/Updating of Guidance Documents (2013)

b. Operation of the Procedure to Update the Guidance on IR and CSA

Moving on to practice, the next two sections will examine the operation of ECHA's consultation procedure on guidance in the adoption of the two guidance documents identified in section II. ECHA publishes drafts developed at the various steps of the procedure on its website as well as the individual comments received at the different consultation levels (including the Agency's responses) 'in order to ensure that the guidance updating process will be kept transparent and open to participation by relevant partners'.[215]

For the update of the Guidance on IR and CSA, the website specifies that ECHA followed a 'fast-track procedure'. Two documents are published for each of the six nano appendices. First, the Agency published the draft appendices that it sent to the CARACAL. Secondly, the Agency made available an excel spreadsheet containing the CARACAL's comments on the draft appendices as well as ECHA's replies to those comments. This means that, out of the various steps of the consultation procedure on guidance, ECHA merely followed two: the Agency drafted the six nano appendices and then—without creating a Partner Expert Group, consulting its committees or the general public—launched the last consultative step by forwarding the drafts to the Member States assembled in the CARACAL.

Indeed, ECHA's consultation procedure on guidance provides for the possibility of a 'fast-track update' when:

> time pressure (or potentially other considerations) requires setting short deadlines and/or streamlining the consultation process. The choice of the fast-track procedure needs to be confirmed by either the ECHA business programme board for foreseeable justifications as listed in 3.1[216] or by the Executive Director in other cases. The ECHA Secretariat shall in all cases provide a written justification for using the fast-track procedure.[217]

The feedback provided by ECHA in response to the CARACAL's comments discloses that the fast-track procedure was considered justified since 'consensus' on the update of the guidance had already been achieved at an earlier stage.[218] In fact, all draft appendices explain that the 'content of the appendi[ces] implements the advice provided by the REACH Implementation Project on Nanomaterials'.

The REACH Implementation Project on Nanomaterials (RIPoN)

The REACH Implementation Project on Nanomaterials (RIPoN) is a project funded and coordinated by the Commission's Joint Research Centre since 2009.

[215] See www.echa.europa.eu/support/guidance/consultation-procedure/closed-reach.

[216] These 'foreseeable justifications' are: (1) 'fast-track updates concerning only legal issues with no major technical implications', (2) 'fast-track updates to guidance targeted mainly at industry, which include technical and other non-legal issues' and (3) 'fast-track updates to guidance targeted mainly at ECHA itself and/or the Competent Authorities', see 'Second Revision to the Consultation Procedure for Guidance' (n 202) 6.

[217] ibid 4.

[218] See document on ECHA website named 'caracal_comments_r8_en' www.echa.europa.eu/support/guidance/consultation-procedure/closed-reach.

It is divided into three sub-projects on substance identity (RIPoN1), information requirements (RIPoN2) and chemical safety assessment (RIPoN3). The mandate of the project is to provide recommendations with a view to updating the current REACH guidance documents to nanomaterials. RIPoN2 and RIPoN3, which have already been completed, constitute the basis for the update of the Guidance on IR and CSA. The sub-projects were carried out by a project consortium, whose members were chosen based on a call for tender by the Joint Research Centre.[219]

The RIPoN reports indicate that, before finalisation, they underwent a two-stage review process. First, the reports were presented to the 'European Commission Steering Group', consisting of the Joint Research Centre, DG Environment, DG Enterprise, and ECHA.[220] Secondly, a 'Stakeholder Consultation Group' reviewed the task reports. This group comprised the CARACAL and 'relevant experts from Member States, industry and NGOs nominated by the CARACAL'.[221] Who exactly participated in this 'Stakeholder Consultation Group' and how it operated in practice will be analysed more closely in section III.B.ii on participation. The final RIPoN reports were subsequently forwarded to ECHA.

Consultation of the Commission Expert Group CARACAL

ECHA, in a next step, converted the RIPoN reports into the six draft appendices. An ECHA staff member confirmed that at this stage only editorial changes were made to the RIPoN reports.[222] The draft appendices were then forwarded, or rather resubmitted, to the Member States sitting in the CARACAL. The CARACAL's comments to the drafts and ECHA's replies are contained in the excel spreadsheets published on ECHA's website.[223] It is important to note that the comments are not made available via a mechanism foreseen in the expert group's own rules of procedure but via ECHA's consultation procedure on guidance. The CARACAL's own minutes do not contain the individual comments submitted by the national representatives. This lack of transparency on the expert group's operation was already remarked upon when analysing its role in the current drafting of the REACH implementing act(s).[224] More generally, it confirms findings of the preceding food case study, where the minutes of the Advisory Group on the Food Chain were also found to be of meagre substance.[225]

The operation of ECHA's consultation procedure in the adoption of the nano appendices to the Guidance on IR and CSA is summarised in Figure 3.

[219] NIA, Safenano and Cefic, 'Specific Advice on Fulfilling Information Requirements for Nanomaterials under REACH (RIP-oN 2)' (Final Project Report, RNC/RIP-oN2/FPR/1/FINAL, 2011) 2.

[220] ibid iv.

[221] ibid.

[222] Interview with an ECHA staff member (Helsinki, 25 November 2013) notes on file with the author.

[223] Accordingly, national representatives provided a total of 52 comments. The Netherlands provided 22 comments, Germany 16, Sweden 6, the UK 4, and Portugal 4.

[224] See above section III.A.i.b.

[225] See above chapter 4, section III.A.ii.

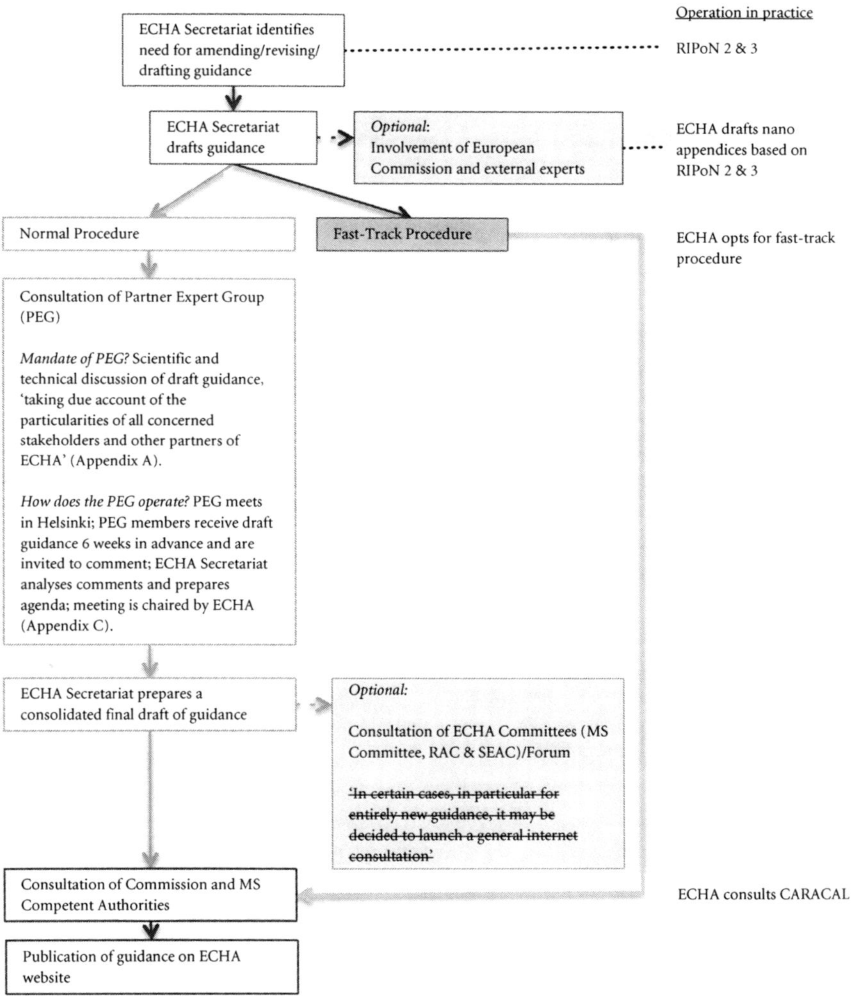

Figure 3: Operation of ECHA's Procedure in Updating the Guidance on IR and CSA

c. Operation of the Procedure in the Adoption of the Guidance on Nanomaterials in IUCLID 5

Contrary to the Guidance on IR and CSA, the Guidance on Nanomaterials in IUCLID 5 did not count as 'guidance' for the purposes of ECHA's consultation procedure on guidance.[226] ECHA confirmed that 'despite the conclusion which

[226] ECHA's consultation procedure on guidance only applies to guidance referred to in Art 77(2)(g) and (h) REACH, see above section III.A.ii.a.

could be admittedly drawn from the inclusion of the words "guidance and support" within its title, the document was not considered as within the scope of the said consultation procedure'.[227] ECHA further explains that the Guidance on Nanomaterials in IUCLID 5 'is a technical manual', which does not fall within the scope of '"formal" ECHA REACH guidance documents' and further that 'there was no specific procedure in place at the time that the document was generated'.[228] While the whole adoption procedure outlined in Figure 3 was hence not considered applicable, there is also no indication as to how the guidance was drafted instead.[229]

d. Evaluation and Comparison with EFSA's Procedure for the Adoption of Guidance Documents

In the abstract, ECHA's consultation procedure on guidance emerges as a complex constellation of consultation levels and opportunities for affected actors, Member States and the Commission to contribute their knowledge to the drafting process. Three features of the procedure stand out, especially in comparison to the manner in which EFSA adopted its nano guidance.[230]

First, the ECHA Secretariat materialises as a key figure not only in the coordination of the procedure but also in shaping the contents of guidance documents. On the one hand, ECHA enjoys the 'right of initiative' to instigate the adoption process. On the other hand, the Secretariat organises the PEG, decides upon the necessity to initiate further consultations[231] and prepares the consolidated and final versions of the guidance. This powerful role is remarkable, potentially worrisome, given the double-hat function that falls on the agency in drafting 'the rules' and, thereafter, in being charged with their implementation.[232] By comparison, although the European Food Safety Authority's Secretariat is initially involved in the selection of the members in the working group,[233] it subsequently serves an

[227] Reply to an access to document request under Regulation 1049/2001 (Regulation (EC) 1049/2001 of the European Parliament and of the Council of 30 May 2001 regarding public access to European Parliament, Council and Commission documents [2001] OJ L145/43). The document is on file with the author.

[228] ibid.

[229] Generally, IUCLID is maintained under the responsibility of ECHA, in collaboration with the OECD. Whether or not the OECD was involved in the adoption process of the guidance is unclear. From the overview of ECHA's organisation, it becomes apparent that the Agency has a specific unit that is charged with the 'specifi[cation] and promot[ion] [of] IUCLID for industry and authority use for reporting, processing, as well as exchanging, chemicals data' and furthermore participates in or chairs the OECD working group related to IUCLID, see Directorate C "Registration", Unit C3 'Computational Assessment', see www.echa.europa.eu/fr/about-us/who-we-are/directorates-and-units/directorate-c.

[230] For an analysis of EFSA's adoption procedure of scientific opinions, see above chapter 4, section III.A.iii and Figure 2.

[231] ie of ECHA's Risk Assessment Committee, the Committee for Socio-Economic Analysis, the Member State Committee and the Enforcement Forum.

[232] See also E Korkea-aho, 'Laws in Progress?' (n 56) 372.

[233] See above chapter 4, section III.A.iii.

administrative support function to the working group's operation. Decisions on the instigation of public consultations, or on whether or not comments provided by affected actors are incorporated into the opinion, are formally taken by the working group itself.

Secondly, ECHA's consultation procedure on guidance places, paradoxically as we go on to argue, a great emphasis on the reconciliation of different knowledge claims. This is most evident from the creation of the PEG, whose consultation constitutes a mandatory step in the 'normal' procedure and whose stated aim is 'to prepare for the necessary buy-in from all ECHA partners'.[234] Having said that, both the actual mandate of the PEG as well as its practical significance are questionable. Approximately 70 accredited stakeholder organisations are currently listed on ECHA's website,[235] all of which can theoretically nominate members to the PEG. To those must be added the appointees of the 'institutional interested parties'. The result is a potentially large group of stakeholders in which it is difficult to imagine that substantive discussions on REACH's details take place. It is therefore hardly astonishing that ECHA's latest revision of the consultation procedure clarifies that in case of 'controversial issues' within the PEG, ECHA can go ahead in the drafting process.[236] Disagreement must not even be recorded in the final guidance document.[237] This raises doubts as to whether the PEG is a true means to gather knowledge from the diversely affected societal actors or rather a tool to signal participation to the outside world in order to foster the acceptability for the guidance (see further section II.B.ii on 'participation'). Leaving the practical operation of the PEG aside for a moment, however, its mere existence and the acknowledgement that it might be faced with 'controversial issues' arguably conflicts with ECHA's formal mandate, namely that of a scientific or technical advisor barred from taking political decisions. The paradox boils down to this: how could one debate the 'scientific truth'? ECHA's consultation procedure thus implicitly acknowledges the (potential) political nature of the content of its guidance documents. Here, EFSA's procedural design is different. In the adoption of its guidance documents such situations do not arise formally. In public consultations launched by EFSA, the emphasis is strictly on 'enhancing the quality and completeness of EFSA's scientific outputs',[238] which is reflected in the absence of a requirement to

[234] 'Second Revision to the Consultation Procedure for Guidance' (n 202) 10.

[235] An updated list of the accredited stakeholder organisations is available through ECHA's website, see www.echa.europa.eu/web/guest/about-us/partners-and-networks/stakeholders/echas-accredited-stakeholder-organisations. It is interesting to note that the 'vast majority' of accredited stakeholder organisations are industry representatives, see also E Stokes and S Vaughan, 'Great Expectations: Reviewing 50 Years of Chemicals Legislation in the EU' (2013) 25 *Journal of Environmental Law* 411, 433.

[236] 'Second Revision to the Consultation Procedure for Guidance' (n 202) 10.

[237] See, on this point, E Korkea-aho, 'Laws in Progress?' (n 56) 371.

[238] European Food Safety Authority, 'Policy on Independence and Scientific Decision-Making Processes of the European Food Safety Authority' (Adopted by Management Board, 15 December 2011) 8.

include all affected actors in EFSA's consultation standards.[239] To exaggerate for the sake of clarity, EFSA sticks to its official mission, which is to collect input in the quest for the scientific truth. This, however, does not alter the fact that both agencies were shown to engage, de facto, in political choices when drafting their guidance documents.

This tension in ECHA's consultation procedure on guidance is also reflected in the fact that both the Commission and Member States, that is, the risk managers, occupy formal roles in the procedure. On the one hand, the Commission may already be involved at drafting stage and, thereafter, has the power to appoint a member to the PEG. On the other hand, the Commission and Member States are mandatorily consulted as a last 'conclusive' step of the procedure. Under EFSA's procedure, whilst the consultation of Member States is merely optional, no formal role is foreseen for the Commission.

In the absence of an impact assessment requirement and a procedure prescribed in the agencies' founding regulations, EFSA and ECHA have hence put in place fundamentally different procedures for the adoption of guidance documents. Partly, these differences also relate to the 'scientific opinion' form[240] in which EFSA adopted its nano guidance. ECHA, to the contrary, follows distinct procedures for the adoption of opinions by its committees, which form part of an authorisation procedure for SVHC[241] (classic scientific opinions as they were called in the context of EFSA), on the one hand, and for its guidance documents, on the other. These procedures diverge substantially. In the adoption of opinions, ECHA follows a procedure which is mainly laid down in REACH itself[242] and which comes much closer to the procedure according to which EFSA adopted its nano guidance.

Having undertaken this abstract analysis of ECHA's consultation procedure, it is time to turn to its operation in practice. Surprisingly, it was observed that the procedure was not followed by the Agency in the adoption of both guidance documents under scrutiny in this chapter. In the case of the Guidance on Nanomaterials in IUCLID 5, the procedure was simply not considered applicable. 'Guidance' does not necessarily equal 'guidance' in ECHA jargon. While it may be justified to have put distinct procedures in place for the adoption of distinct types of documents, the existence of different types of 'guidance' is confusing and gnaws at their transparency.

On the contrary, the update of the Guidance on IR and CSA fell within the scope of application of ECHA's consultation procedure. Here, however, the Agency considered the launch of its 'normal' procedure not necessary given the existence

[239] See above chapter 4, section III.B.ii.b.

[240] See above chapter 4, section II.B.ii. To recall, EFSA's founding regulation, the General Food Law, does not provide for a separate category of guidance documents next to scientific opinions.

[241] European Chemicals Agency, 'Working Procedure for RAC and SEAC for developing opinions on the applications for authorisation' (RAC/14/2010/65, SEAC/08/2010/19_rev.1, 2010).

[242] Art 64 REACH. This procedure has been further elaborated in a document adopted by the RAC and SEAC, see 'Working Procedure for RAC and SEAC (n 242).

of the Commission's foregoing RIPoN project. The option for a 'fast-track update' resulted in the consultations of the PEG, the ECHA committees and the general public being skipped. In other words, the RIPoN process de facto replaced ECHA's own adoption procedure. By inference, the Agency's Secretariat in practice did not assume the key position that may have been expected based on the theoretical analysis of the procedure, but merely converted the RIPoN recommendations into guidance format. Equally, apart from Member States and 'observers' in the CARACAL, affected actors were not involved in the adoption process at ECHA level. The Commission and its expert group CARACAL, on the contrary, were granted a leading role by being consulted twice.

The elephant in the room is, first, why the RIPoN was launched although the responsibility for adopting guidance documents had been delegated to ECHA and, apart from that, whether the RIPoN process was indeed comparable to and consequently capable of substituting the ECHA process—whether the same actors were involved and whether it resulted, as the 'normal' ECHA procedure would foresee, in an exposition of the knowledge gathered.

There seems to be no obvious answer to the first query. To be sure, the REACH Implementation Projects (RIPs) were not invented for nanomaterials but already existed as a tool to craft guidance documents before ECHA started operating—in order to provide guidance to affected actors in the anticipation of their REACH obligations.[243] When the Agency started operating, however, the responsibility for the drafting of guidance was shifted to ECHA.[244] While there is no official reason why the Commission reverted to this pre-ECHA tool to prepare the nano appendices, an ECHA staff member indicated that the RIPoN was launched due to the lack of internal resources within ECHA. In any case, the recourse to the RIPoN confirms the strong control that the Commission exerts on ECHA's guidance drafting process in practice. The second question, to what extent the RIPoN review process was able to substitute ECHA's consultation procedure on guidance, will be resumed in the following sections on 'participation' and 'accountability'.

iii. Synthesis: Pooling Knowledge

The aim of this section was to put to the test the procedures that the EU regulator established in the wake of the European governance debate for pooling the societally fragmented knowledge from affected actors in the drafting of a regulatory framework for nanotechnologies in chemicals. The first point to note is that, in contrast to our observations in the food sector, in the drafting of the forthcoming

[243] The Recitals to REACH clarify that the RIPs 'aim at developing draft guidelines and tools which should help the Commission, the Agency, Member States, manufacturers, importers and downstream users of substances to fulfil, in concrete terms, their obligations under this Regulation. This work should enable the Commission and the Agency to make available appropriate technical guidance, in due time, with regard to the deadlines introduced by this Regulation', see Recital 24 REACH.

[244] In line with Art 77(2) REACH. See also E Korkea-aho, 'Laws in Progress?' (n 56) 366.

REACH implementing act(s) the Commission opted for the performance of an impact assessment. This is remarkable considering that it was concluded that, due to the vagueness of the scope of the 2009 Impact Assessment Guidelines, the Commission could have easily escaped the commitment. Thus the question that arose, why did the Commission choose to do so? Was the impact assessment really a means to pool knowledge? Whilst it seemed that this question could not be answered in the negative, especially in view of the existence of the Joint Research Centre's Nano Support project (which had already analysed the adequacy of current information requirements for nanomaterials in the Annexes for the REACH review),[245] that was not the sole reason. Given the ignited political discussions that accompanied the Commission's decision to only amend the REACH annexes, the impact assessment emerges as a strategic device to pour oil on troubled waters and to present a 'solid evidence base' for the Commission's draft proposal(s) in the comitology procedure.

Of particular note is the omnipresence of the Commission and its expert group CARACAL in the drafting of a regulatory framework for nanochemicals. Not only are the draft proposal(s) of the REACH implementing act(s) intensely discussed in this group, the group and the Commission also dominated the preparation of the nano appendices to ECHA's Guidance on IR and CSA. This is the case even though ECHA, like EFSA in the food sector, developed a complex procedural web for the adoption of guidance documents. In practice, however, large parts of the procedure were skipped due to the possibility of a 'fast track update', recourse to which the Agency justified with the foregoing RIPoN process. Under the tight control of the Commission and CARACAL, the RIPoN therewith effectively replaced ECHA's own procedure. This firm role of the risk manager in the drafting of purportedly scientific or technical guidance documents is remarkable; it even led to the conclusion that this acknowledges, if only implicitly, the political and potentially controversial substance ECHA's guidance document carries in practice. What became clear furthermore is that the role of the CARACAL is substantially different from that of the Advisory Group on the Food Chain discussed in chapter four. While both expert groups are advisory in nature on paper, the fact that most national representatives in the CARACAL wear two hats (as members of the respective comitology committee) renders their advice quasi-binding.

B. Participation

This section turns to input legitimacy and to the analysis of the procedures implemented to ensure the participation of affected actors in drafting the REACH

[245] 'Scientific technical support on assessment of nanomaterials in REACH registration dosssiers and adequacy of available information' (n 108); 'Examination and Assessment of Consequences for Industry, Consumers, Human Health and the Environment of Possible Options for Changing the REACH Requirements for Nanomaterials' (n 137).

implementing act(s) and in updating ECHA's guidance documents. The yardstick will be the two criteria derived from the ideal speech situation: 'full inclusion' of 'all affected actors' and 'equality'.[246] Whereas it was assumed that the representation of affected actors through the European Parliament (political participation) generally approximates the ideal speech situation, their direct participation in the regulatory process (administrative participation) demands closer examination. Indeed, following the White Paper on Governance, the Commission adopted a set of minimum consultation standards.[247] The applicability and practical operation of these standards will be analysed with regard to the Habermasian ideal. To enable a comparison to the food case study, the guiding questions will be the same as those of chapter four:

— Was the European Parliament involved in the adoption of the regulatory options?
— Did affected societal actors have the opportunity to contribute directly to the drafting process?
— If so, were the Commission's minimum consultation standards applicable? If they were applicable, were they complied with in practice?
— If the Commission's minimum consultation standards were not applicable, were other procedures set in place?
— To what extent did administrative participation approximate the criteria derived from the Habermasian ideal speech situation?

i. Participation in the Drafting of REACH's Implementing Act(s)

a. Parliamentary Involvement

Chapter four introduced parliamentary involvement in comitology as the scene of an interinstitutional battleground between Parliament, Council and Commission that has been ongoing for decades.[248] While the cards were lastly reshuffled with the Lisbon Treaty and the distinction between delegated and implementing acts, the REACH implementing act(s) are still adopted under the 'old' regulatory procedure with scrutiny.[249] Whether or not the Parliament will make use of its hard-won veto right granted therein remains to be seen. In the food case study, it was seen, however, that the Parliament did not use its veto right to block the implementing acts under the Food Contact Materials Regulation.[250] The question

[246] See above chapter 3, section II.B.ii.

[247] For a discussion, see above chapter 3, section II.B.ii.b. 'Towards a reinforced culture of consultation and dialogue' COM (2002) 704 final (n 216) 3.

[248] See above chapter 4, section III.B.i.

[249] See Art 5a, Council Decision 1999/468/EC of 28 June 1999 laying down the procedures for the exercise of implementing powers conferred on the Commission [1999] OJ L184/23.

[250] See above chapter 4, section III.B.i.

that lurks in the background is therefore whether the Parliament did not want to make use of its right of scrutiny or could not make use of it, for instance due to a lack of necessary resources. The former reason was considered unlikely due to the Parliament's driver position in the legislative review. The Parliament's behaviour in the drafting of the upcoming REACH implementing act(s) will therefore be telling. Leaving aside the problem of resources, it would only be logical if the Parliament used these act(s), if only symbolically, to express its overall discontent with the Commission's approach to the regulation of nanotechnologies in REACH (and beyond).

So far, however, the Parliament has not seized (or could not seize) opportunities to take part in the drafting process of the implementing act(s). The 2010 revision of the Commission's Horizontal Rules on Expert Groups opened up certain expert groups to parliamentary involvement. Expert groups, which comprise national authorities of all Member States, must provide the Parliament with all documentation sent to the Member States in the run-up to meetings 'where such meetings concern the preparation and implementation of Union legislation, including delegated acts and soft law'.[251] These meetings should furthermore be open for attendance by parliamentary representatives.[252] The CARACAL is beyond doubt one of the expert groups targeted by these specific transparency rules.[253] In practice, however, the Parliament is not attending its meetings.[254] An early-stage participation of the Parliament in the drafting of the REACH implementing act(s) therefore exists only on paper.

b. The Commission's Online Public Consultation

At the administrative level, affected actors were invited to participate in an online public consultation as part of the ongoing impact assessment procedure. Due to the procedural coupling of the Commission's minimum consultation standards to the 2009 Impact Assessment Guidelines, the former were clearly applicable to the present consultation.[255]

To approximate the Habermasian maxim of 'full inclusion' of 'all affected actors', chapter three found that no group of actors should be strategically or systematically excluded from participating.[256] Subjective and objective actor identification processes should be put in place which safeguard, on the one hand, the possibility

[251] 'Framework for Commission's expert groups' C(2010) 7649 final (n 185), rule 12.

[252] ibid rule 13.

[253] The respective rules of the Horizontal Rules on Expert Groups are hence reflected in the CARACAL's rules of procedure, see 'Revised Rules of Procedure for the Competent Authorities for REACH and CLP (CARACAL)' (n 195) Art 13.

[254] Interview with a Commission staff member (Brussels, 21 January 2014) notes on file with the author.

[255] See on the applicability of the Commission's minimum consultation standards above chapter 4, section III.B.ii.b.

[256] See above chapter 3, section II.B.ii.

for societal actors to identify themselves as 'affected' and, on the other hand, the identification of those actors which are obviously impacted by the regulation. Affected actors should furthermore be granted access to the setting of the agenda, be able to substantively contribute to the discussion and influence the final result.

The Commission's online consultation to the forthcoming REACH implementing act(s) was published through DG Environment's website[257] as well as through the 'single access point' *Your Voice in Europe*. Theoretically, the consultation was hence open to 'all interested stakeholders', as DG Environment affirms on its website. The questionnaire, however, reveals the actual target group:

> The scope of the revision is focused on the technical aspects related to nanomaterials set out in the REACH annexes, therefore the questionnaire is also inevitably of a similarly technical nature and is designed primarily for the informed expert user.

In practice, the participation of affected actors was characterised by similar imbalances in representation as those that were already encountered in the food case study.[258] Out of the 142 replies received by the Commission 70 were submitted by private companies or trade associations (ie 50 per cent), while merely 11 submissions came from environmental NGOs or consumer organisations (ie 8 per cent).[259] Comments on the consultation were sought on the basis of 38 very narrowly formulated multiple-choice questions,[260] leaving little room for manoeuvre for participants to raise additional points. However, although the agenda-setting powers were therefore restricted, conclusions as to the ability of participants to influence the final decision are premature in view of the ongoing drafting process.

'Equality', the second criterion derived from the Habermasian ideal speech situation, was found to be fostered by the availability of background information and an appropriate duration of the consultation period.[261] The consultation at issue was launched from 21 June to 13 September 2013, for a period of 13 weeks. While the consultation thus met the minimum period of 12 weeks,[262] the Commission again initiated its consultations during a major holiday period.[263] More generally, when comparing the overall practical operation of this public consultation to the analysis of administrative participation in the food sector, a similar picture emerges. This

[257] See www.ec.europa.eu/environment/consultations/nanomaterials_2013%5Fen.htm.

[258] See above chapter 4, section III.B.ii.c.

[259] 'Impact Assessment of Modifications of the REACH Annexes for Nanomaterials' (n 144) 5.

[260] eg Question 17 'What do you believe would be the impact of the following measures on clarity for registrants?' to which participants could give answers from a (= 'significant increase clarity') to f (= 'don't know'), for the four listed measures of 'more specific ECHA tools and guidance for nanomaterials', 'application of the Commission's definition of nanomaterials', 'introduction of specific requirements in the REACH annexes' and 'other'.

[261] See above chapter 3, section II.B.ii.

[262] The 12-week period has been applicable since 2012, see European Commission, 'Review of the Commission Consultation Policy' (Staff Working Document) SWD (2012) 422 final.

[263] Also in the food case study, it was observed that several online public consultations were launched during a major holiday period, which, according to the Commission's minimum consultation standards, should have resulted in an adequate prolongation of the period, see above chapter 4, section III.B.ii.c.

is despite the fact that the Commission's minimum consultation standards were applicable.

ii. Participation in the Drafting of ECHA's Guidance Documents

The following paragraphs focus on the participation of affected actors in the drafting of ECHA's guidance documents. To be sure, the European Parliament did not occupy a formal role in this drafting process. Yet, the extent to which affected actors were able to contribute directly to the adoption process may be analysed. With regard to ECHA's Guidance on Nanomaterials in IUCLID 5, the straightforward answer is that affected societal actors were not involved. Falling outside the scope of ECHA's consultation procedure on guidance, the Agency confirmed that 'ECHA does not formally consult on *manuals*' (emphasis added).[264] To the contrary, affected actors had the opportunity to participate in the drafting of the nano appendices to the Guidance on IR and CSA. Consultations took place, first, within the scope of the RIPoN project and, secondly, via ECHA's consultation of the Commission expert group CARACAL. The following section will focus on who these affected actors were and how the consultations were conducted in order to determine their value as a source of input legitimacy.

a. The (In)Existence of Consultation Standards

The first question that begs an answer is whether administrative participation in the update of the Guidance on IR and CSA was governed by procedural standards. It is clear that initiatives of EU agencies are not subject to the Commission's minimum consultation standards; this flows from the absence of an impact assessment requirement.[265] Accordingly, the RIPoN review process, which prepared ECHA's guidance, also did not fall within their scope of application. The European Food Safety Authority responded to this procedural lacuna by putting in place its own consultation standards.[266] What has been the reply of the European Chemicals Agency?

In the drafting of certain guidance documents, such as the Guidance on IR and CSA, ECHA, as it was seen earlier, is bound by its 'consultation procedure on guidance'.[267] Closer scrutiny of the document reveals, however, that it does not contain consultation standards comparable to those adopted by the Commission or EFSA. Rather, ECHA's consultation procedure outlines the steps to be followed in the adoption of guidance documents (which EFSA calls a 'workflow'). With the exception of the consultation of the PEG, ECHA's consultation procedure does not offer detailed instructions on how the individual steps are to be performed, for

[264] Reply to an access to document request under Regulation 1049/2001 (Regulation (EC) 1049/2001. The document is on file with the author.

[265] A fact that was already remarked on with respect to EFSA, see above chapter 4, section III.B.ii.b.

[266] See ibid.

[267] See above section III.A.ii.a.

example how much time the CARACAL is granted to comment on draft guidance documents or how a 'general Internet consultation' should be conducted. This latter point has now been addressed with the most recent revision of the consultation procedure on guidance, which no longer provides for the possibility of a general Internet consultation.[268] In the present case, however, the fact that large parts of ECHA's consultation procedure on guidance were replaced by the RIPoN project means that the participation of affected actors took place without any consultation standards being applicable.

b. Administrative Participation in Practice

In both consultations, in the RIPoN review process and in ECHA's consultation of the CARACAL, participation was restricted to invited actors. No subjective actor identification processes were consequently launched. The criteria based on which the CARACAL invited affected actors to participate in the RIPoN review process are not disclosed in the pertinent documents. Also the results of the review process are not publicly available on the Internet. A request for the results of the review process delivered the minutes from 12 teleconferences of the European Commission Steering Group and notes from four meetings of the Stakeholder Consultation Group.[269] While only one of the minutes of the Stakeholder Consultation Group contains a table of comments provided by the individual participants (as well as the project consortium's replies),[270] other minutes do not give the individual comments[271] or do not contain complete lists of participants.[272] The picture of the participants to the consultation and their respective input is hence fragmentary. According to the available information, no more than six stakeholders (in addition to the CARACAL) commented on the RIPoN draft reports: three representatives from industry, one trade union association, one environmental NGO and one consultancy. Not only is this a very limited number of participants, it is also another example of industry preeminence in administrative participation.

On the other hand, all the comments of ECHA's subsequent consultation of the expert group CARACAL, including ECHA's replies, are published via the Agency's website. Accordingly, the CARACAL provided 52 comments. However, only the group's members, that is, the representatives of the Member States, and not its observers, that is, the invited third country authorities, NGOs, international organisations, trade unions and industry associations, could submit comments.[273] Furthermore, it

[268] 'Second Revision to the Consultation Procedure for Guidance' (n 202).

[269] The minutes and notes are on file with the author.

[270] Notes from the 4th Meeting of the Stakeholder Expert Consultation Group (Brussels, 28 February and 1 March 2011) (documents on file with the author).

[271] Notes from the 1st Meeting of the Stakeholder Expert Consultation Group (Brussels, 4 May 2010); Notes from the 2nd Meeting of the Stakeholder Expert Consultation Group (Brussels, 23 and 24 September 2010); Notes from the 3rd Meeting of the Stakeholder Expert Consultation Group (n 164).

[272] Notes from the 3rd Meeting of the Stakeholder Expert Consultation Group (n 164); Notes from the 4th Meeting (n 270).

[273] This has been confirmed in an interview with an ECHA staff member (Helsinki, 26 November 2013) notes on file with the author.

is remarkable that only five out of the then 27 Member States provided the 52 comments.[274] 'Input' at the ECHA level was consequently limited to five Member States.

An interesting observation can be made as regards the participants' agenda-setting powers and their ability to influence the substance of the final nano appendices. The project consortium of the RIPoN had continuously stressed since the very first meeting of the Stakeholder Consultation Group that it is an 'advisory group' and that 'the target [of RIPoN] is not to arrive at a final ECHA Guidance document; *advice* will be handed to ECHA for them to decide if/how/what should be turned into guidance' (emphasis added).[275] Paradoxically, ECHA subsequently rejected 13[276] out of the 52 comments provided by the CARACAL on the draft nano appendices claiming that they would go beyond the scope of the RIPoN or contradict its recommendations.[277] Hence, especially where participants of the Stakeholder Consultation Group struggled with scientific uncertainty and differing perceptions, the RIPoN put off disagreements with the argument that no 'final' decision would be required at this stage.[278] ECHA, in turn, manoeuvred around substantial comments of the CARACAL by relying on the 'consensus' that had already been achieved at the RIPoN level.

In terms of the duration of the consultation period, the minutes of the Stakeholder Consultation Group indicate that, approximately two weeks before its meeting, the project consortium uploaded draft reports to the 'stakeholder consultation platform', a website which was installed for that purpose. Comments could be provided by participants before the meeting in written form. The Stakeholder Consultation Group could furthermore submit comments during the meeting and one week thereafter. Participants thus had three weeks to comment on the different versions of the RIPoN draft reports. While the project consortium hence implemented a complex commenting system, the timeframe of three weeks is short if compared to the minimum of eight weeks (12 weeks since 2012) required by the Commission's consultation standards. This argument is supported by criticism raised by the Stakeholder Consultation Group in its second meeting, in which participants complained about 'insufficient' timeframes and a 'cumbersome' commenting procedure.[279]

There are two questions that now come to the fore. The first picks up on an earlier query, namely whether the RIPoN review process was indeed capable of substituting the 'normal' ECHA consultation procedure on guidance, most notably

[274] Germany, UK, Sweden, the Netherlands and Portugal.

[275] See Notes from the 2nd Meeting (n 271) (documents on file with the author).

[276] 19 comments were rejected in total.

[277] See for instance: 'The justification for adopting the fast-track procedure indicated that text from the RIP-oN reports would be considered as reflecting a consensus. The proposed change cannot therefore justifiably be implemented without further consultation, as it significantly changes the actual meaning of the text. Such changes could be re-considered during a future update for which there would be a full new stakeholder consultation', document on ECHA website named 'caracal_comments_r10_en' www.echa.europa.eu/support/guidance/consultation-procedure/closed-reach.

[278] See, for instance, Notes from the 3rd Meeting of the Stakeholder Expert Consultation Group (n 164) 19/20 (documents on file with the author).

[279] Notes from the 2nd Meeting (n 271) 4 (documents on file with the author).

the consultation of the Partner Expert Group. Could the same affected actors participate under the same conditions?

Table 7: The RIPoN Review Process versus ECHA's Consultation of the PEG

	RIPoN Review Process	**PEG Consultation** (as laid down in ECHA's consultation procedure on guidance)
Selection of affected actors	Objective actor identification process only, criteria for selection are not available.	Objective actor identification process only, based on selection procedure as laid down in ECHA 'consultation procedure on guidance'.
Publication of consultation results	No. Results are, however, available on request. A request thereof did not result in the provision of a complete list of participants, including their comments, for all meetings of the Stakeholder Consultation Group.	Yes. Participants and their individual comments (plus ECHA's replies) are published on the Agency's website.
Duration of consultation period	Project consortia publishes draft reports => 2 weeks of commenting => Stakeholder Consultation Group meeting => 1 week of commenting	ECHA sends draft guidance => 4 weeks of commenting => PEG meeting => 1 week of commenting

The comparison in Table 7 illustrates that for ECHA's consultation of the PEG the selection of affected societal actors follows—at least in theory—a prescribed (and hence transparent) procedure. The comments of the PEG (and ECHA's replies) are directly accessible via the Agency's website and the commenting period is slightly longer. It is therefore arguable that the RIPoN review process was not an equivalent substitute for ECHA's consultation of the PEG.

The second question concerns the comparison with EFSA. The European Food Safety Authority, as was shown in chapter four, can launch general public consultations on draft versions of its guidance documents. Such a general public consultation has not been conducted, so far, for an ECHA guidance document (and will also not be carried out in the future due to the 2013 revision of the ECHA consultation procedure on guidance, which abolished this possibility). The RIPoN review process constituted in practice (as well as the PEG consultation in theory) a 'cosy'[280]

[280] I borrow this term from Mark Dawson who used it in the context of the relationship between Commission, NGOs and Social Partners negotiating in the Open Method of Coordination, see M Dawson, *New Governance and the Transformation of European Law: Coordinating EU Social Law and Policy*, Cambridge Studies in European Law and Policy (Cambridge, Cambridge University Press, 2011) 274.

collaboration between a limited number of selected actors, the project consortium, the Commission and ECHA. The RIPoN Stakeholder Consultation Group met in person four times within a year, giving its participants the opportunity to react to each other's arguments instantly and, importantly, to do so face-to-face. Two entirely different models of administrative participation are present in practice. A (theoretically) open but one-off public consultation without the possibility for debate put in place by EFSA and an exclusive, but potentially more substantive, dialogue instigated by ECHA. Their assessment against the Habermasian ideal speech situation, however, led to sobering results in both cases.

iii. Synthesis: From Parliamentary Absence and a Cosy Stakeholder Collaboration

Parliamentary involvement in the drafting of a regulatory framework for nanotechnologies in chemicals is generally limited due to the Commission's decision not to propose a legislative amendment of REACH. Having said that, in the present adoption of the REACH implementing act(s), the European Parliament holds, de jure, a veto right. Whether it will also (be able to) exercise its right to scrutinise the nano-specific amendments of REACH's annexes remains to be seen. So far, however, the Parliament did (or could) not seize its prerogative to participate in the deliberations on the draft proposal(s) in the expert group CARACAL.

As in the food case study, the question remained: could the absence of parliamentary involvement be compensated by a widespread administrative participation? Although the Commission's minimum standards were applicable to the public consultation conducted in the current drafting process of the REACH implementing act(s), the analysis of its practical operation revealed (if assessed against the criteria derived from the ideal speech situation) shortcomings resembling those in the food sector, ranging from an imbalanced representation of affected actors to narrowly formulated consultation questions and an unfavourable consultation period.

Administrative participation in the adoption of ECHA's nano appendices, on the contrary, largely took place in the absence of procedural standards. On the one hand, this is because ECHA's consultation procedure on guidance was mostly inapplicable due to the Agency's recourse to a 'fast-track update'. On the other hand, the RIPoN project, which de facto substituted ECHA's procedure, was not subject to any consultation standards. Here, a cosy and largely secretive collaboration between a limited number of selected actors, Member States in the CARACAL, the Commission and ECHA emerged in practice. Furthermore the divergence in participatory approaches between the two agencies, ECHA and EFSA, in the adoption of their respective guidance documents is remarkable. All in all, also in the drafting of a regulatory framework for nanotechnologies in chemicals, administrative participation in practice had little in common with the Habermasian deliberative ideal, with accordant consequences for the regulation's input legitimacy.

Table 8: Administrative Participation in Nano Practice

		REACH implementing act(s)	**ECHA Guidance Documents**		
			Nano Appendices to the Guidance on IR and CSA		*Guidance on Nanomaterials in IUCLID 5*
Was a consultation performed?		**Yes**	**Yes**		**No**
			RIPoN Review Process	Consultation of the CARACAL	
Participation standards	*COM minimum consultation standards applicable?*	**Yes**	**No**	**No**	—
	If not, were other standards set in place?	—	**No**	**Yes** (ECHA 'consultation procedure on guidance')	—
1. 'Full inclusion' of all 'affected actors'	*Online consultation?*	**Yes**	**No**	**No**	—
	Publication of results?	Not yet published	Upon request only	**Yes** (individual submissions)	—
	Number of Participants?	142	n/a	5	—
	Balanced representation?	50% industry v 8% NGOs; n/a	n/a	0 of 5 from new MS	—
	Subjective actor identification process?	**Yes**	**No**	**No**	—
	Objective actor identification process?	**n/a**	**Yes** (criteria unclear)	**Yes**	—
	Agenda-setting powers?	**Narrowly framed questions** (multiple-choice)	**Yes**	**Restricted to RIPoN scope**	—
	Influence on final decision?	**n/a**	**n/a**	**Restricted to RIPoN scope**	—
2. Equality	*Background information?*	**Yes**	**Yes**	**Yes**	—
	Duration of consultation period?	**12 weeks** (in summer holidays)	**5 weeks**	**n/a**	—

C. Accountability

This section engages with the question of whether ECHA could—via the political, legal, administrative or social fora[281]—be held to account for its conduct during the drafting process of its guidance documents. Given the fact that the REACH implementing act(s) are still in the making, an analysis of the Commission's accountability for these measure(s) is premature.

i. The Parliament's ex post Scrutiny of ECHA's Guidance Documents

While the Parliament is not involved in the adoption process of ECHA's guidance documents, it is left to be examined whether it could play a role in their ex post scrutiny. A closer look reveals a picture that is in line with the one drawn for EFSA's nano guidance in chapter four. The European Parliament holds a general right to be informed about ECHA's activities, mostly via the submission of annual reports and work programmes.[282] In addition to its supervisory powers over EFSA, however, the Parliament should have further access to information about ECHA's activities via its appointment of two independent persons to ECHA's Management Board.[283] Moreover, REACH obliges ECHA's Executive Director to 'establish and maintain a regular dialogue with the European Parliament',[284] which he fulfils by holding an annual 'exchange of views' with the responsible parliamentary committee, the Committee on Environment, Public Health and Food Safety.[285] This arrangement also exists in practice for EFSA.[286] Yet, at the annual hearing that took place six months after ECHA's nano update to the Guidance on IR and CSA, the MEPs in attendance neither questioned the contents of the nano appendices nor their adoption process.[287]

[281] See above chapter 3, section II.B.iii.

[282] Art 83(3) REACH. ECHA's General Report of 2012 accordingly informed the Parliament that the 'ECHA generated a series of six new appendices to the Information Requirements and Chemical Safety Assessments (IR&CSA) guidance. The Agency conducted the related consultations in the format of a fast-track update procedure that also allowed their publication over one year ahead of the 31 May 2013 REACH registration deadline', European Chemicals Agency, *General Report 2012* (MB/09/2013 final, Helsinki, 2013) 31.

[283] Art 79(1) REACH. In fact, ECHA's Management Board comprises, as well as national and Commission representatives, two members appointed by the European Parliament. These 'independent persons' are currently the former French MEP Anne Laperrouze (ALDE) and the Swedish Professor Christina Ruden, see for list members of ECHA's management board, www.echa.europa.eu/web/guest/about-us/who-we-are/management-board/management-board-members.

[284] Art 83(2)(k) REACH.

[285] See www.echa.europa.eu/about-us/partners-and-networks/eu-bodies.

[286] See above chapter 4, section III.C.i.

[287] Such as the justification for the Agency's choice of a fast-track procedure or the way affected actors were involved in the RIPoN review process, see European Parliament, Committee on the Environment, Public Health and Food Safety (ENVI), Committee Meeting of 29 November 2012, records available www.europarl.europa.eu/ep-live/en/committees/video?event=20121129-1500-COMMITTEE-ENVI and http://www.europarl.europa.eu/ep-live/en/committees/video?event=20121129-0900-COMMITTEE-ENVI.

Finally, the Parliament gives discharge with respect to the implementation of ECHA's budget[288] and may ultimately alter or even terminate the Agency's mandate in case of mal- or underperformance. Yet, both of these parliamentary 'sanction mechanisms' have to date not been used against ECHA. As was observed with respect to EFSA, the Parliament seems to use these powers only in exceptional cases, with respect to sensitive topics that feature high on the political agenda or that refer to systemic deficits in an Agency's overall performance.[289] It is therefore safe to conclude that, in practice, parliamentary accountability is not encompassing the scrutiny of ECHA's day-to-day regulatory conduct, such as (the adoption process of) guidance documents.

ii. In Legal Twilight: The Role of the EU Courts

The EU courts can review and ultimately annul binding acts of EU agencies that constitute an infringement of the Treaties or an essential procedural requirement, a lack of competence and/or create a misuse of power.[290] As was already seen with respect to EFSA's guidance document in the preceding chapter, however, it appears that these measures linger in a legal twilight zone.[291] They are not listed as formal legal instruments in Article 288 TFEU. Instead, they belong to the growing category of 'unidentified legal objects' that were found to be increasingly flying around the EU's legal space.[292] Following the Court's 'substantive approach',[293] these 'unidentified legal objects' should nevertheless be admissible for judicial review if the measure is intended to have binding force and de facto brings about a change in a third party's legal position. Yet, despite its important practical effects on affected actors, in the preceding chapter EFSA's nano guidance was considered unlikely to be admitted before the EU courts. To appraise the reviewability of ECHA's guidance documents, each of the arguments that led to these conclusions with respect to EFSA will be addressed.

First, the fact that EFSA's guidance document was adopted in the form of a scientific opinion was found to thwart the determination of its legal effects.[294]

[288] Art 97(10) REACH. This is even though ECHA was temporarily self-financed until the end of 2013, ie independent from the EU budget, due to fee revenues from REACH, see 'Analytical Fiche no 20: Funding and budget revenues of agencies', fn 2 www.europa.eu/european-union/sites/europaeu/files/docs/body/fiche_20_sent_to_ep_cons_2011-07-20_en.pdf. Furthermore, the Parliament has the power to ask questions to the Agency within the scope of the discharge procedure.

[289] See above chapter 4, section III.C.i.

[290] Art 263(1) TFEU.

[291] See above chapter 4, section III.C.ii.a.

[292] See above chapter 3, section I.C.ii.

[293] ibid.

[294] This is because Agency scientific opinions are generally embedded in a product (or substance) authorisation procedure, which culminates in the adoption of a non-legislative act by the Commission. Previous case law on Agency scientific opinions has exclusively dealt with these classic scientific opinions and has always considered these measures to be mere 'preparatory acts' and hence not reviewable acts in themselves. Only the Commission decision that 'rubberstamps' the Agency opinion

Guidance documents by the European Chemicals Agency, on the contrary, are not only adopted under a different heading than 'scientific opinions' (which ECHA's committees also produce), they also follow a different drafting procedure.[295] Formally, it is therefore much easier to distinguish between opinions adopted by ECHA's committees as part of an authorisation procedure (the classic scientific opinions as they were called in the context of EFSA), which the Court has in the past declared to be mere 'preparatory acts', and the separate category of guidance documents. What remains opaque in the context of ECHA is the existence of different kinds of 'guidance' documents, as was revealed in the analysis of the Guidance on Nanomaterials in IUCLID 5.[296]

Secondly, following the Court's ruling in *Schering-Plough*, measures of EU agencies whose mandate is restricted to the provision of scientific advice, that is, agencies that have no formal decision-making powers, seem categorically barred from judicial scrutiny.[297] Since the General Food Law also formally limits EFSA's mandate to the provision of scientific advice and support,[298] this argument was found to be transferrable to the Food Safety Authority. REACH, however, grants the European Chemicals Agency (certain) decision-making powers.[299] The *Schering-Plough* reasoning hence does not result in categorically excluding legal effects of ECHA's acts.

For the third argument, it is necessary to delve deeper into the content, especially the wording, of EFSA's nano guidance. In line with the Court's 'substantive approach', the challenge is to prove that a guidance document de facto affects the legal position of third parties, by creating a new obligation or by adding to the legal text.[300] Yet, similar to EFSA's nano guidance, the nano appendices to ECHA's Guidance on IR and CSA also claim that they 'have been developed in order to

is reviewable, see Case T-326/99 *Nancy Fern Olivieri v Commission of the European Communities and European Agency for the Evaluation of Medicinal Products* [2003] ECR II-6053, Case T-311/06 *FMC Chemical and Arysta Lifesciences v EFSA* [2008] ECR II-00088*, discussed above in chapter 4, section III.C.ii.a. In the case of EFSA's nano guidance, however, it was concluded that such analogies are confusing as, even though adopted in form of a scientific opinion, the nano guidance not only fulfils a different purpose, but its adoption also completes an administrative procedure—no further act, such as a Commission non-legislative act, directly follows. It was therefore seen as desirable to make this distinction clear, inter alia for purposes of judicial review, by adopting guidance under a heading other than 'scientific opinion'.

[295] See above section III.A.ii.d.

[296] The Guidance on Nanomaterials in IUCLID 5 is not covered by the definition of 'guidance' employed in ECHA's consultation procedure for guidance, see above section III.A.ii.c.

[297] Case T-133/03 *Schering-Plough Ltd v Commission and EMEA* [2008] not published, para 18.

[298] Art 22(2) GFL.

[299] T Ehnert, 'The European Chemicals Agency—Beyond the Scope of the Meroni Doctrine?' (2008) Maastricht University Graduate thesis. See also Case T-96/10 *Rütgers Germany GmbH and Others v European Chemicals Agency (ECHA)* [2013] not published, para 62.

[300] See for an analysis of Cases C-366/88 *French Republic v Commission of the European Communities* [1990] ECR I-03571, para 23; Case C-303/90 *French Republic v Commission of the European Communities* [1991] ECR I-5315, para 24 and C-325/91 *French Republic v Commission of the European Communities* [1993] ECR I-3283, para 14, J Scott, 'In Legal Limbo' (n 181).

provide *advice* to registrants for use when preparing registration dossiers for nanomaterials'; all appendices' titles refer furthermore to '*recommendations* for nanomaterials' (emphases added).[301] ECHA's guidance even goes a step further by additionally including a general disclaimer, which states that:

> [t]his document contains guidance on REACH explaining the REACH obligations and how to fulfil them. However, users are reminded that the text of the REACH regulation is the only authentic legal reference and that the information in this document does not constitute legal advice. The European Chemicals Agency does not accept any liability with regard to the contents of this document.

Indeed, the presence of the disclaimer, supported by the careful wording of the contents of the appendices, renders it unlikely that the latter would be considered to create new obligations before the EU courts.[302] By inference, the legal forum would also not review their adoption process in order to determine, for instance, whether the fast-track procedure in the case of the nano appendices was justified or whether the RIPoN review process provided for an equivalent substitution of ECHA's 'normal' consultation procedure, except where the nano appendices would be considered an 'essential procedural requirement' of a subsequent binding decision of Commission or ECHA.[303]

iii. Administrative Accountability: The Expandable Role of the European Ombudsman

The European Ombudsman opened its investigating into ECHA's administration in 2011. So far, there have been no cases scrutinising (the adoption process of) ECHA guidance documents.[304] Interesting for the purposes of this case study is an own initiative inquiry opened by the Ombudsman in 2012 against ECHA (and 12 further EU agencies) concerning a broad range of topics centring on their independence and impartiality.[305] The initiative evolved from the (highly politicised) allegations contesting EFSA's independence in 2010.[306] Based on this concrete case, the Ombudsman started a horizontal screening, comparing the proceduralisation taking place in various decentralised EU agencies in order to derive 'best practices'. This could be a blueprint for further screening exercises of agency procedural rules, such as on how to draft guidance documents and on how to

[301] For references to the appendices, see above section II.C.i.

[302] See also E Korkea-aho, 'Better Judicial Review?' (n 152) 412.

[303] See Joint Cases T-74/00, 76, 83, 85, 132, 137, 141 *Artegodan GmbH and Others v Commission of the European Communities* [2002] ECR II-4945, para 197.

[304] An ECHA staff member confirmed that the 'Guidance and Forum Secretariat' has as yet no experience with the Ombudsman, Interview with an ECHA staff member (Helsinki, 26 November 2013) notes on file with the author.

[305] Such as the transparency of the Agencies' websites, their handling of access to document requests and declarations of conflict of interest, see the Ombudsman's website on visits to agencies www.ombudsman.europa.eu/en/activities/visits.faces.

[306] See above chapter 4, section III.C.iii.b.

conduct public consultations, where the preceding analysis revealed substantial discrepancies between ECHA and EFSA.

On a more specific note, the Ombudsman investigated a complaint in 2008 in relation to the Commission having deviated from its minimum consultation standards in the drafting of the legislative proposal for a Regulation on tariffs for international roaming services.[307] The Commission's justification was that interested parties had already been consulted before, as the European Regulatory Group had sent out a questionnaire to its members, the National Regulatory Authorities in the field. This, the Commission claimed, was capable of acting as a substitute for its own public consultation. Arguably, the Ombudsman was here confronted with a similar situation to ECHA's 'outsourcing' of its own consultation procedure to an external contractor in the RIPoN project (section III.A.ii.b). In the previous case, however, the Ombudsman did not accept this self-proclaimed substitution. Quoting the Commission's minimum consultation standards, and in particular the provisions on inclusiveness, the Ombudsman concluded that it is 'not convinced that *all interested parties* had the opportunity to express their views …'.[308] An analogous reasoning could be applied to the RIPoN review process based on the comparison with the 'normal' ECHA consultation procedure on guidance that was provided in section III.B.ii.b. In essence, this confirms the observations in relation to the food case study which revealed the Ombudsman as a potentially important accountability forum scrutinising (the adoption process of) agency guidance documents—especially when they are held inadmissible by the EU courts.

iv. Social Accountability: Transparency on Paper

Affected actors constitute the social accountability forum that may scrutinise the regulator's conduct ex post. A precondition therefore was found to be a transparent regulatory process, which is fostered by effective access to documents provisions, reason giving, as well as the availability of regulation (and its preparatory documents) in the EU's official languages.[309]

However, in the preceding chapter on the European Food Safety Authority, it was noted that the scope of application of Regulation 1049/2001 on public access to documents does not extend to EU agencies.[310] Yet, REACH, like the General Food Law, demands that 'Regulation (EC) No 1049/2001 shall apply to documents held by the Agency'.[311] For these purposes, ECHA's Management Board adopted an implementing decision in 2008.[312] Like Regulation 1049/2001, the Agency's

[307] European Ombudsman, Decision 3617/2006/JF of 3 July 2008.

[308] ibid para 2.32.

[309] See above chapter 3, section II.B.iii.d.

[310] See above chapter 4, section III.C.iv.a.

[311] Art 118(3) REACH.

[312] European Chemicals Agency, 'Decision on the Implementation of Regulation (EC) No 1049/2001 of the European Parliament and of the Council regarding Public Access to Documents to European Parliament, Council and Commission Documents' (MB/12/2008 final, 25 March 2009).

implementing decision also draws a distinction between those documents that can be requested by the public and those that must be 'directly accessible'.[313] The Agency's rules of procedure, its work programmes, general reports, final minutes and opinions of the Agency's Committees and its Forum must be directly accessible. Documents drawn up or received in the course of procedures for the adoption of guidance documents are not listed. This gap is filled by ECHA's consultation procedure on guidance, which explicitly requires '[t]he timeline and the main interim documents prepared at different stages of the consultation process [to] be published on the ECHA website in order to keep the process transparent'.[314] In theory, ECHA's implementing rules of Regulation 1049/2001 hence allow for a wide direct accessibility of documents in the preparation of guidance documents. Practice, however, tells a different story.

First, this sobering reality results from the fact that not every guidance document of ECHA is adopted following the Agency's 'consultation procedure on guidance'.[315] More generally, the existence of different kinds of 'guidance documents',[316] to which different types of procedures (or none) apply, is prone to decrease the transparency of ECHA's regulatory output. Secondly, the 'fast-track update' of the Guidance on IR and CSA allowed the bulk of the 'normal' adoption process to be outsourced to external contractors in the RIPoN project, to which ECHA's transparency regime did not apply. Intermediary documents drafted by the RIPoN are therefore not directly accessible.[317] This rendered the adoption of both guidance documents largely opaque.

The transparency of the guidance documents is further compromised by ECHA's language practices.[318] The consultation procedure on guidance foresees that:

> Those guidance documents that are of a general nature and touch upon many downstream user sectors and/or a high proportion of SMEs will be translated from their original into 21 further official EU languages in order to improve the accessibility of guidance to all stakeholders.[319]

While parts of the Guidance on IR and CSA are thus available in all official languages, the six nano appendices were not translated. It is not further specified who takes this decision (not) to translate. Their exclusive availability in English arguably makes the nano appendices inaccessible for a large number of affected actors.

[313] ibid Art 6.

[314] '(Revised) Consultation Procedure on Guidance' (n 202) 4.

[315] The Guidance on Nanomaterials in IUCLID 5 was shown to be an example of this, see above section III.A.ii.c.

[316] This point was made above in section III.C.ii on legal accountability.

[317] Also a request for those documents, via Regulation 1049/2001 did not result in the provision of complete participation lists or a complete overview of the comments submitted.

[318] See, more generally on ECHA's language practices, M Lee, *EU Environmental Law, Governance and Decision-Making*, Modern Studies in European Law vol 43, 2nd edn (Oxford, Hart Publishing, 2014) 210.

[319] '(Revised) Consultation Procedure on Guidance' (n 202) 6.

v. Synthesis: Holding ECHA to Account

Altogether, the preceding analysis has made clear that there are only few opportunities to hold the Agency to account for the drafting of its REACH guidance documents. Even though the European Parliament should theoretically hold more information on (and hence control over) ECHA's activities than on EFSA's activities, in practice, the Parliament did not (or could not) use these channels to question (let alone sanction) the Agency's conduct.

Furthermore, it is unlikely that the EU courts will engage in a procedural review of the Agency's guidance documents, which, like the nano guidance of EFSA, subsist in a legal twilight zone. It is the loose wording of the guidance documents in particular, exacerbated by the presence of a general disclaimer in case of the Guidance on IR and CSA, that makes them predestined to escape the EU courts' scrutiny. The result is the same legal paradox that was observed in the food case study. On the one hand, these formally non-binding measures have a crucial impact on affected actors in practice. They even seem to have (indirect) legal effects, for instance by being relied on in court, as happened with one of the REACH guidance documents. On the other hand, however, affected actors will, in all likelihood, be unsuccessful in challenging these documents in court.

Here again, the Ombudsman emerged as being a valuable, though underused, remedy. The suggestion made in the preceding food case study, namely that the Ombudsman should assume the role of a formulator of best practice in the proceduralisation process taking place in EU agencies, took a more concrete form in this chapter. This chapter showed that the Ombudsman led a horizontal screening activity of rules on independence and transparency. This could be a blueprint for future Ombudsmanian activism also to develop best practices in the adoption of guidance documents, including the involvement of affected actors. So far, these procedures have evolved in a vacuum, where one agency is isolated from the activities (and experiences) taking place in the other agency.

Finally, the transparency of ECHA's guidance adoption process emerged as a matter of concern. This is the case even though the Agency put in place detailed, one could say commendable, transparency provisions. A main reason for the lack of transparency in practice was the Agency's deviation from its standard procedure in both cases. Furthermore, the fact that neither the nano appendices, nor the Guidance on Nanomaterials in IUCLID 5 are available in a language other than English is detrimental to a transparent process. This is a deficiency which also arose in relation to EFSA's nano guidance. Ultimately, this means that ECHA, as well as the other actors involved in the Agency's guidance adoption process, acted largely outside the reach of the pertinent accountability fora and, by implication, remained unchecked for potential abuses of power.

IV. CONCLUSION

Nanotechnologies have become an indispensable part of the European chemicals industry. Due to its gatekeeper position in the industrial value chain, the chemicals sector not only serves as one of the forerunners in nanotechnological research, but it has also become the main stage of nanophobist sentiment. A heated debate has therefore been sparked as to the adequacy of the current EU legislative framework for the specific characteristics of the nanoform—its focus being REACH. While many uncertainties were debated as to whether its provisions are 'fit for nano', ultimately the European Commission decided, under protest from the Parliament, Member States and stakeholders, not to propose a legislative amendment of its legal text, but to concentrate on a (future) amendment of REACH's annexes via implementing acts and an update of ECHA's guidance documents. This second case study also revealed the nano debate's move to the executive sphere.

Since the REACH implementing act(s) are still on the Commission's drawing board, an analysis thereof could only be preliminary. The European Chemicals Agency, on the contrary, has already updated two of its existing guidance documents to the nanoform. A closer look at the content of these documents showed that political decisions seem to be veiled behind scientific or technical language. This, coupled with the fact that ECHA's guidance documents are of crucial practical significance and, beyond that, have started to be invoked before the EU courts, led to some doubt as to whether ECHA, like EFSA, is still acting within the boundaries of its legislative mandate, which formally bars the agency from taking risk management decisions.

At the same time, the importance of decisions taken at the level of the EU administration was found to be unmatched by accordant procedures that would ensure a transparent collection of the fragmented knowledge as well as the legitimacy of the regulatory output. Procedures, set in place for these purposes after the European governance debate, have proved unable to live up to their rationale. Instead, the analysis has revealed a regulatory process dominated by the Commission and its expert group CARACAL. The complex consultation procedure that ECHA instigated for the adoption of guidance documents was in practice not followed by the Agency. The procedure's substitute, the RIPoN review process, was not only conducted in the absence of procedural standards, it also lacked transparency. Administrative participation in the process turned out to be a cosy and essentially secretive collaboration between a number of affected actors (whose selection was not transparent), Member States in the CARACAL, the Commission and ECHA. Overall, if compared to the criteria derived from the ideal speech situation, the participation of affected actors proved unable to compensate for the lack of parliamentary involvement.

At the same time, the accountability mechanisms identified in chapter three were found to apply only sporadically. There are few possibilities to hold ECHA to account for the adoption of its guidance documents. As in the food case study, the

Parliament in practice did not use its supervisory powers to further inquire into their adoption. Their status as 'unidentified legal objects' makes them even more likely to bypass the EU courts' scrutiny. Also the potential of affected actors to hold ECHA to account is restricted due to the largely opaque adoption process that can be seen in practice.

What remains is the aftertaste of controversial issues being shifted to the EU administration, which, largely shielded from the public eye, works out substantive rules in collaboration with a selected number of stakeholders and, thereby, remains largely beyond the control of the pertinent accountability fora.

6

Conclusion

THIS CONCLUDING CHAPTER attempts to weave the various parts of this book into a whole. To that end, it will first return to the point of departure: the problem statement, the social challenges of regulating in today's nano society, the normative answer to that question and the EU's response (section I). Thereafter, the findings of the critical analysis of the current EU risk regulation of nanotechnologies based on the two case studies in the food and chemicals sectors will be addressed (sections II and III). Section IV assesses the repercussions for the meta-theoretical level: does new governance equal better governance? Finally, this chapter looks towards the future. Section V proposes reforms of EU risk regulation within the framework as it stands. More fundamental concerns (and questions) raised by this book are addressed as part of the bigger picture in the final section's identification of three facades of EU risk regulation (section VI). Section VII dares to provide an outlook for the future.

I. REGULATING IN TODAY'S NANO SOCIETY: THE POINT OF DEPARTURE

The original question posed in the beginning of this book was: *How does the EU confront the challenges of today's nano society?* It proceeded from the assumption that the emergence of nanotechnologies is a proxy for broader societal transformations. The image that was drawn of 'today's nano society' was hence characterised by globalisation and the functional differentiation of society into distinct rationalities, as well as the omnipresence of man-made risks. In this climate of uncertainty and competing claims to truth, the point at which nanotechnologies' regulation achieves its desired result—the point at which it can be considered 'effective'—was deemed subjective in nature. The definition of effectiveness depends upon the eye of the beholder.

The description of the societal context led to a search for a normative answer to the research question, how one *should* regulate in 'today's nano society'. To this end, Habermas's discourse theory of law and democracy and Teubner's theory of reflexive law served as theoretical foundation. These approaches claim to observe fundamental deficiencies in the capacity of traditional command-and-control regulation to master the highly specialised and fragmented knowledge(s) of the diversely affected actors, on the one hand, and to ensure the regulation's legitimacy, on the other. Instead, they found that procedures should be set in place that enable affected actors not only to assert their democratic self-determination in the formulation of regulation, but to also increase the latter's effectiveness by remedying the legal system's failure to grasp constantly changing scientific, economic and cultural environments in their entirety. The introduction of this normative perspective allowed, first, this research to be put into context in relation to contemporary literature and, secondly, to develop its analytical lenses, namely those of regulatory capacity.

A translation of those theoretical considerations to the EU level revealed similar concerns and accordant attempts to remedy a perceived lack of legitimacy and effectiveness of the EU and its actions in the debate on European governance. In the late 1990s, reforms were contemplated to bolster regulatory capacity, by allowing for a greater participation of affected actors and a more transparent collection of knowledge within and beyond the classic Community method. A shift towards 'new governance' was conceptualised in numerous academic writings, often, however, with blurring boundaries between normative demands and empirical realities. The endeavour of this book was to investigate the tangible outcomes of the governance debate on how the EU is really regulating in today's nano society. What are the concrete tools—the legal procedures—that the EU institutions have put in place to strengthen their capacity to regulate? To this end, chapter three identified, inter alia, the EU institutions' impact assessment procedure, new procedural frameworks for the creation and operation of Commission expert groups and EU agencies and the Commission's minimum standards for consultation, as well as several accountability mechanisms. It is the application and operation of these legal procedures, against the background of this research's theoretical foundation, that eventually formed the object of analysis in the empirical part.

II. SPOTLIGHT ON THE EU EXECUTIVE

The analysis of the emerging EU regulatory framework for nanotechnologies in food and chemicals revealed a preference on the part of the European Commission to address the issue of nanotechnologies via executive rule making—specifically via comitology, agency guidance documents and Commission recommendations. The Commission hardly used its right of legislative initiative. References to nanotechnologies in the legislative framework for food therefore remain fragmented and inconsistent, since they were pushed into the legal text by the Parliament (and to a lesser extent by the Council) when these frameworks happened to be up for revision in a legislative procedure.

At the same time, executive rule making in the inherently value-laden area of nanotechnologies was shown to accommodate sensitive political choices: how can 'nanomaterial' be defined in the absence of scientific certainty? What information should producers provide in order to register nanomaterials for placement on the EU market? Should one wait for nano-specific risk assessment methods before commercialisation? Political choices were shifted to the EU administration. Even further, independent of their formal (non-) bindingness, these measures were found to have important practical and also (indirect) legal effects for affected actors, for instance when being relied upon before the EU courts.

III. MAIN FINDINGS OF THE CRITICAL ANALYSIS OR THE PITFALLS OF 'NEW GOVERNANCE'

The critical analysis of the case studies sought to scrutinise these regulatory developments through the lenses of regulatory capacity: how the EU regulator, legislature and executive alike, have confronted the challenges of knowledge production in the adoption process, while ensuring the legitimacy of the regulatory output. Overall, the analysis brought to the fore a considerable mismatch between the theoretical raison d'etre of the legal procedures summoned for these purposes and the empirical reality of their operation in practice. Furthermore, more often than not the regulator was (or could) not (be) held to account ex post for its conduct in the regulatory process.

A. The Impact Assessment: Between Empty Proceduralisation and Strategic Choice

The impact assessment was identified as the main procedure that the EU institutions put in place in the wake of the European governance debate to bring together knowledge, in a transparent way, as a foundation for policy initiatives and legislative proposals. It should thereby not only spur the collection of knowledge but equally enhance the democratic legitimacy of the EU regulatory process. So the theory goes.

In practice, the impact assessment procedure as enshrined in the 2009 Guidelines turned out to be largely empty. First, it was observed that the scope of application of the Commission's, as well as the Parliament and Council's, impact assessment commitment was extremely vague (chapter four, section III.A.i). While regulatory output of EU agencies is generally excluded from its scope, the Commission was also not per se required to perform an assessment for regulatory measures in the executive setting but only when implementing acts have a 'significant impact' or non-binding measures 'define future policies'. These triggers remained, however, undefined. As highlighted by the food case study, the Commission used this ambiguity to conduct neither an impact assessment for its recommendation nor for the implementing acts under the Food Contact Materials Regulation. Especially in the latter case the decision appeared arbitrary, given the important—'significant'—impact their nano provisions arguably entail for affected actors. On the contrary, in the current preparation of the REACH implementing act(s), the Commission opted for the performance of an impact assessment. In a climate of fierce resistance towards the Commission's decision not to propose an amendment of the legal text of the REACH Regulation itself, the primary rationale of the impact assessment was found to lie in offering ammunition to uphold the Commission's draft proposal(s) in the comitology procedure.

At the same time, even when the Commission's 2009 Impact Assessment Guidelines were applicable, such as in the case of legislative acts, in practice the impact assessments did not engage with the issue of nanotechnologies. Here, the operating principle of a 'proportionate level of analysis' was found to give the Commission a *carte blanche* in determining the substance, scope and depth of assessment on a case-by-case basis. Although Parliament and Council introduced major nano-specific amendments in the ensuing legislative procedure, the co-legislators also did not conduct their own impact assessment of their substantive amendments. Overall, the vagueness of the procedure's scope of application and operation allowed a shift in rationale of the impact assessment from a tool to pool and expose a proposal's knowledge base to a political device used when acceptability was sought. The substance of the impact assessment fades into the background.

B. The Fragmentary Proceduralisation of EU Agency Rule Making

The key role of EFSA and ECHA guidance documents in the regulation of nanotechnologies directed attention to their adoption processes. Remarkably, the case studies showed that the two agencies follow adoption procedures for guidance documents that could hardly be more different. Completely different approaches to the involvement of affected actors, the role of the agencies' secretariats, Member States and the Commission were apparent in practice. The fact that the agencies' respective founding regulations do not prescribe a particular adoption procedure appeared to be the main reason for these differences, next to the absence of an impact assessment requirement. Instead, the task of producing adoption procedures has been delegated to EFSA's Scientific Committee and ECHA's Management Board, each of which developed their own administrative practices. Furthermore, provisions on transparency and on the translation of regulatory output are not dealt with in a horizontal manner for all EU agencies. This is mainly due to the fact that the scope of Regulation 1049/2001 on access to documents does not extend to EU agencies. Also, agency acts do not need to be published in the Official Journal of the European Union and, in turn, they are not automatically translated into the EU's official languages. Again, each agency has set in place its own rules and procedures to fill these gaps. This fragmented proceduralisation in EU agencies was found not only to distract from the critical impacts their rule making has on affected actors, but also to decrease the transparency of their operations.

C. Depoliticisation: Towards Technocratic Rule?

Contrary to the deliberative account of Habermas and accordant ideas of 'new governance' that controversial questions should be exposed to a meaningful public debate, the shift towards executive rule making resulted in a depoliticisation.

i. The Lack of Parliamentary Involvement

First and foremost, the move towards executive rule making implied a limited role for the European Parliament. Yet, wherever possible, the European Parliament (and to a lesser degree the Council) tried to push the issue of nanotechnologies back onto the political agenda. These attempts were frustrated, first, by the Commission's exclusive right of legislative initiative. Secondly, the case studies revealed that even when the Parliament was formally granted a role in comitology, it seemed incapable of exploiting such opportunities in practice. This became especially clear in the Parliament's inaction in the regulatory procedure with scrutiny leading to the adoption of the plastics implementing act under the Food Contact Materials Regulation, but also in its failure to use its prerogative to attend meetings of the Commission expert group CARACAL in the preparation of the REACH implementing act(s). Hence, the Commission's decision not to propose a revision of the REACH Regulation and the Food Contact Materials Regulation effectively precluded a parliamentary debate on the legislation's nano-fitness.

Also ex post, the Parliament did not seize its powers—its rights to information (annual reports), debate (hearings) and judgment (most notably via its budgetary powers)—to oversee the EU's executive in any of the analysed cases. That the Parliament de jure disposes of these participatory and oversight rights gives the impression of parliamentary involvement that was de facto not taking place. Overall, the limited role of the European Parliament is at odds with its struggle for an increase in its legislative powers over the last few decades. After all, it is only a few years ago that the Parliament became, in most policy areas, co-legislator with the entry into force of the Lisbon Treaty. This status appears hollowed out by the reliance on executive rule making.

ii. The Spectacle of Administrative Participation

Administrative participation was found incapable of making up for the weak parliamentary involvement. The observed trend towards consultation seems far from creating a public sphere a la Habermas that would allow for the development of a joint political will of affected actors. One problem is the erratic applicability of consultation standards. This is primarily because the Commission's minimum consultation standards were procedurally coupled to the 2009 Impact Assessment Guidelines. In practice, the standards were therefore neither applicable to the consultation conducted on a draft of the Commission recommendation for a definition of 'nanomaterial' nor to those conducted by ECHA, EFSA and the scientific committee SCENIHR. Whereas SCENIHR, ECHA and EFSA put in place their own consultation standards, these proved to diverge greatly and to different degrees were less demanding than those of the Commission. The latter point arguably relates to the expert groups and EU agencies' formal mandate as neutral 'sources of knowledge', according to which they are precluded from engaging in political risk management decisions and, by implication, do not 'need' to legitimise their output via a broad involvement of affected actors in their operations. The fact that ECHA nonetheless consults representatives of different affected actors as well as the risk manager revealed this dilemma of reconciling the irreconcilable: the tension between the agency's formal mandate and its actual regulatory function in the adoption of guidance documents (see further section VI.B on the facade of scientific truth).

The fact that consultation standards were applied only sporadically renders it virtually impossible for affected actors to challenge perceived imbalances or unfavourable consultation conditions ex post (although this is also difficult where standards are applicable, see further section III.D). It furthermore impairs the overall transparency of the process. This is especially problematic in view of the practical operation of administrative participation. Whether or not subject to consultation standards, the analysis of the case studies yielded disappointing results when compared to the criteria derived from the ideal speech situation. The dominant consultation format, that is, the online public consultation, was characterised by an unbalanced representation of affected actors, unpublished or merely summarised consultation results, limited agenda setting-powers, too short (or unfavourable) consultation periods and insufficiently transparent actor identification processes. Other formats, such as administrative participation in the drafting of ECHA's nano appendices, emerged as a cosy collaboration between selected stakeholders, national experts and the Commission services. In practice, the Commission's minimum consultation standards, like the 2009 Impact Assessment Guidelines, repeatedly proved empty. Administrative participation meant a confined stakeholder involvement—of stakeholders who were more often than not representing those affected actors with the requisite financial resources—with little potential to stir a European public debate.

D. The (Self-)Tied Hands of the EU Courts

The willingness of the legal forum to hold the regulator to account for its conduct during the drafting process, such as for its collection of knowledge and inclusion of affected actors, is limited. The hands of the EU courts were found to be (self-)tied in two important ways. First, judicial review is restricted to 'reviewable acts'. Non-binding acts, such as Commission recommendations, as well as all the 'unidentified legal objects', including agency guidance documents, are therefore a priori incontestable before the EU courts. The Court's 'substantive approach' to the determination of whether or not an act nevertheless produces legal effects turned out to be inadequate to remedy this gap in practice. Due to their careful wording, all non-binding acts examined in this book were prone to escape the courts' scrutiny.

Yet, even if considered a 'reviewable act', a further important limitation (next to the well-known obstacle of restricted legal standing for individuals) relates to the intensity of review and to what extent the EU courts are willing to review acts, first, based on their collection of knowledge, second, based on (the absence of) participation by societal actors and, finally, based on potential infringements of self-imposed procedures established for these purposes, such as the impact assessment procedure or the Commission's minimum consultation standards. The analysis showed that the courts remained wary of interfering with factual findings and complex assessments made by the regulator, only intervening in the case of a 'manifest error'. The EU institutions, therefore, dispose of broad discretionary powers in collecting (from whom?) and assessing (how?) knowledge. Similarly, the courts have so far denied a general consultation right for affected actors. This discretion, in both cases, is barely narrowed down by the self-imposed consultation standards or impact assessment guidelines. It is again their vague formulation that makes them difficult to enforce (or easy not to enforce) before the courts as an essential procedural requirement. The Ombudsman, albeit generally providing an auspicious remedy to the gaps unfolding in legal accountability, also stumbled over this issue. Despite the existence of these self-imposed rules, it is therefore improbable that the EU institutions could be held to account by the legal forum for the way they have collected knowledge and included affected actors in their drafting process. This grants the EU institutions (and agencies) much leeway in the conduct of their public consultations, but it also grants them the possibility to shield political choices, one-sided or, as in the case of nanotechnologies in food, incomplete analyses behind the elusive notion of 'complex assessments'.

E. (In)transparency

The transparency of the regulatory process proved to be another problem. One reason is certainly the empty proceduralisation that characterises the institutions' impact assessment commitment and the Commission's consultation standards. Of particular concern is again the drafting of non-binding regulation, not least due to the fragmented nature of EU administrative law—the scope of application of Regulation 1049/2001 on access to documents, but also the ambiguous applicability of the duty to state reasons for 'unidentified legal objects' in Article 296 TFEU, to name only two examples.

The distinction between two categories of access to documents rights in Regulation 1049/2001, the right to request documents from the EU institutions (and agencies) and the right to have direct access to certain documents in electronic form via the Internet, emerged as especially detrimental to transparency. Whereas the first category applies to documents drawn up or received in the course of all regulatory options, binding and non-binding alike, the fact that affected actors first have to proactively request documents requires a detailed knowledge of the EU regulatory process (as well as time and patience), hence constituting a true hurdle to transparency in practice. The second category, the right to direct access, on the contrary, applies only to documents drawn up or received in the course of procedures for the adoption of binding acts. Considerably fewer documents are hence directly accessible for non-binding acts. Yet, even when documents were directly accessible on the Internet, such as minutes of meetings of comitology committees or expert groups, in practice they hardly reflected the actual discussions of the meetings; generally, they were brief and of meagre substance. Thus, there is a problem with the 'reality of access'.[1] The 2016 revision of the horizontal rules on expert groups features a new paragraph, requiring that 'minutes on the discussion on each point on the agenda and on the opinions delivered by the group shall be meaningful and complete'.[2] To what extent this addition can change the current practice remains to be seen.

Finally, EFSA's nano guidance and ECHA's nano appendices are not translated. Only acts published in the Official Journal must be translated into the official languages of the EU. This arguably impinges upon the transparency of the guidance documents, by rendering them difficult to access by all affected actors. Equally, most preparatory documents (not only for non-binding acts but for all regulatory measures), including public consultations, are only available in English. This might have been another factor contributing to the observed imbalances in the representation of the different rationalities in the analysed public consultations.

IV. REPERCUSSIONS FOR THE META-THEORETICAL LEVEL: IS 'NEW GOVERNANCE' 'BETTER GOVERNANCE'?

What do these findings tell us? Has the risk regulatory process at the EU level become more effective, more legitimate in the aftermath of the European governance debate? While this book could observe the taking place of an adumbration of proceduralisation on paper—as advocated by the 'new governance' school—this turned out to be empty or highly fragmented (for EU agencies and expert groups) in practice. On the one hand, the procedures that the Commission put in place to guarantee a closer involvement of affected actors were mostly inapplicable due to the Commission's recourse to its executive powers. Paradoxically,

[1] P Craig, *EU Administrative Law*, Collected Courses of the Academy of European Law XVI/1, 2nd edn (Oxford, Oxford University Press, 2012) 362.

[2] European Commission, 'Commission decision of 30.5.2016 establishing horizontal rules on the creation and operation of Commission expert groups' C(2016) 3301 final, Art 13(7).

thus, with its reliance on comitology or non-binding regulation, the Commission escaped the scope of application of its newly instigated procedures. Moreover, the non-bindingness of these procedures, coupled with their imprecise formulations, rendered them in practice, even where applicable, largely redundant. Overall, these procedures proved unable to create an open public discourse on the risks and benefits of nanotechnologies and their regulation. A gap is thus opening up between the theoretical ideas informing the design of the identified procedures and their operation in practice. The analysis revealed that controversial decisions in the area of the regulation of nanotechnologies continue to be taken behind closed doors by experts within the EU administration, suggesting the move towards what Curtin called an 'executive dominance'.[3] This evolution necessarily has repercussions for the capacity of the EU regulator to meet the challenges of today's nano society, to ensure the collection of the societally dispersed knowledge and the legitimacy of the regulatory output. It is here that the ideas of 'new' or, in Commission terminology, 'good' governance diverge from their normative pretensions.

V. STRENGTHENING REGULATORY CAPACITY: PROPOSALS FOR REFORM AT THE MICRO LEVEL

Having identified the shortcomings, the objective of the remaining sections is to advance suggestions for reform. To this end, this section will propose ways to amend existing procedures to patch up the loopholes in the current framework for EU risk regulation as it stands. The subsequent section will then turn to the caveats and to the fundamental problems and questions raised by this book.

A. Impact Assessment Reloaded

Put bluntly, can the impact assessment procedure be saved? To avoid it ending up as an empty procedure, this book showed that efforts are required to clarify its scope of application and, more importantly, to look at its operation and added value in practice. It will be considered to what extent the Commission's reform of the 2009 Impact Assessment Guidelines, as part of the Better Regulation Package of May 2015, addressed the shortcomings revealed in this book.

i. Clarifying its Scope of Application

The ambiguous scope of application of the Commission's 2009 Impact Assessment Guidelines to delegated and implementing acts, but also to non-binding

[3] D Curtin, 'Challenging Executive Dominance in European Democracy' (2014) 77 *The Modern Law Review* 1.

Commission acts, was found to be troublesome. First, the Commission's impact assessment commitment for delegated and implementing acts should therefore be clarified. The pivotal point was the 2009 Impact Assessment Guidelines' undefined trigger of 'significant impact'. Yet, also the 2015 Better Regulation Guidelines state that 'an IA [impact assessment] is required for Commission initiatives that are likely to have significant economic, environmental or social impacts'.[4] The Better Regulation 'Toolbox'—a new online tool detailing the Better Regulation Guidelines for Commission staff—explains that this assessment is to be done on a 'case-by-case basis', taking into consideration whether the Commission actually has a choice, whether impacts can be clearly defined ex ante and taking into account the extent of the impact.[5] Arguably, this leaves the Commission to a large extent with the same discretion that it enjoyed under the 2009 Guidelines. A valuable idea in order to prevent arbitrariness has been advanced by Alemanno and Meuwese. They suggest a shift in attention to the legislator. If, at the time of a delegation, it can be foreseen that the Commission, in the exercise of its implementing powers, will engage in policy choices, Council and Parliament should lay down an impact assessment requirement in the parent legislative act. In this context, Alemanno and Meuwese rightly regret 'that neither the Common Understanding [on delegated acts] nor the new Comitology Regulation addresses the procedural and substantive challenges of rulemaking IA'.[6]

Secondly, the key role played by EU agencies in the regulation of nanotechnologies also raises the impact assessment question for their regulatory output.[7] The answer here largely depends on the adoption procedures put in place by each respective Agency. Where these procedures allow for a transparent generation of knowledge, why bother with a separate impact assessment? The advantage of a common impact assessment requirement would nevertheless be to formally overcome the current fragmentation in agency proceduralisation (see further below section B). It could also lead to the urgently needed acknowledgement that these measures do entail policy choices with far-reaching impacts. This acknowledgement, however, would formalise the conflict with the legislative mandate of EU agencies (see further sections VI.B and VI.C on the facades of scientific truth and non-bindingness). At the same time, there are already agencies performing impact assessments, the prime example being the European Aviation Safety Agency.[8] An opportunity to clarify these questions was not only missed in the 2012 Common

[4] European Commission, 'Better regulation for better results—An EU agenda' (Communication—'Better Regulation Guidelines') COM (2015) 215 final, 17.

[5] European Commission, 'Better Regulation "Toolbox"'—Tool#5 When is an IA necessary? www.ec.europa.eu/smart-regulation/guidelines/docs/br_toolbox_en.pdf.

[6] A Alemanno and A Meuwese, 'Impact Assessment of EU Non-Legislative Rulemaking: The Missing Link in "New Comitology"' (2013) 19 *European Law Journal* 76, 86.

[7] See also P Craig, *EU Administrative Law* (n 1) 179.

[8] See European Aviation Safety Agency, 'Decision of the Management Board amending and replacing Decision 08/2007 concerning the Procedure to be applied by the Agency for the Issuing of opinions, certification specifications and guidance material ("rulemaking procedure")' (MB 01/2012, 2012) art 2.

Approach on decentralised agencies, which does not touch upon the adoption procedures for agency regulatory output, but also in the Better Regulation Package of 2015, which declares that 'whenever specific legislative procedures mandate an EU agency to carry out the main policy-design work and prepare an IA-like document, no Commission IA is necessary a priori'.[9]

ii. The Operation of the Impact Assessment: Proportionate Level of Analysis or Carte Blanche*?*

The added value of clarifying and possibly extending the impact assessment requirement depends upon its practical operation and, ultimately, upon whether it really serves as an adequate procedure for pooling the societally fragmented knowledge. The extension of an empty procedure should be avoided. As regards its practical operation, much of the debate on empty proceduralisation in the case studies was ascribed to the vagueness of the 2009 Impact Assessment Guidelines' operating principle of a 'proportionate level of analysis'.[10] This operating principle also survived the 2015 better regulation reform in form of the principle of 'proportionate analysis'.[11] Arguably, a solution is not readily available. The dilemma is—should the practice of impact assessment be continued—that there surely needs to be a certain degree of discretion for the Commission: different policy initiatives require different assessments. To devise rigid criteria could further turn the procedure into a technical and burdensome 'ticking the boxes' exercise. It is at this point at the latest that serious doubts arise as to whether the impact assessment 'can be saved'.

Is there life in the old dog yet? One final way out is arguably a more effective ex post oversight. Until now, this task has been performed by the Impact Assessment Board. However, since its establishment in 2006, the Board has been severely criticised for being composed of Commission officials[12] but also for its limited powers. The Board could neither oblige the Commission to conduct an assessment, for example for a particular implementing measure, nor did it dispose of veto rights. Proposals for a more independent and binding review therefore were tabled as early

[9] European Parliament, Council of the European Union and European Commission, 'Joint Statement on Decentralised Agencies' (2012) www.europa.eu/european-union/sites/europaeu/files/docs/body/joint_statement_and_common_approach_2012_en.pdf. See also M Chamon, 'Relying on Soft Law to Circumvent the Constitutional Objections to Agencification' (Colloque international de Jeunes Chercheurs 'La Soft Law en droit de l'Union européenne', Rennes, 24 and 25 June 2013) 18. Better Regulation 'Toolbox' (n 5).

[10] These concerns are shared by a 2007 evaluation report of the Commission's impact assessment system, which identified the principle as 'one of the biggest problems on a daily basis'. Not only interviewed stakeholders but also Commission staff criticised the principle as 'too vague', see The Evaluation Partnership, 'Evaluation of the Commission's Impact Assessment System' (Final Report, SG-02/2006, April 2007) 33 www.ec.europa.eu/smart-regulation/impact/key_docs/docs/tep_eias_final_report.pdf.

[11] 'Better Regulation Guidelines' COM (2015) 215 final (n 4) 17.

[12] The European Parliament was again clearest, attacking the Board for its 'information bias' and 'violation of necessary neutrality', see European Parliament, 'Resolution of 8 June 2011 on guaranteeing independent impact assessments' (P7_TA(2011) 0259) para G.

as in 2006, including a role for the Court of Auditors or indeed the creation of a new independent agency.[13] To this end, the 2015 reform of the Impact Assessment Guidelines has established the new Regulatory Scrutiny Board.[14] Unlike the old Impact Assessment Board, the Regulatory Scrutiny Board has to issue a positive opinion in order for an impact assessment to proceed.[15] While the Board is still composed of three Commission officials and chaired by a Commission director general, thus 'retain[ing] very much the character of an "in-house" body',[16] it also includes three members recruited from outside the Commission.[17] Whether the Regulatory Scrutiny Board will indeed be able to remedy the shortcomings of its predecessor, in terms of independence and power, remains to be seen. In view of the empty proceduralisation that was observed in practice—notwithstanding the existence of the Impact Assessment Board—the effective functioning of the new Regulatory Scrutiny Board will be crucial. Alternatively, the EU courts or the Ombudsman could assume a (greater) role in reviewing the quality of impact assessments (see further below sections D and E).

B. Towards a Structured Proceduralisation in EU Agencies

A more structured proceduralisation in EU agencies could be initiated at various levels and through different actors. First, it is surely the agencies themselves that should initiate a mutual learning process, through an exchange of visits, workshops, or the publication of best practices. The diverse procedures for the adoption of guidance documents within ECHA and EFSA left no doubt that agencies could substantially improve their operation when looking beyond their own nose to developments in fellow agencies. Above all, however, it is the legislator that should assume its responsibility. Given the increasing role agency guidance documents play in steering affected actors' behaviour, these (and other) powers should be delegated more carefully. A revealing example is the General Food Law, which does not provide for a separate category of 'guidance documents' in addition to 'scientific opinions'. This proved to make the content of these documents even more opaque, by further disguising their real substance for affected

[13] G Mather and F Vibert, 'Evaluating Better Regulation: Building the System' (London, European Policy Forum, City Research Series 9, 2006) 31. See further on a potential role for the Court of Auditors in reviewing impact assessments, A Meuwese, 'The European Court of Auditors Steps Out of Its Comfort Zone with an "Impact Assessment Audit"' (2011) 1 *European Journal of Risk Regulation* 104.

[14] 'Better Regulation Guidelines' COM (2015) 215 final (n 4) 9; European Commission, 'Decision of the President of the European Commission on the establishment of an independent Regulatory Scrutiny Board' C(2015) 3263 final.

[15] 'Better Regulation Guidelines' COM (2015) 215 final (n 4) 18.

[16] A Meuwese, 'Regulatory Scrutiny in Transition' (2015) 3 *European Journal of Risk Regulation* 359, 359.

[17] European Commission, 'Decision of the President of the European Commission on the establishment of an independent Regulatory Scrutiny Board' C(2015) 3263 final, Art 3(1).

actors but also for accountability fora such as the EU courts. Beyond that, at least the skeleton of an adoption procedure for guidance documents should be laid down in agencies' founding regulations, specifying for instance the involvement of affected societal and institutional actors as well as how the different intermediate steps of the procedure are to be published. Regrettably, the Common Approach on decentralised agencies of 2012,[18] as was noted above when discussing the desirability of an agency impact assessment requirement, is not helpful in this regard.[19] The European Ombudsman can serve as a further important actor in lifting the fog of fragmentation. Whereas the chemicals case study showed that the Ombudsman has already assumed a role in horizontally screening and comparing procedures across agencies, so far its attention has focused on the transparency and independence provisions. It would be desirable for the Ombudsman to expand its activism to further areas (see further below section E).

C. Repoliticising a Depoliticised Political Debate

This research showed that the attempts of the European Parliament (and the Council) to politicise the nano debate failed, first, due to the Commission's exclusive right of legislative initiative and, secondly, due to the Parliament's de facto absence in comitology. To be sure, the Commission possesses the exclusive right of legislative initiative and therewith the control over the legislative agenda. The original rationale for this 'gold standard'[20] is grounded in the belief that the Commission, as guardian of the Treaties, is best suited to represent the common European interest in the legislative process: in order 'to reflect, prepare, think ahead, coordinate and conciliate'.[21] At the same time, it is beyond doubt that the Commission's decision not to revise the text of the REACH Regulation and, in its place, to tackle the issue of nanotechnologies via its executive powers, was highly controversial and hence all but value free.[22] Yet, is this a problem?

The European Parliament may request the Commission to adopt legislative proposals in accordance with Article 225 TFEU. While the Commission has to provide the Parliament with a reasoned justification in case it considers a respective legislative proposal unwarranted, it is not obliged to follow the Parliament's

[18] 'Joint Statement on Decentralised Agencies' (n 9).

[19] See also M Chamon, 'Relying on Soft Law to Circumvent the Constitutional Objections to Agencification' (n 9) 18.

[20] P Craig and G De Búrca, *EU Law: Texts, Cases and Materials*, 5th edn (Oxford, Oxford University Press, 2011) 122.

[21] K Lenaerts and A Verhoeven, 'Institutional Balance as a Guarantee for Democracy in EU Governance' in C Joerges and R Dehousse (eds), *Good Governance in Europe's Integrated Market*, Collected Courses of the Academy of European Law XI/2 (Oxford, Oxford University Press, 2002) 70.

[22] Even in 1997, Craig wrote that 'it is readily apparent that the process of legislative initiation is not value free', see P Craig, 'Democracy and Rule-Making within the EC: An Empirical and Normative Assessment' (1997) 3 *European Law Journal* 105, 117.

request. In the area of nanotechnologies, the European Parliament adopted a resolution in 2009 in which it asked the Commission to review existing legislation in order to adapt it to the specific characteristics of the nanoform. In its reply, the Commission stated that it 'intends to review relevant legislation and instruments of implementation, and report on this in 2011; regulatory change will be proposed where necessary'.[23] In 2012, in the second (delayed) regulatory review on nanomaterials, the Commission announced its decision not to amend the enacting terms of REACH. The elephant in the room is whether it is still justified that parliamentary requests can be put off with a simple explanatory statement, especially in highly controversial areas. This is where the problem lies. Where a majority of members of Parliament identifies the need for legislative action, inaction is problematic from a democratic point of view.

It does not automatically follow that there should be an independent power of legislative initiative for the Parliament.[24] Yet, a respective parliamentary request should be thoroughly explored by the Commission and a rejection carefully reasoned. It might therefore be necessary to reverse the procedure in Article 225 TFEU by granting the Parliament a 'right to co-initiate'.[25] Here, the Parliament would have the power to propose legislation on its own, whereas the Commission would be reserved the privilege of expressing its assent. While this would render it (politically) more difficult for the Commission to turn down an already drafted parliamentary text, it would uphold the Commission's role 'to reflect, prepare, think ahead, coordinate and conciliate'.[26]

To be fair, however, the Parliament in its 2009 Resolution on regulatory aspects of nanotechnology did not explicitly invoke its right in Article 225 TFEU. Nor did it formally request the Commission in the aftermath of the 2012 second regulatory review on nanomaterials to take specific legislative action, for example, to amend the legal text of REACH. This is despite the strong reactions from societal actors, which would have provided a perfect opportunity for the Parliament to exert political pressure on the Commission. Why is the Parliament not relying on Article 225 TFEU to repoliticise the nano debate? Beyond doubt, this omission is regrettable. It concurs, however, with earlier studies attesting its rare use.[27] At the same time, Article 225 TFEU is not the sole area of untapped parliamentary

[23] Follow-up to the European Parliament resolution on regulatory aspects of nanomaterials, adopted by the Commission on 14 July 2009.

[24] Jürgen Habermas recently advocated a reform of the EU Treaties, which would also entail a right for the European Parliament to take legislative initiative, see J Habermas, 'Democracy in Europe: Why the Development of the EU into a Transnational Democracy Is Necessary and How It Is Possible' (2015) 21 *European Law Journal* 546, 554.

[25] K Lenaerts and A Verhoeven, 'Institutional Balance as a Guarantee for Democracy in EU Governance' (n 21) 74.

[26] ibid 75.

[27] From the right's insertion into the Treaties in 1992 up to 2010, it was invoked 29 times, see R Corbett, F Jacobs and M Shackleton, *The European Parliament*, 8th edn (London, John Harper Publishing, 2011) 265.

potential. The Parliament's right of scrutiny under the old comitology system as well as its prerogative to attend expert groups in the preparation of implementing acts also emerged as being under-utilised. These findings must be put in the context of the Parliament's scarce, or at least irregular, use of its ex post scrutiny powers over executive rule making. It is also mirrored in the broad absence of parliamentary impact assessments.[28] In numerous instances in this research it was wondered: where is the European Parliament?

It would be too easy to argue that the Parliament is simply not interested in taking advantage of its privileges in areas of high complexity and technicality. Clearly, the Parliament's activism in nanotechnologies in the two legislative procedures (ie novel foods and food additives) refutes such conclusions. There seems to be a more fundamental problem with the Parliament's institutional capacity, with its ability to actually seize its (limited) powers of involvement in comitology and to live up to its responsibility as an accountability forum. In order to allow for a repoliticisation of the nano debate, the Parliament must also be able to use its powers in practice. This 'mismatch' between the Parliament's (formal) powers and their execution in practice was observed in a 2011 study by Dobbels. As reasons for this mismatch, Dobbels mentioned problems in the Parliament's internal organisation but also a lack of expertise in its comparatively small administration.[29] Although it is beyond the scope of this book to make suggestions for a reform of the Parliament's administration, one way to increase its knowledge base would be to resort to other institutional actors or existent mechanisms as 'fact finders', thereby borrowing institutional capacity. An auspicious instrument in the often complex areas subject to comitology—nanotechnologies being no exception—could be the Commission's impact assessment, provided, of course, that it is more than an empty procedure. So far (and maybe for good reasons), Commission impact assessments are rarely discussed at meetings of parliamentary committees.[30] Also the European Ombudsman could be more systematically mobilised by the Parliament as a fact finder, especially in order to strengthen its oversight of executive rule making (see below section E).

D. From Lapdog to Watchdog: The Catalyst Function of the EU Courts

The role of the EU courts in overseeing the collection of knowledge and participation in the development of the EU regulatory framework for nanotechnologies is

[28] European Court of Auditors, 'Impact Assessments of the EU Institutions: Do They Support Decision-Making?' (Special Report no 3, 2010) 24–25.

[29] M Dobbels, 'The European Parliament: A Giant with Feet of Clay?' (Doctoral Thesis, Maastricht University 2013) 271–73. See also R Corbett et al, *The European Parliament* (n 27) 218.

[30] The 2010 study of the Court of Auditors found that 'an analysis of over 12000 public European Parliament Committee documents of the 2004–2009 parliamentary term revealed that only one document made explicit reference to a Commission IA', see European Court of Auditors, 'Impact Assessments of the EU Institutions' (n 28) 21.

characterised by undue self-restriction. This is regrettable, for the courts could assume a vital role in reviewing the procedures followed in the adoption of the entire spectrum of regulatory measures, thereby not only monitoring but also actively shaping the collection of knowledge and the participation of affected actors, as well as increasing the overall transparency of the process. Scott and Sturm's image of courts as catalysts portrays this ambition.[31] As a response to 'new governance', they argued that courts should 'become a way of publicising and making visible the diversity of governance forms which have emerged'.[32] This would also include reviewing the activities of actors involved in highly complex areas, 'such as the comitology committee and the scientific experts, who participate in normative elaboration and capacity building', without however dictating the substance of the norms.[33] In nano practice, however, the EU courts appeared reluctant, first, to open up towards what Scott and Sturm refer to as 'new forms of governance', of which agency guidance documents are but one example, and, secondly, to take a careful look at the procedural execution of impact assessments or public consultations. While the courts regularly surrender to the smokescreen of 'complex assessments', their substantive approach to the determination of a measure's legal effects also did not allow them to break through the facade of their formal non-bindingness (see further section IV.C).

At the same time, it is arguable that for the EU courts to take an effective role in reviewing the adoption process of regulation, a minimum degree of proceduralisation, that is, of standards whose compliance can actually be verified and further developed by the judiciary, is required. This concerns the creation of adoption procedures for agency guidance documents, but also the involvement of affected societal actors and the pooling of knowledge in the drafting of legislative acts or comitology. Here again, the significance of clarifying the scope of application and operation of the Impact Assessment Guidelines (and the coupled Commission minimum consultation standards) is encountered. It is particularly regrettable in this context that the 2015 Better Regulation Package appears to further obscure the jungle of self-imposed Commission rules. While it repeals the existing Impact Assessment Guidelines, the Commission's 'old' minimum consultation standards seem to co-exist next to a rubric of 'guidelines on stakeholder consultation' in the Better Regulation Guidelines.[34] Moreover, the fact that the Better Regulation Guidelines are detailed in a separate online tool called 'Better Regulation Toolbox' adds to the complexity, not least because they are referred to as 'practical tips' on the Commission's website.[35]

[31] J Scott and S Sturm, 'Courts as Catalysts: Re-Thinking the Judicial Role in New Governance' (2007) 13 *Columbia Journal of European Law* 565.

[32] ibid 571.

[33] ibid 574.

[34] 'Better Regulation Guidelines' COM (2015) 215 final (n 4) Ch VI.

[35] European Commission, Better Regulation: Guidelines and Toolbox www.ec.europa.eu/info/better-regulation-guidelines-and-toolbox_en.

The success of the catalyst court is hence a two-way street. On the one hand, it premises the willingness of the court to assume its constitutive function in the review of 'new forms of governance' and the procedural execution of knowledge collection. On the other hand, the catalyst function preconditions the existence of procedures, which can actually be reviewed, reflected upon and potentially enhanced.

Finally, to enable the EU courts to embrace their catalyst function calls for a rethinking also on the part of societal and institutional actors. For instance, non-binding measures must also be brought before the courts. In this context it is telling that, so far, no agency guidance document has been directly challenged. Applicants also need to change their mind-set and become more audacious. Equally, the courts' catalyst function should not be hampered by constraints in the EU judiciary's institutional capacity to actually fulfil such a role, be it in terms of human or financial resources. This may require concrete reforms to be taken, with the establishment of specialised courts as only one example.[36]

E. Taking the EU Ombudsman Seriously

The EU Ombudsman emerged on several occasions in this book as an underestimated institution. At first, the Ombudsman appeared to be a key figure in compensating for the gaps in legal accountability provided by the existent EU judiciary, whose behaviour diverges substantially from the above-depicted catalyst court. Compared to the EU courts, the Ombudsman is accessible to every citizen residing in an EU Member State, without the need to prove direct and individual concern. Moreover, the Ombudsman scrutinises the administration's behaviour independent of whether it leads to a binding or non-binding act. Unlike the EU courts, the broad understanding of 'maladministration' has furthermore enabled the Ombudsman to look into compliance with self-imposed rules, such as the impact assessment procedure or the minimum consultation standards.[37] Indeed, it may be exactly the formal 'toothlessness' of the Ombudsman, the softer nature of its remedies, that ultimately allows it to go a step further than the Court and to adopt recommendations where the legal situation is not absolutely clear, but where 'good administrative practice' leaves a lot to be desired.[38]

[36] For instance, under Art 257 TFEU, see also E Vos, 'EU Risk Regulation Reviewed by the European Courts' in M Van Asselt, M Everson and E Vos (eds), *Trade, Health and the Environment: The European Union Put to the Test*, Routledge Explorations in Environmental Studies (London, Routledge, 2014) 227.

[37] J Neyer, *The Justification of Europe: a Political Theory of Supranational Integration* (Oxford, Oxford University Press, 2012) 145.

[38] See also M Dawson, *New Governance and the Transformation of European Law Coordinating EU Social Law and Policy*, Cambridge Studies in European Law and Policy (Cambridge, Cambridge University Press, 2011) 298.

Secondly, the EU Ombudsman appeared as an important, though perhaps under-used, fact finder, a 'whistler-blower', for a notoriously under-informed European Parliament in its supervision of the EU executive. Contrary to the Ombudsman's usual depiction as a toothless tiger, the case studies evinced that via further accountability fora, such as the European Parliament or the Court of Auditors and OLAF, the Ombudsman's recommendations are very capable of taking real bites. Even beyond this, much more than the courts, the Ombudsman took a role in pro-actively assessing the adequacy of established procedures. It was in this way that the Ombudsman considered EFSA's conflict of interest rules inadequate to ensure the independence of the agency's administration and, afterwards, started a horizontal screening of transparency and conflict of interest rules across the numerous EU agencies with the aim of establishing best practices. This activism on the part of the Ombudsman was found to constitute a suitable blueprint for further comparative analyses and thus a potentially effective way not only to reveal but also to remedy instances of empty or fragmented proceduralisation. This, however, requires the Ombudsman to be taken seriously by societal actors who have to lodge complaints to its office but also by the EU administration that is targeted by its investigations, has to implement its recommendations and has to provide the Ombudsman with the resources necessary to fulfil its function effectively.

F. Fostering a Transparent Regulatory Process

To a large extent, the achievement of a transparent regulatory process depends upon the effective reform of the impact assessment procedure as discussed above in section A. Beyond that, however, the current fragmented nature of EU administrative law, which was found to hamper a transparent process across the various identified binding and non-binding regulatory measures, needs to be tackled. This is not a blank sheet of paper. Already in 2008 the Commission proposed a recast of Regulation 1049/2001 on access to documents.[39] While the proposal's Lisbon update suggested an expansion of the Regulation's scope to embrace EU agencies, the documents covered by the direct access provision for 'active transparency' remained ambiguous. Indeed, the Commission's proposal foresees direct access to be granted to documents 'which are part of procedures leading to the adoption of EU legislative acts or non-legislative acts of general application'.[40] While this

[39] European Commission, 'Proposal for a Regulation of the European Parliament and of the Council regarding public access to European Parliament, Council and Commission documents' COM (2008) 229 final. The proposal was aligned to the entry into force of the Lisbon Treaty in 2011, see European Commission, 'Proposal for a Regulation of the European Parliament and of the Council amending Regulation (EC) No 1049/2001 regarding public access to European Parliament, Council and Commission documents' COM (2011) 137 final.

[40] 'Proposal regarding public access to European Parliament, Council and Commission documents' COM (2008) 229 final (n 39) 9.

would arguably include Commission recommendations (as non-legislative acts formally listed in Article 288 TFEU), the question remains whether it also includes 'unidentified legal objects', such as agency guidance documents. In any case, the revision is currently deadlocked due to fundamental disagreement between the Parliament, Council and Commission.[41] Should negotiations be resumed, the current non-existent active transparency for preparatory documents generated in the drafting of non-binding measures should also be addressed.

Another construction site is the 'reality of access', meaning the actual content of the available documents, whose often poor quality was found to defy the very idea of active transparency. Yet, the solution to this problem is not obvious. It seems difficult to lay down concrete standards as to the content of these documents. A first step, however, would be to consider these empty documents an instance of 'maladministration' and hence within the investigative mandate of the Ombudsman. Another measure to increase the transparency of the regulatory process would be to codify existing case law in order also to formally require a statement of reasons for instruments not included in Article 288 TFEU. This would need to entail a clarification of the definition of 'legal acts' in Article 296 TFEU. Finally, there is room for reform of the EU institutions' (and agencies') language regimes. An initial step would be to formalise what is already common practice, namely also to publish (and hence translate) opinions and recommendations, that is, the non-binding instruments of Article 288 TFEU, in the Official Journal. Next, attention should be directed towards the various 'unidentified legal objects', such as agency guidance documents. This could be another matter to be addressed horizontally, instead of every single agency adopting its own language regime, as the study of EFSA and ECHA demonstrated. Perhaps even more important, the common practice of the Commission (and EU agencies) publishing preparatory documents, including public consultations, only in English should be tackled.[42]

VI. THREE FACADES OF EU RISK REGULATION

Having proposed reforms within the framework of EU risk regulation as it stands, this section turns to the caveats and to the more fundamental problems raised

[41] Despite a joint motion for a resolution of the European Parliament in June 2013 in which it 'ask[ed] all the EU institutions to work together to find a way out as soon as possible', see European Parliament, 'Resolution of 12 June 2013 on the deadlock on the revision of Regulation (EC) No 1049/2001' (P7_TA(2013)0271) para 2. The question of block exceptions to access to documents and the very definition of 'document' are hotly debated.

[42] This has been heavily criticised by the Ombudsman as 'restricted multilingualism', which would result in only a limited number of EU citizens being able to exercise their right 'to participate in the democratic life of the Union', as provided for in Art 10(3) TEU, thereby constituting an 'unequal treatment', see European Ombudsman, Draft Recommendation 640/2011/AN, 24 November 2011, paras 32 and 35. See for a discussion, N Vogiatzis, 'The Linguistic Policy of the EU Institutions and Political Participation Post-Lisbon' (2016) 41 *European Law Review* 176.

by this book. Three facades of EU risk regulation appeared to run like a thread throughout this book. On occasion, these facades met or overlapped. Separately, however, they can be captured under the headings of participation, scientific truth and non-bindingness. These are the three aspects of EU risk regulation that should be the focus of future research.

A. The Facade of Participation

The heavy reliance placed by the European Commission on regulatory options in the executive setting raised fundamental concerns as to the legitimacy of these measures. In their adoption, the European Parliament naturally plays a negligently small role. To ensure democratic self-determination of affected actors in today's nano society, however, requires their input in the regulatory process at the European level; a mere focus on the regulation's output legitimacy was found deceptive in the highly uncertain and controversial area of nanotechnologies. Yet, the procedures that were devised in the wake of the European governance debate to foster the involvement of affected actors, such as the impact assessment procedure and the integrated public consultation, bitterly failed when measured against the criteria derived from the ideal speech situation. These procedures seem far from creating a European public space that would enable a joint political will formation and, hence, compensate for the absence of political participation.

The question left is therefore: administrative participation, *quo vadis*? Arguably, two broad directions are conceivable. One is to attempt to reform the current non-binding system of administrative participation in the EU regulatory process. The existing standards could be sent back to the drawing board in order to clarify their scope of application but also their vague contents. A continued reliance on these (revised) rules would furthermore require enhanced possibilities for their ex post oversight, most notably by the EU courts assuming their catalyst function as expounded above in section V.D. Having said this, thorough reforms of the Commission's consultation practices are not foreseen in the near future. Whilst a 2012 review conducted by the Commission acknowledged several of the shortcomings identified here,[43] overall the Commission concluded that the 'consultation policy and its tools remain valid and fulfil international best standards'.[44] This is also reflected in the 'guidelines on stakeholder consultation' that are part of the 2015 Better Regulation Guidelines.[45]

The other broad direction would be to bow out of current practices altogether. Their abolition would imply a refocus on political participation in order to ensure input in the regulatory process by affected actors. This, of course, raises different

[43] European Commission, 'Review of the Commission Consultation Policy' (Staff Working Document) SWD (2012) 422 final, 10–16.

[44] ibid 17.

[45] 'Better Regulation Guidelines' COM (2015) 215 final (n 4) Ch VI.

issues, be it the feasibility (in terms of resources) of a role for the Parliament in executive rule making[46] or, vice versa, a retreat from such mechanisms back to regulation via legislation. At least such a move would end the pretence of legitimate regulation based on an opaque, arguably unequal and often exclusive stakeholder consultation. One is almost inclined to argue that both regulator and participants would save valuable time and resources if the current spectacle of administrative participation was no longer performed.

Alternatively, current consultation practices could be replaced with the adoption of legally binding rules by the EU legislature. Based on the insertion of Article 11 TEU into the Lisbon Treaty, a current strand in EU scholarship argues for a juridification of participation.[47] The basic argument is that the direct link drawn in Article 11 TEU between participation and democracy designates a normative shift from the hitherto instrumental usage of participation to participation as a means to further participatory democracy.[48] As the legal basis for such a law, Mendes proposes Article 298(2) TFEU, which enables Parliament and Council to adopt a regulation to further 'an open, efficient and independent European administration'.[49]

Article 298 TFEU is a new addition to the Lisbon Treaty that has revived a debate[50] on the desirability of a 'General Law of Administrative Procedure'[51] or a 'European Administrative Procedure Act'.[52] Depending on its scope and substance, such a general law could be a remedy to various problems encountered in this research, well beyond consultation practices, ranging from the fragmentary proceduralisation in EU agencies and a repeatedly empty impact assessment procedure to loopholes in the present access to document system, language policies and reason-giving requirements. There is hence the potential to kill not only two birds with one stone but a whole flock. In January 2013, the European Parliament requested the Commission to submit a respective legislative proposal.[53] While the Parliament envisages that such a law should apply to all EU institutions, bodies,

46 The topic was touched upon in a 2010 Framework Agreement between Parliament and Commission, in which the institutions declared that 'in areas where the Parliament is usually involved in the legislative process, the Commission shall use soft law, where appropriate and on a duly justified basis after having given the Parliament the opportunity to express its views', Framework Agreement on relations between the European Parliament and the European Commission [2010] OJ L 304/47, para 43.

47 J Mendes, 'Participation and the Role of Law After Lisbon: A Legal View on Article 11 TEU' (2011) 48 *Common Market Law Review* 1849.

48 ibid 1850.

49 ibid.

50 The debate has its origins in the late 1990s, see eg C Harlow, 'Codification of EC Administrative Procedures? Fitting the Foot to the Shoe or the Shoe to the Foot' (1996) 2 *European Law Journal* 3.

51 P Craig, 'A General Law on Administrative Procedure, Legislative Competence and Judicial Competence' (2013) 19 *European Public Law* 503.

52 A Meuwese, Y Schuurmans and W Voermans, 'Towards a European Administrative Procedure Act' (2009) 2 *Review of European Administrative Law* 3.

53 European Parliament, 'Resolution of 15 January 2013 with recommendations to the Commission on a Law of Administrative Procedure of the European Union' (P7_TA(2013)0004).

offices and agencies, the proposal only covers single case decision making.[54] Rule making, which is of particular relevance in the context of this book, is not covered by the Parliament's proposal. A group of scholars has, however, taken rule making on board in its current project,[55] which has as its aim to advise on the development of such a general law. Yet, this project also only considers rule making leading to the adoption of binding acts. Obviously, this limitation to binding rule making would leave unaddressed many of this book's concerns or pitfalls of new governance.

Whether or not there are legally binding rules for participation, be it in the form of a European Administrative Procedure Act or not, the question that lurks in the background is whether a reform of administrative participation would indeed pave the way for the development of a European public sphere. Would such rules lay the foundation for a true deliberation to take place at European level? Habermas imagines the formation of a civic solidarity at the European level[56] that, in turn, would create the conditions for communication in a political public sphere. The crux of the matter is only how to achieve this transnational form of civic solidarity. Habermas envisions this solidarity to be stimulated by 'legal-administrative means', steered, inter alia, by media, migration, the Internet and tourism. If we look at participation in current public consultations at the European level (leaving aside the shortcomings of current practices for a moment), however, only a narrow group of stakeholders is identifiable, mostly with economic interests, but there is hardly a balanced representation of 'all affected actors' that seize the opportunity to participate. The essential question is, therefore, are we faced with such imbalances only because of problems in scope and content of present impact assessment rules and consultation standards? Would this be different if participation was juridified? To say the least, it is difficult to imagine a wider array of affected actors contributing to a consultation at the European level only because legally binding rules were adopted. Yet, are these not the 'legal-administrative means' Habermas speaks of to stimulate a civic solidarity? Arguably, a fundamental tension emerges here in his post-national constellation, which is based on a theory of deliberative democracy developed in the context of the nation-state, in which a public sphere exists. The real question that remains is therefore how to develop a European public sphere, which seems indispensable for a meaningful participation.

B. The Facade of Scientific Truth

The artificial separation between risk assessment and risk management—between scientific and political decision making—has been a thorn in many commentators'

[54] ibid Annex Recommendation 1.

[55] Research Network on EU Administrative Law, ReNEUAL. See for further information www.reneual.eu.

[56] J Habermas, *Zur Verfassung Europas* (Berlin, Suhrkamp, 2011) 62 and J Habermas, 'Democracy in Europe: Why the Development of the EU into a Transnational Democracy Is Necessary and How It Is Possible' (n 24) 553.

sides for a long time.[57] Nevertheless, the instigation of the principle of risk analysis as the Grundnorm[58] of EU risk regulation has reinforced the leitmotif of 'speaking truth to power' with the turn of the 2000s (chapter two, section III.B.i). This is inter alia manifested in the 'agency phenomenon'[59] and in the mushrooming of EU agencies, such as EFSA and ECHA after 2001, which are meant to supply the regulatory process with scientific and technical advice. They follow the ideal model of independent regulatory agencies that derive their legitimacy from effective problem solving.[60] Yet, this struggle for effectiveness was found to be illusory in the context of the regulation of nanotechnologies. The nano guidance of EFSA and ECHA's REACH guidance documents proved to accommodate normative choices, which are shielded behind the notion of technical specifications and the accordant labels of 'scientific opinion' and 'technical and scientific guidance'.

Their classification as scientific or technical specifications distracts societal (eg consumers, industry or environmental NGOs) and institutional actors, including the EU legislature, national authorities and the judiciary, from their actual content. This, in turn, hinders not only their transparency but it also reduces the room for public participation and political contestation. After all, how could one challenge the truth? Agencies are hence torn between their formal role as 'neutral' sources of knowledge and their de facto assumption of regulatory tasks. One is confronted with the 'paradox of a politicised depoliticised administration',[61] which begs for an acknowledgment of agencies as 'political creatures'.[62] In Beck's words, politics has 'migrated from the official arenas'.[63] This acknowledgement, however, not only implies a rethinking of the role of agencies in the EU's institutional structure and balance (see further section VI.C), it also means to question the very foundation of EU risk regulation: the principle of risk analysis.

To be sure, this book is far from proposing a new framework for EU risk regulation. However, it would like to join a recent call by Elizabeth Fisher to actually resume debates on its adequacy, debates that started in the 1990s.[64] Now, Fisher notes, over a decade later, 'while there are many policy documents and scholarly articles on the topic of risk regulation there is far less debate about the frameworks

[57] eg S Jasanoff, *The Fifth Branch: Science Advisors as Policy Makers* (Cambridge, Harvard University Press, 1994) 230.

[58] A Alemanno, 'Regulating the European Risk Society' in A Alemanno, F Den Butter, A Nijsen and J Torriti (eds), *Better Business Regulation in a Risk Society* (New York, Springer, 2013) 41.

[59] M Busuioc, M Groenleer and J Trondal, *The Agency Phenomenon in the European Union*, European Policy Research Unit Series (Manchester, Manchester University Press, 2012).

[60] G Majone, *Regulating Europe*, European Public Policy (London, Routledge, 1996) 296.

[61] M Everson, C Monda and E Vos, 'What is the Future of European Agencies?' in E Everson, C Monda and E Vos (eds), *European Agencies in Between Institutions and Member States*, European Monographs 85 (Alphen aan den Rijn, Wolters Kluwer, 2014) 236.

[62] ibid 239.

[63] U Beck, *Risk Society: Towards a New Modernity* (M Ritter (tr), London, SAGE Publications, 1992) 188.

[64] E Fisher, 'Framing Risk Regulation: a Critical Reflection' (2013) 2 *European Journal of Risk Regulation* 125. For the debates of the 1990s, see most notably S Jasanoff, *The Fifth Branch* (n 57).

under which it should operate. This is not to say that there are no contributions, but rather that the risk assessment/risk management framework has become the dominant account of risk regulation'.[65] Fisher admits that there are good reasons for this, most notably because the principle of risk analysis has become enshrined in legislation (such as the General Food Law), because it speaks to the rational paradigm of bureaucracy and because it conveys the impression of neutrality.[66] This, however, should not prevent a critical reflection on this framework's advantages and, of course, its disadvantages.[67]

C. The Facade of Non-Bindingness

The fact that the EU legislator has endowed agencies merely with the power to issue non-binding, technical guidance documents must also be considered in the context of the ambiguous constitutional position of agencies in the EU's legal order. In fact, the EU Treaties neither explicitly foresee the possibility to create an EU agency nor do they provide for a delegation of powers to the latter.[68] Paradoxically, however, Article 263 TFEU enables the EU courts to review the legality of acts of EU agencies intended to produce legal effects vis-a-vis third parties. The Lisbon Treaty hence implicitly recognises EU agencies' lawful existence and engagement in activities that may result in the adoption of binding acts.[69]

In the absence of a Treaty basis, the delegation of powers to EU agencies has so far been regulated by the Court. In its *Meroni* case law of the late 1950s, the Court strictly prohibited the possibility of delegating discretionary powers to bodies other than those established by the Treaties. In its recent case *UK v Parliament and Council*, the Court of Justice further elaborated on the definition of 'discretionary powers'.[70] The UK Government claimed that the powers delegated to the European Securities and Markets Authority (ESMA) would constitute a breach of *Meroni*.[71] ESMA's powers to adopt binding measures to fine economic operators[72] would, the UK argued, entail 'a very large measure of discretion',[73] requiring a

[65] E Fisher, 'Framing Risk Regulation' (n 64) 128.

[66] ibid 128–30.

[67] ibid 132.

[68] M Chamon, 'EU Agencies between Meroni and Romano or the Devil and the Deep Blue Sea' (2011) 48 *Common Market Law Review* 1055, 1056.

[69] 'Otherwise these Treaty amendments would be meaningless', see Case C-270/12 *United Kingdom of Great Britain and Northern Ireland v European Parliament and Council of the European Union* [2014] not published, Opinion of AG Jääskinen, para 74.

[70] For a discussion, see CF Bergström, 'Shaping the New System for Delegation of Powers to EU Agencies: *United Kingdom v. European Parliament and Council (Short selling)*' (2015) 52 *Common Market Law Review* 219.

[71] Case C-270/12 *United Kingdom of Great Britain and Northern Ireland v European Parliament and Council of the European Union* [2014] not published.

[72] Regulation (EU) No 236/2012 of the European Parliament and of the Council of 14 March 2012 on short selling and certain aspects of credit default swaps [2012] OJ L 86/1, Art 28.

[73] Case C-270/12 *United v European Parliament and Council* (n 71) para 28.

subjective and potentially controversial judgment as to whether or not there is a threat to the functioning of the financial markets.[74] The Court, however, could not find a violation of the *Meroni* requirements. Since the ESMA's powers 'are precisely delineated and amenable to judicial review',[75] they would neither be discretionary nor of a 'quasi-legislative nature'.[76] On the contrary, following Advocate General Jääskinen's opinion in this case, the powers delegated to the Commission under Article 290 TFEU, which enable the adoption of 'non-legislative acts of general application to supplement or amend certain non-essential elements of the legislative act' are discretionary. Measures that can alter the normative contents of legislative acts, according to AG Jääskinen, 'must be exercised by an EU institution that is democratically accountable, in other words by the Commission, which is ultimately accountable to the European Parliament'.[77]

From a purely formal angle, the guidance documents adopted by ECHA and EFSA are non-binding, technical specifications, and fully in line with *Meroni*. This, however, proved to be a farce. These documents are neither void of (indirect) legal effects nor are they mere technical specifications. Looking at ECHA's nano appendices, one could even go a step further: they were shown to supplement the information requirements in the REACH Regulation's annexes with two additional nano-specific endpoints. In the language of the Treaties, this would be nothing less than a 'supplement to a non-essential element of the legislative act' and hence, according to AG Jääskinen, necessarily of a discretionary or quasi-legislative nature. Combined with practical and even indirect legal effects of the guidance, it is difficult not to call them a veiled delegated act *but* a delegated act that is not reviewable by the EU courts, not subject to the Parliament and Council's right to objection, not even potentially within the scope of the Commission's impact assessment requirement, participation standards and transparency provisions. Here, institutional and legal practice hides behind the facade of formal non-bindingness.

There are two ways to break this facade. The first one is to abide by the *Meroni* doctrine and to comply with its requirements—not only on paper but also in practice. Arguably, this leaves one to wonder what kind of tasks EU agencies such as EFSA and ECHA could still perform in areas where not only scientific considerations and value judgements (see above section B on the facade of scientific truth) but also the boundaries between binding and non-binding regulatory output incessantly blur. It appears inevitable for agencies operating in the area of risk regulation to engage in political choices, the potential (indirect) legal effects of which cannot be excluded. Everything else would be a 'rhetorical illusion'.[78]

[74] ibid para 29.

[75] ibid para 53.

[76] ibid paras 63–67 with reference to *Romano*, Case C-98/80 *Guiseppe Romano v Institut National d'Assurance Maladie-Invalidité* [1981] ECR 1241.

[77] Case C-270/12 *UK v Parliament and Council* (n 71) para 85.

[78] M Everson, 'Agencies: The 'Dark Hour' of the Executive?' in HCH Hofmann and AH Türk (eds), *Legal Challenges in EU Administrative Law: Towards an Integrated Administration* (Cheltenham, Edward Elgar Publishing, 2009) 128.

The other, arguably only, direction is then to overturn *Meroni* and to concede the delegation of discretionary powers also formally to EU agencies, correspondent to those in Article 290 TFEU and with equivalent control mechanisms set in place by Parliament and Council.[79] This, however, would require the constitutional recognition of agencies, as regards their creation, but also the delegation of powers to the latter. The mention of EU agencies in Article 290 TFEU (or in a corresponding new Article) seems inevitable. Such a move appears necessary to prevent *Meroni* from being 'dismantled from within, invisibly, through empirical evidence'.[80] The continuation of the status quo would uphold a facade that shields a growing executive power from parliamentary and judicial control mechanisms.

VII. OUTLOOK

To look beyond the facades of participation, scientific truth and non-bindingness arguably is a particular challenge for legal scholars and their fondness for black-and-white pictures. To climb these facades, a leg-up by other disciplines, most notably by political science, is therefore indispensable. Only the recognition that de jure does not equal de facto may alter the EU regulator's steady course towards an executive dominance. The important task of the lawyers here is to adapt the existing constitutional framework to a new social reality: procedures must be (re)designed, institutional actors must be recognised and resources must be (re)distributed in order to ensure the EU's regulatory capacity in today's nano society.

[79] The weak institutional capacity of the Parliament to exploit such control mechanisms in practice remains problematic here, see above section V.C.

[80] D Curtin and R Dehousse, 'European Agencies: Tipping the Balance' in M Busuioc, M Groenleer and J Trondal (eds), *The Agency Phenomenon in the European Union*, European Policy Research Unit series (Manchester, Manchester University Press, 2012) 198. In a similar vein, M Lee, *EU Environmental Law, Governance and Decision-Making*, Modern Studies in European Law vol 43, 2nd edn (Oxford, Hart Publishing, 2014) 47.

Bibliography

AFP, 'Inquiétudes autour des nanomatériaux dans les aliments' *Le Monde* (Paris, 29 February 2012).

Alemanno, A, 'EU Risk Regulation and Science: The Role of Experts in Decision-Making and Judicial Review' in E Vos (ed), *European Risk Governance—Its Science, Its Inclusiveness and Its Effectiveness* (Mannheim, CONNEX Report Series, 2008) 37–88.

——, 'The Better Regulation Initiative at the Judicial Gate: A Trojan Horse within the Commission's Walls or the Way Forward?' (2009) 15 *European Law Journal* 382.

——, 'Regulating the European Risk Society' in A Alemanno, F Den Butter, A Nijsen and J Torriti (eds), *Better Business Regulation in a Risk Society* (New York, Springer, 2013) 37–57.

——, 'How Much Better is Better Regulation?' (2015) 3 *European Journal of Risk Regulation* 344.

—— and Meuwese, A, 'Impact Assessment of EU Non-Legislative Rulemaking: The Missing Link in 'New Comitology'' (2013) 19 *European Law Journal* 76.

Armstrong, K and Kilpatrick, C, 'Law, Governance and New Governance? The Changing Open Method of Co-ordination' (2007) 13 *Columbia Journal of European Law* 649.

Asselt, M van, Vos, E and Rooijackers, B, 'Science, Knowledge and Uncertainty in EU Risk Regulation' in M Everson and E Vos (eds), *Uncertain Risks Regulated*, Law, Science and Society (Abingdon, Routledge Cavendish, 2009) 359–88.

Baldwin, R, Cave, M and Lodge, M, 'Introduction: Regulation—The Field and the Developing Agenda' in R Baldwin, M Cave and M Lodge (eds), *The Oxford Handbook of Regulation* (Oxford, Oxford University Press, 2010) 3–16.

Bartolini, S, 'New Modes of European Governance: An Introduction' in A Héritier and M Rhodes (eds), *New Modes of Governance in Europe: Governing in the Shadow of Hierarchy*, Palgrave Studies in European Union Politics (Basingstoke, Palgrave Macmillan, 2011) 1–18.

Bast, J, 'New Categories of Acts After the Lisbon Reform: Dynamics of Parliamentarization in EU Law' (2012) 49 *Common Market Law Review* 885.

Bauchmüller, M and Blawat, K, 'Rätsel um das Nano-Risiko' *Süddeutsche Zeitung* (Munich, 1 September 2011).

Beck, U, *Risk Society: Towards a New Modernity* (M Ritter (tr), London, SAGE Publications, 1992).

——, *Weltrisikogesellschaft* (Frankfurt am Main, Suhrkamp, 2008).

Belgian EU Presidency, 'Towards a regulatory framework for the traceability of nanomaterials' (Workshop organised by the Belgian EU Presidency, Brussels, 14 September 2010).

Belton, C, '*Nanotechnology: Plans for the Next Stage in Humanity's Development' Financial Times* (London, 14 April 2009).

Bengtsson, G, 'Global Trends in Chemicals Management' in J Eriksson, M Gilek and C Rudén (eds), *Regulating Chemical Risks: European and Global Challenges* (Dordrecht, Springer, 2010) 179–215.

Bergkamp, L and Penman, M, 'Conclusions' in L Bergkamp (ed), *The European Union REACH Regulation for Chemicals: Law and Practice* (Oxford, Oxford University Press, 2013) 410–30.

Bergström, CF, 'Shaping the New System for Delegation of Powers to EU Agencies: *United Kingdom v. European Parliament and Council (Short selling)*' (2015) 52 *Common Market Law Review* 219.

Better Regulation Task Force, *Principles of Better Regulation* (London, Cabinet Office, 1998).

——, *Imaginative Thinking for Better Regulation* (London, Cabinet Office, 2003).

Black, J, 'Constitutionalising Self-Regulation' (1996) 59 *Modern Law Review* 24.

——, 'Proceduralising Regulation: Part I' (2000) 20 *Oxford Journal of Legal Studies* 597.

——, 'Proceduralising Regulation: Part II' (2001) 21 *Oxford Journal of Legal Studies* 33.

——, *Critical Reflections on Regulation* (ESRC Centre for Analysis of Risk and Regulation, London School of Economics and Political Science, 2002).

——, 'The Role of Risk in Regulatory Processes' in R Baldwin, M Cave and M Lodge (eds), *The Oxford Handbook of Regulation* (Oxford, Oxford University Press, 2010) 302–48.

Blagescu, M, Las Casas, L de and Lloyd, R, *Pathways to Accountability: A Short Guide to the GAP Framework* (London, One World Trust, 2005).

Bogdandy, A von, 'The European Lesson for International Democracy: The Significance of Articles 9 to 12 EU Treaty for International Organisations' (2011) Jean Monnet Working Paper no 02/11, 11.

Booth, J, 'Scientists call for stricter safeguards on nanotechnology' *The Times* (London, 29 July 2004).

Bovens, M, 'Analysing and Assessing Accountability: A Conceptual Framework' (2007) 13 *European Law Journal* 447.

——, Curtin, D and 't Hart, P, *The Real World of EU Accountability: What Deficit?* (Oxford, Oxford University Press, 2010).

Bowman, DM and Hodge, GA, 'Counting on Codes: An Examination of Transnational Codes as a Regulatory Governance Mechanism for Nanotechnologies' (2009) 3 *Regulation & Governance* 145.

Brandsma, GJ, 'Accountable Comitology?' in M Bovens, D Curtin and P 't Hart (eds), *The Real World of EU Accountability: What Deficit?* (Oxford, Oxford University Press, 2010) 150–73.

——, Curtin, D and Meijer, A, 'How Transparent are EU "Comitology" Committees in Practice?' (2008) 14 *European Law Journal* 819, 826.

Breggin, L, Falkner, R, Jaspers, N, Pendergrass, J and Porter, R, 'Securing the Promise of Nanotechnologies—Towards Transatlantic Regulatory Co-operation' (Project of the London School of Economics and Political Science, Chatham House, the Environmental Law Institute and the Project on Emerging Nanotechnologies, 2009).

Brooks, H, 'National Science Policy and Technological Innovation' in R Landau and N Rosenberg (eds), *The Positive Sum Strategy: Harnessing Technology for Economic Growth* (Washington D.C., National Academy Press, 1986) 119–67.

Búrca, G de and Scott, J, 'Introduction' in G De Búrca and J Scott (eds), *Law and New Governance in the EU and the US*, Essays in European Law no 10 (Oxford, Hart Publishing, 2006) 1–12.

Burgess, J, Stirling, A, Clark, J, Davies, G, Eames, M, Staley, K and Williamson, S, 'Deliberative Mapping: A Novel Analytic-Deliberative Methodology to Support Contested Science-Policy Decisions' (2007) 16 *Public Understanding of Science* 299, 300.

Burgraff, E, 'Les nanotechnologies ont envahi notre vie quotidienne' *Le Soir* (Bruxelles, 27 May 2010).

Busuioc, M, 'European Agencies: Pockets of Accountability' in M Bovens, D Curtin and P 't Hart (eds), *The Real World of EU Accountability: What Deficit?* (Oxford, Oxford University Press, 2010) 87–116.

——, *European Agencies: Law and Practices of Accountability*, Oxford Studies in European law (Oxford, Oxford University Press, 2013).

——, Groenleer, M and Trondal, J, *The Agency Phenomenon in the European Union*, European Policy Research Unit Series (Manchester, Manchester University Press, 2012).

Cafaggi, F, 'Rethinking Private Regulation in the European Regulatory Space' in F Cafaggi (ed), *Reframing Self-Regulation in European Private Law*, Private Law in European Context Series vol 9 (Alphen aan den Rijn, Kluwer Law International, 2006) 3–75.

——, 'Private Regulation, Supply Chain and Contractual Networks: The Case of Food Safety' (2010) European University Institute Working Paper, RSCAS 2010/10.

Calliess, C and Lais, M, 'REACH Revisited—Der Verordnungsvorschlag zur Reform des Chemikalienrechts als Beispiel einer neuen europäischen Vorsorgestrategie' (2005) 5 *Natur und Recht* 290.

—— and Stockhaus, H, 'Precautionary Principle and Nanomaterials: REACH Revisited' (2012) 9 *Journal for European Environmental & Planning Law* 113.

Calster, G van, 'Regulating Nanotechnology in the European Union' (2006) 15 *European Environmental Law Review* 238.

——, 'The Role of the World Trade Organisation in Nanotechnology Regulation' in G Hodge, D Bowman and K Ludlow (eds), *New Global Frontiers in Regulation: The Age of Nanotechnology*, Monash Studies in Global Movements (Cheltenham, Edward Elgar Publishing, 2007) 287–319.

——, Bowman, D and D'Silva, J, 'Protecting Consumers or Failing Them? The Regulation of Nanotechnologies in the EU' (2011) 1 *European Journal of Consumer Law* 85.

Centre for Strategy & Evaluation Services, 'Interim Evaluation: Impact of the REACH Regulation on the Innovativeness of the EU Chemical Industry' (Final report, June 2012).

Chalmers, D, Davies, G and Monti, G, *European Union Law*, 3rd edn (Cambridge, Cambridge University Press, 2014).

Chamon, M, 'EU Agencies between Meroni and Romano or the Devil and the Deep Blue Sea' (2011) 48 *Common Market Law Review* 1055.

——, 'Relying on Soft Law to Circumvent the Constitutional Objections to Agencification' (Colloque international de Jeunes Chercheurs 'La Soft Law en droit de l'Union européenne', Rennes, 24 and 25 June 2013).

Chang, K, 'In Study, Researchers Find Nanotubes May Pose Health Risks Similar to Asbestos' *The New York Times* (New York, 21 May 2008).

Chaudhry, Q, 'Nanotechnology' (Presentation held at ICoMST, Copenhagen, August 2009).

——, Scotter, M, Blackburn, J, Toss, B, Boxall, A, Castle, L, Aitken, R and Watkins, R, 'Applications and Implications of Nanotechnologies for the Food Sector' (2008) 25 *Food Additives and Contaminants* 241.

——, Castle, L and Watkins, R, 'Nanotechnologies in the Food Arena: New Opportunities, New Questions, New Concerns' in Q Chaudhry, L Castle and R Watkins (eds), *Nanotechnologies in Food*, RSC Nanoscience & Nanotechnology no 14 (Cambridge, Royal Society of Chemistry Publishing, 2010) 1–17.

Christensen, FM, 'Nano–silver—Feasibility and Challenges for Human Health Risk Assessment Based on Open Literature' (2010) 4 *Nanotoxicology* 284.

Corbett, R, Jacobs, F and Shackleton, M, *The European Parliament*, 8th edn (London, John Harper Publishing, 2011).

Council for Science and Technology, 'Nanosciences and Nanotechnologies: A Review of Governments Progress on its Policy Commitments' (Report, 2007).

Craig, P, 'Democracy and Rule-Making within the EC: An Empirical and Normative Assessment' (1997) 3 *European Law Journal* 105.

——, *EU Administrative Law*, Collected Courses of the Academy of European Law XVI/1, 2nd edn (Oxford, Oxford University Press, 2012).

——, 'A General Law on Administrative Procedure, Legislative Competence and Judicial Competence' (2013) 19 *European Public Law* 503.

—— and Búrca, G de, *EU Law: Text, Cases, and Materials*, 5th edn (Oxford, Oxford University Press, 2011).

Curtin, D, 'Holding (Quasi-) Autonomous EU Administrative Actors to Public Account' (2007) 13 *European Law Journal* 523.

——, *Executive Power of the European Union, Law, Practices, and the Living Constitution*, Collected Courses of the Academy of European Law XII/4 (Oxford, Oxford University Press, 2009).

——, 'Challenging Executive Dominance in European Democracy' (2014) 77 *The Modern Law Review* 1.

——, and Dekker, I, 'Good Governance: The Concept and its Application by the European Union' in DM Curtin and RA Wessel (eds), *Good Governance and the European Union: Some Reflections of Concepts, Institutions and Substance*, Ius Commune Europaeum 49 (Antwerpen, Intersentia, 2004) 3–20.

—— and Senden, L, 'Public Accountability of Transnational Private Regulation: Chimera or Reality?' (2011) 38 *Journal of Law and Society* 163.

—— and Dehousse, R, 'European Agencies: Tipping the Balance' in M Busuioc, M Groenleer and J Trondal (eds), *The Agency Phenomenon in the European Union*, European Policy Research Unit Series (Manchester, Manchester University Press, 2012) 193–206.

——, Hofmann, R and Mendes, J, 'Constitutionalising EU Executive-Rulemaking Procedures: A Research Agenda' (2013) 19 *European Law Journal* 1.

Dahl, RA, *On Democracy* (New Haven, Yale University Press, 1998).

Dawson, M, 'New Governance and the Proceduralisation of European Law: The Case of the Open Method of Coordination' (Law Department PhD, European University Institute, 2009).

——, *New Governance and the Transformation of European Law Coordinating EU Social Law and Policy*, Cambridge Studies in European Law and Policy (Cambridge, Cambridge University Press, 2011).

——, 'Better Regulation and the Future of EU Regulatory Law and Politics' (2016) 53 *Common Market Law Review* 1209.

Dehousse, R, 'Misfits: EU Law and the Transformation of European Governance' in C Joerges and R Dehousse (eds), *Good Governance in Europe's Integrated Market*, Collected Courses of the Academy of European Law XI/2 (Oxford, Oxford University Press, 2002) 207–29.

——, 'Delegation of Powers in the European Union: The Need for a Multi-principals Model' (2008) 31 *West European Politics* 789.

——, 'The Community Method at Sixty' in R Dehousse (ed), *The Community Method: Obstinate or Obsolete?*, Palgrave Studies in European Union Politics (Basingstoke, Palgrave Macmillan, 2011) 3–13.

Dietz, T, 'Preface: Democracy and Science' in O Renn, T Webler and P Wiedemann (eds), *Fairness and Competence in Citizen Participation*, Technology, Risk, and Society vol 10 (Dordrecht, Kluwer Academic, 1995) xvii–xix.

Dobbels, M, 'The European Parliament: A Giant with Feet of Clay?' (Doctoral Thesis, Maastricht University, 2013).

DPA, 'Umweltbundesamt warnt vor Nanotechnik-Produkten' *Die Zeit* (Hamburg, 21 October 2009).

Drexler, KE, *Engines of Creation* (New York, Anchor Books/Doubleday, 1986).

——, 'Nanotechnology: From Feynman to Funding' in G Hunt and MD Mehta (eds), *Nanotechnology: Risk, Ethics and Law*, Science in Society Series (London, Earthscan, 2006) 25–34.

Dunsire, A, 'Modes of Governance' in J Kooiman (ed), *Modern Governance: New Government–Society Interactions* (London, SAGE Publications, 1993) 21–34.

Ehnert, T, 'The European Chemicals Agency—Beyond the Scope of the Meroni Doctrine?' (2008) Maastricht University Graduate Thesis.

——, 'The Legitimacy of New Risk Governance: A Critical View in Light of the EU's Approach to Nanotechnologies in Food' (2015) 21 *European Law Journal* 44.

Esteban, M, Webersik, C, Leary, D and Thompson-Pomeroy, D, 'Innovation in Responding to Climate Change: Nanotechnology, Ocean Energy and Forestry' (UNU-IAS Report, United Nations University Institute of Advanced Studies, 2008).

ETC Group, 'The Big Down: From Genomes to Atoms' (Report, 2003).

ETC Group, 'Down on the Farm: The Impact of Nano-Scale Technologies on Food and Agriculture' (Report, November 2004).

EU Observer, 'EU food agency criticised over GMO lobbying' *EU Observer* (Brussels, 14 December 2011).

Euractiv, 'Parliament calls for EU ban on cloning for food' *Euractiv* (Brussels, 8 July 2010).

European Chemical Industry Council (Cefic), 'Press Release: Practical Nanomaterials Definition Needed to Push Forward Next Great Innovation Breakthroughs' (18 October 2011).

——, 'Facts and Figures 2012: The European Chemicals Industry in a Worldwide Perspective' (June 2012).

European Consumers' Organisation (BEUC), 'Plenary Vote on a Resolution Opposing the Draft European Commission (EC) Delegated Regulation Updating the Definition of 'Engineered Nanomaterials' in Food' (Letter sent to the Members of the European Parliament, 10 March 2014).

—— and European Consumer Voice in Standardisation, 'Nanotechnology: Small is Beautiful but is it Safe?' (Joint ANEC/BEUC Position, 2009).

—— and ——, 'NANO Very Small and Everywhere: A Technological Magic Silver Bullet or a Serious Safety Risk?' (2012).

European Environmental Bureau, 'Nano Definition Too Narrow Says EEB' (Press release, 18 October 2011).

European Food Safety Authority, 'The Potential Risks Arising from Nanoscience and Nanotechnologies on Food and Feed Safety' (2009) 7 *EFSA Journal* 1.

European Food Safety Authority, 'Scientific Opinion on Guidance on the Risk Assessment of the Application of Nanoscience and Nanotechnologies in the Food and Feed Chain' (2011) 9 *EFSA Journal* 2140.

Everson, M, 'Agencies: the "Dark Hour" of the Executive?' in HCH Hofmann and AH Türk (eds), *Legal Challenges in EU Administrative Law: Towards an Integrated Administration* (Cheltenham, Edward Elgar Publishing, 2009) 116–35.

—— and Vos, E, 'European Risk Governance in a Global Context' in E Vos (ed), *European Risk Governance—Its Science, Its Inclusiveness and Its Effectiveness* (Mannheim, CONNEX Report Series, 2008).

——, Monda, C and Vos, E, 'What is the Future of European Agencies?' in E Everson, C Monda and E Vos (eds), *European Agencies in Between Institutions and Member States*, European Monographs 85 (Alphen aan den Rijn, Wolters Kluwer, 2014) 231–40.

Falkner, R, and Jaspers, N, 'Regulating Nanotechnologies: Risk, Uncertainty and the Global Governance Gap' (2012) 12 *Global Environmental Politics* 30.

FAO/WHO, *FAO/WHO Expert Meeting on the Application of Nanotechnologies in the Food and Agriculture Sectors: Potential Food Safety Implications* (Rome, FAO/WHO, 2010).

Feder, BJ, 'Technology's future: a look at the dark side' *The New York Times* (New York, 17 May 2006).

Fedrigo, D and Senjen, R, 'Shaping Innovation—Policy Approaches on Innovation Governance: The Case of Nanotechnology' (European Environmental Bureau, Issue 4, 2010).

Feynman, R, 'There's Plenty of Room at the Bottom' (1960) 23 *Engineering and Science* 22.

Fisher, E, 'The European Union in the Age of Accountability' (2004) 24 *Oxford Journal of Legal Studies* 495.

——, *Risk Regulation and Administrative Constitutionalism* (Oxford, Hart Publishing, 2007).

——, 'The "Perfect Storm" of REACH: Charting Regulatory Controversy in the Age of Information, Sustainable Development, and Globalisation' (2008) 11 *Journal of Risk Research* 541.

——, 'Risk and Governance' in D Levi-Faur (ed), *The Oxford Handbook of Governance*, Oxford Handbooks in Politics & International Relations (Oxford, Oxford University Press, 2012) 417–26.

——, 'Framing Risk Regulation: a Critical Reflection' (2013) 2 *European Journal of Risk Regulation* 125.

Fischer-Lescano, A and Teubner, G, 'Regime-Collisions: The Vain Search for Legal Unity in the Fragmentation of Global Law' (2004) 25 *Michigan Journal of International Law* 999.

Fleurke, FM and Somsen, H, 'Precautionary Regulation of Chemical Risk: How REACH Confronts the Regulatory Challenges of Scale, Uncertainty, Complexity and Innovation' (2011) 48 *Common Market Law Review* 357.

Flinders, M, 'Distributed Public Governance in the European Union' (2004) 11 *Journal of European Public Policy* 520.

Follesdal, A, 'The Legitimacy Challenges for New Modes of Governance: Trustworthy Responsiveness' (2011) 46 *Government and Opposition* 81.

FoodDrinkEurope, 'MEPs' Vote on "Engineered Nanomaterials" Regrettable for Europe's Food and Drink Industry' (Statement, 13 March 2014).

Food Standards Agency, 'A Review of Potential Implications of Nanotechnologies for Regulations and Risk Assessment in Relation to Food' (Report, August 2008).

Franco, A, Hansen, SF, Olsen SI and Butti, L, 'Limits and Prospects of the 'Incremental Approach' and the European Legislation on the Management of Risks Related to Nanomaterials' (2007) 48 *Regulatory Toxicology and Pharmacology* 171.

Friends of the Earth, 'Out of the Laboratory and on to our Plates: Nanotechnology in Food and Agriculture' (Report, March 2008).

Funtowicz, S, Shephard, I, Wilkinson, D and Ravetz, J, 'Science and Governance in the European Union: A Contribution to the Debate' (2000) 27 *Science and Public Policy* 327.

GAIA, 'Study on REACH Contribution to the Development of Emerging Technologies' (Final Report, DG Enterprise and Industry, 2012).

Gergely, A, Bowman, D and Chaudhry, Q, 'Small Ingredients in a Big Picture: Regulatory Perspectives on Nanotechnologies in Foods and Food Contact Materials' in Q Chaudhry, R Watkins and L Castle (eds), *Nanotechnologies in Food*, RSC Nanoscience & Nanotechnology 14 (Cambridge, Royal Society of Chemistry Publishing, 2010) 151–81.

German Federal Institute for Risk Assessment, 'BfR rät von Nanosilber in Lebensmitteln und Produkten des täglichen Bedarfs ab' (BfR discourages nanosilver in food and everyday products) (Stellungnahme Nr 024/2010 des BfR vom 28. Dezember 2009).

Gestel, R van and Micklitz, HW, 'Why Methods Matter in European Legal Scholarship' (2013) 20 *European Law Journal* 292.

Giddens, A, *Runaway World: How Globalisation is Reshaping Our Lives* (London, Profile Books, 1999).

——, 'Risk and Responsibility' (1999) 62 *The Modern Law Review* 1.

Grant, RW and Keohane, RO, 'Accountability and Abuses of Power in World Politics' (2005) 99 *American Political Science Review* 29.

Grave, L, '15th Anniversary: Why the Future Still Needs Us a While Longer' *Wired Magazine* (San Francisco, 24 March 2008).

Grobe, A, Kreinberger, N and Funda, P, 'Synthesis Report—Stakeholder's Attitudes towards the European Code of Conduct for Nanosciences & Nanotechnologies Research' (Report, FP7 NanoCode Project, March 2011).

Haas, EB, *The Uniting of Europe: Political, Social and Economic Forces 1950–1957* (Stanford, Stanford University Press, 1958).

Habermas, J, *Between Facts and Norms: Contributions to a Discourse Theory of Law and Democracy*, Studies in Contemporary German Social Thought (W Rehg (tr), Cambridge, The MIT Press, 1996).

——, *The Postnational Constellation: Political Essay*, Studies in Contemporary German Social Thought (M Pensky (tr), Cambridge, Polity, 2001).

——, 'Why Europe Needs a Constitution' (2001) 11 *New Left Review* 5.

——, *Zwischen Naturalismus und Religion* (Frankfurt, Suhrkamp, 2005).

——, *Zur Verfassung Europas* (Berlin, Suhrkamp, 2011).

——, 'The Crisis of the European Union in the Light of a Constitutionalisation of International Law' (2012) 23 *The European Journal of International Law* 335.

——, 'Democracy in Europe: Why the Development of the EU into a Transnational Democracy Is Necessary and How It Is Possible' (2015) 21 *European Law Journal* 546.

—— and Rosenfeld, M, 'Paradigms of Law' (1996) 17 *Cardozo Law Review* 771.

Hansen, BG and Blainey, M, 'REACH: A Step Change in the Management of Chemicals' (2006) 15 *Review of European, Comparative & International Environmental Law* 270.

Harden, I, 'Legal implications: non-representative rulemaking procedures' (3rd ACELG Annual Conference on 'Postnational Democracy: Beyond Representation in the EU', University of Amsterdam, 22 November 2013).

Harlow, C, 'Codification of EC Administrative Procedures? Fitting the Foot to the Shoe or the Shoe to the Foot' (1996) 2 *European Law Journal* 3.

——, *Accountability in the European Union*, Collected courses of the Academy of European Law Series XI/3 (Oxford, Oxford University Press, 2002).

—— and Rawlings, R, 'Promoting Accountability in Multi-Level Governance: A Network Approach' (2006) European Governance Papers (EUROGOV) no C-06-02.

Hassi, S, 'Towards an Effective Governance of Nanomaterials: First Reaction to the Second Regulatory Review on Nanomaterials' (Workshop 'Second Regulatory Review of Nanomaterials', European Commission, Brussels, 30 January 2013).

Heselhaus, S, 'Risk Management of Nanomaterials: Environmental and Consumer Protection under Existing EC Legislation on Chemicals, Pesticides and Biocides' (2010) 12 *Environmental Law Review* 115.

Hey, C, Jacob, K and Volkery, A, 'Better Regulation by New Governance Hybrids? Governance Models and the Reform of the European Chemicals Policy' (FFU-Report 02/2006, Environmental Policy Research Centre, Freie Universität Berlin, 2006).

Heyvaert, V, 'The EU Chemicals Policy: Towards Inclusive Governance?' in E Vos (ed), *European Risk Governance—Its Science, its Inclusiveness and its Effectiveness* (Mannheim, CONNEX Report Series, 2008).

——, 'Regulating Chemical Risk: REACH in a Global Governance Perspective' in J Eriksson, M Gilek and C. Rudén (eds), *Regulating Chemical Risks: European and Global Challenges* (Dordrecht, Springer, 2010) 217–38.

High-Level Group on the Competitiveness of the Agro-Food Industry, 'Report on the Competitiveness of the Agro-Food Industry' (European Commission, DG Enterprise and Industry, March 2009).

High-Level Group on the Competitiveness of the European Chemicals Industry, 'European Chemicals Industry: Enabler of a Sustainable Future' (Final Report, European Commission DG Enterprise and Industry, 2009).

Hix, S and Lord, C, 'The Making of a President: The European Parliament and the Confirmation of Jacques Santer as President of the Commission' (1996) 31 *Government and Opposition* 62.

Hodge, Graeme A, Bowman, D and Ludlow, K, 'Introduction: Big Questions for Small Technologies' in GA Hodge, D Bowman and K Ludlow (eds), *New Global Frontiers in Regulation: The Age of Nanotechnology*, Monash Studies in Global Movements Series (Cheltenham, Edward Elgar Publishing, 2007) 3–26.

——, —— and Maynard, AD (eds), *International Handbook on Regulating Nanotechnologies* (Cheltenham, Edward Elgar Publishing, 2010).

Hofmann, HCH, Rowe, GC and Türk, AH, *EU Administrative Law and Policy* (Oxford, Oxford University Press, 2011).

Hood, C, Rothstein, H and Baldwin, R, *The Government of Risk: Understanding Risk Regulation Regimes* (Oxford, Oxford University Press, 2001).

Hooghe, L and Marks, G, *Multi-level Governance and European Integration* (Lanham, Rowman and Littlefield, 2001).

Inglis, D and Gimlin, D, 'Food Globalisations: Ironies and Ambivalences of Food, Cuisine and Globality' in D Inglis and D Gimlin (eds), *The Globalisation of Food* (Oxford, Berg Publisher, 2009) 3–42.

Institute of Technology Assessment of the Austrian Academy of Sciences, 'NanoTrust Dossiers: Carbon Nanotubes—Part II: Risks and Regulation' (No.024en, February 2012).

International Risk Governance Council, 'Policy Brief—Appropriate Risk Governance Strategies for Nanotechnology Applications in Food and Cosmetics' (2009).

Jachtenfuchs, M, 'The Governance Approach to European Integration' (2001) 39 *Journal of Common Market Studies* 245.

Jacobs, F, 'EU Agencies and the European Parliament' in M Everson, C Monda and E Vos (eds), *European Agencies in Between Institutions and Member States*, European Monographs no 85 (Alphen aan den Rijn, Wolters Kluwer Law & Business, 2014) 201–28.

Jasanoff, S, *The Fifth Branch: Science Advisors as Policy Makers* (Cambridge, Harvard University Press, 2004).

——, *Science and Public Reason*, The Earthscan Science in Society Series (London, Routledge, 2012).

Joerges, C, 'The Law's Problems with the Governance of the European Market' in C Joerges and R Dehousse (eds), *Good Governance in Europe's Integrated Market*, Courses of the Academy of European Law XI/2 (Oxford, Oxford University Press, 2002) 3–31.

Joy, B, 'Why the Future Doesn't Need Us' *Wired Magazine* (San Francisco, 1 April 2000).

Kampers, F, 'Potential Benefits and Market Drivers for Nanotechnology Applications in the Food Sector' in Q Chaudhry, R Watkins and L Castle (eds), *Nanotechnologies in Food*, RSC Nanoscience & Nanotechnology 14 (Cambridge, Royal Society of Chemistry Publishing, 2010) 102–19.

Keading, M and Hardacre, A, 'The European Parliament and the Future of Comitology After Lisbon' (2013) 19 *European Law Journal* 382.

Keohane, RO, 'Accountability in World Politics' in S Gustavsson, C Karlsson and T Persson (eds), *The Illusion of Accountability in the European Union*, Routledge Advances in European Politics (London, Routledge, 2009) 11–22.

Kim, SH, 'Max Weber', *The Stanford Encyclopedia of Philosophy* (Fall edn, 2008).

Kjaer, PF, 'Rationality within REACH? On Functional Differentiation as the Structural Foundation of Legitimacy in European Chemicals Regulation' (2007) European University Institute Working Paper, LAW 2007/18.

Klabbers, J, 'Informal Instruments Before the European Court of Justice' (1994) 31 *Common Market Law Review* 997.

Klöckner, L, 'Wie umweltschädlich sind Nanoteilchen?' *Die Zeit* (Hamburg, 20 November 2012).

Knight, FH, *Risk, Uncertainty and Profit* (Boston, Hart Shaffner and Marx, 1921).

Kohler-Koch, B, 'The Commission White Paper and the Improvement of European Governance' in JHH Weiler, C Joerges and Y Meny (eds), *Symposium: Mountain or Molehill? A Critical Appraisal of the Commission White Paper on Governance* (2001) Jean Monnet Working Paper no 6/01.

——, 'Civil Society Participation: More Democracy or Pluralisation of the European Lobby?' in B Kohler-Koch and C Quittkat (eds), *De-Mystification of Participatory Democracy: EU Governance and Civil Society* (Oxford, Oxford University Press, 2013) 173–91.

——, 'Colliding Visions of Representation and Participation' (3rd ACELG Annual Conference on 'Postnational Democracy: Beyond Representation in the EU', University of Amsterdam, 22 November 2013).

——, 'Governing with the European Civil Society' in B Kohler-Koch and C Quittkat (eds), *De-Mystification of Participatory Democracy: EU Governance and Civil Society* (Oxford, Oxford University Press, 2013) 18–40.

—— and Rittberger, B, 'Review Article: The 'Governance Turn' in ES Studies' (2006) 44 *Journal of Common Market Studies* 27.

Kooiman, J, 'Social-Political Governance: Introduction' in J Kooiman (ed), *Modern Governance: New Government-Society Interactions* (London, SAGE Publications, 1993) 1–8.

Korkea-aho, E, 'Better Judicial Review? EU Courts and the Smart Regulation Agenda in Implementing Chemicals Regulation' (2012) 6 *Legisprudence* 397.

——, 'Laws in Progress? Reconceptualizing Accountability Strategies in the Era of Framework Norms' (2013) 2 *Transnational Environmental Law* 363.

Kratochwil, F, 'Globalization: What It Is and What It Is Not. Some Critical Reflections on the Discursive Formations Dealing with Transformative Change' in D Fuchs and F Kratochwil (eds), *Transformative Change and Global Order: Reflections on Theory and Practice*, Fragen politischer Ordnung in einer globalisierten Welt no 2 (Hamburg, Litt, 2002) 25–43.

Kreuter, J, Shamenkov, D, Petrov, V, Ramge, P, Cychutek, K, Koch-Brandt, C and R Alyautdin, R, 'Apolipoprotein-mediated Transport of Nanoparticle-bound Drugs across the Blood-Brain Barrier' (2002) 10 *Journal of Drug Targeting* 317.

Ladeur, KH, *Proceduralization and its Use in Post-Modern Legal Theory* (1996) European University Institute Working Paper, LAW 1995/05.

——, 'Kommunikation über Risiken im Rechtssystem. Das Beispiel Nanotechnologie' in C Büscher and KP Japp (eds), *Ökologische Aufklärung* (Wiesbaden, VS Verlag für Sozialwissenschaften, 2010) 131–55.

Landesanstalt für Umwelt, Messungen und Naturschutz Baden Württemberg, '*Nanomaterialien: Regulierungen national-international*' (Bericht, June 2012).

Lebessis, N and Paterson, J, 'Evolution in Governance: What Lessons for the Commission? A First Assessment' (1997) Forward Studies Unit, European Commission Working Paper.

—— and ——, 'The Future of European Regulation' (1997) Forward Studies Unit, European Commission Working Paper.

—— and ——, 'A Learning Organisation for a Learning Society: Proposals for Designing Tomorrow's Commission' (1998) Forward Studies Unit, European Commission Working Paper.

—— and ——, 'Improving the Effectiveness and Legitimacy of EU Governance: a Possible Reform Agenda for the Commission' (Report CdP(99)750), Forward Studies Unit, European Commission, 1999).

—— and ——, 'Developing New Modes of Governance' (2000) Forward Studies Unit, European Commission Working Paper.

Lee, M, 'Risk and Beyond: EU Regulation of Nanotechnology' (2010) 35 *European Law Review* 799.

——, *EU Environmental Law, Governance and Decision-Making*, Modern Studies in European Law vol 43, 2nd edn (Oxford, Hart Publishing, 2014).

Lenearts, K, 'The European Court of Justice and Process-oriented Review' (2012) College of Europe Research Paper in Law 01/2012.

—— and Verhoeven, A, 'Institutional Balance as a Guarantee for Democracy in EU Governance' in C Joerges and R Dehousse (eds), *Good Governance in Europe's Integrated Market*, Collected Courses of the Academy of European Law XI/2 (Oxford, Oxford University Press, 2002) 35–88.

Levi-Faur, D, 'Regulation and Regulatory Governance' in D Levi-Faur (ed), *Handbook on the Politics of Regulation* (Cheltenham, Edward Elgar Publishing, 2011) 3–21.

Lindseth, P, 'Agents without Principals? Delegation in an Age of Diffuse and Fragmented Governance' in F Cafaggi (ed), *Reframing Self-Regulation in European Private Law*, Private Law in European Content Series vol 9 (Alphen aan den Rijn, Kluwer Law International, 2006) 107–30.

Luhmann, N, 'Differentiation of Society' (1977) 2 *The Canadian Journal of Sociology/ Cahiers canadiens de sociologie* 29.

——, 'Closure and Openness: On Reality in the World of Law' in G Teubner (ed), *Autopoietic Law: a New Approach to Law and Society*, European University Institute—Series A Law no 8 (Berlin, De Gruyter, 1987) 335–48.

Magnette, P, 'Between Parliamentary Control and the Rule of Law: The Political Role of the Ombudsman in the European Union' (2003) 10 *Journal of European Public Policy* 677.

Mahony, H, 'Nanofoods—coming to a plate near you?' *EU Observer* (Brussels, 18 October 2011).

Majone, G, 'The Rise of the Regulatory State in Western Europe' in WC Müller and V Wright (eds), *The State in Western Europe: Retreat or Redefinition?*, West European Politics Series vol 17 no 3 (Ilford, Frank Cass, 1994) 77–101.

—— (ed), *Regulating Europe*, European Public Policy (London, Routledge, 1996).

——, 'What Price Safety? The Precautionary Principle and its Policy Implications' in G Majone (ed), *Risk Regulation in the European Union: Between Enlargement and Internationalisation* (Florence, European University Institute, 2003).

Malkiewicz, K, Pettitt, M, Dawson, KA, Toikka, A, Hansson, SO, Hukkinen, J, Lynch, I and Lead, J, 'Nanomaterials in REACH' (Project Report, SKEP ERA-NET, August 2011).

Marchant, GE, Sylvester, DJ and Abbott, KW, 'Risk Management Principles of Nanotechnology' (2008) 2 *NanoEthics* 43.

Marxsen, C, 'Open Stakeholder Consultations at the European Level—Voice of the Citizens?' (2015) 21 *European Law Journal* 257.

Mather, G and Vibert, F, 'Evaluating Better Regulation: Building the System' (London, European Policy Forum, City Research Series 9, 2006).

Maynard, AD, 'Nanotechnology: The Next Big Thing, or Much Ado about Nothing?' (2006) 51 *Annals of Occupational Hygiene* 1.

Meisterernst, A, Daniel, H and Thron, M, 'Nanoparticles in Food and Cosmetics—Scientific and Legal Aspects' (2006) 2 *European Food & Feed Law Review* 69.

Mendes, J, 'Participation and the Role of Law After Lisbon: A Legal View on Article 11 TEU' (2011) 48 *Common Market Law Review* 1849.

Menon, A and Weatherill, S, 'Democratic Politics in a Globalising World: Supranationalism and Legitimacy in the European Union' (2007) LSE Law, Society and Economy Working Papers 13/2007.

Meuwese, A, *Impact Assessment in EU Law-Making*, European Monographs no 61 (Alphen aan den Rijn, Kluwer Law International, 2008).

——, 'The European Court of Auditors Steps Out of Its Comfort Zone with an "Impact Assessment Audit"' (2011) 1 *European Journal of Risk Regulation* 104.

——, 'Regulatory Scrutiny in Transition' (2015) 3 *European Journal of Risk Regulation* 359.

——, Schuurmans, Y and Voermans, W, 'Towards a European Administrative Procedure Act' (2009) 2 *Review of European Administrative Law* 3.

Meyer, J, 'To Czech industry, everything is nano' *The New York Times* (New York, 22 May 2012).

Milieu Ltd, 'Technical Assistance Related to the Scope of REACH and Other Relevant EU Legislation to Assess Overlaps' (Final Report (revised), European Commission, DG Environment, 2012).

—— and RPA Ltd, 'Proposal for an EU Reporting System for Nanomaterials' (Study commissioned by the European Commission—DG Environment, 2010).

Möllers, C, 'European Governance: Meaning and Concept' (2006) 43 *Common Market Law Review* 313.

Montfort, JP, Indirli, G, Georgieva, D and Carrega, CM, 'Nanomaterials under REACH: Legal Aspects' (2010) 1 *European Journal of Risk Regulation* 51.

Müller-Lissner, A, 'Verdächtige Zwerge' Die Zeit (Hamburg, 24 June 2009).

NanoKommission, 'Review of Nanomaterial and Nanoproduct Regulation' (Working Group Report of three of the German Federal Government's NanoKommission, 2010).

National Research Council, *Risk Assessment in the Federal Government: Managing the Process* (Washington D.C., National Academies Press, 1983).

Nestler, R and Schäuble, J, 'Wie gefährlich ist die Nanotechnologie?' *Die Zeit* (Hamburg, 19 November 2009).

Neyer, J, *The Justification of Europe: A Political Theory of Supranational Integration* (Oxford, Oxford University Press, 2012).

NIA, Safenano and Cefic, 'Specific Advice on Fulfilling Information Requirements for Nanomaterials under REACH (RIP-oN 2)' (Final Project Report, RNC/RIP-oN2/FPR/1/FINAL, 2011).

Nowotny, H, Scott, P and Gibbons, M, *Re-Thinking Science: Knowledge and the Public in an Age of Uncertainty* (Cambridge, Polity Press, 2001).

ObservatoryNano, 'Development in Nanotechnology Regulation and Standards' (FP7 Report, May 2009).

ObservatoryNano, 'General Sector Reports: Chemistry & Materials' (FP7 Report, June 2009).

ObservatoryNano, 'Focus Report 2010: CNT and Nanodiamond' (FP7 Report, June 2009).

ObservatoryNano, 'Agrifood Sector: Report on Economic Impact of Nanotechnologies' (FP7 Report, April 2010).

ObservatoryNano, 'Nanotechnologies for Food Packaging: Reporting the Science and Technology Research Trends' (FP7 Report, August 2010).

OECD, 'Fostering Nanotechnology to Address Global Challenges' (Report, OECD, 2011).

Palacios-Huerta, I, 'Time-Inconsistent Preferences in Adam Smith and David Hume' (2003) 35 *History of Political Economy* 241.

Peers, S and Costa, M, 'Court of Justice of the European Union (General Chamber), Judicial review of EU Acts after the Treaty of Lisbon; Order of 6 September 2011, Case T-18/10 Inuit Tapiriit Kanatami and Others v Commission & Judgment of 25 October 2011, Case T-262/10 Microban v Commission' (2012) 8 *European Constitutional Law Review* 82.

Pesendorfer, D, 'EU Environmental Policy under Pressure: Chemicals Policy Change Between Antagonistic Goals' (2006) 15 *Environmental Politics* 95.

Peters, A and Pagotto, I, *Soft Law as a New Mode of Governance: A Legal Perspective* (NEWGOV: New Modes of Governance, 2006).

Peter, F, 'Political Legitimacy', *The Stanford Encyclopedia of Philosophy* (Summer edn, 2010).

Poggi, G, *Weber: A Short Introduction* (Cambridge, Polity Press, 2006).

Poland, CA, Duffin, R, Kinloch, I, Maynard, A, Wallace, WA, Seaton, A, Stone, V, Brown, S, MacNee, W and Donaldson, K, 'Carbon Nanotubes Introduced into the Abdominal Cavity of Mice Show Asbestos-like Pathogenicity in a Pilot Study' (2008) 3 *Nature Nanotechnology* 423.

Popelier, P, 'Governance and Better Regulation: Dealing with the Legitimacy Paradox' (2011) 17 *European Public Law* 555.

Posner, RA, 'The Decline of Law as an Autonomous Discipline' (1987) 1000 *Harvard Law Review* 761.

Purcell, K, Clarke, L and Renzulli, L, 'Menus of Choice: The Social Embeddedness of Decisions' in MJ Cohen, (ed), *Risk in the Modern Age: Social Theory, Science and Environmental Decision-Making* (London, Palgrave MacMillan, 2000) 62–79.

Quittkat, C, 'Consultation in Daily Practice: An In-Depth Analysis' in B Kohler-Koch and C Quittkat (eds), *De-Mystification of Participatory Democracy: EU Governance and Civil Society* (Oxford, Oxford University Press, 2013) 61–84.

——, 'New Instruments Serving Democracy: Do Online Consultations Benefit Civil Society?' in B Kohler-Koch and C Quittkat (eds), *De-Mystification of Participatory Democracy: EU Governance and Civil Society* (Oxford, Oxford University Press, 2013) 85–113.

—— and Kohler-Koch, B, 'Involving Civil Society in EU Governance', in B Kohler-Koch and C Quittkat (eds), *De-Mystification of Participatory Democracy: EU Governance and Civil Society* (Oxford, Oxford University Press, 2013) 41–61.

Radaelli, CM and Meuwese, A, 'Hard Questions, Hard Solutions: Proceduralisation through Impact Assessment in the EU' (2010) 33 *West European Politics* 136.

Renn, O, *Risk Governance: Coping with Uncertainty in a Complex World*, Risk in Society Series (London, Earthscan, 2008).

—— and Roco, MC, 'Nanotechnology and the need for risk governance' (2006) 8 *Journal of Nanoparticle Research: an interdisciplinary forum for nanoscale science and technology* 1.

RIVM, 'Nanomaterials under REACH: Nanosilver as a Case Study' (Report 601780003/2009, 2009).

——, 'Development of an inventory for consumer products containing nanomaterials' (Final report, European Commission—DG Environment, 2011).

——, 'Interpretation and Implications of the European Commission Recommendation on the Definition of Nanomaterial' (RIVM Letter Report 601358001, 2012).

Rogers, MD, 'The European Commission's White Paper 'Strategy for a Future Chemicals Policy': A Review' (2003) 23 *Risk Analysis* 381.

Royal Society & The Royal Academy of Engineering, *Nanoscience and Nanotechnologies: Opportunities and Uncertainties* (London, The Royal Society, 2004).

Scharpf, FW, *Demokratietheorie zwischen Utopie und Anpassung* (Konstanz, Universitätsverlag, 1970).

——, *Governing in Europe: Effective and Democratic?* (Oxford, Oxford University Press, 1999).

Schmitter, PC, *How to Democratise the European Union ... And Why Bother?*, Governance in Europe (Lanham, Rowman & Littlefield Publishers, 2000).

Scott, C, 'Accountability in the Regulatory State' (2000) 27 *Journal of Law and Society* 38.

——, 'Reflexive Governance, Regulation and Meta-Regulation: Control or Learning?' in O de Schutter and J Lenoble (eds), *Reflexive Governance: Redefining the Public Interest in a Pluralistic World*, Modern Studies in European Law no 22 (Oxford, Hart Publishing, 2010) 43–63.

Scott, J, 'REACH: Combining Harmonisation and Dynamism in the Regulation of Chemicals' in J Scott (ed), *Environmental Protection: European Law and Governance*, Collected Courses of the Academy of European Law XVIII/3 (Oxford, Oxford University Press, 2009) 56–92.

——, 'In Legal Limbo: Post-Legislative Guidance as a Challenge for European Administrative Law' (2011) 48 *Common Market Law Review* 329.

—— and Sturm, S, 'Courts as Catalysts: Re-Thinking the Judicial Role in New Governance' (2007) 13 *Columbia Journal of European Law* 565.

—— and Trubek, DM, 'Mind the Gap: Law and New Approaches to Governance in the European Union' (2002) 8 *European Law Journal* 1.

Senden, L, *Soft Law in European Community Law: Its Relationship to Legislation* (Nijmegen, Wolf Legal Publishers, 2003).

——, 'Soft Post-Legislative Rulemaking: A Time for More Stringent Control' (2013) 19 *European Law Journal* 57.

Sens, A and Stoett, P, *Global Politics: Origins, Currents, Directions*, 3rd edn (Scarborough, Nelson Thomson Learning, 2004).

Singer, N, 'New products bring side effect: nanophobia' *The New York Times* (New York, 3 December 2008).

Smismans, S, *Law, Legitimacy, and European Governance: Functional Participation in Social Regulation*, Oxford Studies in European Law (Oxford, Oxford University Press, 2004).

——, 'New Modes of Governance and the Participatory Myth' (2006) European Governance Paper (EUROGOV) N-06-01.

Smolander, M and Chaudhry, Q, 'Nanotechnologies in Food Packaging' in Q Chaudhry, R Watkins and L Castle (eds), *Nanotechnologies in Food*, RSC Nanoscience & Nanotechnology 14 (Cambridge, Royal Society of Chemistry Publishing, 2010) 86–101.

Snyder, FG, *New Directions in European Community Law*, Law in Context (London, Weidenfeld & Nicolson, 1990).

——, 'Soft Law and Institutional Practice in the European Community' in S Martin (ed), *The Construction of Europe: Essays in Honour of Emile Noël* (Dordrecht, Kluwer Academic Publishers, 1994) 197–226.

Ştefan, O, 'European Union Soft Law: New Developments Concerning the Divide Between Legally Binding Force and Legal Effects' (2012) 75 *The Modern Law Review* 879.

——, *Soft Law in Court*, European Monographs no 81 (Alphen aan den Rijn, Wolters Kluwer Law International, 2013).

Stiglitz, JE, 'The Invisible Hand and Modern Welfare Economics' (1991) NBER Working Paper Series no 3641.

Stokes, E, 'Regulating Nanotechnologies: Sizing Up the Options' (2009) 29 *Legal Studies: The Journal of the Society of Public Teachers of Law* 281.

——, 'Nanotechnology and the Products of Inherited Regulation' (2012) 39 *Journal of Law and Society* 93.

—— and Vaughan, S, 'Great Expectations: Reviewing 50 Years of Chemicals Legislation in the EU' (2013) 25 *Journal of Environmental Law* 411.

Sunstein, CR, *Laws of Fear: Beyond the Precautionary Principle*, John Robert Seeley lectures no 6 (Cambridge, Cambridge University Press, 2005).

Svilpaite, E, 'Legal Evaluation of the Selected New Modes of Governance: The Conceptualisation of Self- and Co-Regulation in the European Union Legal Framework' (University of Basel, NEWGOV: New Modes of Governance, 2007).

Szajkowska, A, 'Different Actors, Different Factors—Science and Other Legitimate Factors in the EU and National Food Safety Regulation' (2011) 4 *European Journal of Risk Regulation* 523.

——, *Regulating Food Law: Risk Analysis and the Precautionary Principle as General Principles of EU Food Law*, European Institute for Food Law series vol 7 (Wageningen, Wageningen Academic Publishers, 2012).

Tamanaha, B, 'Understanding Legal Pluralism: Past to Present, Local to Global' (2008) 30 *Sydney Law Review* 375.

The Economist, 'Has All the Magic Gone?' *The Economist* (London, 12 April 2006).

The Evaluation Partnership, 'Evaluation of the Commission's Impact Assessment System' (Final Report, SG-02/2006, April 2007).

Teubner, G, 'Substantive and Reflexive Elements in Modern Law' (1983) 17 *Law & Society Review* 239.

——, 'Das Regulatorische Trilemma: Zur Diskussion um post-instrumentale Rechtsmodelle' (1984) *Quaderni Fiorentini per la Storia del Pensiero Giuridico Moderno* 109.

——, 'Introduction to Autopoietic Law' in G Teubner (ed), *Autopoietic Law: A New Approach to Law and Society*, European University Institute—Series A Law no 8 (Berlin, De Gruyter, 1987) 1–11.

——, 'Regulatory Law: Chronicle of a Death Foretold' (1992) 1 *Social & Legal Studies* 451.

——, 'The Two Faces of Janus: Rethinking Legal Pluralism' (1992) 13 *Cardozo Law Review* 1443.

——, 'Fragmented Foundations: Societal Constitutionalism Beyond the State' in P Dobner and M Loughlin (eds), *The Twilight of Constitutional Law: Demise or Transmutation?*, Oxford Constitutional Theory (Oxford, Oxford University Press, 2009) 327–41.

Torfing, J, Peters, BG, Pierre, J and Sørensen, E, *Interactive Governance: Advancing the Paradigm* (Oxford, Oxford University Press, 2012).

Türk, AH, 'Oversight of Administrative Rule-Making: Judicial Review' (2013) 19 *European Law Journal* (2013) 126.

Verhey, L, 'Fostering Executive Accountability in the EU: A Key Issue' in J Wouters, L Verhey and P Kiiver (eds), *European Constitutionalism Beyond Lisbon* (Antwerp, Intersentia, 2009) 239–58.

——, Claes, M and Broeksteeg, H, 'Political Accountability in the European Union: Conceptual Analysis and Future Prospects' (2008) in L Verhey, H Broeksteeg and I Van den Driessche (eds), *Political Accountability in Europe: Which Way Forward?* (Groningen, Europa Law Publishing, 2008) 301–44.

Verhoeven, A, *The European Union in Search of a Democratic and Constitutional Theory*, European Monographs no 38 (The Hague, Kluwer Law International, 2002).

Visser, M de, *Network-Based Governance in EC Law*, Modern Studies in European Law no 19 (Oxford, Hart Publishing, 2009).

Vogelezang-Stoute, E, 'Regulating Nanomaterials: Bottlenecks and Perspectives in EU Legislation on Chemicals and Products' (2012) 21 *European Energy and Environmental Law Review* 41.

——, 'Regulating Uncertain Risks of New Technologies: Nanomaterials as a Challenge for the Regulator' in M Peeters and R Uylenburg (eds), *EU Environmental Legislation. Legal Perspectives on Regulatory Strategies* (Cheltenham, Edward Elgar Publishing, 2014) 211–32.

Vogiatzis, N, 'The Linguistic Policy of the EU Institutions and Political Participation Post-Lisbon' (2016) 41 *European Law Review* 176.

Vos, E, 'Reforming the European Commission: What Role to Play for EU Agencies?' (2000) 37 *Common Market Law Review* 1113.

——, 'European Agencies and the Composite EU Executive' in E Everson, C Monda and E Vos (eds), *European Agencies in Between Institutions and Member States*, European Monographs no 85 (Alphen aan den Rijn, Wolters Kluwer Law & Business, 2014) 11–47.

——, 'EU Risk Regulation Reviewed by the European Courts' in M Van Asselt, M Everson and E Vos (eds), *Trade, Health and the Environment: The European Union Put to the Test*, Routledge Explorations in Environmental Studies (London, Routledge, 2014) 213–32.

—— and Wendler, F, 'Food Safety Regulation at EU Level' in E Vos and F Wendler (eds), *Food Safety Regulation in Europe, A Comparative Institutional Analysis*, Ius Commune Europaeum 62 (Antwerp, Intersentia, 2006) 65–138.

Waldmeir, P, 'Brave new risks of nanotechnology' *Financial Times* (London, 18 September 2007).

Walker, N and Búrca, G de, 'Reconceiving Law and New Governance' (2007) 13 *Columbia Journal of European Law* 519.

Wallbraun, S, 'Immer kleiner, immer feiner' *Die Zeit* (Hamburg, 12 January 2011).

Waters, R, 'Why nanotechnology is the next big thing' *Financial Times* (London, 29 March 2005).

Weatherill, S, 'The Challenge of Better Regulation' in S Weatherill (ed), *Better Regulation*, Studies of the Oxford Institute of European and Comparative Law no 6 (Oxford, Hart Publishing, 2007) 1.

—— and Beaumont, P, *EU Law*, 3rd edn (London, Penguin, 1999).

Weber, M, 'Die drei reinen Typen der legitimen Herrschaft' (1922) 187 *Preußische Jahrbücher* 1.

——, *The Theory of Social and Economic Organization* (T Parsons and AM Henderson (trs), New York, Free Press 1964).

——, 'Wissenschaft als Beruf' in D Kaesler (ed), *Max Weber Schriften 1894–1922* (Stuttgart, Kröner, 2002) 474–511.

——, *The Protestant Ethic and the Spirit of Capitalism* (T Parsons (tr), Mineola, Dover Publications, 2003).

Webler, T, '"Right" Discourse in Citizen Participation: An Evaluative Yardstick' in O Renn, T Webler and P Wiedemann (eds), *Fairness and Competence in Citizen Participation*, Technology, Risk, and Society vol 10 (Dordrecht, Kluwer Academic, 1995) 35–86.

Weiler, JHH, 'The Commission as Eurosceptic: A Task-Oriented Commission for a Project-Based Union—A Comment on the First Version of the White Paper' in JHH Weiler, C Joerges and Y Meny (eds), *Symposium: Mountain or Molehill? A Critical Appraisal of the Commission White Paper on Governance* (2011) Jean Monnet Working Paper no 6/01.

——, Haltern, UR and Mayer, F, 'European Democracy and Its Critique' (1995) 18 *West European Politics* 4.

——, Joerges, C and Meny, Y, (eds), *Symposium: Mountain or Molehill? A Critical Appraisal of the Commission White Paper on Governance* (2001) Jean Monnet Working Paper no 6/01.

Weimer, M, 'EU Risk Governance of "Cloned Food"—Regulatory Uncertainty between Trade and Non-Trade' in M Van Asselt, E Versluis and E Vos (eds), *Balancing Between Trade and Risk: Integrating Legal and Social Science Perspectives* (Abingdon, Routledge, 2013) 33–58.

Weinberg, AM, 'Science and Trans-Science' (1972) 10 *Minerva* 209.

Wilkinson, M, 'Three Concepts of Law: Towards a Jurisprudence of Democratic Experimentalism' (2010) 2 *Wisconsin Law Review* 673.

Wille, A, 'The European Commission's Accountability Paradox' in M Bovens, D Curtin and P 't Hart (eds), *The Real World of EU Accountability: What Deficit?* (Oxford, Oxford University Press, 2010) 63–86.

Winckelmann, J, *Legitimität und Legalität in Max Webers Herrschaftssoziologie* (Tübingen, J.C.B. Mohr, 1952).

Witte, B de, 'Executive Accountability under the European Constitution and the Lisbon Treaty' in P Kiiver, S Loeffen and L Verhey (eds), *Political Accountability and European Integration* (Groningen, Europa Law Publishing, 2009) 139–51.

World Bank, *Sub-Saharan Africa: From Crisis to Sustainable Growth* (Washington, The World Bank, 1989).

Zander, J, *The Application of the Precautionary Principle in Practice, Comparative Dimensions* (Cambridge, Cambridge University Press, 2010).

Zumbansen, P, 'Governance: An Interdisciplinary Perspective' in D Levi-Faur (ed), *The Oxford Handbook of Governance*, Oxford Handbooks in Politics & International Relations (Oxford, Oxford University Press, 2012) 83–96.

Index